Leila Alikarami holds a PhD from SOAS. She is a practicing lawyer and human rights activist who grew up in Tehran, where she completed her legal training with Nobel Peace Laureate Shirin Ebadi. Since 2001, Alikarami has focused on women's and children's rights and in 2009 she accepted the RAW in War (Reach All Women in War) Anna Politkovskaya Award on behalf of the women of Iran and the One Million Signatures campaign.

WOMEN AND EQUALITY IN IRAN

Law, Society and Activism

Leila Alikarami

I.B. TAURIS
LONDON • NEW YORK • OXFORD • NEW DELHI • SYDNEY

I.B.TAURIS
Bloomsbury Publishing Plc
50 Bedford Square, London, WC1B 3DP, UK
1385 Broadway, New York, NY 10018, USA
29 Earlsfort Terrace, Dublin 2, Ireland

BLOOMSBURY, I.B.TAURIS and the Diana logo are trademarks of
Bloomsbury Publishing Plc

First published in Great Britain 2019
Paperback edition published 2021

Copyright © Leila Alikarami 2019

Leila Alikarami has asserted her right under the Copyright, Designs and Patents Act, 1988, to be identified as Author of this work.

Cover design: Simon Levy
Cover image © epa european pressphoto agency b.v. / Alamy Stock Photo.

All rights reserved. No part of this publication may be reproduced or transmitted in any form or by any means, electronic or mechanical, including photocopying, recording, or any information storage or retrieval system, without prior permission in writing from the publishers.

Bloomsbury Publishing Plc does not have any control over, or responsibility for, any third-party websites referred to or in this book. All internet addresses given in this book were correct at the time of going to press. The author and publisher regret any inconvenience caused if addresses have changed or sites have ceased to exist, but can accept no responsibility for any such changes.

A catalogue record for this book is available from the British Library.

A catalogue record for this book is available from the Library of Congress.

ISBN: HB: 978-1-7845-3316-8
PB: 978-0-7556-4120-8
ePDF: 978-1-7883-1887-7
eBook: 978-1-7883-1886-0

Series: International Library of Iranian Studies

Typeset in Garamond Three by OKS Prepress Services, Chennai, India

To find out more about our authors and books visit www.bloomsbury.com and sign up for our newsletters.

To my son, Parsa, who gives me courage to never give up

'*The Islamic Republic has not opened the gates. Women are jumping over the fences.*'

Haideh Moghissi

CONTENTS

Note on Transliteration x
*Glossary of the Most Commonly Used Persian and
   Arabic Terms and Abbreviations* xi
Acknowledgements xiii
Preface xv

Introduction and Theoretical Framework 1

1. The Development of Universal Standards on Gender Equality: The Convention on the Elimination of All forms of Discrimination Against Women 9
   Introduction 9
   The global movements for women's rights: Muslim women's experience 11
   The Beijing platform for action: Moving Muslim women from the periphery to the centre 20
   The concept of equality in the international and the Islamic framework 24
   The Convention on the Elimination of All Forms of Discrimination Against Women: An overview 32
   Conclusion 45

2. The Political and Legal System of the Islamic Republic of Iran 47
   Introduction 47

The legislative system and codification of law in Iran: Historical background	48
The Islamic definition of the state: Principles, goals and tasks	56
Legislation in Iran	60
Sources of law	65
Conclusion	74

3. **Deliberation Over the Adoption of CEDAW by the Islamic Republic of Iran** — 75
   Introduction — 75
   The emergence of the women's movement and the CEDAW — 76
   Debating ratification of the CEDAW in Iran — 82
   The debate over Iran's accession to the CEDAW: Opponents and supporters — 92
   Conclusion — 100

4. **Iranian Women's Struggle for Gender Equality: The Case of Iran's Civil Code** — 103
   Introduction — 103
   A review of Iran's civil code — 104
   Equal rights in marriage — 105
   Polygamy — 117
   The dissolution of marriage — 122
   Temporary marriage and its dissolution — 132
   Inheritance — 136
   Conclusion — 138

5. **Iranian Women Demanding Equal Rights: The Case of Iran's Criminal Code** — 140
   Introduction — 140
   An overview of Iran's criminal code — 141
   The age of criminal responsibility — 142
   Testimony — 145
   Laws that support honour killings — 148
   Blood money (*diyeh*) — 151
   Conclusion — 157

CONTENTS

6. **The One Million Signatures Campaign: Domestic Discourse on Gender Equality** — 159
   Introduction — 159
   The birth of the campaign — 160
   The major goals of the campaign — 164
   The methods and strategies of the campaign — 165
   The campaign's successes and achievements — 171
   Challenges faced by the campaign — 189
   Women's rights activists beyond the campaign: The coalition of women before the 2009 presidential election — 196
   Conclusion — 209

Conclusion — 211

Notes — 216
Bibliography — 288
Index — 333

NOTE ON TRANSLITERATION

This book follows the transliteration system currently adopted in the journal *Iranian Studies*. The names of persons are exempt from the diacritic rules and are at times written in the most common form. Some nouns and widely adopted terms, such as *Islam* and *Imam*, are also written without diacritics.

GLOSSARY OF THE MOST COMMONLY USED PERSIAN AND ARABIC TERMS AND ABBREVIATIONS

Ādel	Just
Āqel	Be cognisant and aware
Blugh	Child's puberty
Diyeh	Compensation for murder or injuries under Islamic law, also known as blood money
Eddeh	The legal period during which a wife is not allowed to remarry, and her husband can return to the marriage whenever he desires
Efsād-e felarz	Spreading corruption on earth
Ejtehād	Juridical reasoning of a qualified Islamic jurist
Faskh	Judicial annulment of a marriage
Fatwā	Legal or religious opinion by a qualified Islamic jurist
Feqh	Islamic jurisprudence
Foqahā	Jurists
Hadd	Fixed punishments
Hadd-e Jald	Punishment by lashes
Hejāb	Compulsory prescribed dress for women
Ijāb	Offer
Ejmā'	Juristic consensus
Lavāt	Male homosexuality, sodomy

Khul'	Dissolution of a marriage, initiated by the wife
Majles	The Iranian Parliament
Mahdur-o dam	Deserving death
Mahriyeh	Marriage portion payable to the wife
Maslahat	Benefit, advantage
Mohārebeh	Sedition
Mojtahed	A high-ranking religious scholar who has attained the right to engage in *ejtehād*, or independent reasoning in Islamic jurisprudence
Nafaqeh	Maintenance
Naskh	Abrogation
Nekāh	Marriage
Nezārat-e Estesvābi	Approbatory supervision
Olamā	High-ranking religious figures
Qabul	Acceptance
Qavvādi	Pandering
Qazf	Slanderous accusation of fornication
Qesās	Retaliation
Qiyās	Legal analogy
Rajm	Punishment by stoning
Roshd	Maturity
Ruju'	Husband's right to cancel divorce
Saqir-e qeir-e momayez	Undiscerning child
Shari'a	The divine source of Islamic law (Qur'an and Sunna)
Shi'ite	The minority branch of mainstream Islam, formed in the aftermath of the death of Prophet Mohammad by those Muslims who recognised his nephew Ali as the rightful successor; Shi'ites currently account for around ten per cent of the worldwide Muslim population
Sunna	The teachings, deeds and sayings of the Prophet Mohammad
Talāq	Divorce
Talāq-e Raj'i	Revocable divorce
Ta'zir	Discretionary punishment
Zenā	Adultery

ACKNOWLEDGEMENTS

The initial ideas for this book were developed after the widespread arrests of women's rights activists following the Haft-e Tir Square demonstration in Tehran in 2006, which I observed closely while representing a number of activists in the revolutionary courts in Tehran.

There are many people to whom I owe my thanks. First and foremost, I would like to express my sincere appreciation and gratitude to Dr Shirin Ebadi, from whom I have learned so many things in my personal and Professional life. Special thanks to Professor Martin Lau, Professor Lynn Welchman, Dr Nazila Ghanea, Dr Anicee Van England and Dr Siavush Ranjbar-Daemi who have given me tremendous support and encouragement, and have devoted considerable energy, enthusiasm and academic assistance to my project. I am grateful to Jody Williams and the Nobel Women's Initiative for the generous support of my work.

I further acknowledge and thank several friends for their intellectual support and generosity. My understanding of Islamic law, its application in Iran and the contemporary history of Iran have been greatly enhanced by conversation and interaction with Dr Alam Saleh, Mehrangiz Kar and Dr Ziba Mir-Hosseini among others. I am thankful to many friends and colleagues who have been indispensable in their intellectual support, constructive criticism and encouragement. I am grateful to Neda Shahidyazdani, Simin Fahendej, Masih Alinejad, Taimoor Aliassi, Azadeh Pourzand, Yousef Namin, Farnoosh Hashemian, Parvin Zabihi, Nooshin Ahmadi Khorasani, Mansoureh Shojaei, Khadijeh Moghadam, Asieh Amini, Parvin Ardalan, Mahnaz Parakand, Shima Ghoosheh,

Sussan Tahmasebi, Tara Sadooghi, Elenara Velivasaki, Ridvan Karpuz, Parisa Tolou Hayat, Nargess Tavassolian, Saba Zavarei, Ahad Ghanbary, Mani Mostofi, Nadia Novibi, Shadi Safavi, Sara Zavarei and Fazel Hawramy.

This book would not have been completed without my family. I owe boundless thanks to my parents: my mother Fakhrosadat, who has been an inspiration to me in my fight for gender equality, and my father Mohammad, who has empowered me to stand up against injustice and inequalities.

I am grateful to my sisters, Ashraf, Shima, Sahar and Elaheh, and my brothers, Hamidreza and Alireza, for their continued support. I owe a special thanks to my son's father, Vahid for his support during the most difficult and challenging years of my life. Last and not least, my son Parsa, who has made me a better person and a proud mother.

PREFACE

Iranian women have suffered legal discrimination both before and after the 1979 Revolution. This book aims to determine the extent to which subsequent bargaining by women's rights activists has led to a significant and tangible change in the legal status of women in Iran. This book strives to prove that while Iranian women have not yet obtained legal equality, they have not been passive either. As a result, the gender bias of the Iranian legal system has been successfully challenged and has lost its legitimacy. More pertinently, the social context has become more prepared to accommodate equal rights for women.

The most important international instrument for ensuring women's rights is the Convention on the Elimination of All Forms of Discrimination Against Women (CEDAW), to which Iran is not yet a party. The failure of Iran to ratify the CEDAW and remove discriminatory laws stands in stark contrast to the advances that Iranian women have made in other spheres during the past three decades and is a valid illustration of their present paradoxical condition. This book aims to ascertain the causes of Iran's failure to ratify the CEDAW and, in particular, to analyse whether Islamic principles prevent Iran from ratifying the Convention. It analyses some of the key challenges that proponents of gender equality face in the Muslim context, to explore the possibility of reforming women's rights within an Islamic and domestic framework. For instance, the One Million Signatures Campaign launched in 2006 to put an end to legal discrimination against women in Iran is an illustration of the contextualisation of the international discourse on gender equality by Iranian women.

To study the legal situation of Iranian women, this book relies mainly on feminist legal theory to criticise and re-evaluate the underlying principles that have shaped the struggle for equal rights between the sexes.

INTRODUCTION AND THEORETICAL FRAMEWORK

In early 1979, a revolutionary movement spearheaded by male Shi'a clergy succeeded in bringing an end to the Pahlavi monarchy, a secular-leaning regime committed to the elimination of organised religion from government and public life. As a girl born in Tehran two years earlier, I became part of the generation that had to pick up the mantle of the feminist movement that had progressively emerged since the Constitutional Revolution of 1906. Even before 1979, any attempt to shift entrenched moral and social conduct – strictly policed by senior religious figures – required aggressive political mobilisation. Progress in advancing gender-balanced civil rights did not come easy in such hostile terrain. With a brief exception during the administration of the Tabriz Democratic League (1945–6), women in Iran were denied the right to vote in parliamentary elections until 1963, thereby beating Switzerland to the punch by seven years. However, women's rights activists did play a commanding role in enactment of the Family Protection Law in 1967, the amendment of which in 1976 led to the further strengthening of women's rights.

My generation was supposed to inherit this progressive, albeit starkly imperfect, legacy of women's activism in Iran. But I was born on the cusp of the most consequential social, political and legal transformation in twentieth-century Iranian history, the 1979 Revolution. The revolution stopped the drive toward further female emancipation in its tracks. Rather than taking up the inheritance bequeathed by the generations of Iranian women before me, I was instead confronted with the Iran–Iraq War and the long shadow cast by Islamic puritans in the public square, all of which constricted the space for debate and mobilisation for the expansion of women's rights. In fact, I didn't personally become acquainted with the women's movement and its activities until 1995, when I began my undergraduate studies in the school of law at the University of Tehran.

The course of events after the revolution did not favour women's rights. Most of the gains of previous decades – including rights painstakingly achieved through the long and difficult process of prying concessions from a Shah whose commitment to modernisation was often more apparent than real – were rolled back. Shirin Ebadi, the Nobel Peace Prize laureate, captured the situation accurately when she observed that 'the 1979 Revolution was a revolution staged by men against women'.[1] The formation of an Islamic republic with a Shariʿa-based[2] constitution stipulating that all laws and regulations must be in accordance with Islamic principles had a detrimental effect on the legal status of Iranian women. The revolution saw the Shi'ite clergy and their allies and supporters assume complete control of the executive, legislative and judicial branches of the State, and the Shariʿa elevated to the principal source of law in Iran.

The result has been a significant and sustained attack on the rights of Iranian women over nearly four decades. At the heart of this offensive is the claim of the Shi'ite clergy that men and women do not have equal rights under Islam.[3] As one of the most prominent scholars on the relationship of Islam and human rights argues, 'Shariʿa family law is fundamentally premised on the notion of male guardianship over women and is consequently characterised by many features of inequality between men and women in marriage, divorce, and related matters.'[4] When Iranian women have questioned the iniquities of Islamic law as applied in Iran, they have frequently been cast as miscreants, accused of defying sacred law and even of threatening national security. However, despite the government's inclination to criminalise advocacy of women's rights, the women's movement has not only persisted but has become more insistent over time.

Paradoxically, the revolution itself played a crucial role in opening opportunities and encouraging women to participate in the public and social spheres. Historically, the women's movement lacked the momentum to penetrate the rural parts of the country – where until comparatively recently most Iranian women lived – and so was largely an elite mobilisation. The revolution changed all that. Women who had long been marginalised in rural and religious communities were able to find their place in public life. The war and the reconstruction that followed, including the expansion of women's education, meant women from all walks of life were increasingly drawn into the workforce and the community more generally to contribute to the national cause. This participation saw women – particularly religious women – forced to confront every day the callousness of Iran's myriad discriminatory laws. Such women could no longer deny that a dogmatic interpretation of Islam was a fundamental roadblock to equal rights. As a result, women belonging to traditional, modern, religious and secular families came together to demand equality. The universal participation of women catapulted the movement into new spheres of discourse.

When I entered the women's movement in 1995, I quickly realised that through all the challenges of the post-revolutionary period, Iranian women had not assumed a negative and passive attitude. Instead, they had made use of every local and international strategy available to confront and combat legal discrimination. As a woman, I had personally experienced discrimination in my daily life but I only began to come to terms with this when I entered university. My study of the law in particular showed me that the legal and social climate was not as closed as it might have been, and the many opportunities available to fight for equality of rights, which I felt were innate to me as a human being, no matter the culture or religion I had happened to be born into. This book is the culmination of the stories of the struggle waged by Iranian women for legal equality. It seeks to assess the success of the various strategies that women's rights activists' have deployed – appealing to international law and mobilising for changes to domestic legislation, re-interpreting the Qur'an, exercising *ejtehād* and activism – in the quest to achieve significant and tangible changes in the legal status of women in Iran. As a student, and later practitioner, of law I not only observed these strategies but made them part of my advocacy toolkit. After nearly two decades working on women's rights in Iran – challenging judges in family courts and defending women's rights activists in revolutionary courts, reflecting on the causes and consequences of the status of women in Iran, analysing discourse and surveying literature and theories relevant to women's rights and feminist analysis of the legal situation of women – it has become clear to me that the current political context of Iran constitutes the 'clear and present danger' to the advance of women's rights in the country. It became my mission to determine whether – despite not being fully grounded within the canons of Islamic law – legal reform could succeed within the framework of an Islamic state. The question therefore must be asked: to what extent is bottom-up, grassroots effort and activism by women's rights activists and organisations capable of securing top-down political support for the advancement of women's rights in Iran?

I have written this book, in large part, to answer this question. In so doing, I focus particular attention on the One Million Signatures Campaign, which emerged in 2006 aiming to put an end to discriminatory laws and attracting the participation of women from all walks of life. As a member of the campaign's legal committee, I was 'present at the creation', to coin a phrase. As one of the campaigns lawyers, I took part in seminars aimed at educating Iranian men and women regarding discriminatory laws against women. But this was no academic exercise either; I was often called from the classroom to the court to defend campaign activists charged with that vaguest of catch-all allegations, deployed by authoritarians everywhere: 'threatening national security'. As one of the leading attorneys for the One Million Signatures Campaign, I was confronted with just how resistant the current regime is to address discriminatory laws against women, a reticence that ultimately doomed the campaign to failure. Iran's refusal to sign the Convention on the Elimination of All Forms of Discrimination Against Women (CEDAW) – which the Guardian Council argues contravenes Shari'a law even though it has been ratified by many Muslim nations – constitutes the signal international manifestation of the regime's intransigence in this regard. The story of the movement to see Iran accede to the CEDAW – culminating in the One Million Signatures Campaign – thus forms the core of this book.[5]

The argument put forward in this book draws heavily upon feminist legal theories, which provide useful tools to place the existing, marginalising structures of law and society under a clear critical spotlight and to propose alternatives. Feminist legal theories foreground the issue of gender in law by highlighting the ways in which dominant frames and discourse silence or obscure the voice and interests of women and by developing extensive proposals for legal reforms to reduce these inequities.[6] Feminist legal theorists analyse law from the perspective of all women and criticise law as a patriarchal institution that contributes to the subordination of women.

The nexus between gender and law is complex, and a substantial and impressive body of feminist legal theory has developed that helps us come to grips with that complexity. The feminist critique of international law deconstructs the international legal regime by highlighting its limitations and the narrow scope on which it is grounded. It also seeks to reconstruct a framework that is not predicated upon the domination of women by men. Moreover, that critique – which addresses the position of women within international legal structures – questions 'who' (and, indeed, who is *not*) is involved in creating international law and whose concerns are heard and addressed within international legal structures. To assess the extent to which women's voices and concerns have been included within the international legal system, feminist scholarship has examined linkages between the 'who' and the 'where'.[7]

Throughout the 1990s, the feminist challenge to international law produced real gains, including affirmative changes in international institutions and in the substance and procedures of the international human rights regime. As a result, women's human rights have increasingly come to be recognised and protected, despite the huge amount of work that is yet to be done. Historical gains were seen at the Vienna Conference on Human Rights in 1993, which declared that the 'human rights of women and of the girl-child are an inalienable, integral and individual part of universal human rights'[8] and when the 1994 Conference on Population and Development in Cairo guaranteed women's reproductive rights.[9] In 1999, the enforcement mechanism of the CEDAW was enhanced by the adoption of its Optional Protocol, allowing individual complaints in case of violations of the Convention and empowering the Committee to launch an inquiry in the face of reliable information of grave or systematic violation.[10]

These great achievements notwithstanding, the struggle for women's rights remains a key concern in the realm of international affairs. In today's Western political perspectives, we find examples of key instances, such as the War on Terror, where women and their individual freedoms – while ostensibly integral to the discourse – are used to justify military interventions in places such as Afghanistan. Examples like this show that the rhetorical placement of women at the heart of mainstream human rights discourse contrasts with reality, where they are used as a façade to frame intervention. Women's rights are therefore overlooked for the sake of security concerns once the 'liberation' operation has been minimally achieved.[11] In fact, when women become 'insiders' in human rights discourse, human rights become an 'outsider' discourse.[12]

Feminists have developed different methods to challenge existing legal structures. The first of these is the 'women question', an approach that casts a bright light on whether women's interests have been considered in every legal analysis.[13] The 'woman question' has a long and rich history that has evolved throughout centuries, having also reached post-colonial contexts. In the case of Iran, in particular, the 'woman question' is a rather recent perspective – introduced with the 1906 Constitutional Revolution – and will be examined in more depth, as it has played out after 1979, in this book.

The second method consists of engaging in feminist practical reasoning, which seeks to heighten the sensitivity of legal decision-making to those matters which legal doctrine has tended to ignore, to obscure or to silence. Consciousness-raising, which 'offers a means of testing the validity of accepted legal principles through the lens of the personal experience of those directly affected by those principles',[14] constitutes the third method. These methods will be employed throughout this book and each chapter benefits from one method or a combination of them.

Following feminist methodology, this book questions the very boundaries of legal gender discourse and praxis set by the current state system in Iran. It is crucial to ground a feminist analysis of that system on a commitment to challenge the possible dominance of men over women within Iranian society. Success can be achieved in this arena through the implementation of educational changes from within; that is, by changing the method and not the objective. Systematic and consistent pressure for cooperation from malleable and receptive parts of the Islamic Republic's political elite – such as the inner-establishment reformists, which implements restrictions – will result in reforms and changes.

With that critical commitment squarely in mind, this book draws heavily on the range of investigative methods that inform Margaret Radin's analytical approach of *situated judgment*. The legal situation of Iranian women cannot be adequately analysed without considering the political context of the country. By using the feminist legal theories and applying its different methods, I take the reader through a process of exploring how Iranian women have applied different strategies, including international law, domestic law, Islamic law, social discourse and political mechanisms while appealing to higher authorities to change the laws that discriminate against them. Furthermore, I will look at how these women have responded to the political context and what experiences they have gained from it. Nonetheless, feminist theory is only a vehicle. The diversity of cultural, national, spiritual (religious), economic and public concerns and interests and, of course, women's own stories will also be considered.

This book assesses the failures of Iran's legal and political system, under which the rights of Iranian women are subject to severe restrictions. Within the context of the academic literature on women's rights in Iran, this study seeks to contribute to the field by analysing the current situation, which presents considerable differences with respect to the period in which many of the previous academic works were produced. Women are more educated these days and their awareness of discriminatory laws has increased. I argue that the latter — developed during the expansion of civil society under the presidency of Mohammad Khatami (1997–2005) — mobilised Iranian women to the extent that even restrictions re-enacted and augmented during the presidency of Mahmud Ahmadinejad have not prevented them from demanding their rights. By steering away from ideological idealism towards political activism, the women's movement has equipped itself with the ability to collaborate with the broader democracy movement, and to prepare the ground for eventually achieving gender equality. This book aims to explore the level of engagement and impact of women's rights activists, in their quest to bring about positive changes in the Shari'a-based civil and criminal codes of Iran. For this reason, the focus of this book is mainly on state laws and will not analyse the personal status laws of recognised religious minorities.[15]

I believe that the existing literature has not adequately examined the struggle of Iranian women and the different strategies and methods they have applied to eradicate discrimination and achieve gender equality. Rather, its focus is entirely on the discriminatory legal situation of Iranian women.[16] This book contributes to the literature by examining the struggle of Iranian women to achieve gender equality from several vantage points: legal, political and socio-religious. It combines the detailed legal analysis of the discriminatory status of women, which is obtained through a close study of a variety of relevant Iranian written primary material, such as legal documentation, official records of the Iranian Parliament, the Majles, and the remarks, periodicals and memoirs of relevant personalities within the socio-religious and political context in which attempts to tackle discrimination have been made. It also makes use of a wide range of personal interviews[17] conducted between 2009 and 2013 with people from different groups, including women's activists,[18] lawyer,[19] and some of the sixth Majles representatives who support Iran ratifying the CEDAW.[20] Parliamentary terms in Iran run for four years. The first session of the Majles in the post-revolutionary period ran from 1980 to 1984, during the height of the Iran–Iraq War. At the time of writing, the Majles was in its ninth session (2012–16). Most of the 'action' in the book took place in the sixth Majles (2000–04).

The book argues that, even though Iran has not yet ratified the CEDAW, the discourse of universality regarding gender equality that it reflects has enabled Iranian women to fight for equal rights. Women have played an active role in the struggle to eradicate discrimination and contextualise internationally accepted standards on equality and non-discrimination within Iranian society. According to Shirin Ebadi, 'human rights discourse is alive and well at the grassroots level; civil society activists consider it to be the most potent framework for achieving sustainable [...] reforms.'[21] Iranian women have used a progressive interpretation of Islamic discourses on gender equality to demonstrate that it is possible to be both a Muslim and a believer in gender equality.

CHAPTER 1

THE DEVELOPMENT OF UNIVERSAL STANDARDS ON GENDER EQUALITY: THE CONVENTION ON THE ELIMINATION OF ALL FORMS OF DISCRIMINATION AGAINST WOMEN

Introduction

In several instances, Iranian women's rights activists have demonstrated on the streets of Tehran and demanded that the government take action end to discrimination against women. The fact that every protest has been brought to an end through suppression by the security forces underscores the extent to which human rights in general – and women's rights in particular – are seen as a challenge to be faced down by the Iranian Government. Traditionally, in some Islamic countries like Iran, human rights are considered a Western invention with limited or no connection to the fabric of Muslim societies.[1] The reason for this view may be the fact that no educational or awareness-raising measures can be effective in a community that regards the values reflected in human rights instruments as alien and imposed on them from the outside.[2]

The principal argument advanced in this chapter is that, despite the traditional view of some Islamic governments that human rights discourse is a Western phenomenon, international standards of human rights extend beyond national borders. This chapter examines the development of international standards on women's human rights to highlight the presence and participation of Muslim women in this process. The aim is to demonstrate that gender equality standards are not alien to Muslim women.[3]

Equality and non-discrimination are fundamental principles of human rights. With respect to the human rights of women, the Convention on the Elimination of All Forms of Discrimination Against Women (CEDAW), which was adopted by the UN General Assembly in 1979, stands out as the most influential instrument yet devised by the international community. Although the CEDAW is designed to eradicate discrimination against women and improve the individual, family, social, political, economic and cultural aspects of women's lives in the ratifying country, the contradictions between the CEDAW and the Shari'a remain a primary concern in many Muslim states.

The CEDAW urges States Parties to amend laws, practices and customs that discriminate against women.[4] Whilst the CEDAW's objectives appear capable of universal acceptance, they have nevertheless been controversial in the Muslim world. The central basis of the convention is the demand for gender equality as expressed in Articles 2 and 16 of the CEDAW.

This chapter briefly analyses the CEDAW to assess the extent to which this comprehensive and well-targeted international convention focusing on non-discrimination against women can be effective in improving the status of women worldwide. It argues that the convention provides effective legal language and a framework which can be used as a legal tool by advocates for gender equality for addressing the issue of discrimination against women. It also provides minimum common standards on gender equality to persuade the States Parties to the convention to ensure and guarantee the protection of women's rights. In the words of Indira Jaising, 'the implementation of human rights norms for women can only be effective if it is in furtherance of preserving and according to women a life of dignity. The role of laws in such matters has to rise above the level of a tool of adjudication to a tool to ensure the provision of justice'.[5]

The global movements for women's rights: Muslim women's experience

While gender equality carries a certain modern quality, the fact is women began the struggle for equality long before the adoption of the UN Charter. Consider the International Alliance of Women (1904) and the Women's International League for Peace and Freedom (1915), both organised by women, including Muslim women.[6] Of course, solidarity, as they say, begins at home, and women were involved in social and political movements seeking equality within national borders dating back to the turn of the twentieth century. Iranian women, for example, played essential roles in the political events that occurred in the country during and after the Constitutional Revolution of 1906.[7]

The preamble of the United Nations Charter affirms 'faith in fundamental human rights, in the dignity and worth of the human person, in the equal rights of men and women of nations large and small.'[8] The purpose of the United Nations, according to Article 1 of the charter, is 'to achieve international cooperation [...] in promoting and encouraging respect for human rights and for fundamental freedoms for all without distinction as to race, sex, language or religion.'[9] To promote the implementation of the principle that men and women have equal rights and to develop proposals to give effect to such recommendations, the Commission on the Status of Women (CSW) was set up by United Nations Economic and Social Council (ECOSOC) in accordance with Article 68 of the UN Charter, in 1946.[10] During its first session in February 1947, the CSW declared as one of its guiding principles:

> [To] raise the status of women, irrespective of nationality, race, language or religion, to equality with men in all fields of human enterprise, and to eliminate all discrimination against women in the provisions of statutory law, in legal maxims or rules, or in interpretation of customary law.[11]

The CSW has played a significant role in setting new international standards on women's human rights during 1946–62. A number of international conventions were held with sponsorship from the commission, namely the 1952 Convention on the Political Rights of Women,[12] the 1957 Convention on the Nationality of Married

Women[13] and the 1962 Convention on Consent to Marriage, Minimum Age for Marriage, and Registration of Marriage.[14] The commission, therefore, was successful in elaborating and adopting specific conventions on the rights of women before the UN Commission on Human Rights, founded in 1946, succeeded in drafting the Covenant on Economic, Social and Cultural Rights and the Covenant on Civil and Political Rights, both of which contain non-discriminatory provisions.[15]

The commission had observer status in the Human Rights Committee (HRC) of the UN during the drafting process of the Universal Declaration of Human Rights (UDHR). Although the CSW did not have an independent vote in the HRC, its presence and lobbying encouraged the incorporation of the equality of rights discourse into the UDHR.[16]

Women's rights were discussed significantly during the drafting process of the UDHR, in one of the most essential debates of the drafting process. Reference to gender equality in the UN Charter's opening affirmation of faith was left out and replaced with the gender-neutral term 'everyone' in the fourth draft submitted to the HRC by the drafting committee.[17] This provoked objections from the delegations of some countries during the discussion in the Third Committee of the General Assembly. Lakshimi Menon, the delegate from India, objected to the omission of gender equality, arguing that its absence invited discrimination against women. Minerva Bernardino from the Dominican Republic, supporting Lakshmi's position, insisted that:

> [In] certain countries the term 'everyone' did not necessarily mean every individual, regardless of sex. Certain countries claimed to recognise the rights of 'everyone' but experience has shown that women did not enjoy those rights in the same capacity as men – as, for instance, voting rights.[18]

The explicit term 'gender equality' was re-inserted into the text by a vote of thirty-two to two, and three abstentions that came from the United Kingdom, Canada and Ethiopia. The United States and China cast the two opposing votes.[19] It is interesting to note that no representative from Muslim countries voted against the text on gender equality. The representatives from the Muslim world, however, did not have a unified position on the issue of gender equality. According to Waltz, while most

The Development of Universal Standards on Gender 13

representatives from Muslim countries hoped to limit the strong language of gender equality inserted in the UDHR, some Muslim delegations, including those of Iraq and Pakistan, strongly advocated for women's rights.[20]

Article 16 of the UDHR guarantees both sexes equal rights in marriage, including the right to choose whom to wed, and the right to dissolve a marriage contract. This was one of the debated issues that attracted significant attention during the drafting process of the UDHR. The CSW, in its report submitted to the HRC in mid-1947, suggested including a clause to the UDHR in relation to family issues. The commission suggested that the clause mention freedom of choice, the dignity of the wife, the right to keep one's nationality, the right to make contracts and equal rights to divorce, guardianship of children and the ownership of property.[21] The draft of Article 16 discussed at the Third Committee contained three paragraphs: 1) 'Men and women of full age have the right to marry and to found a family and are entitled to equal rights as to marriage'; 2) 'Marriage shall be entered into only with the full consent of both intending spouses'; and 3) 'The family is the natural and fundamental group unit of society and is entitled to protection.'[22]

Equal rights to divorce constituted the most controversial issue for the delegates to the Third Committee. It is interesting to note that 'much of the opposition to the explicit mention of divorce came from delegates from Christian countries and organisations'.[23] M. Amado, the Panamanian representative, argued, for instance, 'some States were bound by laws based on Concordats with the church and had, in respect of religious marriage and divorce, obligations which would not permit them to accept the proposal text.'[24]

Some Muslim delegations were also active in these discussions. Saudi Arabia and Egypt, for example, proposed amendments to the text of Article 16.[25] The Saudi Arabian delegation strongly criticised the article, stating that Western standards on the family were given priority over 'more ancient civilisations that had passed the experimental age, and the institution of which, for example, had proven their wisdom through the centuries'.[26] Lebanon and Syria were the only Muslim countries supporting Saudi Arabia's position. Interestingly, no other Muslim states backed it. Yet, Shaista Irkamullah of Pakistan raised the point with other Muslim representatives that the term 'equal rights' was not equivalent to 'identical rights.' She stated that Article 16 was drafted 'to prevent child marriage and marriages without the consent of both parties, and also to ensure the protection of women after divorce.'[27]

When the text of UDHR Article 16 was forwarded to the General Assembly in December 1948, the phrases 'without any limitation due to race, nationality or religion' and 'during marriage and its dissolution' were added to the first paragraph. The word 'free'[28] was added to the second paragraph to make the consent full and free. In the third paragraph, the terms 'by society and the state' were added to the idea of protection.[29] Therefore, the final text of Article 16 in the UDHR included provisions for equal rights to marriage, during marriage and its dissolution, the free and full consent of both parties and prohibited limitations based on race, nationality and religion. It is important to note that Muslim states, with the sole exception of Saudi Arabia, voted for Article 16. The latter was approved through the positive vote of, amongst others, Egypt, Iran, Iraq, Pakistan, Turkey, Lebanon and Syria. Therefore, one may agree with Morsink when he states:

> The question of human rights cannot be settled on religious grounds. The human rights enunciated in the UDHR are not linked to religion. The drafters did not think that to accept the existence of any one of the rights one had to be an adherent of a certain faith.[30]

The CSW 'aimed at improving the status of women in all fields of human rights irrespective of their nationality, language or religion and therefore in its view democracy is the only way in which women can enjoy their full rights as human beings.'[31]

Muslim states also advocated for gender equality during the adoption of the International Covenant on Civil and Political Rights (ICCPR) and the International Covenant on Economic, Social, and Cultural Rights (ICESCR). The Human Rights Commission did not initially provide for a separate article on gender equality in an earlier draft of covenants. Rather, the provisions guaranteeing gender equality were attached to other articles of the covenants.[32] The Iraqi delegation, headed by Bedia Afnan, insisted on the incorporation of a separate article on gender equality within the covenant drafts.[33] Although the delegations of both Western and Muslim states argued against the Iraqi delegation's position, Afnan's idea attracted more positive support and resulted in

The Development of Universal Standards on Gender 15

adoption of a common Article 3 in both covenants that urges the State Parties to ensure the equal rights of men and women to the rights set forth in both covenants.[34]

Muslim delegates also played active roles during the world conferences on women. The members of the CSW agreed to hold the first World Conference on Women (WCW) in June 1975, in Mexico. At the end of the conference, a world 'plan of action' was adopted by the delegates with the aim of promoting 'equality between men and women; to ensure the integration of women in the total development effort; and to increase the contribution of women to the strengthening of world peace'.[35] The plan acknowledged the differences between countries and between women in the same country and therefore proposed that each nation individually develop distinct strategies and activities. However, these had to be in line with the ones mentioned in two specific UN plans, that is, the International Development Strategy for the Second Development Decade and the World Population Plan of Action adopted at the Bucharest conference. The plan provided for realistic and pragmatic guidelines and recommendations including the establishment of local women's bureaus, commissions and committees with adequate staffing and budgets.[36] Alongside the world plan of action, the FWCW adopted a declaration that clearly sent a message to the world that:

> [W]omen of the entire world, whatever differences exist between them, share the painful experience of receiving or having received unequal treatment, and that as their awareness of the phenomenon increases they will become natural allies in the struggle against any form of oppression.[37]

According to Afkhami, the Women's Organisation of Iran (WOI) played a major role in the formulation of the world plan of action.[38] The WOI subsequently used the world plan of action to formulate and implement Iran's national plan of action, which opened space for the WOI to be involved in the political decision-making process.[39] The WOI was a non-profit organisation created in 1966, working mostly through volunteers, with local branches and centres for women all over the country, determined to enhance the rights of women in Iran. According to Afkhami, the WOI gradually 'convinced the government that its services were necessary for national development and that the government was obligated to assist the organisation in the best possible manner.'[40] The WOI was successful in bringing together Iranian women from different parts of the country and from different social strata based on a common belief in their unsatisfactory and unfair situations. By 1975, the WOI had succeeded in creating a network of 349 branches and 120 centres that compelled it to become aware of the challenges and demands faced by different groups of women. Subsequently, it established a network with women's organisations in other countries including China, France, Iraq, Pakistan and the Soviet Union. With the support of the WOI, the Iranian delegation played a key role in the first WCW. Ashraf Pahlavi, the twin sister of the late Shah of Iran, was the head of Iran's delegation. She was appointed to chair the consultative committee producing the draft of the world plan of action. Afkhami describes the conference in the following terms:

> During the conference in Mexico City, the main resolution, which committed member nations amongst others to attending a mid-decade world conference to monitor national progress and establish the International Research and Training Institute for the Advancement of Women (INSTRAW), was initiated by Iran. Iran was to host the mid-decade conference in 1980 and to provide a permanent home for INSTRAW. The final draft of the World Plan of Action adopted by the UN General Assembly in 1975 reflected many ideas researched and tested in Iran.[41]

The WOI worked extensively with the government as well as women's groups to prepare the national plan of action that was, in fact, a response to UN demand from member states to advance women's status over the ten-year period of 1975–85. To foster an agreement between different women's groups on a national plan of action, the WOI managed and financed more than 700 panels, which consequently led to the creation of a preliminary draft plan of action. The WOI was also successful in drawing government attention to women's issues and the adoption of a national plan of action through the establishment of a high council of cooperation consisting of eight cabinet ministers, the directors of Iranian national radio and television, the civil service commission, the national committee for world literacy programme and the WOI itself. The final document, approved in May 1978, included the basic goals and broad

The Development of Universal Standards on Gender 17

guidelines necessary to advance the women's status, as well as mechanisms for implementation, evaluation and monitoring.[42]

The mid-term World Conference of the United Nations Decade for Women and the parallel NGO forum were held in in Copenhagen July 1980. The objectives of the conference were to reaffirm the importance of the CEDAW, to indicate the extent to which the goals of the first WCW had been achieved and to update the world plan of action agreed in Mexico.[43] The unequal representation of the participants and disagreement about the topics chosen by women from Western and non-Western countries at the NGO forum transformed the conference into a highly politicised event and the 'most conflictive' of all of the conferences of the women's decade.[44] The participation of Iranian women at the NGO forum added to these tensions.

The Copenhagen conference took place one year after the revolution in Iran. It is evident that the new Iranian Government paid careful attention to selecting representatives for its first ever presence on this international platform. A press conference was held by Iranian representatives at the parallel NGO forum, in which Iranian participants celebrated the outcomes of the 1979 Revolution. Women participating in that press conference called for a return to the *hejāb* as a symbol of anti-colonialism.[45] In fact, the Iranian Government took advantage of the presence of Iranian participants in the second world conference to spread the idea that women's liberation was being advanced by Iran's anti-imperialist project. This view was challenged by a number of Iranians at the time.[46] As argued by Nayereh Tohidi, 'Iranian women were prevented from conceptualising their own answers, developing their own movement or defining their own identities independent of the national movement and the question of national identity.'[47] She suggests 'intertwining the liberation of women with national liberation and feminism with nationalism further complicated the conceptualisation of feminism and the course of women's emancipation in Iran.'[48] The oppression of Iranian women after the revolution reflects the fact that Iran's representative to the conference did not necessarily represent all Iranian women. The disruption of the celebration of 8 March 1979 and the accusation that feminism and women's rights are part of a 'Western conspiracy' is illustrative in this regard.[49]

Due to the political tensions surrounding the conference, the programme of action did not attract a consensus. The final document of the conference acknowledged the needs and requirements of women in different national and regional contexts. It was agreed to by a roll-call vote of 94 in favour and 4 against, with 22 delegations abstaining. The programme of action recognised the everyday realities of women and suggested that improving the status of women required action at the national, local and family levels.[50] In spite of all the frustration and confusion, the conference turned into a positive experience and cultural differences did not separate women. Instead they realised that there was so much in common to unite them, to feel the bond of sisterhood, to break the isolation of women and to feel the growing power within women.[51] It was in this spirit that the third WCW was organised.

Concluding the decade of women, the third WCW was held in Nairobi, Kenya in 1985. The conference aimed to establish concrete measures to overcome the persistence of underdevelopment and mass poverty, the continuation of subordinate roles for women in the development agenda and ongoing threats to international peace, all obstacles to the advancement of women. After two weeks of negotiations, the 'Nairobi Forward-Looking Strategies for the Advancement of Women to the Year 2000' was adopted by the state representatives. The document provided a series of measures for implementing equality at the national level. It explained, 'Since countries are at various stages of development, they should have the option to set their own priorities based on their own development policies and resource capabilities'.[52] In response to the results of the Nairobi conference, the General Assembly in a resolution of 13 December 1985 urged governments 'to establish collaborative arrangements and to develop approaches' in their national programmes towards the implementation of Nairobi strategies.[53] The commission's mandate was expanded in 1987, in the aftermath of the third WCW.[54]

The United Nations' fourth World Conference on Women[55] took place in Beijing between 4 and 15 September 1995 in conformity with General Assembly resolutions 45/129 and 46/98.[56] Prior to the conference, representatives from government agencies, NGOs, women activists and the private sector worked together to prepare themselves for what had become a very prominent public global event. Their efforts led to the establishment of national multidisciplinary committees, which proved effective entities for cross-border networking. Muslim women were also active in establishing such networks amongst themselves and the United Nations Development Fund for Women (UNIFEM), established to give the world's women a space within the United Nations system, helped them prepare to work within the context of a UN conference.[57]

The Iranian delegation, including 100 women, was headed by Shahla Habibi, the presidential advisor on women's affairs. According to Jamshid Sharifian, the participation of 100 active women from the state and the non-governmental sectors with an Islamic dress code greatly improved the negative image of the Iranian Government within the international community. It was the first time after the Revolution that Iranian women had successfully presented themselves in an international conference.[58] To describe Iran's participation in the conference, Shahla Habibi considers three different stages. The first was the stage at which a variety of activities were carried out to prepare the delegation for the conference. The second consisted of activities during the conference and the third included plans and strategies to be carried out after the conference. Habibi explains that the time framework was very limited, around two years, to make necessary arrangements and preparations for the conference. However, the responsible sectors under the presidential office managed to recognise non-governmental organisations and different women's groups and to link them to state agencies working in the field of women's rights. The other important issue for Habibi was the success enjoyed by her office in alerting Iranian politicians to women's issues and making them consider possible steps that should be taken to improve the status of women within the country. For this reason, some Iranian women participated in regional and international preparatory conferences prior to the Beijing conference; this enhanced their capacity to contribute substantively at the global gathering in the Chinese capital.[59] According to Habibi, Iranian delegates, both governmental and non-governmental, were very active during the conference and its NGOs Forum.

During her speech at the conference, while stating that it provided a unique opportunity to thoroughly review the status of women worldwide, Habibi criticised the draft platform for action. In her view, 'there exists a trend of confrontation between men and women in defining their roles in the society. This trend can overshadow many positive elements embodied in the text and accordingly undermine the full and expeditious implementation of the provisions of the Platform'. She stated that 'the draft Platform has not properly underlined the motherhood role of women.' She believed that a 'delicate balance can be established between the family as well as social roles of women.'

She noted, 'An active minority is trying to impose its certain sets of ideas on the majority of the international community. They have established a yard-stick and are applying it to measure the commitment of others to the cause of women.' She ended her speech with a statement by the late founder of the Islamic Republic of Iran, Imam Khomeini, who stated, 'The woman is the source of all virtues'.[60]

The outcome of twelve days of NGO lobbying and intense internal discussion was the final document of the Fourth WCW; the Beijing declaration and platform for action were declared to be 'the two fundamental documents to guide women's advancement into the twenty-first century.'[61] One hundred and eighty-nine countries, including the Islamic Republic of Iran, unanimously adopted these documents.[62]

The Beijing platform for action: Moving Muslim women from the periphery to the centre[63]

The Beijing conference 'was an important catalyst for defining women's issues, establishing the language of women's rights as human rights and planning action in various Muslim countries.'[64] Following the Beijing conference, national mechanisms for addressing women's issues were established across the Middle East and Central Asia. In Jordan, a national strategy was formulated to advance the status of women. A national commission for women was established in Palestine. Women in Lebanon, Kuwait and Qatar drew on their ministers of social affairs to formulate a welfare model of support for women.[65] These activities demonstrate the fact that international agreements on certain minimal standards are very important for the improvement of women's rights. As Afkhami and Friedl aptly state, the documents that comprise the international framework on women's human rights 'provide women everywhere with models they can use to compare and assess their situation. They also provide international standards by which every nation [that is] a signatory to them must measure its performance.'[66] However, according to Afkhami, the following must apply for Muslim women to benefit from human rights policies:

> They must be able to learn about these rights and how they fit local traditions, including religious ones; they must be able to

The Development of Universal Standards on Gender 21

compare their own situations to the postulates of 'rights' and to form and formulate their own opinions and arguments.[67]

To realise the importance of international human rights standards for the advancement of women's rights in Islamic countries, it is useful to elaborate on the case of the Islamic Republic of Iran. During the presidency of Mohammad Khatami, as part of the Beijing + 5 and Beijing + 10 initiatives, the Iranian Government submitted two reports to the UN's Division for the Advancement of Women (DAW).[68] In October 1998, as part of the preparatory process for the Beijing + 5 conference in the year 2000, DAW sent a questionnaire to governments around the world requesting information on the implementation of the Beijing platform for action. Iran's response gave significance to the work of the national committee, which represented the Iranian Government during the Beijing conference, to guarantee the implementation of the Beijing platform for action. To increase public awareness and to familiarise state actors with the Beijing platform for action, the national committee launched a media campaign and translated the Beijing platform for action and the Beijing declaration into Persian. It also drafted the national plan for action.[69] Iran's response consisted of 12 sections reflecting on critical areas of concern outlined in the Beijing declaration. In the area of 'human rights of women' the report notes the importance of promoting the human rights of women, just as the national plan emphasised.

The Beijing conference had a positive impact on improving the status of Iranian women. According to Iran's report, 'since 1995, attention to the advancement of women has been reinforced in both government policies and public perception.'[70] However, the report acknowledged that:

> In areas such as the elimination of legal obstacles, the eradication of poverty, changing negative perceptions and patriarchal attitudes, closing the gender gap at high levels of decision-making, bringing a gender perspective into the mainstream has been least successful. The revision of laws and legislation on women is a long-term complex procedure, which makes the modification of laws arduous.[71]

Despite all these obstacles, the report suggests that the government has made a serious effort to bring a gender perspective into all national, economic, legal, social and political policies. The bureau for women's affairs was expanded into the Centre for Women's Participation (CPW) headed by a member of the cabinet. This enabled the centre to review budget bills and to lobby for a larger allocation in the budget for women's issues.[72]

The role and function of the CPW in improving the situation of Iranian women was covered in more detail in a 2005 report of the Iranian Government to DAW.[73] The Centre for Women's Participation was recognised as a support organisation within the government, identifying and discussing issues of concern for women, to offer solutions through executive organisations. It also made policies and plans and coordinated, supervised and monitored the activities of the executive regarding women's affairs. The report suggests that Iran was taking progressive steps in bringing women's issues from the margins to the centre. It was acknowledged that the award of the 2003 Nobel Prize to Shirin Ebadi, an Iranian Muslim lawyer, had increased the Iranian Government's commitment to ensuring women's rights.

The 2005 report listed laws that had been changed or amended since the victory of the 1979 Revolution in general and the Beijing conference in particular. These included the conditions set by a bride at the time of her marriage contract on the basis of Article 1119 of the Iran's civil code (1982), a law that gave the right of custodianship of minor or sick children to their mothers (1985), an amendment to Article 1041 of the civil code raising the minimum age of marriage for girls and boys (1991), an amendment to Article 1110 of the civil code regarding the provision of necessary support to the wife during the waiting period (*eddeh*) after the death of husband (2002) and an amendment to Article 1130 of the civil code determining cases of distress and constriction of women (2002).[74] Although the CPW tried to pave the way for Iran to join the Convention on the Elimination of all Forms of Discrimination Against women, the complexity of Iran's legislative system stymied its efforts.

After the rise to power of a traditionalist-oriented right-wing government in 2005, the Ahmadinejad administration, issues pertaining to women's rights were once again attached to interpretations over the role of family. In 2008, the delegation of the Islamic Republic of Iran to the fifty-second session of the Commission on the Status of Women made it clear that 'the effort of the Islamic Republic of Iran in the area of women's issues are based on the principles, values, and moral foundations of the nation and are geared to address our own domestic problems'. In the view of this delegation, 'by offering a new model of contemporary women who are pious and chaste and possess political wisdom, are accountable, self-sacrificing and promoters of spirituality in families, a new civilization will emerge'.[75] In 2013, Maryam Mojtahedzadeh, head of the Centre for Women and Family Affairs[76] and advisor to President Ahmadinejad, presented the general approach of the Islamic Republic of Iran towards women and their dignity to the fifty-seventh session of the Commission on the Status of Women. In her statement, she said 'we believe that Almighty God has created both man and woman equally from essence and for perfection and growth, complementary to each other, whereby each has been given a specific role to play'.[77]

As part of the UN reform agenda in July 2010, the General Assembly created UN Women, the United Nations body responsible for gender equality and the empowerment of women. This new initiative merges and builds on the important work of four previously distinct parts of the UN system, including DAW, which focused exclusively on gender equality and women's empowerment.[78] In 2014, Iran won a seat on the executive board of UN Women with a four-year term ending in 2018. UN Women has a number of roles and responsibilities. It is charged with supporting inter-governmental bodies, such as the Commission on the Status of Women, in their formulation of policies, global standards and norms. The body is also tasked with helping member states implement these standards – standing ready to provide suitable technical and financial support to those countries that request it – and forge effective partnerships with civil society. Finally, UN Women is the agency charged with leading and coordinating the UN system's work on gender equality, including promoting accountability through regular monitoring of system-wide progress. It was my hope that Iran, as one of the board members of this UN body responsible for promoting UN work on gender equality, would itself become a party to the CEDAW, the UN convention on women's rights.

In 2016, Gholamali Khoshroo, ambassador and permanent representative of the Islamic Republic of Iran to the United Nations, presented the view of the new moderate administration of Hassan Rowhani before the sixteenth session of the Commission on the Status of Women. Commenting on the importance of the advancement and empowerment of women, Ambassador Gholamali stated:

[Relying] on its basis, which is reflected in articles 20 and 21 of [the] Iranian Constitution, the Islamic Republic of Iran has launched efforts in the past 37 years in line with promotion of women's status, women's empowerment, family sustainability, and bridging gaps and disparities between men and women. It has always considered this issue in all national development programs and policies.[79]

While listing positive developments, he admitted: 'Nonetheless, the government is not negligent to the need to further promote women's participation in political and decision-making areas and in the labor market'.[80]

The concept of equality in the international and the Islamic framework

There is no consensus on the meaning of equality in international human rights law as well as within political and legal theory.[81] Although most international human rights conventions and covenants include articles that protect the right to equality, they fail to address the specific content of equality.[82] Different approaches to equality have been discussed to a great extent in the literature, but go beyond the scope of this study. Two approaches emerge in this regard: a formal one, according to which equality is seen to require equal treatment, and a substantive one, which 'is not simply with the equal treatment of the law, but rather with the actual impact of the law', hold dominant positions within legal jurisprudence.[83] According to Kapur 'CEDAW has primarily adopted a substantive model of equality',[84] which is affirmed in CEDAW General Recommendation No. 28 on States Parties' 'core obligation' under Article 2 of the convention.[85] General Recommendation No. 28 explains that:

> Article 2 calls on States parties to condemn discrimination against women in 'all its forms', while article 3 refers to appropriate measures that States parties are expected to take in 'all fields' to ensure the full development and advancement of women. Through these provisions, the convention anticipates the emergence of new forms of discrimination that had not been identified at the time of its drafting.[86]

The Development of Universal Standards on Gender

Gender equality has also been a contested issue, which has not attracted consensus amongst feminist legal theory scholars. Protectionism, sameness and compensation are amongst different approaches which arose in the question of gender differences. According to the protectionist approach, women are different to men and considered to be weaker, subordinate and in need of protection. Based on this approach, any law treating women and men differently could be justified based on the existing differences between two sexes and the idea that women need to be protected. The equal treatment considers men and woman the same that must be treated with legal equivalence. The third approach takes into consideration the historically disadvantaged position of women and therefore asks for compensatory or corrective treatment.[87] The CEDAW has adopted a more robust approach to gender equality and 'acknowledges the role of gender differences in producing disadvantage, without reinforcing those differences to preclude women from access to and enjoyment of equality.'[88]

The Universal Declaration on Human Rights 'envisages equal protection under a neutral law, a law that does not deny rights to members of weaker or disfavoured categories of society, according all people equal treatment'.[89] The general human rights treaties, namely the International Covenant on Social, Economic and Cultural Rights (ICSECR) and the International Covenant on Civil and Political Rights (ICCPR), both of which have been ratified by Iran, embody the fundamental principles of equality and non-discrimination on grounds such as gender. Moreover, Article 3 of both covenants in particular obliges States Parties to ensure equal enjoyment of all rights set forth in the covenants for men and women.[90] The Human Rights Committee (HRC), in its general comment on Article 3, observed that:

> Inequality in the enjoyment of rights by women throughout the world is deeply embedded in tradition, history and culture, including religious attitudes. The subordinate role of women in some countries is illustrated by the high incidence of parental sex selection and abortion of female foetuses. States Parties should ensure that traditional, historical, religious or cultural attitudes are not used to justify violations of women's right to equality before the law and to equal enjoyment of all Covenant rights. States parties should furnish appropriate information on those

aspects of tradition, history, cultural practices and religious attitudes that jeopardize, or may jeopardize, compliance with Article 3, and indicate what measures they have taken or intend to take to overcome such factors.[91]

Moreover, Articles 2(1) and 26 generally prohibit discrimination on grounds such as race, colour and sex. According to Article 26 of the ICCPR, all persons are equal before the law, and are entitled without any discrimination to the equal protection of the law. This article has a broad meaning. The HRC has made it clear that Article 26 is not limited to the rights already provided for in the ICCPR: 'It prohibits discrimination in law or in fact in any field regulated and protected by public authorities'. Therefore, state legislation must comply with the requirement of Article 26 that its content should not be discriminatory.[92] According to the CEDAW, any distinction made based on sex that has the intention or outcome of affording women unequal rights in comparison with men is discriminatory.[93]

The concept of equality, however, is interpreted differently in Islamic countries. Some, including the Islamic Republic of Iran, have benefitted from debates over the universality[94] or relativism[95] of human rights discourse to challenge the normative structure of international human rights law. At the heart of this challenge is the presentation of Islam as a supreme cultural principle, with priority above all other ethical constructs not based on revelation.[96] Ayatollah Ali Khamenei, the Supreme Leader of the Islamic Republic of Iran, in rejecting the 'Western notion of human rights', claimed that:

> Today the Islamic system is questioning the identity, goal, and capability of the Western system, and the most superior Western thinkers are gradually realising the tediousness of the Western system. Thus, the civilisation that began with the Renaissance is coming close to an end. Human beings today are searching for a substitute for the Western system, and inclination toward Islam in the United States, Europe and Africa emanates from this situation.[97]

The Supreme Leader and some other religious figures in Iran have tried to establish that the West is indebted to Islam. Ayatollah Jannati, for

The Development of Universal Standards on Gender 27

instance, insisted that 'Islam had best defined all aspects of human rights and that the human rights proposed by the United Nations merely recapitulated rights propounded over a thousand years earlier'.[98] Due to various historical, cultural, social, political and economic differences, the implementation of Islamic law differs among different Islamic countries. Moreover, there has always been a conflict between traditionalists and reformists regarding Islamic law. Some interpretations of Shari'a law insist that these laws are fundamental and divine, which implies that they cannot be challenged.

Others challenge this approach and ask whether or not these discriminatory laws are actually derived from the Shari'a. These implementation challenges have a direct effect on the way the concept of equality is interpreted in Islamic countries such as Iran. The Iranian Shi'ite clergy maintains that the international principle of equality violates Islam because according to the latter, women and men should not be treated equally; there are different roles and responsibilities for each. For example, the late Ayatollah Fazel Lankarani, one of the most prominent experts in the field of Islamic law, stated, while addressing theology students, that:

> Being students of theology, you must not get the impression that intellectualism necessitates violating certain Islamic principles. Who said there is no difference between men and women? There are many differences [...] We don't want to say that women are intellectually and socially inferior, but God has set aside some exclusive advantages for men, and vice versa.[99]

Iranian laws mostly follow this school of thought and do not provide equal rights for women. Iran's constitution does not identify any rights for a woman as an independent person. However, it has recognised some rights for married and pregnant women.

One should bear in mind that prominent female members of the Iranian political elite actively promote the opinion that 'in most parts of the world, particularly in the Western countries, women are merely objects of collective materialistic values'.[100] Those espousing this opinion believe that family values have been changed in the West and that commitments to change the situation in favour of women have resulted in exploitation, injustice, oppression, aggression, harassment, neurosis and indignity.[101] The Iranian Government takes the view that the West aims to control its women by turning them into 'Western dolls'. It is also claimed that the concept of 'equality' is confused with 'similarity' in the West. Therefore, it is argued that Western women struggle to achieve rights similar to those of men. The West's attempt to provide equal rights for women is seen as 'degrading woman to a mere means of promoting consumer goods and perpetual sexual slavery'.[102]

Some senior clerics' resistance to support the adoption of CEDAW, is rooted in the prevailing notion that the convention is inconsistent with the principles of Shari'a. For instance, Ayatollah Hossein Mazaheri, head of the Islamic Seminary of Isfahan and a traditionalist religious jurist, stated:

> If there is any carelessness, we will all be held accountable. This convention, which denies any difference between men and women's rights and duties, is in fact a grave step by the UN towards establishing Western dominance and global hegemony of Western materialistic culture. And unfortunately, some of the people in charge, particularly women, are for ill-founded and baseless reasons trying to persuade Iran to join a Convention that guarantees problems with religious jurisprudence.[103]

On the other hand, a number of jurists believe that Islam has, by its very nature, abolished discrimination between men and women, and has provided equal rights between the two sexes. Therefore, Iran like other Muslim countries that have ratified the CEDAW may become a party to the convention without infringing upon Islam. Among those jurists is Ayatollah Bojnurdi, who believes that 'Changes can be made in many of the laws that are considered discriminatory'. In his view, 'the rights that currently exist for women in Shi'ite jurisprudence are not fixed and may be modified.'[104] He supports Iran's accession to the CEDAW without stating any reservation, as, in his view, many of the domestic laws of Iran are in the process of being modified.

Contemporary academics have taken different approaches when it comes to deciding whether the principle of equality recognised internationally is compatible with Islamic legal tradition. Some scholars, while arguing that Islam recognises equal rights for women, emphasise that equality in Islam is not necessarily conducive to women having the

The Development of Universal Standards on Gender 29

same rights as men. Mashood Baderin has done significant work on the issue of the compatibility of Islam and human rights law. In one of his works he compares women's rights in Islam with international human rights law.[105] He emphasises that Islam provides equal rights for men and women and points out that 'Islam was the first to liberate women more than fourteen hundred years ago from the inhumane conditions they were in'. However, he reiterates that the roles and responsibilities of women and men are different in Islam; especially in matters relating to the family, it could be argued that they are 'equal but not equivalent'.[106] Baderin uses the example of the equality provision in Article 6 of the Organisation of the Islamic Cooperation's (OIC) Cairo Declaration on Human Rights in Islam, which states that:

> Woman is equal to man in human dignity and has rights to enjoy as well as duties to perform; she has her own civil entity and financial independence, and the right to retain her name and lineage. And husbands are responsible for the support and welfare of the family.[107]

Anne Elizabeth Mayer, who has written extensively on issues of Islamic law in contemporary legal systems, argues that equality 'in human dignity', which is also mentioned in Islamic provisions, does not guarantee equality of all civil and political rights as defined under the ICCPR.[108] For example, Article 1(a) of the Cairo Declaration states that 'all human beings are equal in terms of basic human dignity and basic obligation'. Mayer considers this language to be misleading and argues that the words 'dignity' and 'obligation' do not have the same meaning as rights. She points out that under Islamic law not everyone has equal rights. In addition, Mayer argues that the meaning of equal protection is vague under Islamic law. She refers to authors such as Sultanhussein Tabandeh, for whom equal protection means that Muslims should be treated equally under the Shari'a and concludes that the equal protection of women and men, who do not have equal rights under Shari'a law, is not possible.[109]

Another approach argues that Islamic legal tradition, like any other legal tradition, holds within itself different perspectives on gender rights and is open to change. Ziba Mir-Hosseini, a social anthropologist, divides gender perspectives in Islamic law into three categories:

traditionalist, neo-traditionalist and reformist.[110] She argues that, under the first category, women are generally seen as sexual beings whose rights are not equal to those of men. Mir-Hosseini argues that jurists supporting the traditionalist view follow patriarchal assumptions and interpret Qur'anic verses according to these assumptions; women at that time did not have any problem with those rules because they were in line with existing values. The second group, the neo-traditionalists, do not accept equality because they consider it a Western phenomenon not relevant to Islamic law. In the course of the twentieth century, when modern legal systems based on Western models were created, many changes occurred in the laws of Muslim countries. Countries such as Turkey, for example, generally put aside Islamic law in their legislative processes. Other countries, such as Saudi Arabia, kept Islamic law in their legislation, while yet another set of countries applied Islamic principles only within family law, setting it aside in all other legislative spheres. The most striking feature in this category are the hybrid laws created as a result, neither Western nor classical Islamic laws. The other important factor to consider is the participation of non-jurists in dealing with the rights of women under Islamic law. Patriarchal interpretations of Islamic law, as elaborated by jurists, are now implemented by the State, representing a great risk for the protection of women's rights. It may be argued that the neo-traditionalists believe in fairness, claiming that Islam considers men and women as equal creatures while assigning different roles to them. Mir-Hosseini emphasises that neo-traditionalists by contrast have 'an oppositional stance and a defensive or apologetic tone'. The former trait is due to the fact that they do not believe in change and believe that equality is a Western concept, alien to Muslim society, and the latter one because they refer to *feqh* to defend the discriminatory rules of Islamic law.

The reformist view is the third category. Mir-Hosseini argues that by the early 1990s, as a response to political Islam, this new way of thinking about gender appeared on the scene. This new mind-set, which builds on earlier reformist discourses, argues for gender equality in all aspects of public and private life, using Islamic sources to defend women's rights in Islam. Its advocates did not try to establish the genealogy of every concept in the Qur'an and made a clear distinction between religion and religious knowledge. The reformists also argued that notions like equality and human rights were compatible with the principles of Islam.[111]

Mir-Hosseini follows the reformist trend and makes a distinction between Shari'a and *feqh*. In her view, what we get from Shari'a is always an interpretation; the dominant interpretations, as reflected in classical *feqh*, are no doubt patriarchal. But this does not mean that we cannot have an egalitarian interpretation. The new reformist and feminist voices in Islam are now offering this egalitarian interpretation.

The late Fatima Mernissi, a well-known Islamic feminist whose earlier writings suggest that gender issues cannot be solved through Islam, later adopted a reformist approach, according to which she proposed that the future of Muslim societies should be based upon a 'liberating memory' of Islam.[112] In her view, there are different verses in the Qur'an that assign rights to women, and one should reconsider and rethink the verses that are not compatible with the situation of women in modern societies. She claims that the problematic position of women in Muslim societies is a result of male manipulation of the sacred text. In *The Veil and the Male Elite*, she recommends that:

> The answer without doubt is to be found in the time-mirror wherein the Muslim looks at himself to foresee his future. The image of 'his' woman will change when he feels the pressing need to root his future in a liberating memory. Perhaps the women should help him do this through daily pressure for equality, thereby bringing him into a fabulous present and the present is always fabulous, because there everything is possible – even the end of always looking to the past and the beginning of confidence, of enjoying in harmony the moment that we have.[113]

In the case of Iran, women's rights activists have adopted the reformist view to challenge discriminatory laws. They have risked imprisonment, torture and even death to stand up for their human rights while maintaining their religion. Shirin Ebadi, the Nobel Peace Prize laureate, in an interview expresses her view on the compatibility of Islam and human rights:

> I am a Muslim, to begin with. It's perfectly OK that there are certain people who do not accept Islam at all. Therefore, to announce that I am a Muslim can rub some people the wrong way. But my aim is to show that those governments that violate the

rights of people by invoking the name of Islam have been misusing Islam. They violate these rights and then seek refuge behind the argument that Islam is not compatible with freedom and democracy. But this is basically to save face. In fact, I'm promoting democracy. And I'm saying that Islam is not an excuse for thwarting democracy.[114]

I agree with the view of scholars who 'argue for gender equality using the conceptual tools and legal theories of the tradition, such as the distinction between Shari'a and *feqh* and the notion of *ejtehād*, thereby defusing opposition from defenders of traditional *feqh*, who invoke cultural relativist arguments for gender inequality disguised in Islamic terminology.'[115]

The Convention on the Elimination of All Forms of Discrimination Against Women: An overview

The most important instrument in ensuring women's rights is the Convention on the Elimination of All Forms of Discrimination Against Women (CEDAW), which was adopted by the UN General Assembly on 18 December 1979, through Resolution 34/180 (1979).[116] The women's convention entered into force on 3 September 1981, after its ratification by the twentieth State Party.[117] As of January 2018, there were 188 State Parties to the convention.[118] The adoption of the Optional Protocol through General Assembly Resolution 54/4, on 6 October 1999, strengthened the CEDAW through special procedures to ensure the supervised compliance of States Parties with it. The optional protocol entered into force on 22 December 2000; as of January 2017, there were 104 States Parties to this protocol.[119]

The CEDAW consists of a preamble and thirty articles and is divided into six parts: part I (Articles 1–6) contains definitions and general provisions, part II (Articles 7–9) contains guarantees of equality in political and public life, part III (Articles 10–14) addresses the social and economic rights of women, part IV (Articles 15 and 16) provides for equality before and under the law, and for equality in marriage and family life, Part V (Articles 17–22) establishes a Committee on the Elimination of Discrimination Against Women, the international monitoring mechanism, and part VI (Articles 23 and 24–30) deals with formal and procedural matters such as entry into force and reservations. The CEDAW defines discrimination against[120] women as:

> [A]ny distinction, exclusion or restriction made on the basis of sex which has the effect or purpose of impairing or nullifying the recognition, enjoyment or exercise by women, irrespective of their marital status, on a basis of equality of men and women, of human rights and fundamental freedoms in the political, economic, social, cultural, civil or any other field.[121]

The convention considers both equality of opportunity and equality of outcome.[122] It guarantees equality and freedom from discrimination by the state and by private actors in all areas of public and private life. The convention is a legal instrument but may also be considered a political manifesto, championing equal rights for women. It aims to provide equal enjoyment of civil and political, as well as economic, social and cultural rights.[123]

However, examining the CEDAW in more detail indicates that many of its provisions only express vague intentions rather than concretely identifying binding legal obligations. This ambiguity is the result of two issues: the need to achieve agreement between states to adopt the convention and the pressure of time. First, the idea of having a convention specific to women was considered controversial, and many voices rose to express disagreement with such a convention. This controversy continued during the discussion of the text of the convention, reflecting an ideological and religious confrontation that resulted in the 'constructive ambiguity' of the women's convention. The second issue is related to the temporal framework during which the convention was discussed. The UN announced the year 1975 as International Year of Women and the beginning of the United Nations Decade for Women (1975–85); therefore, the women's convention was adopted very quickly, and hence was kept vague on certain issues to achieve agreement. These developments affected the structure of the convention and caused a lack of clarity in its general terms and, more specifically, in the preamble of the CEDAW.[124]

The legal situation of Iranian women under the civil and criminal codes of Iran will be examined in Chapters 4 and 5. To understand the extent to which the laws affecting the legal position of Iranian women contradict accepted international norms on gender equality, Articles 2 (f)–(g) and 16 (1) (a), (b) and (c) of the CEDAW are of particular relevance, because they require States Parties to amend or repeal laws, regulations and customs that discriminate against women.

Article 2 (f)–(g)

The underlying commitment of Article 2(f)–(g) is 'to take all appropriate measures, including legislation, to modify or abolish existing laws, regulations, customs and practices which constitute discrimination against women and to repeal all national penal provisions that discriminate against women'.[125] As Article 2 is the core provision of the CEDAW, states failing to comply with these commitments are regarded by the committee as in breach of their obligations under the convention. The legal grounds and procedures for divorce,[126] laws on inheritance that give more rights to men than to women[127] and laws allowing polygamy[128] are amongst key areas identified by the committee as discriminatory towards women.[129] The committee has encouraged States Parties to pay particular attention to the gender impact of new and existing legislation[130] and to review laws on a regular basis.[131] The committee considers discriminatory practices and customs as elements that delay the advancement of women and prevent them from acquiring full equality of rights with men. Article 2 (e) and (f)[132] are interpreted by the committee 'to impose an obligation on States Parties to intervene positively in the activities and practices of religious, cultural or ethnic groups that either directly or indirectly discriminate against women'.[133] The committee has drawn states' attention to the importance of taking steps to address discriminatory attitudes embodied in personal status laws and religious law.[134]

The committee introduced several measures to be taken by states to eliminate discrimination against women and to identify and establish a non-discriminatory regime. Amongst others are the criminalisation of discriminatory practices, the provision of civil remedies for the victims and the adoption of awareness-raising programmes about the convention.[135]

During the drafting process of the convention, many states argued that since the CEDAW's general provisions required States Parties to modify or abolish discriminatory legislation including penal laws, Article 2(g) did not need to be inserted into the convention.[136] On the contrary, on the basis that 'rules of a discriminatory nature abounded in penal codes in particular',[137] Egypt, supported by India and Senegal and other delegations, successfully argued for the retention of Article 2(g).[138] According to the committee these laws amongst others fell under the provision of Article 2(g): laws that allowed a defence of honour to a charge of homicide or assault,[139] the law of evidence discriminating against women[140] and laws that failed to prohibit marital rape.[141]

Although any state that fails to comply with the undertakings of Article 2 is in breach of other provisions of the convention, states are accorded great discretion in implementing it into domestic law. Despite this advantage given to states by the convention, Article 2 in particular is one of the contested provisions of the convention that prevents the Iranian Government from adhering to the CEDAW. The provisions of Article 2 are targeted precisely at eliminating discrimination against women and identifying and establishing a non-discriminatory regime, which moves in the opposite direction from the Iranian Government's policy on gender equality. As will be discussed in Chapter 4, there are several provisions within the Iranian criminal code that discriminate against women, such as *diyeh* and testimony. The incompatibility of these laws with Article 2 of the CEDAW and the obligation of Iran to change them upon the ratification of the convention was discussed during the process of ratification of the latter in the sixth Majles.[142] Therefore, one possible reason of missed ratification of the CEDAW may be that the Iranian Government is unwilling to be bound by another international obligation in relation to gender equality.[143]

Marriage and family life: Article 16(1) (a), (b), (c)
In accordance with the provisions of Article 16, States Parties shall take 'all appropriate measures to eliminate discrimination against women in all matters relating to marriage and family relations'. According to Article 16 (1) (a), states 'shall ensure, on a basis of equality of men and women, the same right to enter into marriage'. In some countries, women's enjoyment of the right to enter into marriage is limited either by formal legislation or by religious and customary practices and social attitudes.[144] For instance, in some states a divorced woman is required to see out a waiting period before she can remarry. However, similar restrictions are not imposed on men.[145] As discussed in Chapter 2, the observation of a waiting period is necessary for a divorced woman according to Iran's civil code.[146] Moreover, there are other legal

restrictions that deny Iranian women the same rights as men to enter into marriage.[147]

According to Article 16 (1) (b), states shall ensure, on a basis of equality of men and women, 'the same right to enter into marriage, the same right to freely choose a spouse and to enter into marriage only with their free and full consent'. General Recommendation No. 21 provides that:

> A woman's right to choose a spouse and enter freely into marriage is central to her life and to her dignity as a human being. An examination of States parties' reports discloses that there are countries which, on the basis of custom, religious beliefs or the ethnic origins of particular groups of people, permit forced marriage or remarriages. Other countries allow a woman's marriage to be arranged for payment or preferment and in others, women's poverty forces them to marry foreign nationals for financial security. Subject to reasonable restrictions based, for example, on women's youth or consanguinity with her partner, a woman's right to choose when, if, and whom she will marry must be protected and enforced at law.[148]

As the committee expressed in General Recommendation No. 21, women often are not in the same position as men to negotiate marriage. Gendered role expectations and economic inequality impose pressures on women and limit their bargaining power.[149]

According to Article 16 (1) (c), states agree that both spouses should enjoy 'the same rights and responsibilities during marriage and its dissolution.' The committee has noted that the 'husband being accorded the status of head of household and primary decision maker [...] contravene the provisions of the convention'. In the view of the committee:

> Many countries in their legal systems provide for the rights and responsibilities of married partners by relying on the application of common law principles, religious or customary law, rather than by complying with the principles contained in the convention. These variations in law and practice relating to marriage have wide-ranging consequences for women, invariably restricting their rights to equal status and responsibility within marriage.[150]

The committee emphasised the equal treatment of women in the family both in law and in private. General Recommendation No. 21 stressed that human activity in public and private life has been viewed differently and the roles of women in the private or domestic sphere treated as inferior.[151] The committee highlighted that 'such activities are invaluable for the survival of society and that there can, therefore, be no justification for applying different and discriminatory laws or customs to them'.[152] Based on reports of States Parties the committee declared that:

> There are still countries where de jure equality does not exist. Women are thereby prevented from having equal access to resources and from enjoying equality of status in the family and society. Even where de jure equality exists, all societies assign different roles, which are regarded as inferior, to women. In this way, principles of justice and equality contained in particular in article 16 and also in articles 2, 5, and 24 of the convention are being violated.[153]

The general recommendation identified the following practices as violating the provisions of Article 16: polygamous marriage, forced marriage, forced pregnancy, abortion or sterilisation, considering the husband as head of the family, the obligation for a woman to change her name upon marriage or at its dissolution and granting to men a greater share of property at the time of the dissolution of marriage.[154] Article 16 (1) is the most controversial provision of the convention for the Islamic states and has therefore attracted many reservations. In the case of Iran, the realm of family as covered by Article 16 is moulded by a number of violations of the rights of women.[155]

The ratification of the CEDAW by Muslim countries and Shari'a-based reservations to it[156]

Approximately 837 million Muslims live around the world.[157] Of the Muslim countries in which over 70 per cent of the population adheres to the Islamic faith, only Iran, Sudan and Somalia are not parties to the CEDAW. However, those Muslim countries that have ratified the convention have excluded themselves from the application of some of its provisions by entering reservations.[158] Articles 2,[159] 9,[160] 15,[161] and 16[162] have attracted the most reservations on the grounds of contradiction with the principle of the Shari'a.[163] Using Morocco and Saudi Arabia as case studies, this section assesses the effect of the CEDAW in these two different Muslim countries. Comparing how each of these countries, which share a common Islamic law and tradition in different political, social and economic contexts, treat women, demonstrates that mere ratification of the CEDAW is not enough to advance women's rights in the ratifying country. The convention can only be 'an effective tool for advocacy where the State has demonstrated the political will to comply with the convention – a will that is discounted by reservations'.[164] Taking Iran's political context into account, its failure to ratify the CEDAW even with reservations is motivated by ideological or political considerations that preclude the advancement of women's rights.[165]

Saudi Arabia

The status of women in Saudi Arabia is affected by traditional and religious practices sanctioned by law. Discriminatory attitudes characterise not only 'the private or family sphere as in the majority of Muslim states, but also extend to almost all areas of public life, such as education, political activities, employment and even the simple participation in the life of the society.'[166]

Saudi Arabia is a monarchy with a Shari'a-based system of government. The Basic Law of Governance of Saudi Arabia was adopted in 1992 and formally declared Saudi Arabia an Islamic state. According to Article 1 of the Basic Law, the religion of Saudi Arabia is Islam and its constitution is God's Holy Book, the Qur'an, and His Prophet's Sunna, which also constitute a source of the law, according to Article 7.[167]

Therefore, 'Saudi Arabia is an Islamic State, with the laws of Islam as its foundation; consequently any criticism or questioning of Saudi laws is often viewed as a criticism of Islam'.[168] Article 26 of the basic law declares that the State shall protect human rights according to the Shari'a. Although this provision may be a positive step toward recognising and guaranteeing the human rights of citizens, including women, the reference to Shari'a may restrict its scope for two possible reasons. First, the Shari'a is uncodified and second, it is subject to the interpretation of the Council of Senior Scholars.[169] The council, consisting only of men, 18 of whom are appointed by the king, has the authority to interpret the laws of the kingdom.[170]

As a result of omissions in the basic law on women's rights and the non-codification of the family and personal status laws, women's rights in Saudi

Arabia are 'a permanent hostage to the vicissitudes of public sentiment or pressure from interest groups'.[171] An illustration of this is the victory of the Council of Senior Scholars in preventing the Saudi Government's participation in the UN Population and Development Conference (calling for 'freedom and equality between men and women and the total elimination of differences between them') held in Cairo in September 1994. In the view of the council, equality between men and women is against God's law and the conference agenda was therefore an insult to the values of Muslims. The conference was also accused of attacking Muslim society by seeking to transform it from a culture in which 'chastity and purity prevail' to one afflicted with 'perversion'.[172] Therefore, the advancement of women's rights in Saudi Arabia, according to Sifa Mtango, 'is left to government-appointed individuals, whose agenda often suppresses women's rights in the name of religion'.[173]

Saudi Arabia ratified the CEDAW on 7 September 2000 with a general reservation that declares: 'In [the] case of contradiction between any term of the convention and the norms of Islamic law, the Kingdom is not under obligation to observe the contradictory terms of the convention.' In a country like Saudi Arabia, with a long history of patriarchy and strong traditions, it is not incorrect to assume that most of the CEDAW's provisions related to the private and public spheres of women's lives will contradict the Shari'a.[174] The reservation is described by the government as follows:

> The Kingdom's ratification of the convention is based on the fact that its general content is consistent with the country's approaches to safeguarding the rights of women. To talk about the philosophy of domestic and international law and the application thereof in the Kingdom of Saudi Arabia in isolation from the Islamic Shari'a is inconceivable. Law-making in an Islamic state proceeds from the Islamic Shari'a [...] As such, the country's laws cannot transgress the framework of the Islamic Shari'a and, consequently, may not be changed or developed by the legislative authority in the Kingdom in a manner which would lead to the creation of new principles, inconsistent with the basis of the Islamic Shari'a, in letter and spirit [...] This is what is made clear, albeit in condensed form, by the Kingdom's explanatory reservation to the provisions of the convention.[175]

The views of the Saudi Government on the concept of equality are described in its combined initial and second periodical report to the CEDAW committee:

> Islam's view of woman derives from her shared humanity with man. However, proceeding from a basis of realism, Islam holds that full likeness between men and women is contrary to the reality of their being [...] Scientific studies attest to the physiological difference between them [...] the Islamic Sharia respects these natural differences and accords woman a privileged position to achieve justice for her.[176]

Therefore, the Saudi Government believes that existing discriminatory practices against women are not to be considered violations of their rights. Having this understanding of equality in mind, the Saudi Government provided no detailed information on the situation of women in its combined initial and second periodic report to the CEDAW committee. It was also reluctant to answer the committee's questions or to map out clearly women's status. For instance, when the committee asked for more information about 'whether women are ensured the same rights as men to vote and to be eligible for election at all levels', the Saudi Government's response was very general, as follows:

> Women have the same political rights as men and are ensured the same right as men to participate in the decision-making process. The law does not prohibit women from participating in elections, although, in practice, that participation is not completely possible. Women also have the right to participate in elections of the councils of chambers of commerce and have won seats in a number of those councils.[177]

The Saudi Government did not provide a clear response to the committee's question, and instead made it obvious that women are not able to fully practise their political rights.

By nature of absolute monarchy, in Saudi Arabia official state positions, either advisory or executive, are by royal appointment only. This creates a restriction of political rights for men and women, and presents a particular challenge to changes in women's political positions and basic freedoms of expression and association.

The 2013 decree issued by King Abdullah, requiring at least 20 per cent of the 150 seats in the Council of Senior Scholars to be reserved for women, may be considered positive. However, the restrictions imposed on the thirty women who were appointed to the Shura Council suggest that no progressive changes have happened, in the view of the Saudi Government, towards gender equality. It is worth noting that women members of the council have not been able to drive themselves to work as the law has forbidden women from driving in Saudi Arabia. In September 2017 Saudi King Salman ordered that this restriction be removed, with the order scheduling legalisation for women drivers no later than 24 June, 2018. All this being said, the positive aspect of the appointment of these women may be the fact that their presence in public life will gradually change the mind-set of conservatives by showing them that women can perform the same jobs as men.

In addition to allowing women to drive cars, Saudi started to prepare a law to combat harassment. It seems that more positive changes are on the way to facilitate the inclusion of women in public life. The recent move toward reforms in Saudi Arabia is a clear sign of the political will of the Saudi Government to change the face of the country when it comes to half of its population. Central to the reforms has been the apparent break between the state and hard-line clerics. To move ahead with its reforms, the kingdom understands that it has no choice but to part ways with such voices and rather move to more tightly control them. This is not without its challenges however. The head of supreme scholars, the mufti, and some appointed scholars maintain a strict view of women's rights, including the resistance to abolish the male-guardianship system and accusing activists who try to challenge the system of being dangerous to the state and Islam. In a conversation Hala Aldosari, a fellow at the Radcliffe Institute for Advanced Study at Harvard researching gender dynamics in Saudi Arabia, concluded that 'the move to arrest clerics is rooted in switching the authoritarianism of the state from a religious-based one to a more nationalist: stifling the independent voice on the pretext of betraying the state, rather than offending Islam. The state's move to reduce public spending and allow the private sector to become the main generator of jobs meant that women must be allowed to become workers and tax-payers to offset the reduction in the state-funding of citizens through subsidies and public jobs'.[178]

In Iran, there remains a challenge where strong connections between hard-line clerics and the ruling authorities persist to put forth obstacles for women's advancement in this arena, though one cannot separate religion and tradition from either society. Similar to King Salman bin Abdul-Aziz Al Saud of Saudi Arabia, the last Iranian monarch was no supporter of feminism, but did believe that development was impossible without the full participation of women and a complete change in their social status. Indeed, despite opposition by the clergy, the legal status of women improved during the Shah's rule (1941–79). After Iran became an Islamic Republic, women were once again side lined in Iran, losing most of the rights they had achieved. For instance, women lost equal rights in family matters – including divorce, marriage settlements and the custody of children.

Without doubt, the push by civil societies and women activists for the ratification of the CEDAW by Saudi Arabia has influenced the government to reach a level of understanding that women should be present in public life. Economic, political and social changes have also been important factors to push the Saudi Government to open up opportunities for women and start to realise that their country cannot advance until women's rights are improved in the kingdom. Nevertheless, there has been ongoing crackdown on women activists and civil society since King Salman came to power, a clear demonstration that despite giving the appearance of supporting women's rights, albeit for economic reasons, the monarchy is determined to control and manage reform without the participation of civil society. In its constant consolidation of power, the Saudi Arabian government attempts to shrink the space for discourse on women's rights, however the ratification of CEDAW will be a point of reference for advocates and has established the necessary tool for public mobilisation to advance women rights.

Morocco

To understand the status of women in Morocco, reference should be made to the complexity of Moroccan society. In the words of Rachel Newcomb:

The Development of Universal Standards on Gender 43

Morocco is a country of multiple contexts, often extremes – between rural and urban, poor and wealthy, religious and secular, provincial and cosmopolitan, Berber and Arab – and there are just as many identities between those ranges, which are intended here as guides and not binaries.[179]

It seems that this complex and varied context of social and religious traditions has promoted greater tolerance of woman's rights in Morocco, in comparison with less-diverse societies. However, while it has helped to advance women's rights, at the same time, this diversity has stymied efforts to promote gender equality within Moroccan society itself.[180] As observed by John Hursh, 'while liberal women's rights reformers currently appear to have the upper hand, a conservative backlash is possible'.[181]

Ninety-nine per cent of Morocco's population is Muslim and it is therefore correct to claim that 'Islam and Islamic values are a priority for numerous Moroccan women'.[182] However, adherence to Islamic values has not prevented Moroccan women from demanding modernisation and reform. Rather, it has encouraged them to find a balance between the two. As Mernissi rightly observed, Moroccan women want 'the mosque and the satellite, both at the same time'.[183]

The attempt to advance women's status within the Shari'a has resulted in reforming the Code of Personal Status of Morocco (the Mudawana), the only religion-based law in the secular legal system of Morocco. It covers family-related regulations including marriage, divorce and the custody of children. The first personal status law was codified in 1957 and reformed in 1993 by a royal decree. In the view of most Moroccans, the reform – which was not achieved through any parliamentary process – was insufficient, lacking the necessary elements of meaningful change.

To reflect the demands of women for equality and to prove its good intentions to reform their status within the country, Morocco ratified the CEDAW on 21 June 1993, with three reservations and two declarations.[184] In its reservation to Article 2, Morocco expressed its readiness to apply the provisions of this article, provided that they are without prejudice to the constitutional requirements that regulate the rules of succession to the throne of the Kingdom of Morocco and that they do not conflict with the provisions of the Islamic Shari'a. Morocco's reservation to Article 16 addresses the equality of men and women, in respect of rights and responsibilities on entry into and at dissolution of marriage and states that Article 16, which specifically deals with the dissolution of marriage, is considered incompatible with the Shari'a, which guarantees rights and responsibilities to each of the spouses within a framework of equilibrium and complementarity to preserve the sacred bond of matrimony.[185] Ekaterina Yahyaoui argues that Morocco did not provide sufficient information about the issue of the dissolution of marriage in its combined third and fourth periodic report submitted to the CEDAW committee. The text of the reservation, however, presents a vivid description of the obstacles encountered by women in obtaining a divorce.[186]

Morocco's ratification of the CEDAW, even with the Shari'a-based reservations, strengthened women's rights activists in their demand for gender equality; this fortunately attracted a positive reaction from the government. In August 1999, just one month after ascending to the throne, King Mohammad VI challenged the status of women, declaring: 'How can society achieve progress, while women, who represent half the nation, see their rights violated and suffer as a result of injustice, violence, and marginalisation, notwithstanding the dignity and justice granted them by our glorious religion?'[187] In March 2001, King Mohammad VI announced his intention to reform the personal status law and to proceed with his reform policy of improving women's status, he appointed several women to high-level government posts. He also established a royal commission, three members of which were women, to review the personal status law in light of religious law, *ejtehād* (legal reasoning), Islamic principles of fairness and universal human rights standards.[188]

In October 2003, while opening the new session of the parliament, King Mohammad VI proposed substantial reforms, that were advocated for by the women's movement in the 1980s and further developed by his father King Hassan II in the 1990s, to the personal status law and urged parliament to adopt a modern revision of the same. To back his reform proposal, the King quoted the Prophet Mohammad as stating that men and women are equal before law. He explained that the purpose of the new code should be to eliminate discrimination against women, to protect children's rights and to preserve the dignity of men.[189]

The king's proposal to reform the personal status law attracted resistance from conservatives within Moroccan society, who saw the reforms as illegitimate, owing to their perceived contradiction with the Shari'a. The king cleverly reached out to Moroccan women and civil society to gain support for his proposed reforms and overcome the opposition from conservatives. More importantly, he used Islam as a point of reference and justification to legitimise the need to reform the personal status law. The new law was ratified by parliament in January 2004 and it introduced a range of measures to advance women's equality in marriage, divorce, child custody and other aspects of family life.[190] For instance, according to Article 18 of the Mudawana, the age of marriage for both girls and boys is eighteen.[191] According to the provisions of the new law, the husband is no longer considered the head of the family and spouses share their rights and responsibilities.[192]

On 10 December 2008, Morocco withdrew its reservations to the CEDAW.[193] During his speech on the occasion of the celebration of the sixtieth anniversary of the Universal Declaration of Human Rights, King Muhammed VI, while announcing Morocco's withdrawal of its reservations to the CEDAW, stated: 'Our reservations have become obsolete due to the advanced legislation which has been adopted by our country'.[194]

Although Moroccan women still face serious problems,[195] the evolution that has occurred in Morocco's legislation after the country's ratification of the CEDAW highlights the significant role of the convention in encouraging member States to eradicate discrimination against women. This demonstrates that there are no direct contradictions between international standards and the Islamic principles of Shari'a. In many Muslim countries, the absence of democratic space for debate and negotiation, combined with the lack of commitment to gender equality, enables governments to leave intact laws that discriminate against women, and to continue using these unjust laws. It should be noted, this push for change is made possible when a political space is opened to civil society and women's groups who can contribute to the discourse for reform. Therefore, Morocco could be an excellent example for Muslim states – including Iran – to follow the same policy as Morocco and amend discriminatory rules against women without infringing on Islam.

Conclusion

The women's movement around the world has become stronger since the 1970s. The United Nations Decade for Women (1975–85) and its associated women's world conferences paved the way and led to the emergence of the global movement for women's human rights in the

1990s.[196] The global network of women that emerged after the Nairobi Conference challenged the assumption that feminism and women's rights were Western concepts. It was understood that global feminism and international women's networks should go beyond the notion of solidarity, information-sharing and support mechanisms. It was acknowledged that events in different parts of the world affected each other. The growth of 'fundamentalism anywhere, for instance, has implication for its growth in other countries and the instability and violence of armed conflicts spill over many borders'.[197]

In the view of many Muslim women, 'Islam forbids injustice against people, against nations and against women. It shuns race, colour, and gender as bases of discrimination among fellowmen'.[198] The Iranian Government's involvement in the reporting procedure to the United Nations division on the status of women delivers this important message: that international standards on equality of rights between men and women are relevant to Iranian women. It demonstrates that the Iranian Government's claim that human rights is a Western concept should be treated only as a political statement aimed at restricting the rights of Iranian citizens. Iran's reliance on Islam to justify inequality between men and women has been challenged by Iranian women of both secular and religious leanings.[199]

This examination of the CEDAW sheds light on the fact that the convention provides a foundation of mutual collaboration between State Parties. While the adverse consequences of globalisation and extremist ideologies aim to undermine the importance of the CEDAW, reassertion and reaffirmation of the convention's principles are more important than ever for the advancement of women's status throughout the world.[200]

Given that most Islamic countries have ratified the CEDAW, it might be claimed that the reason why countries such as Iran have not ratified it is not due to its possible incompatibilities with Islam, but to the fact that women's rights conflict with the interests of the predominantly male political elite. The political and legal system of the Islamic Republic of Iran is complicated to a large extent that makes slow the progress of any changes in favour of women.

CHAPTER 2

THE POLITICAL AND LEGAL SYSTEM OF THE ISLAMIC REPUBLIC OF IRAN

Introduction

To gain a better understanding of the legal situation of women in Iran, an in-depth analysis of the foundation and structure of the Iranian legal system is necessary. The normative structure of Iranian law has failed to accommodate the realities of women's lives; it contains ambiguous and complex legislation, which ultimately discriminates against women. The government justifies gender-based discrimination through principles derived from the Shari'a. Ironically, some religious scholars, such as Grand Ayatollah Sanei, believe that the extent of this discrimination is in fact incompatible with a true and objective interpretation of the Shari'a.[1]

This chapter examines the political structure of the State after the 1979 Revolution and further analyses the processes through which Iranian legislation is produced. The purpose of this analysis is to measure the success and failure of government policies adopted in the course of the past three decades. The objective is to outline the existing obstacles and restrictions that prevent any changes to or amendment of discriminatory laws against women. This will be achieved by examining whether there has been any political will to support a process of legal reform aimed at changing the discriminatory laws and adapting them to international standards on equal rights for men and women.

The following section scrutinises legislation in Iran by first examining the historical background of Iran's legislative system and the changes that have occurred up to the current period of the Islamic Republic. To analyse the current system and the role of so-called Islamic law, this chapter will elaborate on the Islamic notion of the state and its principles and goals, to expose the extent to which the Iranian political and legal system is based on the principles of the Shari'a. It will demonstrate that the particular interpretation of Islam adopted by the Iranian Government to justify its legislation is one of the main obstacles preventing any reform or change within Iran's legal system. The chapter will then examine the process of law making in Iran to shed more light on the complexity of the Iranian legislative system.[2]

The definition of law employed throughout this study describes it as the product of an authority that has the power to adopt it.[3] This chapter will further analyse the sources of Iranian laws, to explore the methods used by different social elements to draft new legislation. It may seem that codified laws are a set of regulations issued by a legislature in accordance with a special procedure. However, societies sometimes follow regulations that do not appear in the law but have been established spontaneously, without interference from the legislature. As they have remained in place over time and with use, people feel obligated to abide by them. These regulations are called customs. Moreover, legislated law cannot foresee all problems and issues that may arise in the everyday life of people within society. For instance, if the law is silent on a certain matter, the presiding judge must interpret existing law and consider current conditions, according to official procedures. On the other hand, the opinions of scholars and legal experts are the guiding lights for judges and the legislature in solving social questions. All these elements serve as sources of codified law, and each influences the legal process differently.[4] According to Iran's constitution, all laws and regulations should be compatible with Islam. For this reason, the sources of Islamic law should also be considered in examining the foundations of Iranian laws.

The legislative system and codification of law in Iran: Historical background

The foundations of Iran's legal system date back to the early stages of the country's national history.[5] The earliest documented appearance of codified law and courts date back to 3200 BC, in the Book of a Thousand Judgements, a systematic collection of legal rulings devised to aid the decision-making of judges.[6] Iran's legal history is traditionally divided into five eras: the period prior to the advent of Islam in the seventh century; the period of modernisation and the Constitutional Revolution of 1871–1906; the post-constitutional revolution era of 1906–1921; the era of authoritarian modernisation of 1921–79; and the post-Islamic Revolution era (1979 to the present).[7]

Prior to Islam, Iranian society was regulated by rules and laws based on decrees by the king, religious texts, customs and traditions.[8] The first legal system was established in Iran by the Elamites around 3200 BC. The invention of written language in Sumer encouraged them to establish a system to keep legal records in a written format.[9] Prior to Islam, religion did not play a significant role in the ruling system of the country. It was only during the Sassanid period – when Zoroastrianism was recognised as the official religion of the country – that state and religion intertwined.

Islamic law was imposed as the law of the country following the Arab invasion of Iran in seventh century. This development effectively brought an end to the process of codification. Islam became the official religion of the country and the Shari'a developed as the main source of applicable laws and regulations. Since then, the Shari'a has remained an important factor in the political, social, cultural and legal affairs of the State. The clergy, religious figures, were appointed to serve as judges during this period and Shari'a courts were created alongside state courts. During this period and moving forward, the clergy profoundly influenced the Iranian judiciary, to such an extent that there was never an attempt to separate them from the judiciary. During the Safavid period, the Shi'ite faith became the officially imposed religion in Iran, and a distinction was made between the state courts and those governed by Shari'a.[10] The jurisdiction of the Shari'a courts was limited to private matters such as marriage, divorce, wills and inheritance. Restrictions on *olamā* authorities increased until the eighteenth century, when the Afshārids and Zandids weakened the Shi'ite *olamā* by confining their authority to religious acts, and preventing their interference in other matters, such as the administration of justice.[11]

During the rule of the Qajar Dynasty (1796–1921), a mutual interdependence was maintained between the State and the Shi'ite *olamā*.[12]

Parvin Paidar argues that 'despite occasional conflicts of interest, the State needed the support of the religious establishment for legitimacy, and the clergy needed the support of the State to strengthen their social position'.[13] In the mid-Qajar era, the need to codify laws emerged in response to growing communication with Western countries, in particular France. The lack of codified laws was seen as one of the main factors holding back Iranian society from modernisation. To establish a modern state based on democratic elements, such as equal rights among citizens, freedom of religion, state secularisation, social rights, state responsibility and the separation of powers, a constitution consisting of ten articles was drafted in 1871. Articles of the constitution relating to social rights and the separation of powers prevented Naser al-Din Shah from ratifying it. The constitution was then adeptly redrafted to minimise any risk of displeasing the Shah.[14] The second draft received a positive response from the Shah and became a key point of reference in Iran's evolving legal and political system.

The main purpose of the law was to keep the concentration of political power in the hands of a responsible government. The constitution provided for the ratification of other necessary laws to facilitate the management of the country. Qānun-e Tanzimāt, the law of adjustments, consisting of forty-seven articles, came into existence in 1873. It aimed to draw boundaries between rulers and people, creating Majles-e Tanzimāt, a single executable organ, and establishing a centralised state system.[15] The Majles-e Tanzimāt successfully managed the affairs of the land and supported the process of codification that created regulations relating to due process, scientific investigation and prison reform.[16]

Despite introducing these reforms, the Qajars were unable to build an effective administration and failed to establish a centralised state. Attempts to bring reform to crucial sectors of the state bureaucracy, such as the customs division, compelled the merchant classes to join elements of the intelligentsia and clergy in supporting modernist ideas that limited the powers of the monarch, establishing other permanent state institutions, such as a parliament and the office of prime minister. This campaign, which became known as the constitutionalist movement, brought modernity into Iranian political culture.[17] The movement succeeded in bringing together a variety of different forces, which in turn created a cross-societal alliance that, while not fully aligned in its objectives, made significant changes to the structure of the state:

'On 5 August 1906, Muzaffar al-Din Shah signed the royal proclamation to hold nationwide elections for a Constituent Assembly.'[18] The Constitutional Revolution of 1906 moved Iran into a new era during which the constitution and a set of supplementary fundamental laws were drafted and approved.[19] As a result, the absolute monarchy was at least nominally replaced by a constitutional one.[20] The constitution provided a formal separation of powers and the judiciary was based on a new framework.[21] Due to the prominent role played by the clergy during the revolution, Islamic principles were significantly integrated into the legal and judicial frameworks of the state. The judiciary was divided into state and religious courts and Article 2 of the supplementary fundamental laws provided for a board (panel) consisting of five clerics entrusted with the examination of all bills approved by parliament; this panel had the right to veto any bill which was in conflict with the Shari'a. Article 2 stipulated that decisions of the board should be followed and obeyed.[22]

The constitution provided for public education, and women took advantage of this provision to promote education for girls. Women challenged the status quo, insisting that unless Iranian women were educated, Iran could not advance.[23] However, one should bear in mind that, according to the constitution, women – along with criminals and people with mental problems – were still deprived of the right to vote. This naturally restricted their ability to participate actively in public life.

The office of drafting laws was established in 1908 to accomplish a variety of tasks, including: 'translating laws, providing regulations for the Office of the Attorney General, defining the attributes and status of heads and members of the courts and judiciary staff, establishing the reconciliation courts, and answering the judicial questions of the courts'.[24] The idea that Islamic laws were not sufficient to regulate a modern society encouraged the process of codification. According to Mohammadi, 'Islam, in the context of the Constitutional Revolution, was "a" source of law, not "the" source of law'. As well as the Shari'a, European laws also influenced Iranian legislation. The 1906 constitution, for instance, was mainly translated from the Belgian and French constitutions.[25] It was soon discovered that the new government could not proceed with any reform agenda owing to its lack of centralised machinery. This fact, together with its financial straits, external pressures and wartime disruptions, alongside bad harvests and diseases, caused Iran to become a 'failed state' by 1920.[26]

On 21 February 1921, General Reza Khan, commander of the Cossack garrison in Qazvin, took control of Tehran and ushered in a new era in the history of Iran. The dream of a powerful central government became a reality with Reza Shah. As Abrahamian aptly states 'Reza Shah came to power in a country where the government had little presence outside the capital. He left the country with an extensive state structure – the first in two thousand years.'[27] During the era of modernisation, a new judicial system was established in 1926, in line with Reza Shah's policy and strategy for reform.[28] The process of modernisation moved the Iranian legislative regime towards a national legal framework in which the State not only created the law but also guaranteed its application.

However, the conditions and context surrounding this process could not be compared with European legal positivism. The State did not consider itself bound by its legislation. Mohammadi calls this 'rule of law for the ruled and not for the rulers'.[29] In 1927, Ali Akbar Davar and Firuz Farmanfarma, both European-educated lawyers, became responsible for reforming the legal system of Iran. A new court system that included local, county, municipal, provisional and supreme courts replaced the old system. The laws were amended to become more compatible with modern regulations; as a result, certain punishments derived from the Qur'an and ancient tribal customs, such as stoning and lashing, were abolished.[30] The religious establishment opposed this development.

Reza Shah tried to limit the influence of the clergy in political, social, cultural and legal affairs, as well as in other spheres. He dismissed the clergy from their high positions within the judiciary and limited the jurisdiction of the Shari'a courts to just three civil matters.[31] A 1936 law addressed the employment of judges and required them to have a law degree from the Tehran Faculty of Law or from a foreign university. A secular legal system was seen as a tool to establish and maintain a centralised state. The political elite assumed that the concerns of both the modernist and traditional strata of society could be met by presenting religious law within the guise of a secular legal system.[32] New legal frameworks, including a criminal code (1926), a civil code (passed 1928 and amended in 1934 and 1935), a commercial code and a code of civil procedure (1939) were devised through reliance on European models.

By the end of Reza Shah's era, the process of codification was to a great extent completed, thereby proving Watson's theory on the context of codification:

> [The] impetus towards codification of the law in the interest of clarity or simplicity often does not come from lawyers or legislatures and traditional lawmakers but dictators or other powerful leaders who have made their reputation in other activities.[33]

Although Reza Shah was successful in his state-building policy and changed Iran into a modern state, he failed to establish the rule of law within the country, attracting the opposition of the intelligentsia. The policy of removing the female veil, adopted by Reza Shah in 1936, was the most visible example of the non-democratic nature of Iranian governance at the time. In 1941, the Soviet Union and the Great Britain, with the help of the USA, invaded Iran and removed Reza Shah from power.

The modernisation of the legal system and judiciary continued during Mohammad Reza Shah's reign between 1941 and 1979. One important aspect of this policy was the government's focus on modernising laws pertaining to women. Although the Shah himself was not a supporter of feminism, he believed that development was impossible without the full participation of women and a complete change in their existing situation. In his speech at the general congress of the Women's Organisation of Iran (WOI) on 27 February 1978, he said: 'Let us not forget that problems such as human rights, family planning, campaign against illiteracy and poverty, on which the fate of the human rights depends, cannot be resolved without the complete and effective participation of women'.[34] Despite opposition by the clergy, the legal status of women improved during this period. The most significant improvement, which in fact had a key role in improving the status of women, was the extension to women of the right to vote. Ayatollah Khomeini expressly objected to the enfranchisement of women and sent a long telegram to Alam, the prime minister at the time, warning him that:

> Your illegal bill [on local elections] is contrary to Islamic law, the Constitution and the laws of the Majles. The *olamā* have publicly

stated that the franchise for women and the abrogation of the condition that one must be a Muslim in order to be allowed to vote or to run in an election is contrary to Islam and the Constitution.[35]

On 26 January 1963, women were allowed to take part in voting. In subsequent elections, six women were elected to parliament and two were appointed to the Senate.[36] When the Family Protection Law was adopted in 1967 (amended 1975), women were given equal rights in family matters, including divorce, marriage settlements and the custody of children. The age of marriage increased to eighteen and men were forced to get permission from the court to marry more than one wife. The new family law reflected the needs of Iranian women and to a great extent was successful in presenting a more tolerant reading of Islam on issues related to women. By 1977, the cultural contours of Iranian society were dominated by the Shah's 'great civilisation' ideology. In the words of Paidar

> the Shah devised the larger than life ideology of 'Great Civilisation' to accompany the arrival of Iranian society into the ranks of prosperous countries. The Iranian calendar was changed to reflect the image of a continuous non-Islamic civilisation in Iran. A single political party, the Rastākhiz-e Melli, or National Resurgence, replaced the two existing ones, the Iran-e Novin, or New Iran and the Mardom, or People to lead the country into the Age of 'The Great Civilisation'.[37]

Political influence was extremely restricted, and the Shah became the sole source of power. Most of the nation's prominent Marxist-Leninist militant activists were killed in guerrilla operations or under torture by the Shah's secret police, SAVAK.[38] Opposition Shi'ite leaders such as Ayatollah Khomeini, Ayatollah Taleghani and Ali Shariati were in internal or external exile. While the State strongly limited the political power of the Shi'ite leaders, it allowed Islam to spread at the grassroots level.[39] As Mohammadi aptly stated 'alongside with the centralisation of the State and secularisation of the society and polity, the authority of the religious leadership was also centralised and the ideology of the traditional opposition gradually Islamicized'.[40]

In addition, the rise in monetary liquidity within society during the 1970s extended the gap between the rich and the poor, and between those living in the capital city and people in villages or small towns.[41] Frances FitzGerald's contemporary report summarised the overall disparities as follows:

> Iran is basically worse off than a country like Syria that has had neither oil nor political stability. The reason for all this is simply that the Shah has never made a serious attempt at development [...] The Wealth of the country has gone into private cars rather than buses, into consumer goods rather than public health, and into the salaries of soldiers and policemen rather than those of teachers.[42]

Political and social tensions caused mass public protest, which led to emergence of an anti-Shah movement with the single goal of removing the Shah from the country's political scene. The movement's leadership eventually narrowed down, by 1978, to the figure of Ayatollah Khomeini, a veteran opposition figure who had been in exile since 1964 and was perceived as being uninterested in monopolising political power after the overthrow of the Shah.[43] A few months after the 1979 Revolution, clerics took control of the most powerful institutions of the country. Many members of the Shah's government were either executed or forced into exile; opposition groups were eliminated. All secular parties and groups which represented ethnic minorities were declared illegal. The clerics in power claimed that Islamic law was all-encompassing and that there was no need to adopt legislation from other countries. According to Ebadi 'in Mehr 1358 [21 September to 21 October 1979] the Revolutionary Council (which was in charge of running the country's affairs) approved a bill which in effect revived the provisions of the Civil Law on family issues, and in that way, it took the women and their rights some 70 years back'.[44]

In July 1982, Ayatollah Khomeini issued an order to modify all the laws deemed to be contradictory to the Islamic Shari'a. After this decree, the Supreme Judiciary Council issued a circular and ordered all the courts to use authentic Islamic texts and reliable *fatwās*, mainly Khomeini's main jurisprudential book, *Tahrir al-Wasila (Drafting the Means)*.[45]

The Islamisation of the legal system focused on two crucial elements. The first step concerned the Islamisation of pre-revolutionary legislation. The second involved the injection of thousands of clerics and revolutionaries into a variety of positions within the legal system, from the judicial to the administrative. The most important laws, approved by the Majles during the Islamisation process, were the comprehensive *Hudud* and *Qesās* Law (25 August 1982), Islamic Punishment Law (13 October 1982), Blood Money Law (*diyāt*) (15 December 1982) and *Ta'zirāt* Law (9 August 1983).[46] This Islamisation drive was the last stage in the construction of the post-revolutionary state order. It represented an attempt by the Khomeinist political elite who had, by the mid-1980s, gained full control over the state system, to extend their worldview and ideological leanings into the judicial framework, thereby consolidating their control over society.

The Islamic definition of the state: Principles, goals and tasks

Ayatollah Khomeini returned to Iran from exile on 1 February 1979. His declared intention was to strictly follow an Islamic policy and therefore, with the slogan *'Na sharqi, na qarbi, jomhuri Islami'* ('Neither West nor East, Only the Islamic Republic'), he proposed the outline of a *hukumat-e Islami*, or 'Islamic State', but he never clarified the institutional configuration of this political system. Previously Khomeini had stated that: 'The *olamā* (clerics) themselves will not hold power in the government. They will exercise supervision over those who govern and give them guidance'.[47] He had never before expressed any interest in exercising political power. In an interview he declared: 'Neither my age nor my inclination and position would allow me to do something like that.'[48]

The outcome of the 1979 Revolution was endorsed by a majority of 98.2 per cent of the people who voted for the Jomhuri-ye Islami, or 'Islamic Republic', in the national referendum held on 30–31 March 1979. The new Iranian constitution was ratified in November of the same year and amended in 1989. The process of drafting the constitution from first to final version was complex.[49] The first preliminary outline was prepared while Khomeini was still in Paris, and was revised shortly thereafter by a commission consisting of six prominent civil society personalities: Hassan Habibi, Ahmad Sadr Hajj Seyed Javadi, Naser Katuzian, Mohammad Jafar Langarudi, Abdolkarim Lahidji and Abbas Minachi.[50] A first completed draft was given to Khomeini in the city of Qom in late February 1979.

Ayatollah Khomeini tasked Bazargan,[51] the prime minister of the provisional revolutionary government, with preparing the final draft of the constitution. This version was to be ratified swiftly by the Revolutionary Council and approved by the people through a national referendum.[52] To implement this decree, on 5 July 1979, the Revolutionary Council passed a bill scheduling election for an assembly to ratify the constitution. Article 2 of the bill allocates one member of the assembly of experts to every 500,000 citizens, resulting in an assembly of approximately seventy-three members elected as the people's representatives on 29 July 1979.[53] Of the seventy-three, fifty-five were clerical figures that were mostly supportive of Khomeini. Some members of the opposition objected to the result and the way the election had been carried out. For example, it was claimed that false information was disseminated, and the results were fraudulent (for instance, in the case of two Shi'ite candidates elected in the predominantly Sunni region of Kurdistan).[54]

The composition of the assembly gave the impression that the so-called 'representatives of the population' had been chosen by Khomeini. In a message on 19 August, issued on the occasion of the first meeting of the Assembly of Experts, Khomeini instructed its members to create a '100 per cent Islamic Constitution' and asked them to do so openly and 'without any fear of the uproar this may cause in the press or amongst Westernised writers.'[55] In the same decree, Khomeini declared:

> Determining whether principles laid down in the Constitution are or are not in conformity with Islamic requirements is exclusively reserved for the revered jurists, who, thanks to God, form a particular group in the Assembly.[56]

Taking into consideration the context of this decree, the Assembly of Experts decided to put aside the preliminary draft altogether and ignore it as a working document. The Revolutionary Council discussed and adopted the principles of the constitution in sixty-seven sessions. The national referendum on the constitution took place on 2–3

December 1979. Of 21 million eligible voters, 15.6 million voted in favour of the constitution.

Article 1 of the constitution defined the form of government of post-revolutionary Iran as an Islamic republic.[57] The Twelver Ja'fari School of Shi'ite Islam was adopted as the official religion of the State.[58] The state system was grounded upon the Islamic principles presented in Article 2:

> There is only one God [...] who has exclusive sovereignty and right to legislate, and man must submit to His commands.
> Divine revelation and its fundamental role in the promulgation of laws.
> The essential role of the resurrection in the course of man's ascent towards God.
> God's justice in his creation and his legislation.
> The Imamate's leadership and its essential role in the progress of the Islamic revolution.
> The exalted dignity and value of man. His freedom entails responsibility before God.

Both the preamble and the main articles of the constitution define the Islamic character of the state and Article 3 lists its goals. Among them is the creation of 'an exemplary society' based on 'Islamic principles'. The legislative power is bound by the Shari'a and Article 4 of the constitution declares that all laws should be based on the Shari'a, and that the Guardian Council is responsible for judging whether or not laws are compatible with Shari'a.[59] In other words, the Majles is prevented from enacting laws that are contrary to the principles of Shari'a.[60] Moreover, judges and courts are obliged to refrain from enforcing statutes and regulations that are contradict the Shari'a.[61] Although Iran's constitution provides for the principles of non-discrimination/non-privilege[62] and equality before the law,[63] these rights are regulated, according to Article 4, by 'Islamic criteria'.[64] However, there is no definition of 'Islamic criteria' in the constitution itself. Therefore, different interpretations of these criteria may be used to prevent criticism of the laws and, by implication, of the government. For the purpose of this book, it is important to acknowledge the fact that 'the Constitution constructed the new "Islamic" link between nation and gender and specified a corresponding position for women'.[65]

The constitution recognised women and family as two specified characteristics of the 'Islamic nation'.[66] Therefore, Article 10 states that all pertinent laws, regulations and programmes must tend to facilitate the foundation of the family, as well as to protect the sanctity and stability of family relations on the basis of the law and the ethics of Islam. Moreover, the constitution privileges women as a particular section of Islamic society and states that:

> Through the creation of Islamic social infrastructures, all the elements of humanity that served the multifaceted foreign exploitation shall regain their true identity and human rights. As a part of this process, it is only natural that women should benefit from a particularly large augmentation of their rights, because of the greater oppression that they suffered under the old regime.[67]

Article 21 contains a substantive provision on women's rights. According to this article the government must ensure the rights of women in all respects, in conformity with Islamic criteria, and accomplish certain goals.[68] Four of the five objectives of Article 21 concern a woman's role as mother and wife. As Paidar argues 'women were granted social and political rights because they were mothers and potential mothers'.[69] She aptly explains how the constitution constructed a particular set of patriarchal gender relations.

Women's loyalty could now be shared between the family and the nation. The woman was constructed as a mother; the mother as creator of the Islamic family; and the family as the foundation of the Islamic nation. Women were granted rights and obligations as the creators and nurturers of the Islamic family and nation. The state was given the task of creating 'Muslim mothers' and of putting them in the service of the Islamic nation. The rights and responsibilities of 'Muslim mothers', however, were left to be determined by the Islamic state in conformity with an unspecified Islamic law.[70]

The drafters of the constitution prided themselves on the ideological and 'Islamic nature' of their struggle.[71] They saw themselves as the guardians of Islamic tenets and, as such, all principles were drafted with an eye to the religion's stricter mandates. For instance, Article 20 of Iran's constitution states that:

All citizens of the country, both men and women, equally enjoy the protection of the law and enjoy all human, political, economic, social, and cultural rights, in conformity with Islamic criteria.

It might be argued that the constitution does not grant the same rights to men and women even though it states that they enjoy equality under 'the protection of the law'. Many religious scholars and Islamic jurists believe that men and women should not have equal rights. It is therefore safe to say that the drafters of the constitution did not believe that women should enjoy the same rights as men. Rather, for every right accorded to men, women should have their own unique rights. As an example, the right of sexual intercourse belongs to men – wives cannot refuse the desires of their husbands.[72] In return, men must pay *nafaqeh* (maintenance)[73] to their wives. Since women have the right to maintenance, the two rights are equated in value. This is the 'equality' that is enshrined under the protection of the law.

Legislation in Iran

The Iranian constitution enshrines the principle of the separation of powers. However, this is contradicted by Article 57, which states that all three powers (executive, legislative and judiciary) should be under the supervision of the Supreme Leader.[74] Legislation is mainly introduced and produced by Iran's parliament, the *Majles-e Showrā-ye Islami* (Islamic Consultative Assembly), usually referred to simply as the Majles. The Guardian Council (GC) is constitutionally mandated to ensure the compatibility of all laws approved by the Majles with either the constitution or its own interpretation of the Shari'a.[75] The Majma'-ye Tashkhis-e Maslahat-e Nezām, or Expediency Council for the Discernment of the Interest of Islamic Order, is generally referred to as the Expediency Council. It was created in 1988 by the late Supreme Leader, Ayatollah Khomeini, to overcome disputes between the Majles and the GC.[76]

The Majles

The ICA has 290 members, elected by a direct vote of the people for a four-year term. Due to the fact that the candidates' qualifications are subject to *nezārat-e estesvābi* ('approbatory supervision') by the Guardian

Council, the choice of candidates does not reflect popular will. The Majles has different powers, among which are debating the motions tabled by the government upon the cabinet's approval, as well as bills tabled by at least fifteen members of parliament (MPs), approving international treaties, protocols, agreements and contracts, examining and approving the national budget, investigating all national affairs, approving state-of-emergency declarations, approving foreign loans and subjecting cabinet ministers or the president to impeachment proceedings. Moreover, the interpretation of ordinary laws falls within the remit of the Majles.[77]

The Majles has several commissions – the most important for our purposes being the cultural commission – which carry out initial discussions about the bills and motions.[78] All bills approved by the Majles are sent to the Guardian Council for final ratification.[79] The power and authority of the Majles is therefore greatly limited by the Guardian Council. The intervention of the Supreme Leader's office in the legislative processes through a so-called *hokm-e hukumati* ('state order') mechanism is another obstacle to the functioning of the Majles.[80] This practice came to force when Ayatollah Khomeini issued a letter in January 1988 to President Khamenei, declaring that: 'the State is the most important of God's ordinances and has precedence over all other derived ordinances of God'.[81] With this *fatwā*, the State was given the power to suspend 'the derived ordinance' of the Shari'a whenever necessary. In the view of Khomeini, 'safeguarding Islam is a higher duty than safeguarding the Islamic ordinances'.[82] According to Ayatollah Rasti Kashani, a prominent political figure in the 1980s, by safeguarding Islam, Khomeini meant 'safeguarding the Islamic state'.[83] According to Akbar Hashemi Rafsanjani, an influential political player and Majles speaker during the first decade of the revolution, the Imam (Khomeini) had responsibility over state ordinances and was empowered to confer them to whichever government authority he desired.[84] As a result, the Supreme Leader's state decrees have the power to annul or suspend decisions made by the Majles and the Guardian Council. The High Council of Cultural Revolution, created by Imam Khomeini in December 1984, is another institution with legislative power over cultural and educational issues.[85] These parallel law-making institutions restrict the Majles' independence.

2.3.2 The Guardian Council (Showrā-ye Negahbān)[86]

The Showrā-ye Negahbān (Guardian Council, GC) is a constitutional council made up of twelve male jurists. Six of these are religious men (*faqih*)[87] selected by the Supreme Leader and reputed to be conscious of the needs and issues of present-day society; the other six are specialists in different areas of law, chosen by the Majles from a list of Muslim male jurists proposed by the head of the judiciary[88] who is nominated by the Supreme Leader. Therefore, the Supreme Leader in effect appoints all the members of the Guardian Council. Its members are appointed to serve for a period of six years, but after the first three-year term, drawing lots will change half of the members of each group and new members will be elected in their place.[89] Appointment, dismissal and the resignation of religious members of the Guardian Council are amongst the powers and prerogatives of the Supreme Leader.[90] However, the constitution does not deal with the appointment, dismissal and resignation of the other six jurists nominated by the head of the judiciary. On this subject, Article 7 of the internal regulations of the council states that a member of the council who wants to resign should give his request in writing to the secretary, who will read it out during the first session of the council. If the member does not withdraw his request within a week, his resignation will be relayed to the heads of both the judicial and legislative branches.[91]

The Guardian Council's responsibilities include interpretative pronouncements on and safeguarding of Islamic ordinances and the constitution;[92] these require the consent of three-quarters of its members. It is responsible for supervising elections for the Assembly of Experts, President and the Majles, as well as supervising referenda.[93] Moreover, the GC examines the compatibility of Majles bills with the principles of the Shari'a.[94] After the victory of the Islamic Revolution in February 1979, the legitimacy of laws passed before the revolution came into question. In response, the GC declared:

> Given the fact that current laws of the country are only void when they violate articles of the Constitution and that questions of constitutionality require the interpretation of the Guardian Council, until a law has been interpreted by the Guardian Council, that law is valid and its enforcement remains intact.[95]

The Guardian Council controls Majles decision-making through two different procedures. First, as already noted, the GC is responsible for approving the qualifications of all candidates who intend to stand for election to the Majles. This means that the GC initially decides who is eligible to be a potential Majles representative. Only at this stage does the public have a right to vote for candidates previously approved by the council. The 2004 election provides an example. Arguing that the 'first and foremost' requirement for any candidate for elected office in Iran was unwavering loyalty to the absolute rule of the Supreme Leader, the Guardian Council disqualified a peak of 3,600 of approximately 8,000 Majles candidates (some of whom were reformists) in the run-up to the vote. However, the qualifications of a third of the disqualified candidates (1,200) were approved after some pressure from the reformist president at the time, Mohammad Khatami.[96] In later parliamentary elections in 2008 and 2012, at least 30 per cent of registered candidates were disqualified in each round.[97] In the 2016 parliamentary elections, 49 per cent of registered candidates – mostly reformists – were disqualified.[98]

As mentioned, the Guardian Council examines Majles enactments to ascertain their compatibility with the constitution and Shari'a principles. Article 4 of the constitution requires the GC to examine the compatibility of Majles enactments with the principles of the Shari'a and to veto any laws that are inconsistent with the provisions of the constitution and the Shari'a. A deadline of ten days, extendable for a further ten, is set for the Guardian Council's review. If it finds legislation incompatible, it returns it to the Majles for amendment, otherwise the law shall be deemed enforceable.[99] Ordinary sessions of the GC take place twice a week behind closed doors.[100] Extraordinary sessions may be held if necessary upon the request of three members of the council.[101]

The members of the GC adopted a restrictive and narrow interpretation of Islam. They could veto certain Majles bills citing incompatibility with Shari'a. For instance, the council rejected a bill approved in July–August 2003 by the Majles for Iran's accession to the Convention on the Elimination of All Forms of Discrimination Against Women, on the ground that it was incompatible with Shari'a.[102] Although reformist deputies have always had a presence in the Majles and have tried to introduce modifications to the existing laws and regulations, the Guardian Council has consistently deployed its veto power to stymie change.

The Expediency Council (Majma'-ye Tashkhis-e Maslahat-e Nezām)

The Expediency Council (EC) was established on 6 February 1988 upon the orders of the late Supreme Leader, Ayatollah Khomeini, to overcome a stalemate between the Majles and the Guardian Council.[103] The Expediency Council acts as an arbitrator, drawing on the concept of 'expediency' to vote in favour of either the Majles or the Guardian Council when there is a conflict between them. According to Mohammadi, 'These two had lots of friction due to the reading by the *foqahā* of Islam and the reading of realities by MPs'.[104] The Council consists of forty-five members, including the heads of the judiciary, the executive and the legislature, and the six clerical leaders of the GC. Taking into consideration the fact that permanent and non-permanent members of the Council are appointed by the Supreme Leader, one can begin to understand how complicated the legislative system in Iran is. The intrinsic contradictions encoded in Iran's constitution have produced these complexities.

The main questions that arise are: what precisely is 'expediency'? What are the issues that come under the provision of 'expediency of the State'? Does the Majles have the power to refer all bills refused by the GC to the EC? Unfortunately, these questions find no clear answer in the constitution. One of its most consequential shortcomings in fact concerns precisely this issue of expediency.

A key cause of concern is that EC has the potential to act as a parallel legislative body, thereby restricting the functioning of the Majles as the main legislative authority. As discussed previously, the EC intervenes where there is a dispute between Majles and the GC over an act approved by the former. The Expediency Council may agree with either the GC or the Majles – or, it may disagree with both and declare its own opinion about the disputed matter. In the latter case, the EC may amend the disputed law or add something new. This initiative is considered to be an act of legislation, potentially contradicting the function of the Majles.[105] Following a dispute between Majles and the Guardian Council regarding the age of marriage, on 22 June 2002, the EC amended Article 1041 of the civil code as follows: 'Marriage for girls younger than 13 full solar years and for boys younger than 15 full solar years requires the guardian's permission, but on condition of expediency, as determined by a competent court'.[106] The Expediency Council is known for taking its time in delivering decisions on occasion. The bill for Iran's accession to the Convention on Elimination of All Forms of Discrimination Against Women has remained with the Council since 2003.

Sources of law

The sources of law in Iran can be divided into two groups – namely codified legislation and Islamic sources.

Sources of Iran's codified law

The word law, in its general sense, includes parliamentary legislation, decrees, statutes, injunctions, circulars, ordinances and directives.[107] In particular, according to the Iranian constitution, law in its strict sense refers to texts that have been passed by the Majles and approved by the Guardian Council[108] or accepted by a majority vote through a referendum.[109] In fact, within Iran's legal system, law in its general sense can be hierarchically ordered as follows: the constitution, ordinary law, treaty law, administrative procedures and regulations and circulars.[110]

The constitution is the most important legislative document in Iran and has priority over all other legal sources. It determines the legal organisation of the State, the authority vested in the three branches of government, and their relationship to the people. In relation to treaties, Article 9 of Iran's civil code proclaims:

> Treaty regulations that have been signed, accordant to the Constitution, between the government of Iran and other governments are considered law.' Therefore, the executive and judicial branches must enforce the content of treaties as if they were ordinary laws. Administrative procedures and regulations are another category of law, which includes the ratified procedures of the Council of Ministers. The executive branch's authority to write procedures is not limited to those explicitly delegated by ordinary laws, and each minister may draft regulations that will better fulfil the administrative responsibilities of his/her office.[111]

Further, Article 138 of the constitution proclaims:

> In addition to instances in which the Council of Ministers or a single minister is authorised to frame administrative procedures for the implementation of laws, the Council of Ministers has the right to lay down rules, regulations, and procedures to perform its administrative duties, ensure the implementation of laws, and structure administrative bodies. Every minister also has the right to frame regulations and issue circulars on matters within his/her jurisdiction and in conformity with the decisions of the Council of Ministers. However, the content of such regulations must not violate the letter or the spirit of the law.

Thus, the contents of rules and procedures should not contradict the law. Article 170 of the constitution further proclaims: 'Judges of courts are obliged to refrain from executing administrative procedures and regulations of the government that are in conflict with the laws or norms of Islam, or that lie outside the authority of the executive power. Any person has the right to request the annulment of any such regulation from the Court of Administrative Justice.' Furthermore, officials heading administrative bodies can issue instructions to their employees to better enforce laws and procedures. These instructions are called circulars. Circulars cannot contradict laws or procedures.

Judicial procedure is the second source of Iranian law and its sources are the conventions and methods practised by judges and magistrates. It is notable that, except in very specific circumstances, the purview of every ruling is limited to the case for which it was issued. No single court can establish judicial practices for itself or for other courts. However, in practice, courts tend to follow procedures laid down by higher courts. As such, it often happens that the opinions of judges regarding a specific issue become similar. This means that judicial practice is spontaneous in nature, much like common law.[112] There are two instances in which the judge is obliged to follow judicial practice. The first is in accordance with the amendment to Article 20 of the Law of the Court of Administrative Justice (1999). This specifies that when conflicting opinions on similar cases are given by one or several branches of the Court of Administrative Justice, the head of the court is obliged to hold discussions with the general board of the Court of Administrative

Justice. For the board to convene, at least three-quarters of the judges from the lower branches and courts of appeal must be present. The majority ruling of the board is ineffective for cases that have already been decided but binding in future cases.

The second instance is according to the single-article Uniformity of Jurisprudence Act (1949). Here, the justice ministry, head of the court or prosecutor general can ask the general board of the Supreme Court to hold a meeting to investigate an issue and agree on a ruling at any time, should conflicting procedures be adopted by one or several branches of the Supreme Court regarding similar cases. The majority ruling of the said board, which requires the presence of three-quarters of the heads and judges of the courts to convene, is binding for branches of the Supreme Court and other courts.[113]

The third source of codified law in Iran is custom, which can be interpreted and defined as the public morality shared and respected by society, from which deviations are considered immoral and improper by the collective conscience.[114] In many instances, the legislature has subscribed to custom. For example, Article 667 of the civil code proclaims, 'The agent must, in his handlings and performances, act in the interests of his principal, and must not exceed the limits of the authority which the principal has explicitly given him, or the authority which is inferred by custom, usage, and circumstantial evidence.' Custom should not conflict with the law, since in the Iranian legal system – a system of written or redacted laws – codified law is the most important source of the legal corpus. Other sources do not coexist with the written laws. Therefore, if an issue has become accepted as custom but contradicts law, adherence to the law takes precedence. For instance, it is customary for women not to request *mahriyeh*, a form of dowry the groom commits to pay to the bride. However, according to Article 1082 of Iran's civil code, the wife becomes the owner of the *mahriyeh* immediately after the performance of the marriage contract. Therefore, if she asks for her *mahriyeh*, the husband should pay it and cannot refer to the custom. However, there are instances in which the law itself gives priority to the custom. For example, Article 382 of the civil code accords priority to custom if custom lays down some rules regarding the expenses of the transaction or the place of delivery contrary to those detailed in previous articles, or if in the contract some stipulations to the contrary are made.

The set of opinions consisting of explications, expressions or interpretations of laws by legal experts and scholars is called 'the opinion of scholars' or 'doctrine' and this constitutes the fourth source of codified law in Iran. These opinions can be articulated through a variety of means; academic scholars can express them in lectures, lawyers in legal arguments and writers in books and articles. Sometimes they are presented in speeches delivered in national or international gatherings.[115] In fact, as judges officially interpret the meaning of laws, legal scholars participate in this scientific and technical undertaking by offering new suggestions, criticising court rulings and clarifying the positive and negative aspects of ratified laws. Even though scholarly opinion is neither official nor supported by governmental institutions, it still affects the thinking and practices of judges and lawmakers. It is possible to claim that these opinions indirectly influence the application of codified laws, and as such, become a source of law.[116]

Islamic sources

Although Islamic law has always played an important role in the Iranian legislative process, it was officially accepted as one of the sources of legislation by the constitution only following the 1979 Revolution. Shari'a is made up of main and secondary sources. Due to limited space, only the main sources will be analysed here. However, as the role of *ejtehād* is of great importance in reforming discriminatory laws against women, it will be also discussed in this section. The main sources of Shari'a are the Qur'an, Sunna, *ejma'* and reasoning for Shi'ite Muslims or analogy for Sunnis.[117]

The Qur'an is the primary source of the Shari'a and Muslims believe that it is divine and constitutes the words of God as directly revealed to the Prophet Mohammad. The Qur'an cannot be considered legal code as such; only an estimated 350–500 of approximately 6,666 verses contain legal elements.[118] According to An-Na'im, 'the Qur'an primarily sought to establish certain basic standards of behaviour for the Muslim community rather than express those standards as rights and obligations.'[119] However, the Qur'an's influence in the establishment of the Islamic legal framework should not be disregarded. It is evident that the non-legal verses of the Qur'an were used as guidance to form legal content. Although the words of the Qur'an are divine and immutable, its application has faced many different interpretations since the

THE POLITICAL AND LEGAL SYSTEM OF THE ISLAMIC   69

aforementioned revelation.[120] Different interpretations of the Qur'an contain some contradictions. For example, the Shari'a interpretations that have been adopted within the Iranian legal system cannot be considered identical to the ones in use in Malaysia. It has been claimed that an objective interpretation was produced during the Prophet Mohammad's lifetime. He was the receiver of its revelation and accordingly he was the best person to interpret the Qur'an.

The Sunna is the second primary source of the Shari'a, and has been defined as 'anything that could be proven to have been the practice of the Prophet and his oldest disciples'.[121] According to Imam al-Shafi'i the Sunna of the Prophet is of three types:

> First is the Sunna which prescribes the like of what God has revealed in His Book; next is Sunna which explains the general principles of the Qur'an and clarifies the will of God; and last is the Sunna where the Messenger of God has ruled on matters on which nothing can be found in the Book of God.[122]

In more than one instance, the Qur'an considers the Sunna a source of law which should be strictly followed by Muslims. For instance, it states:

> There has certainly been for you in the Messenger of Allah an excellent pattern for anyone whose hope is in Allah and the Last Day and [who] remembers Allah often.[123]

The Sunna has different meanings for Shi'ite and Sunni Muslims. According to the former, the Sunna only contains the sayings and deeds of the Prophet Mohammad, his daughter Fatima and the twelve Imams, who are free from sins. However, Sunni Muslims also consider sayings and deeds by the companions of the Prophet as Sunna.

In applying a Sunna, two main points should be noted. First, it is important to note that only acts and sayings with intent to make a rule or a law should be considered Sunna.[124] Therefore, when there is no such intention, those acts and sayings may not constitute Sunna. Second, due to the fact that Sunna is the second source of Shari'a, its authenticity should be beyond doubt.[125] It has been claimed that some of the Sunna relayed by Muslims is inauthentic material that has been considered legitimate.[126] Strict criteria were put into place to verify the authenticity of the Sunna. Due to the Islamic theory of evidence, these criteria were not successful. The Islamic theory of evidence presumes that 'a respectable man who would not willingly tell a lie is therefore necessarily telling the truth.'[127] Considering these two points may discredit many of the Sunna.

Ejmā' (juristic consensus) is the third source of Shari'a which is also mentioned in the Qur'an.[128] The Prophet Mohammad announced, 'My people shall never be unanimous in error'[129] According to An-Na'im, *ejmā'* is an independent source of Shari'a for several reasons. It is a tool for verifying the reliability of Sunna and it is considered a means of interpreting the Qur'an.[130] However, the nature and scope of *ejmā'* have been – and continue to be – controversial.

Reasoning for Shi'ite and *qiyās* (analogy) for Sunni Muslims constitutes the fourth main source of the Shari'a and underscores the acceptance of rationality in Islam. There is a principle in Shari'a that states: 'Whatever is implied by *aql* shall be implied by the Shari'a too and whatever the Shari'a praises shall be acknowledged by reason'.[131] By applying *qiyās*, a jurist may conclude from an agreed principle within a precedent that a new case falls under another principle or is similar to another precedent due to shared fundamental elements. For example, according to Shari'a, a husband should pay *nafaqeh*, or maintenance expenses, to his wife. Moreover, he may provide his wife a nurse if needed. However, Shari'a does not oblige a man to pay for the surgical expenses of his wife when she is sick and needs to be cared for in hospital. Although there is no Shari'a-based rule in this regard, one could infer the rule through the use of *qiyās*. The same reasoning (the duty to pay living expenses and to care for one's wife in time of illness) requires the husband to provide for the hospital expenses when and if needed.[132] *Qiyās* might therefore be used in different cases which are not explicitly mentioned in the Shari'a.

The role of ejtehād

Ejtehād technically means exercising independent juristic reasoning to provide answers when the Qur'an and Sunna have no direct explanation for a pressing theological issue.[133] After the death of the Prophet and in fact with the end of the divine revelation, the need for *ejtehād* emerged as a response to new questions arising from the growth of Islam within societies and cultures. As a result of the exercise of *ejtehād*, four schools of

The Political and Legal System of the Islamic 71

jurisprudence mainly followed by the majority of Sunni Muslims today came into existence. These are the Hanafi, Maliki, Shafie and Hanbali schools.[134] However, this process of *ejtehād* did not last for long and 'as Shari'a matured as a legal system, and the need for developing fresh principles and rules was perceived to be diminishing, room for *ejtehād* was seen to be narrowing to the point of extinction. This phenomenon is known in the history of Islamic jurisprudence as the closing of the gates of *ejtehād*'.[135] Some Sunni jurists, such as An-Na'im, argue that 'the gates of *ejtehād* have remained closed since the tenth century A.D. up to the present time.'[136] Despite An-Na'im's analysis, some other scholars argue that *ejtehād* has always been a fundamental concept among Sunni jurists.[137] And in fact 'the legal basis of Shi'ite jurisprudence is no different from the Sunnis, at least in practice'.[138]

Ejtehād developed as a juridical doctrine over the centuries, increasingly following the advent to power of the Zand Dynasty in Iran. There is no consensus amongst Shi'ite jurists on this issue. The Akhbari school of jurispruence has opposed the concept of *ejtehād*, while the Usuli school advocate active *ejtehād* and its implications for the religious and social roles of the *olamā*.[139] Shaykh Mohammad Sharif Astarabadi, the founder of the Akbari school, rejected the principle of *ejtehād* on the basis that it was incompatible with the authority of the Hidden Imam. In the view of the Akbari school, the entire community are followers of the Hidden Imam's teachings, which provide sufficient guidance for understanding the Shi'ite faith and doctrine. Therefore, the position of the *mojtahed* is unnecessary.[140] In contrast, the advocates of *ejtehād*, the Usulis, believe that the *mojtahed*s act as legislators for their followers.[141] The struggle and dispute between these two different viewpoints concerning *ejtehād* has led to violent disputes in the streets of Najaf and Karbala in Iraq and in some big cities in Iran. The Usuli *mojtahed*s ensured their direct influence upon their followers' conduct, and provided a basis for their power, by making *taqlid* (following the directives of one particular *mojtahed* whom the believer considered most worthy) incumbent upon believers.

By the nineteenth century, when an official hierarchy of orthodox *olamā* had come into being, the entire Shi'ite community came to be regarded as consisting of two distinct groups: the small group of *mojtahed* acting as guides, and the majority of their dutiful followers. Although some Sunni Muslims believe that the gates of *ejtehād* have long been permanently closed, the doors of *ejtehād* were opened – from the Shi'ite perspective – with the emergence of the Usuli school in the mid-nineteenth century.[142]

Classical jurists held that 'for the sake of the public welfare the ruler can restrict some matters as long as the matters are not mandatory in Islam'.[143] The relevant example in line with the scope of this study is the second caliph, Omar Ibn Al-Khattab, who used *ejtehād* to ban temporary marriage or marriage of pleasure which was valid and practised during the life time of Prophet Mohammad.[144] *Ejtehād* has also been an effective tool in contemporary Muslim countries to reform laws concerning women. For instance, *ejtehād* has played an important role in reforming the Mudawana in Morocco and, in the words of Amina Arshad, 'the drafters explicitly invoked and utilised *ejtehād* in their revisions, as evidenced by the radical changes to the law'.[145] Therefore, she believes that 'ijtihad was present in the new Mudawana and was the impetus for the improvement in women's status in Morocco'.[146]

Accordingly, Islamic feminists consider *ejtehād* to be an effective tool for dealing with status changes or a tool for leveraging Islamic law to advance the status of women in the broader context of rapid social and technological change in the contemporary era. For example, how would Islamic law address the issue of women acting as head of a household and being the breadwinner when this was once a role reserved for men? How would Islamic law react to the misuse of polygamy and divorce by men in the modern Islamic societies? According to Amira Mashhour, 'when the law fails to respond to the needs of the society and to reflect social change, the law becomes obsolete and the society will seek other informal strategies to fill the gap between the law and development in society'.[147] For example, in the absence of equal rights for men and women in divorce within Iran's civil code, asking for a higher amount of *mahriyeh* from the husband becomes a means for women to guarantee security. Iran, which is a Shi'ite State, considers the importance of the *ejtehād* in its constitution. Iran's constitution emphasises the necessity of *ejtehād* and states that:

> The Islamic Republic is a system based on belief in [...] the exalted dignity and value of man, and his freedom coupled with responsibility before God; that are secured by recourse to: a)

continuous *ejtehād* of the qualified *mojtahed*s, exercised on the basis of the Qur'an and the Sunna, upon all of whom be peace.[148]

Therefore, the gates of *ejtehād* are open in the view of Shi'ite jurists and Iran's constitution provides provisions supporting the use of *ejtehād*. The question arises as to why the Iranian Government doesn't take advantage of this principle to reform its discriminatory laws. It is a fact that radical reforms have occurred in some Muslim countries. As mentioned previously it is claimed that the Maliki-based family law reforms enacted in Morocco have opened the gates of *ejtehād* in this Islamic country.[149] It is therefore the *mojtahed*'s duty to extract the rules from the Shari'a which have more compatibility with the current status of Iranian society.

In the words of the renowned Islamic intellectual Ali Shariati, the existing dogmatic interpretation of Islam which violates the rights of women and reduces their abilities and their potential to those of a 'washing machine' and their human personality to that of a 'breeding machine' may not be tolerated by most of the Iranian population.[150] Although Shariati tackled this problem many years ago, the dogmatic interpretation of Islam still remains one of the main obstacles to any reforms of discriminatory laws against women.

One possible strategy that has resulted in other Muslim countries like Morocco in reforming legislation related to women, as discussed above, is feminist *ejtehād*. It is crucial that women become engaged 'in a process of understanding Islamic law, its interpretations, and Islamic jurisprudence as well as to articulate counter arguments to prove that patriarchal viewpoints are unwarranted and inconsistent with Islamic teaching'.[151] A great number of Muslim women and men adopted this approach to press for a more egalitarian Islam. In the words of Roudi-Fahimi:

[A] growing number of male and female Islamic scholars have been studying religious teachings to justify equal treatment for men and women, and fight discrimination [...] MENA [Middle Eastern and North African] women activists and their supporters are now looking to the Quran and the Sunnah [...] to develop new interpretations of family law. These activists believe that Islam is at heart egalitarian, and that parts of the Shari'a codified in family laws were interpretations by men whose views were rooted in the patriarchal traditions of former times.[152]

It should be noted, however, that the feminist reading of the Qur'an will be opposed by the conservatives who are supporters of patriarchy. The application of *ejtehād* in area of family and women's rights have significant cultural and political implications. With the permissibility of *ejtehād* the clerics will lose their monopoly on legal interpretation of Islamic texts, a fact that is likely to prompt conservative clerics to reject the legitimacy of *ejtehād*.[153] Therefore, achieving gender equality within Muslim societies is not an easy task and requires social and political action as well as a strong legal basis in Islamic law.

Conclusion

It can be inferred from the above expositions that, due to several political, social and religious factors, the normative structure of the contemporary Iranian legal system has failed to accommodate gender equality. The discretionary supervision of the Guardian Council over the Majles and the absolute power of the Supreme Leader have created major obstacles to the reform of Iran's legal system following the 1979 Revolution. Moreover, the hard-line interpretative approach to Islamic law that has been adopted by the Iranian Government prevents the rise of any demands for the reform of the existing Shari'a based discriminatory laws against women. Qualifications such as 'in conformity with Islamic criteria',[154] 'not detrimental to the fundamental principles of Islam',[155] 'sanctioned' or 'provided by law'[156] that are attached to the constitutional rights accorded to Iranian citizens, limit the application of these rights. Therefore, it is not Islam *per se* which prevents progressive changes in the legal system of Iran, but the current regime, which adopts and applies the laws in a manner that restricts the application of human rights, particularly equal rights for men and women, in the name of Islam. One might conclude that, once the contradictions in Iran's constitution are removed, a new, open-minded interpretation of the Shari'a could be applied to the Iranian legal system, effectively eliminating discriminatory laws and practice.

CHAPTER 3

DELIBERATION OVER THE ADOPTION OF CEDAW BY THE ISLAMIC REPUBLIC OF IRAN

Introduction

In Islamic jurisprudence, at least according to most Western-based scholars, the legal principle of equality before law is rejected in favour of the principle of equal but not equivalent.[1] In Iran, conservative politicians, leaders and religious figures reject international demands for gender equality and instead propose Islamic alternatives. By way of introduction, reference can be made to the view of the Supreme Leader of the Islamic Republic of Iran, that the 1979 Revolution set women on the right path: 'Islam introduces Fatima [the daughter of the Prophet Mohammad] the outstanding and distinguished celestial being – as a model and an ideal for Muslim women.'[2] By citing the example of Fatima, Ayatollah Khamenei rejects the secular understanding of women's rights and instead provides for a religiously based alternative to the Western model of equality.

This chapter analyses the process of ratification of the CEDAW by the Iranian Government to explore and analyse the discourse about women's right to equality in Iran. Issues pertaining to Iranian women have always been intertwined with politics. As a result, safeguarding women's rights in Iran depends on the ideological perspective of the ruling authorities. This chapter will, moreover, provide a detailed discussion of the ratification of the CEDAW in the Majles to demonstrate that its representatives could not escape political and religious pressures to enact laws in line with social needs.

The emergence of the women's movement and the CEDAW

The women's movement after the 1979 Revolution emerged in the 1990s, not long after suppression of the non-clerically oriented political activists and dissidents during the previous decade. Consequently, there were still fears of arrest and repression in society, especially amongst civil and political activists. In the early 1990s, most meetings were held around 8 March, to mark International Women's Day, and had the format of private and friendly gatherings in women's homes. In fact, their homes became a refuge for women's rights activists, who gathered under the umbrella of book reading sessions and poetry recitals and film reviews to discuss women's issues and engage in feminist debates. The important lesson to be taken from that era is that women from various social and political backgrounds who were somehow suppressed and forbidden to express themselves publicly in the aftermath of the 1979 Revolution, created a new movement in the 1980s in private gatherings beyond the prying eyes of the state. Irrespective of internal differences in beliefs and viewpoints, the women adopted International Women's Day as a common ground to give meaning to their private meetings and cast a spotlight on their domestic activities.

From the 1990s, a gradual expansion of the non-state media occurred in Iran (albeit from a very low base), and women were able – through the above-mentioned community-building – to carve out a small niche within it. In the early 1990s, *Salām* newspaper was amongst the first publications to include a section to address women's issues. Other publications such as *Iran-e Fardā, Ādineh, Jāme-e ye Sālem, Ketāb-e Towseeh* and *Donyā-ye Sokhan* also directly or indirectly addressed the issue of women, but only so far; none wanted to risk closure by the authorities. But in general, four publications represented the major trends in women's movement at that time: *Jense Dovom (The Second Sex), Farzāneh, Payām-e Hājar (Hājar's Message)* and *Zanān (Women)*. These four publications each for their own part have had an impact on the formation, function and follow-up of the demands of the women's movement.

The Second Sex was actually representative of marginalised women, those who were repressed during and after the revolution because of their secular views. Nooshin Ahmadi Khorasani, a prominent feminist and writer, established *The Second Sex*, which later became a bridge between secular women inside and outside the country. However, due to existing and uncontrolled state-imposed limitations, the outreach of the publication was limited to secular and intellectual women. The imposed state limitation was extensive, to the extent that for the release of any new edition of *The Second Sex*, the ministry of culture had to issue a licence. Nooshin Ahmadi Khorasani in her book, *The Spring of the Iranian Women's Movement*, explains the difficulties she went through to obtain a permanent licence for the *Second Sex* during the presidency of Mohammad Khatami. Yet her efforts were fruitless. In her view, *The Second Sex* at that time 'was a sign of powerlessness of a large section of women's society in Iran'.[3]

Farzāneh was representative of technocrat women close to the Kārgozārān-e Sāzandegi party, which insisted on expert oriented and development-based discourse to advance women's rights. Sixteen members of the cabinet founded Kārgozārān-e Sāzandegi in February 1996, the final year of the second term of Akbar Hashemi Rafsanjani's presidency. In fact, Kārgozārān was the first political party established within the government. Owing to its focus on expert-oriented material, *Farzāneh* played a significant role in introducing up-to-date women's debates to Iranian society, which subsequently proved to be fundamental in the establishment of a women's studies unit at universities. Faezeh Hashemi Rafsanjani, the daughter of President Rafsanjani, was the most prominent woman associated with this group. She was instrumental in attracting international attention to women's sport in Iran. She assumed the management of the *Zan (Woman)* newspaper in 1998.

Payām-e Hājar was another publication addressing women's issues. The publication represented the Melli-Mazhabi (National-Religious) group under the leadership of Azam Taleghani. Although this publication to some extent paid attention to women's issues, especially the problems of women belonging to the working class, in general it did not have a strong focus on issues pertaining to women.

The most important occurrence concerning the promotion of women's issues was the emergence of *Zanān* magazine in 1991 under the leadership of Shahla Sherkat. The main themes of *Zanān* were family-related legal issues and rules governing them. The publication's outlook was in line with those who pressed for a modernist reinterpretation of religious texts, such as the Noandishan-e Dini movement. Therefore, from the Islamic Republic's internal factional perspective, *Zanān* was close to the reformist left. The emergence of *Zanān* advanced discussions surrounding women's rights and equality. Women's rights defenders and female lawyers made advantage of this platform to raise public awareness about issues pertaining to women.

The role of two female lawyers, Shirin Ebadi and Mehrangiz Kar, was significant in enlivening the debate about women's rights within Iranian society. Mehrangiz Kar depicted women's daily problems caused by discriminatory laws and legal arguments in her reasoned articles and thereby tried to provide solutions to improve the situation of women affected by discriminatory laws. It was her legal articles, published during the 1995–2002 period, that educated me on how to propose practical solutions for improving the situation of female victims of discriminatory legislation. Kar eloquently discussed the cases of domestic violence against women for the readers and at the same time alerted the authorities to the necessity of establishing safe houses to protect women victims of domestic violence. Kar's reasoned and insightful articles encouraged me to explore in more depth the legal texts and legislation to find the best legal way to restore justice to oppressed women.

Shirin Ebadi was an active lawyer defending human rights activists and dissidents pro bono. Through defending sensitive cases and spotlighting them in the media, Ebadi was trying to raise public awareness about the suffering of victims of discriminatory laws and educate citizens not to be indifferent to injustices their compatriots were being subjected to. I met Ebadi in 1999 at the office of the Society for the Protection of the Rights of the Child (SPRC), a non-profit organisation established by Ebadi and some of her colleagues to protect the rights of children. I became a member of that NGO as a law student and civil rights activist and became involved in its activities.

The political atmosphere opened during the second administration of President Rafsanjani and this led to new possibilities for civil society mobilisation. However, women's issues were still considered sensitive and therefore it was not easy to manoeuvre. To avoid any risks associated with being seen as associating too closely with the women's rights movement, activists shaped their actions around other justice questions. For example, children's rights were a less controversial issue, as Iran was a signatory to the UN Convention on the Rights of the Child. The SPRC, which by the nature of its mandate required pursuing issues which affected women, was born in this context through the work of women's rights activists like Mahdokht Sanati and Shirin Ebadi.

There are a number of cases that exemplify the work of the society during this period. For example, Leila Fathi's case,[4] which brought the debate on gender discrimination of the *diyeh* regulation to the fore in Iranian society, coincided with my attendance at law school. This case allowed Ebadi to gain public support by demanding a change in *diyeh* regulations. In fact, this case caused a precedent for such extreme discrimination and engaged public opinion in the quest to mobilise change. In the case of Arian Golshani, a nine-year-old girl who died as a result of the conduct of her abusive father and stepmother, Ebadi demonstrated the negative consequence of discriminatory custody law and the need for reform.[5] The latter case became grounds for a social movement to change custody law to favour best interest of the child. In fact, the case was the first civic experience for women's movement to change discriminatory laws.[6] A ceremony was organised by the SPRC at the Al-Ghadir mosque in Tehran. The SPRC invited people to participate in the event. During the ceremony, when the crowd became emotional and began crying, Ebadi strode up to the microphone in the women's section and said, 'Today we are here to defend the rights of other Arians. We must reform the law that led to her death'.[7] After her intervention all people in the mosque and surrounding streets chanted slogans to the effect that that the law should be changed. I was impressed by Ebadi's courage and on this same day I pledged to myself that I too would become a lawyer and like her defend victims of discrimination. For this reason, after admission to the bar association, I asked Ebadi to be my supervisor. After beginning my training with Ebadi, I started to defend human rights cases.

One very powerful legal strategy that female lawyers pursued to shed light on the stark discrimination of many laws was through bringing cases to public attention. The advantage here was that the everyday impacts of discrimination could be brought into the open in the court in detail. The Women's Cultural Centre was successful in this area, raising public awareness by publicising paradigmatic cases that showcased clearly how egregious some laws could be for ordinary women, casting this legal cruelty against the ordinary sense of justice and fair play within Iranian society. The Women's Cultural Centre was established in 1999 by nine women's rights defenders with a mandate to raise public awareness about women's demands. In the view of Nooshin Ahmadi Khorasani, one of the founding members of the centre:

> [Following] the legal cases of ordinary women was an effective strategy that started in 1995 and merged with civil and street protests in 1997 and reached its pick during the years 2000 to 2005 by widely adopting civil and non-violent methods such as holding meetings, rallies and protests. This strategy was able to a large degree to tie the demand for legal equality with women's everyday challenges.[8]

Along with these activities, the accession to the CEDAW has always been one of the main demands of women's rights activists. During the 1990s, women's rights defenders and lawyers argued for Iran's accession to the CEDAW through articles, conferences and public meetings.

Despite the importance of this grassroots activism, political developments within the Rafsanjani administration – particularly its desire for a conflict-free foreign policy – were formative in creating an opportunity structure for the public manifestation of this demand and open discussion about it to emerge. In 1995, a network of women's NGOs of the Islamic Republic was established to organise and send some non-governmental organisations to the WCW in Beijing. Some of these actors called for Iran to join the convention. Women's rights activists welcomed this initiative of women within the political structure and used that to make their own demand open and public. For example, the Cultural Centre for Women in its newsletter, *Nameh-ye Zan*, published in March 2001, clearly emphasised the importance of Iran's accession to the CEDAW. In the winter of the same year, the centre drafted a petition and asked for public support through the collection of signatures from citizens; more than 100 were collected. On 8 March 2001, during a ceremony marking International Women's Day, the centre showed a documentary about the history of the day, during which the CEDAW was discussed as well.

In the 2002 celebrations of 8 March, the centre prepared a petition asking Iran to join the CEDAW without any reservation and distributed a petition to its members in other cities, including Tabriz, Sanandaj, Isfahan, Zanjan and Semnan to collect signatures from citizens in support of Iran's accession. The centre published the text of the convention in a booklet and distributed it widely. From 2001, the centre prepared and published a calendar reviewing women's events in Iran and around the world. The focus of initial calendar was on the CEDAW and Iranian laws. To further discuss the CEDAW between 2002 to 2007 the centre organised and held workshops on the CEDAW despite considerable restrictions.

Demands for Iran to join the CEDAW came from other quarters as well. Women's rights activists, academics, women's groups and some women within the political establishment were also active. Mehrangiz Kar wrote a comprehensive book analysing Iranian laws in line with the CEDAW to highlight the extent to which they violated it, and to lay out potential avenues of reform without provoking disagreement from religious establishment. Women's groups such as Zanān-e Esfand published pamphlets on the CEDAW and in their events celebrating International Women's Day urged Iran to join the convention.

Iran's accession to the CEDAW therefore became one of the main demands of the women's movement in Iran between 1999 and 2004. In 2002, the main theme of the 8 March gathering in Tehran and other cities was the importance of Iran being party to the convention. For example, in the Pārk-e-Lāleh gathering in Tehran, Shirin Ebadi and Nooshin Ahmadi Khorasani were among the main speakers who spoke on this subject. In that year, Faranak Farid and Zohreh Moini, two Azerbaijani women's rights activists, organised an event in a women's prison in Tabriz. During this gathering, Zohreh Arzani – a lawyer and member of the Women's Cultural Centre – brought awareness about the CEDAW to the jailed women.

In October 2003, supporters of Iran's accession to the convention gained more influence when Shirin Ebadi was awarded the Nobel Prize. During her first press conference following the award on 23 October 2003, Ebadi urged Iran to join the convention. But the Khatami government's perception about the Nobel Peace Prize and its impact on the women's movement was different from that of women's rights activists. In fact, religious leaders did not change their views on the

CEDAW after award to Shirin Ebadi. Despite all restrictions, women have continued their demands during the discussion of Iran's accession to the CEDAW in parliament.

Debating ratification of the CEDAW in Iran

CEDAW and the executive

According to the 1989 constitution, Iran's president or his legal representative are endowed with the authority to sign treaties, protocols, contracts and agreements concluded by the Iranian Government with other governments, as well as agreements pertaining to international organisations, after obtaining the approval of the Majles.[9] Therefore, in relation to Iran's accession to international treaties, the executive will first decide whether it is necessary for the State to become a party to the treaty and then seek approval from the Majles. The procedure calls on the executive to prepare a bill and send it to the Majles. If the latter ratifies it and the GC approves the bill, the executive can then sign the treaty. A treaty concluded between the Iranian Government and any other government shall bear the force of law.[10]

The ratification of the CEDAW has been at the forefront of discussion in two distinct periods in Iran. The first period (1995–7) was at the end of the presidency of Hashemi Rafsanjani, when Iran's postwar economic and social reconstruction of the country was still the greatest political priority. Ratifying the CEDAW was proposed by Aliakbar Velayati, then Iran's foreign minister, arguing that most Islamic countries had already ratified the convention, albeit with reservations. In his letter to Hashemi Rafsanjani, he referred to twelve issues embedded in Iranian domestic laws that contravened CEDAW, suggesting that it might be possible to amend six of the issues that concerned domestic laws.[11] In 1996, the Supreme Council of Cultural Revolution (SCCR) was asked to examine the foreign minister's proposition and the SCCR appointed a committee to deal with this issue.[12] At the same time, opponents and supporters of the ratification of the CEDAW expressed, as shall be seen below, their differing opinions in the press.[13] The Supreme Leader of Iran as well as a number of Islamic jurists disagreed with the ratification of the CEDAW, and stated that it was against the principles of the Shari'a.[14] On 13 October 1997, the general secretary of the SCCR's committee presented a report containing the opinions of its members for the SCCR.

On 3 February 1998, a few months after the start of Mohammad Khatami's presidency, the Supreme Council of Cultural Revolution rejected Iran's ratification of the CEDAW without subjecting the question to detailed scrutiny.[15] At this stage, the bill of accession was discussed within the executive branch of State and not submitted for the examination of the Majles. This process suggests that women's rights did not yet feature as a prominent issue for the new reformist administration of the time.

The ratification of the CEDAW was discussed again between 1999 and 2003, when the reform era had developed further and when more attention was paid to advancing civil and political rights within an Islamic framework. In the words of Mir-Hosseini, 'Reformist efforts to reconcile Islam with democracy and human rights brought to the surface the inherent contradiction between the construction of gender rights in Shari'a law and democratic ideals'.[16] The issue of accession to the CEDAW was raised, this time around, by the Centre for Women's Participation, which sent a letter to President Khatami in May 1999 demanding that the previous decision opposing the ratification of the CEDAW be overturned.[17] President Khatami was open to this request, and requested further examination of the issue. On 26 September 1999, the president of the Centre for Women's Participation issued a letter to the first vice president of Iran concerning a demand made by the UN Secretary-General regarding Iran's accession to the CEDAW.

The first vice president referred the issue to the Komisiyon-e Lavāyeh, the body responsible for drafting legislation, and six months later, on 16 February 2000, the latter created a subcommittee to analyse Iran's accession to the CEDAW.[18] Among the members of the subcommittee, the legal and parliamentary affairs division of the office of the president voiced its objection to Iran's accession to the CEDAW as follows:

> Most of the obligations in relation to the elimination of discrimination against women and granting them their rights, which are included in articles 1–16 of the CEDAW, are in contradiction with the principles of Islamic legal regime, the principles of the Constitution, our national culture and religious beliefs. Even reservations would not be helpful and therefore, the Majles and the Guardian Council will not approve Iran's accession to the CEDAW.[19]

To minimise the negative impact of Iran's disapproval of the CEDAW, the legal and parliamentary affairs bureau in the presidential office proposed that the foreign affairs office draft a proper document as an alternative to the CEDAW with the assistance of the Islamic Culture and Relations Organisation[20] and the judiciary. This document was to contain provisions on gender equality based on Islamic principles and was to be presented to the Organisation of the Islamic Conference (OIC).[21]

The subcommittee was of the view that Article 1 of the CEDAW was in contradiction with ninety-five issues covered by Iranian domestic law, including the constitution, civil code, Islamic criminal code and other regulations. The Komisiyon-e Lavāyeh recommended that Iran join the CEDAW subject to some conditions and the establishment of a reservation according to which:

> The Islamic Republic of Iran applies the provisions of the convention as long as they are not in conflict with Islam and the Islamic Republic of Iran is not bound by paragraph 1 of article 29 of the convention concerning the settlement of disputes through arbitration or referral to the International Court of Justice.

The Komisiyon-e Lavāyeh noted that the CEDAW had been ratified by most countries, including many Muslim states, since entering into force in September 1981. Moreover, the subcommittee insisted that Iran's accession to the CEDAW with a general reservation would have positive consequences for the country.[22] On 19 January 2002, the government ratified a bill of accession to the CEDAW containing a general Shari'a-based reservation and sent it to the Majles.

Contestation over the CEDAW after approval by the executive

This ratification triggered a wave of concern among different groups of women about the reaction of the *foqahā*, or religious jurists, to Iran's accession to the CEDAW. The president of the Centre for Women's Participation issued a letter explaining why Iran should join the CEDAW to convince the *foqahā* that the government's Shari'a-based reservation was the best option for joining the CEDAW without infringing on Islamic principles.[23] In spite of some negative voices from the *foqahā*, the cultural commission of the Majles approved the bill of accession to the CEDAW on 12 February 2002 and the bill was tabled for debate.

In February 2002, the Centre for Women's Participation hosted a conference to discuss the CEDAW. Some deputies of the Majles and some representatives from both government and non-government organisations participated in this conference. Elaheh Kulaei, a reformist deputy in the Majles, stated that the convention's main message was not to promote identical rights between men and women. 'Rather, the treaty seeks to remove the chains and shackles from the hands and feet of women'. Zahra Ayatollahi, a representative from the Women's Social and Cultural Council, represented the conservative view when she stated: 'We should improve women's status according to the expectation of God and his Prophet, not on the basis of international pressure'.[24] Jamileh Kadivar, a reformist deputy in the Majles, responded: 'Many reforms occurred after the Revolution only in response to international pressures'.[25] On 23 March 2003 the bill was tabled for debate in the Majles, but the presiding board of the Majles put it aside immediately. Kulaei considered the reaction of the *olamā* (and the wish to prevent any dispute between the *olamā* and the Majles) the main reason for postponing the debate until a suitable future time.[26] Ayatollah Meshkini, the chair of the Society of Seminary Teachers of Qom, sent a confidential letter to the Majles outlining the concerns of the *olamā* about Iran's accession to the CEDAW. A year-and-a-half later the *Jomhuri-ye Islami* newspaper published a letter justifying the *olamā's* decision to prevent Iran from ratifing the CEDAW on the basis that the latter was in conflict with the Shari'a and *maslahat*, or 'expediency'. The letter argued:

> If Iran, which leads the Islamic resurgence in the world, joins the CEDAW, consensus would be reached that the Western model of equality that supports the idea of similarity is the only model and Islam itself does not have an alternative one. Therefore, Islamic governments would be expected to amend their laws on the basis of the similarity model, not on Islamic values and the *maslahat*. As a result of the fact that the CEDAW is in contravention with the Islamic principle, our Islamic system would be accused of making distance from the Shari'a.[27]

The CEDAW's supporters tried to convince their opponents with little success. Akram Mosavari Manesh, a deputy from Isfahan in the sixth Majles, stated:

> We have done whatever was possible in our capacity, and we have had sessions with the *olamā*. The presiding board should also carry out some activities in this regard. We were informed that a committee was set up to discuss this issue with *olamā*, however, more detailed information was not provided.[28]

Four *maraje*'[29] – high-ranking clerics – namely, Jawad Tabrizi, Makarem Shirazi, Fazel Lankarani and Safi Golpayegani, issued a *fatwā* in April 2002, which once again prevented the Majles from debating the delayed bill of accession to the CEDAW. In his own *fatwā*, Ayatollah Lankarani highlighted his concerns about the contradictions between the CEDAW with the Islamic Shari'a. Ayatollah Makarem Shirazi believed that a Shari'a-based reservation would not solve the problem because the convention explicitly proclaimed that reservations which were incompatible with the object and purpose of the convention were not permitted. He further pointed out that this convention not only failed to afford any additional support for women in society but also introduced the same difficulties that Western women were facing in their societies, which undermined the family union. He further elaborated that the West wanted to impose its cultural values upon Iran; the government should be alert and not be exploited by the West. Ayatollah Tabrizi believed that the West wanted to remove Islam from the scene.[30]

The supporters of Iran's accession to the CEDAW complained that the Majles were not discussing the bill. Azam Naseri Pur, an MP for West Islam Abad, accused the Majles speaker of acting against the laws of the country. Karubi, Majles speaker at the time, responded,

> I was informed by the head of the Cultural Commission that the bill has some defects and therefore needs to be amended. He asked me to not debate the bill in the session and I did so to help the Commission amend the bill for the next consideration in the Majles. I have received two letters from Qom and I gave them to the representatives from the government and the Cultural

Committee. I have asked some diplomats from the Foreign Ministry to go to Qom to discuss the issue with the *olamā*.[31]

The advocates of accession to the CEDAW were disappointed with the points made by the *olamā*. In an interview with the Iranian Students' News Agency, Mosavari Manesh concluded that *olamā* disagreed with the bill due to a lack of understanding of its context.[32] Fatemeh Rakei, the president of the *ferāksiun-e zanān* (women's caucus) in the Majles, stated that the 'views of some *olamā* in the seminary are not compatible with Ayatollah Khomeini's perspective. They believe that the old laws should be applicable in the twenty-first century without any revision'.[33] The supporters of accession also criticised political groups, such as the Reformists, who were not actively involved in the discussions. Elaheh Kulaei claimed that those political groups did not want to involve women's issues in their own problems.[34]

CEDAW and the legislature

The sixth Majles (2000–04) was dominated by reformists. As aptly stated by Mir-Hosseini, 'the sixth Majles was a turning point for women and the politics of gender'.[35] Thirteen women deputies active within it, including Elaheh Kulaei, Jamileh Kadivar and Fatemeh Haqiqatjoo, played an important role in addressing gender inequalities in law and society. These three MPs were at the forefront of attempts to redress the gender inequalities through corrective legislation and often spread news of this initiative through the media. Haqiqatjoo acquired the sobriquet *shir-zan* ('lion woman') due to her passionate activism and fearless attitude.[36] Thirty-three bills were introduced by members of the *ferāksiun-e zanān* during this session. Sixteen of these became law after an intervention by the EC, while the rest were rejected by the GC on grounds of incompatibility with the Shari'a. The amendment of laws concerning the custody of children (increasing the age to seven for both girls and boys) was amongst the defeated bills.

In early April 2003, it was announced that the bill of accession to the CEDAW was ready for debate. The Centre for Women's Studies sent a letter to the Majles speaker to respond in more detail to the views of CEDAW opponents, urging the parliament to undertake more studies in this regard. The cultural commission and the women's caucus in the parliament invited three experts from the Centre of Women's Studies, established by the management of women's seminaries in 1998,[37] to discuss the perspectives of opponents and supporters of the bill. Hojat-ol-Islam Zibaei Nejad, the president of the Centre presented the views of the opponents alongside Fariba Alasvand and Mostafa Fazaeli while Fatemeg Rakei, Elahe Kulaei and Ali Shakoori elaborated the views of the supporters.[38]

In May 2003, Ayatollah Makarem Shirazi expressed his view of the convention during a speech to a group of women, stating that 'to impose its culture upon us, the West created this Convention which encompasses all of their cultural traits. They have asked other countries to sign the convention to become civilised. We must either ignore our honour, esteem, independence, dignity, religion, faith and principles or obey the West'.[39]

On 23 July 2003, the bill was debated for the first time in the Majles. Two events paved the way for progress on this issue in parliament. The tragic death in prison of Zahra Kazemi, an Iranian-Canadian journalist who had been illegally detained, charged the political atmosphere against Iran in the international media, to an extent that made it seem inauspicious to add to the negative flow of news coming out of Iran. This coincided with an academic break at the Qom seminary, which made it easier to discuss such issues without interference from the *olamā* based there.

Ahmad Pur Nejati, the head of the parliament's cultural commission, reported on the six-year-long process of drafting the bill of accession to the CEDAW between 1995 and 2001. He noted that, due to the current political situation, it was necessary for Iran to ratify the CEDAW. He pointed out that 168 countries had joined the convention and only eighteen countries had refused to be a party to it, with forty-four of the fifty-six members of the OIC signing. He assured the Majles that ratifying the convention with a general Shari'a-based reservation would enable Iranian women to benefit from the privileges and capacities of the convention without jeopardising Iran's religious values and beliefs. He emphasised that by joining the CEDAW, Iran could minimise propaganda against the country while providing reliable reports to the monitoring body of the CEDAW, that is, the Committee on the Elimination of Discrimination against Women In his view, rejection of the CEDAW reinforced the stereotype of Iran as an Islamic State willing to discriminate against women. At the end of his report, he asked the

Majles to trust the decision of the Majles cultural commission and to vote in favour of ratification of the CEDAW.⁴⁰

In opposition, Hassan Sobhani gave a detailed account of the negative effects of joining the CEDAW. He argued that if the Majles were to adopt the bill, it would also be forced to change the current laws that differentiate the men from women, which include differences in ways to prove crimes, to carry out *qesās*, women's testimony and the amount of *diyeh* between men and women. Namely that under the law women would have to be treated equally to men.⁴¹ Voting for the bill would give women equal rights with men in marriage, during marriage and at its dissolution.⁴² He argued that the convention did not serve women's interests. It tried to push women to achieve the same situation as men. Feminists did not want to improve women's status, but to change the world built by men. They wanted to introduce a new definition of power relations by bringing women from the private sphere into public life. They wanted to restructure the family union and minimise the importance of the woman's role as a mother in the family. 'Are we ignoring the rights of women?' he asked. To answer this question, he referred to Morteza Motahhari, who stated that equality between men and woman as well as their freedom as human beings is obvious. Both share the same dignity and human values. However, they are two different creatures, with two different characteristics. Equality and freedom are therefore necessary – but not sufficient – conditions. Women and men are equal but not similar. He also quoted Ayatollah Fazel Lankarani and Ayatollah Makarem Shirazi, who objected to Iran's accession. He concluded that women would be insulted if Iran joined the convention, as it would provide them with fewer rights than those afforded them by the Shari'a.⁴³

Elaheh Kulaei, on the other hand, spoke in favour of ratification. In her view, the 1979 Revolution and the subsequent crisis – the Iran–Iraq War above all – had prevented Iran from discussing the convention seriously during the first years of its ratification. She posed the issue as one of national honour. She insisted that in lining up to ratify the CEDAW, the international community had affirmed a common view that discrimination against women violates the principles of equality and human dignity, thereby preventing women from participating in public life as actively as their male counterparts. Would Iran not be able to join this consensus by ratifying the convention, thus putting the lies to the distorted view of the situatino of Iranian women the country's enemies were trying to show.

To generate further discord regarding the CEDAW, another MP, Musa Ghorbani, pointed out that Islam does not recognise discrimination and that this concept is based on a Western notion of legal norms. For instance, matters such as inheritance that the West considers discriminatory, do not, in fact, constitute discrimination against women. It would be most damaging if we were to change first our constitution and then our laws and then even our customs and practices, she argued. Eventually, the bill was passed by a majority of 196 deputies on 23 July 2003.[44]

Opposition to Majles' decision on the CEDAW opponents began to heat up. On 1 August 2003, during Friday prayers in Qom, a protest rally was organised to condemn the Majles for its decision.[45] Similar demonstrations were held in Tabriz, Hamedan, Semnan, Rasht and Ahvaz. On 2 August 2003, Ayatollah Mesbah Yazdi, a prominent hawkish cleric, criticised the government for ratifying a bill that, in his opinion, contradicted ninety Iranian laws. He questioned the wisdom of the government's decision to submit this bill for parliamentary approval. Widespread demonstrations took place across the country following Mesbah's criticism.[46] State TV hosted a limited roundtable which featured only opponents of the bill, including Zahra Ayatollahi, Fariba Alasvand and Mohammadreza Zibaei Nejad. They criticised the concept of equality under the convention and declared that ignoring the differences between sexes was not in conformity with Islam. This programme compelled the *ferāksiun-e zanān* in the Majles to take legal action against state TV, the result of which has never been made public.[47]

Due to extreme opposition from different groups and some clerics, the Guardian Council rejected the bill one month after its ratification by the parliament, preventing Iran's accession to the convention. Ayatollah Jannati, the head of the council, stated that the provisions of the convention were, to a very large extent, in contradiction with the Shari'a and the constitution.[48] Some days later Ayatollah Rezvani and Ebrahim Azizi, both members of the Guardian Council, addressed the Majles' cultural commission to present this reasoning in person.

The cultural commission of the Majles discussed the concerns of the Guardian Council in two sessions. During the second, on 7 October

2003, the head of the cultural commission, Ahmad Pur Nejati, stated that the council had returned the bill of accession to the CEDAW, asking the Majles to specify those articles of the CEDAW that contradicted the Shari'a, to enable the council to decide whether Iran could join.[49] Pur Nejati declared, on the Majles floor, that parliament had followed the same general procedures in ratifying other international instruments that the council had accepted. He explained that the proposed reservation to the CEDAW meant none of the provisions deemed in conflict with Islam would apply to Iran. Additionally, Iran would not be compelled to accept the settlement of disputes through arbitration or referral to the International Court of Justice. He explained that the Majles was not responsible for ascertaining which articles of the CEDAW contradicted the Shari'a; this is the Guardian Council's constitutional duty. He reaffirmed the cultural commission's decision, ratified by the Majles, and suggested that the Expediency Council intervene to provide another possible way forward. Finally, he urged the members of the Majles to vote in favour of the cultural commission's decision.[50]

Hassan Sobhani spoke against the decision of the cultural commission and stated that the Majles should heed the GC's request to specify the articles contravening the Shari'a. He pointed out that the GC had not given an opinion on whether the bill went against the Shari'a or the constitution. The GC had asked the Majles to answer questions about which articles of the CEDAW went against the Shari'a and who should decide on this issue. Therefore, in his view, there was no text to be sent to the EC. Mohammad Reza Khatami, first deputy speaker of the parliament, responded that, based on his discussions, this bill should be considered law because the GC did not examine it within the specified time framework mentioned in Article 94 of the constitution. The bill would have been deemed enforceable if they had listened to his comments. This could not be done, given the current situation of the country. He maintained that the bill should be sent to the Expediency Council and its decision upheld.[51] It was ultimately agreed that the bill should be sent to the EC for a resolution of the dispute between the Majles and the GC, as indicated by the constitution.

It is interesting to note that the bill has been held within the Expediency Council ever since. It seems that the issue of women's rights is not high enough on the government's agenda to force the EC to take action regarding the CEDAW. Hassan Rowhani's accession to the presidency in June 2013 potentially raised new prospects for the approval of the CEDAW. It was presumed that his moderate stance on social issues and his long-standing collaboration and association with the head of the EC, Hashemi Rafsanjani, would be conducive to women's rights activists succeeding in exerting pressure, in turn leading to the re-examination of the case of accession to the CEDAW by the EC itself. Such auspices had been strengthened by the nomination of Shahindokht Molaverdi, a long-standing women's rights activist, as vice-president of Iran for women affairs in August 2013. However, no serious action regarding the CEDAW took place until the end of the first term of Rowhani's administration.

The debate over Iran's accession to the CEDAW: Opponents and supporters[52]

Traditionalists and religious figures who support the current Supreme Leader's interpretation of Islam may be considered the main group opposed to the ratification of the CEDAW. During the debate over the ratification of the bill of the accession to the CEDAW in the Majles, many conservative newspapers – including *Resālat*, *Jomhuri-ye Islami*, *Keyhān* and *Khorāsān*, among others – published the arguments of opponents to deliver the messages that the CEDAW would have a substantial, negative impact on the individual, social and family life of citizens of member states, and that it is to a large extent incompatible with *feqh* and Islamic rules that Muslims must obey. The opponents of accession buttressed their arguments by referring to the apparent incompatibility of the CEDAW with Islamic principles, the lack of identification of the CEDAW with women's interests, its failure to support the unity of the family, its conflict with Iran's national interest and the inadequacy of the reservations.[53]

On the other hand, some reformist newspapers and magazines – including *Yās-e Now*, *Zan-e Rooz*, *Zanān* and *Sharq*, among others – reflected the arguments of supporters, who argued that the opponents had politicised the issue of Iran's accession to the CEDAW. In their view, the conservative newspapers employed different strategies to undermine the positive impact of the convention. One strategy consisted of persuading religious figures to denounce the convention as an anti-Islamic instrument. One of the male preachers before Friday prayers asked, 'where in the world are women allowed to marry up to four husbands, for us to become the second one?'[54] Zahra Shojaei, the women's affairs advisor to President Khatami, criticised this way of introducing the convention and stated that Iran's government should avoid reactions based on ridicule: 'Where does the CEDAW speak about such rights for women? Why do you define the convention in such a way? What are the benefits of such definitions?'[55] To respond to opponents, the supporters of accession argued that the CEDAW is not inconsistent with the Shari'a; it is a legal framework for the support of women's rights and would strengthen the family union. They furthermore argued that CEDAW would improve Iran's reputation in the international community, and that the reservation would help Iran to ratify the convention without infringing on Islamic principles.[56]

Apparent contravention of Islamic principles by the CEDAW
The opponents of accession to the CEDAW claimed that its provisions contravened Islamic principles. As previously mentioned, many *olamā* expressly raised concerns about the incompatibility of the CEDAW with Islamic rules, arguing that it is not permissible for Muslims and Islamic governments who believe in Islam to join the convention.[57] In the view of the opponents, the narrow and limited definition of discrimination against women adopted by the convention, based on the idea of similarity, contradicts the Islamic definition of discrimination.[58] The opponents believed that the convention is designed to eradicate natural differences between men and women, which cannot be accepted by Islam.[59]

According to the view of the opponents, the CEDAW contravenes forty principles of Islamic law.[60] For instance, compulsory *hejāb* for women, which is mentioned in verses 24:31 and 33:59 of the Qur'an, might be considered a form of gender-based discrimination in contravention of Article 1 of the CEDAW. In the view of these opponents, Articles 1 and 15 of the convention were incompatible with the Qur'anic verse 2:282, which accepts differences in testimony for men and women. Moreover, verses 4:34 and 2:228 recognise the guardianship of men, which would have differing consequences in family life. For instance, a wife should have her husband's consent before leaving home, in violation of Article 1 and 7 (b) of the convention.[61] The guardianship of men mentioned above is also incompatible with Articles 9, 11 (a) and 15 (4) of the CEDAW.[62] According to Articles 1 and 16 of the convention, men and women shall enjoy equal rights in the family. However, these provisions do not reflect the guidance given in Qur'anic verse 4:34.[63] Restrictions on sexual activity during a woman's monthly period are derived from Qur'an 2:222; according to Article 1 of the CEDAW, this would be considered an example of gender-based discrimination. The right to polygamy, given to men by Qur'an 4:3, contradicts Articles 1 and 16 (a) of the convention. Differences in men and women's right to inherit are derived from Qur'an 4:11 and 4:12. However, this Islamically based principle contravenes provisions contained in the CEDAW.[64] The Islamic rules concerning divorce, custody and the marriage of a Muslim woman with a non-Muslim man, a father's guardianship and consent and other issues do not conform to the CEDAW. Therefore, according to the opponents, the extent to which the CEDAW contradicts the Shari'a is sufficiently extensive that Muslims cannot accept it.

In contrast, supporters of accession argued that that the incompatibility between the CEDAW and Islamic principles is not significant, being limited to some minor issues. They argued that, in an Islamic system, women have the same rights as men in education, work, political participation, ownership and many other aspects of public life.[65] Most importantly, in Islam men and women are equal in creation. The Qur'an as the main source of Islamic law declares: 'O mankind! Be careful of your duty to your Lord Who created you from a single soul and from it created its mate and from them twain hath spread abroad a multitude of men and women'[66] and the noblest person in the sight of the God is the best in conduct.[67]

CEDAW's supporters argued that feminism initially emerged as a struggle against the tyranny and oppression that women suffered in the West. Earlier declarations of human rights did not consider women as human beings or accord any rights for their support.[68] Hashemi Rafsanjani believed that the women's rights movement in the West was a result of the gradual influence of Islam in the Western societies. Supporters argued that the convention did not attempt to provide similar rights for men and women in all domains; it rather intended to improve the situation of women and eradicate any kind of discrimination imposed on them because of their sex. To back up their view, the supporters argued that the CEDAW itself recognised the differences between men and women and reflected this issue in its Articles 4, 11 and 12, which provided special support for women because of their sex. In reality, the convention not only highlights the biological and natural difference between men and women, but also acknowledges social and acquisitive differences. Discrimination that deprives women of freedom and human rights is forbidden; this view is totally accepted by the Shari'a.[69]

The CEDAW's faliure to identify with women's interests

In the view of Hojat-ol-Islam Mohammadreza Zibaei Nejad, the head of the Centre for Women's Studies in the Qom seminary, the CEDAW not only fails to provide any rights for Muslim women, but also deprives them of many rights that Islam has accorded them.[70] Instead of adopting the similarity approach to bring women up to the level of men, the proper policy is to take into account the natural differences between men and women and legislate accordingly. For instance, if women's family roles as wives and mothers were not considered by the legislators, the outcome would be harmful for women, imposing more responsibility on them.[71] Due to some limitations, which the article does not specify, women could not undertake every profession available to the opposite sex. However, the convention asked them to do so, when it urged member states to take all appropriate measures for the elimination of discrimination against women in rural areas to ensure, on the basis of equality of men and women that they participated in and benefited from rural development. Such women were promised the right to participate in designing and implementing development planning at all levels.[72] It is clear that the opponents believe that women are not always capable of doing the same jobs as men; in their view, the convention seeks to encourage Marxism. It was even claimed that the CEDAW had been written by Marxists, as the USSR was still in existence at this time.[73] As an instrument with legal force, it would empower men to ask women to do their jobs, for instance, sending them to fight in wars. This idea had previously been discarded in socialist countries.[74]

Supporters countered that, in addition to the legal equality of rights between men and women, the convention took into account the importance of equal treatment of both sexes in society and for this purpose urged States Parties to take all appropriate measures to modify the social and cultural patterns of conduct of men and women, with a view to eliminating prejudice and customary practices based on ideas of the inferiority or superiority of either sex or on stereotyped roles for men and women.[75] According to Shadi Sadr, a prominent lawyer, the amendment of patriarchal culture and the eradication of gender-biased clichés is a long-term process that cannot be dealt with overnight. Discrimination against women is rooted very deeply in Iranian society; it cannot be eradicated through the adoption of one or two laws or regulations in favour of women. The CEDAW could therefore only be used as a legal instrument by Iranian women to combat discriminatory laws and practices.[76] Other strategies, including raising awareness, raising legal equality consciousness through mass campaigns, some of which conducted through social networks, should be adopted at the same time to foster the emergence of a public discourse on gender equality and increase as a consequence the cumulative pressure in favour of the adoption and full implementation of the CEDAW.

The CEDAW's conflict with Iran's national interest

According to Article 21 (3) of the Universal Declaration of Human Rights, the will of the people shall form the basis of the authority of the government. This will shall be expressed in periodic and genuine elections which shall be by universal and equal suffrage and shall be held by secret vote or by equivalent free voting procedures.[77] However, the opponents of Iran's accession to the CEDAW argued that the latter ignores the right of nations and specifically Muslim nations through its Article 18, which states:

(1) States Parties undertake to submit to the Secretary-General of the United Nations, for consideration by the Committee, a report on the legislative, judicial, administrative or other measures which they have adopted to give effect to the provisions of the present Convention and on the progress made in this respect:
    (a) Within one year after the entry into force for the State concerned;
    (b) Thereafter at least every four years and further whenever the Committee so requests.
(2) Reports may indicate factors and difficulties affecting the degree of fulfilment of obligations under the present Convention.

Through accession to the CEDAW, Iran would be expected to amend its discriminatory laws and practices and to ask every organisation or enterprise to cooperate. Iran would also report to the committee of the CEDAW on the actions it had taken to improve the status of women.[78] Considering Articles 23 and 24 of the CEDAW, in the view of the opponents, it was clear that the convention imposed its will on nations without taking their interests into account.[79] It is important to note, in accordance with the Islamic principle of *nafye sabail*, a non-Islamic country should not have any advantage over an Islamic one.[80] By accepting the convention, states are obliged to amend laws that contradict the CEDAW; the committee set under the convention would supervise their activities, a potential conflict with the national interest of the respective country.[81] In the case of Iran, as has been argued, the CEDAW contravenes approximately eighty-eight articles of the civil code, twenty articles of the criminal code and twenty articles of the constitution.[82] The amendment of a vast amount of legislation would become essential if Iran decided to ratify the CEDAW. Although the opponents do not object to changing or amending the laws concerning women, the model they introduced is based on Islamic principles and not international standards.[83] In the view of Zohreh Tabibzadeh Nuri, women have adopted the wrong strategy. It is not necessary to rely on the CEDAW to prove that domestic violence against women is unacceptable. The West itself, according to this thinking, violates women's rights; Muslims should take advantage of Islamic principles to block this form of behaviour against women. She emphasised that 'as long as I am in my post, I will not allow Iran to join to the CEDAW'.[84]

To reject the opponents' argument, Elaheh Kulaei, a deputy of the Majles, proclaimed that accession to the CEDAW would be a great opportunity to show the world the real face of Iranian women. In the process of globalisation, in her view, Iran is in transition and the importance of the women's issue should be considered. It is important to understand women's needs and to facilitate their participation in all national affairs.[85] In her view, if Iran refused to join the CEDAW, it would be disconnected from the outside world and accused of violating women's rights.[86] Akram Mosavari Manesh, a member of the *ferāksiun-e zanān* in the Majles, stated that 'the United Nations' Human Rights Committee always criticises the Iranian government for violating women's rights. Joining the CEDAW will improve Iran's reputation in the international community.'[87] In the view of Behnaz Ashtari, a legal expert, women's rights are human rights and accession to the CEDAW would prove that Iran respects international human rights standards.[88]

The CEDAW's deviation from the interests of the family union
The CEDAW supports the idea that the role of the mother in the family is not a natural right of women; rather, it is a social function which is a common responsibility of men and women participating in the upbringing and development of their children. It is important to note that the convention requests that States Parties ensure appropriate services for women in connection with pregnancy, convalescence and the postnatal period, granting free services where necessary, as well as adequate nutrition during pregnancy and lactation.[89] In the view of the opponents, this provision expunges men's responsibility to support their wives during pregnancy and after, urging the government instead to provide proper services and adequate care for women during pregnancy and lactation. This shift in practice would be harmful for relationships within the family, decreasing the level of care and friendship which spouses are supposed to have for each other, it was argued.[90]

It is also interesting to note that the convention urges states to eliminate any stereotypical concept of the roles of men and women at all levels and in all forms of education by encouraging coeducation and other types of education that will help to achieve this aim. A particular request is to revise textbooks and school programmes and adapt teaching methods.[91] Some years earlier, in Iran, a special education policy had been introduced to highlight the role of women in the family. There is a lesson entitled '*bābā nān dād*', or 'father provides the bread', in a textbook for the first year of primary school, and another lesson for year three about a lady called Kokab who is a very good housewife and makes delicious food. Hojat-ol-Islam Zibaei Nejad criticised those who believe that such lessons promote stereotypical concepts of the roles of men and women within the family or who seek to remove them from the educational system. Therefore, in the view of Hojat-ol-Islam Zibaei Nejad, accession to the CEDAW would have a huge cultural impact on Iranian society, undermining its strong Islamic tradition.[92]

To counter the opinion of Zibaei Nejad and those who believe that the CEDAW undermines the family, one should note that the CEDAW claims that discrimination against women, which violates the principles of equality of rights and respect for human dignity, hampers the growth and prosperity of society and the family and makes it more difficult to fully develop the potential of women in the service of their countries and humanity.[93] It takes into account the great contribution of women to the welfare of the family and to the development of society, which has not been fully recognised thus far. The CEDAW stressed the social significance of maternity and the role of both parents in the family and in the upbringing of children. It argued that the role of women in procreation should not become a basis for discrimination, as the upbringing of children requires the sharing of responsibility between men and women and society as a whole.[94] In no way does the CEDAW undermine the importance of the family union; rather, it tries to strengthen it through specific and supportive provisions.

The inadequacy of the reservations[95]

The concept of a reservation and the conditions under which it is acceptable under the international law of treaties were discussed earlier; as mentioned, reservations that contradict the main purpose of the convention are not permissible. The main purpose of the CEDAW is equality of rights between men and women. During the presidency of Mohammad Khatami, it was proposed that Iran join the CEDAW with a reservation. Approximately twelve provisions of the CEDAW were problematic for the Iranian Government. President Khatami supported the idea of a general reservation to avoid disputes among different groups and religious figures. However, the opponents of the CEDAW argued that Iran could not join the convention with the proposed general Shari'a-based reservation, as the latter was too vague and would generate many objections from other member States to the CEDAW. In the view of Hojat-ol-Islam Zibaei Nejad, joining the convention with reservation would not be a correct decision by the Iranian Government as after accession it would face pressure to withdraw. He argued that many positive changes in Iranian culture and to regulations concerning children had flowed after Iran joined the Convention on the Rights of the Child in 1994. Minors have become educated about the rights they are entitled to and how to challenge inadequate laws and practices that are not in their interests.[96] His analysis demonstrates how the impact of the awareness-raising in relation to the rights of the children within the framework of that convention had facilitated the reform of practices and regulations. The same might happen if Iran joined the CEDAW, a development that would not be tolerated by the Supreme Leader and his supporters.

In the view of supporters, there should be nothing to worry about; by a general reservation, Iran would prevent the application of any provisions of the convention that contradicts Islamic principles. Iran could easily respond to criticism from the international community and at the same time safeguard its Islamic principles, they argued. Fatemeh Khatami, a member of the Majles' women's caucus, reiterated that Iran should join the CEDAW with reservation.[97] The supporters argued that Iran had joined the Convention on the Rights of the Child with a general Shari'a-based reservation; according to Article 51 (2) of the latter, reservations that contradict the purpose of the convention are not permissible. The supporters questioned CEDAW's opponents as to why the issues of women should be treated differently.[98]

On the other hand, some supporters of accession argued that the proposed general Shari'a based reservation by the Iranian Government was too vague. For instance, Mehrangiz Kar, a prominent lawyer and legal expert argued that, as is clear from the Iranian regulations, there is no definition either for Islamic criteria or for the authority that can define them.[99] Therefore, this reservation gives those who object to improving women's status the authority to boycott any reforms on the pretext of their lack of conformity with Islamic principles.[100] Given such a reservation, the extent to which the Iranian Government would have to accept any provisions of the CEDAW was not clear; it provides no clear answer as to which provisions of the CEDAW would have to be applied inside the country.[101] Some supporters of the accession, like Shadi Sadr and Mehrangiz Kar, therefore urged the Iranian Government to join the CEDAW without reservation.

Conclusion

The reformists aspired, in their own words, to make use of the capacities of the constitution to modify the power structure of Iran and to bring transparency and accountability into the political arena. To address the gender inequalities contained within the Shari'a, some reformist figures have openly advocated for a 'pluralistic and tolerant Islam, based on human rights and democratic values'.¹⁰² Their conservative opponents opposed such plans through a variety of means. Nevertheless, although 'the sixth Majles failed to make political power accountable, it went a long way towards demystifying the way in which elite play power games in religious language and use the Shari'a instrumentally to justify autocratic rule and patriarchal culture'.¹⁰³

The accession to the CEDAW has attracted considerable attention from different political and religious groups. After a long process within the cabinet and the Majles, the bill of accession to the CEDAW was ratified by the Majles but rejected by the GC. However, the GC did not openly declare the bill to contravene Islam and astutely sent it back to the Majles for clarification to avoid putting itself in a contrarian position with respect to the reformist majority of the time. The bill is currently blocked in the Expediency Council and, due to the inadequacy of the law, it is not clear for how long the EC can remain idle on the matter. The victory of Rowhani, a moderate cleric, in the 2013 and 2017 presidential elections has raised the question of how a broader process of political change might pave the way for Iran to become a party to the CEDAW.

The debate surrounding the implications of the CEDAW for Iran after ratification proves that religiously conservative forces, both within the Majles and other bodies, such as the Guardian Council and the network of national Friday prayers leaders, were instrumental in preventing the definitive accession of Iran to the CEDAW. This opposition was successful due to several factors: first and foremost, that the GC shared the political outlook of the those who believed that accession to the CEDAW would mark a surrender of adherence to the Shari'a in favour of the acceptance of Western and secular norms governing the legal status of women vis-à-vis men. Other crucial elements in the failed drive for full accession to the CEDAW were the reformist factions' lack of influence within key decision-making state institutions, such as the GC, and their failure to press successfully for their stance within the wider society. Additionally, the unbiased coverage from state media, which was then dominated by a conservative management aligned to the GC, was a key factor.

The ratification of the convention should be considered from two perspectives: international and domestic. Should Iran ratify the convention, the Iranian Government would take a positive step towards improving its reputation and responding to the adverse publicity generated by its violations of human rights in general and women's rights in particular. The convention imposes responsibility on signatories to take all appropriate measures to ensure equality of rights between men and women and to eradicate any kind of gender-based discrimination. The CEDAW establishes a monitoring framework to give these stipulations some 'bite'. At the national level, states are held responsible for amending or reforming and practices that discriminate against women. The social, political, economic and cultural structure of each society plays an important role in the process of improving of the status of women. The accession of Iran to the CEDAW could bring about considerable changes in the legal status of Iranian women. This could include acceleration in the pace of reform of laws concerning gender inequality.

CHAPTER 4

IRANIAN WOMEN'S STRUGGLE FOR GENDER EQUALITY: THE CASE OF IRAN'S CIVIL CODE

Introduction

'What justice is this? What an unfair law is this?', Parichehr, a sixty-year-old woman whose husband had gone to court to seek permission to marry a second woman, asked me, wearily. 'My husband is marrying a second woman now, without my consent and there is nothing I can do about it'. This was my first case as a lawyer in training. I had previously witnessed a myriad of cases of discrimination against women. In fact, making the voices of women in Iran heard was the main reason why I chose a career in law. Now, here I was dealing with a case of polygamy.

Parichehr and Ali had been married for nearly forty years. Everything was fine until Ali fell in love with a younger woman and decided to take advantage of the law recognising polygamy in his favour. My client predictably disapproved of the decision. However, the court did not consider her opinion and, due to Ali's financial situation, it ruled in his favour and allowed him to take a second wife.

Sadly, Parichehr's case is not unique. Millions of women in Iran either face similar issues related to polygamy or have to grapple with other discriminatory laws and policies affecting their daily lives. The Iranian civil code not only covers different aspects of civil matters but also deals with general principles of law that must be analysed to understand other domestic laws and regulations. The code is a mixture of Shi'ite and

Western law. The code was drafted in 1935 by a committee composed of Shi'ite jurists as well as lawyers familiar with the more prominent modern legal systems of that time, such as the French.[1] Therefore, Islamic laws and Shi'ite principles were presented in articles and sections of the code using the format of the French civil code. For instance, the part of the code dealing with obligations was based on the French. However, the section containing family related articles was a 'simplification and codification of classical Ithna Ashari law'.[2]

The aim of this chapter is to provide an in-depth analysis of Iranian laws that offer less protection to women than men, according to international standards on gender equality. Proposals and recommendations for legal reform can only be made after close scrutiny of the existing legal regulations.[3] As Ayatollah Sanei, a prominent cleric in Iran, has aptly stated, 'the current civil laws of Iran are in line with the traditional society of the past, instead of being in tune with contemporary realities and relations in Iranian society'.[4] He continues that 'since the subject (the situation of women) has changed, the framework of civil laws must change too'.[5]

This chapter will review certain controversial issues relating to the rights of women in Iran, through discussion of factors such as equal rights in marriage, the marriage of a Muslim woman to a non-Muslim man, the marriage of a virgin girl, polygamy, dissolution of marriage, temporary marriage and its dissolution and inheritance.

A review of Iran's civil code

Iran's civil code was adopted in three stages: part 1, on properties, which includes Articles 1–955, was enacted in 1928; part 2, on persons, spans Articles 956–1256 and was enacted in 1934. Finally, part 3, on evidence in proving claims, is covered by Articles 1257–1335 and was enacted in 1935. The only articles not derived from the Shari'a were those provisions setting the minimum age for marriage, which prohibit marriage for girls under thirteen and require court permission for those under fifteen to marry.[6] In 1931, the Qānun-e Ezdevāj (Law on Marriage) was enacted with the aim of reforming laws dealing with marriage and divorce.[7] The Family Protection Law,[8] which introduced a radical reform in marriage and divorce practices, was enacted in 1967. The Family Protection Law of 1975 largely retained the provisions of the 1967 law, but modified those articles covering child custody and the financial maintenance of divorced wives.[9] The minimum age of marriage was raised as well – from fifteen to eighteen for girls and from eighteen to twenty for boys. Some religious figures opposed the law, arguing it contradicts the Shari'a.[10] The Family Protection Law of 1975 was abrogated after the 1979 Revolution and some articles of the civil code, particularly in relation to family matters, were also changed to accommodate principles more in tune with Islamic, rather than Western, law. On 26 February 1979, Ahmad Sadr Hajj Seyyed Javadi, the interior minister, officially declared the abrogation of the Family Protection Law; he repeated his statement on 9 August 1979 in his capacity as minister of justice.[11] The Civil Court Act, according to which all family cases would be removed from the ordinary civil courts and dealt with by a court presided over by religious judges, was passed by the Revolutionary Council on 21 September 1979.[12] Other laws were also enacted to emphasise Shi'ite law as the main source of the Iranian legal system. Article 3 of the Civil Procedural Law refers to Shi'ite law as a source to be relied on when existing laws are unclear, contradictory or not comprehensive enough to cover the case before the court, or when there exists no applicable law.[13]

Articles 1195–1256 in part 2 of the civil code deal with family matters. The present chapter will analyse some of these articles to highlight the legal status of Iranian women under the civil code. As mentioned in the introduction, the personal status laws pertaining to recognised religious minorities falls outside the scope of this study, in which only state law is analysed.[14]

Equal rights in marriage

In Iran's legal system, a family may be formed only through marriage. Extramarital[15] relations between women and men and co-habitation, no matter how harmonious and enduring, are not legally recognised. Under Iran's legal system, marriage must be between a woman and a man; same-sex relationships are a criminal offence punishable by law.[16]

Marriage is a civil contract and takes place by *ijāb* (offer) and *qabul* (acceptance), which explicitly conveys the intention of marriage.[17] The proposal and acceptance may be uttered by the parties themselves or by persons who are legally empowered to perform the act.[18] By proposing, one of the parties expresses the desire and intention to enter into the marriage contract and by accepting, the other party agrees to this specific proposal. For the marriage contract to be valid, the husband and wife should be identified in such a way that neither party is in doubt as to the identity of the other.[19] The other important issue that needs to be clarified is that the acceptance should shortly follow the proposal, in accordance with custom. In other words, the proposal and acceptance must be made at the same meeting.[20]

An essential issue in relation to the equality of men and women in marriage is the right to enter into marriage and to choose a spouse freely. To some extent Iranian law has provided for and addressed this vital matter. According to Article 1070 of Iran's civil code, consent of the marrying parties is the condition upon which the enforcement of the marriage contract depends.[21] As mentioned above, marriage takes place by means of proposal and acceptance, through the utterance of words, which explicitly convey the intention of marriage.[22] Therefore the marriage contract is not considered valid without the full and free consent of both parties. This is the only aspect of the marriage process which requires equal participation of both the man and woman. Despite this equal treatment of man and woman in the marriage contract, some asymmetry persists in rights and relations between the sexes. This section attempts to examine these imbalances and to shed some light on their repercussions. Discrimination against Iranian women and the denial of equal rights upon entering a marriage lead to problematic and destructive marriages that can severely impact the family and children. This is particularly true when the husband is not an Iranian national or a non-Muslim. These two topics will further be examined in the next two sections.

The marriage of a Muslim woman to a non-Muslim

Mina was a student in Italy. She fell in love with Marco, an Italian man. They decided to get married. For their marriage to be recognised by Iranian law, they needed to obtain an Iranian marriage certificate. However, as he was not Muslim, Iranian law did not permit their marriage, which would require him to convert to Islam.

Article 1059 of Iran's civil code prohibits the marriage of a female Muslim to a non-Muslim man.[23] According to this article, an Iranian Muslim woman is not even allowed to marry a non-Muslim Iranian national unless the latter has previously converted to Islam. This provision is based on the Qur'an. Muslim jurists – both Shi'ite and Sunni – contend that Muslim women are not allowed to marry non-Muslim spouses. This, they believe, is a form of protection for women.[24]

Article 1059 thus constitutes a major restriction on a woman's free choice of spouse. There are two particular areas of concern. The first deals with women who live in Iran and attempt to marry Iranian non-Muslims. It is important to note that around two per cent of Iran's population consists of religious minorities, including Bahá'ís, Mandeans, Yarsanis, Zoroastrians, Jews and Christians. Iran's constitution has recognised the latter three minority religions and guarantees their rights.[25] However, Mandaeans, Yarsanis and Bahá'ís, the latter being the largest non-Muslim religious minority in Iran, are not officially recognised.[26] The second area of concern relates to women who live abroad and are in contact with non-Muslim men. They also face two major obstacles in reaching a decision: the faith as well as the nationality of their future husbands. This means that in reality, Iranian women are only permitted by Iranian law to marry Iranian Muslim men. The issue of nationality will be further explained in the next section.

Article 1059 does not provide guidance on the issue of marriage between a Muslim man and a non-Muslim woman. As mentioned previously, jurists should refer to Shi'ite principles as a source of law in cases for which the existing laws are not comprehensive enough.[27] Mohaqeq Damad, an Islamic jurist and prominent legal expert, argues that there is consensus amongst both Sunni and Shi'ite jurists that a Muslim man is prohibited from marrying a woman who is not from among the 'people of the book' (*ahl-e ketāb*), that is to say Jews, Zoroastrians and Christians.[28] He argues, however, that there are different opinions amongst Islamic jurists regarding the marriage of a Muslim man with a non-Muslim woman from the *ahl-e ketāb*. One opinion is that permanent marriage is not allowed, but temporary marriage is permitted.[29] Sheykh Mofid, Seyed Morteza and Ebne Edris, other Islamic jurists, believe that the marriage of a Muslim man with a non-Muslim woman from the *ahl-e ketāb* is prohibited whether it is permanent or temporary.[30] Mohaqeq Damad finally concludes that, as Article 1059 of the civil code does not cover the marriage of a Muslim man with a non-Muslim woman, one should look for a solution in *feqh*. He explains that his understanding is that a Muslim man is only allowed to marry a non-Muslim woman from amongst 'the people of the book'.[31]

The marriage of an Iranian woman with a foreign national

Article 1060 of Iran's civil code holds that the marriage of an Iranian woman with a foreign national – even where no specific legal impediment exists – must first receive special permission from Iran's ministry of foreign affairs.[32] Increasing numbers of Afghan and Iraqi men have married Iranian women in Iran since 2001. Nevertheless, approximately 70,000 marriages of Iranian women with Muslim Afghan men are not registered.[33] Moreover, Iran's interior ministry has declared invalid all marriages between Iranian women and Afghan men that took place after 2001.[34] Some Afghan and Iraqi men who married Iranian women without permission from the ministry of foreign affairs asked the civil court to permit the registration of their marriages. An opinion from the legal department of the judiciary in support of this reads as follows:

> The marriage should be registered in Iran and the registration of a marriage is a matter of public order. If the marriage ceremony is administered properly, a lack of prior registration does not annul it and it can not be deemed illegal by the courts. However, a punishment may be imposed as contained in article 17 of the Marriage Law of 1931 on the offending party.[35]

In the view of the late Naser Katuziyan, a prominent legal jurist in Iran, the marriage of an Iranian woman with a non-Iranian man without previous permission from the ministry of foreign affairs is not valid.[36] However, other jurists, such as Hossein Safai and Asadollah Emami, believe that such a marriage is valid.[37] Based on the opinion of the latter jurists, and also on the view of the aforenoted legal opinion from the judiciary, it seems that the substantial and procedural aspects of marriage contracts are different. Acquiring permission from the ministry of foreign affairs may be viewed as a procedural issue that does not affect the substance of the marriage contract. In the view of Safai and Emami, Article 1060 has both a political and protective character, serving the interests of government and also protecting the rights of Iranian women.[38]

Iranian men may marry Muslim or non-Muslim women (from among 'the people of the book') or Iranian or non-Iranian women without requiring permission from the ministry of foreign affairs. The only restriction is Article 1061 of the civil code, according to which the government can require special permission for the marriages of certain civil servants, officials and students financially supported by the government with female foreign nationals.[39] In January 1967, a law was passed forbidding the marriage of a ministry of foreign affairs' employee with a non-Iranian national or with a person who had previously obtained Iranian nationality. Breaching this provision will not annul the marriage; it only results in the dismissal of the employee from his job at the ministry of foreign affairs. On 10 April 2003, a regulation was ratified requiring Iranian men wanting to obtain permission from the interior ministry to marry migrant women holding foreign national identity cards.[40] Therefore, the restrictions imposed on Iranian men are limited and specified by the law, while in the case of Iranian women, the restrictions are broad, preventing them in general from marrying non-Iranian men without permission.

Since there is no Qur'anic or religious base for this discriminatory provision, it seems that the prohibition of the marriage of an Iranian woman with a non-Iranian man results from a traditional perspective towards women and their rights, intertwined with politics. The traditional understanding of marriage in the Iranian context enables men to be the head of the family; this provision is codified in Iran's civil code.[41] By a broad interpretation of this provision, it is assumed that the domination of a foreign husband may be expanded to include his government's control over the Iranian authority. The Iranian Government is therefore not willing to provide equal rights for women in relation to nationality for political reasons.

According to the Iranian civil code, marriage is one of the ways to acquire or retain nationality. However, different legal systems apply to foreign women marrying Iranian men, and to Iranian women marrying foreign men. According to Article 976 (6) of the code, every woman of foreign nationality who marries an Iranian man automatically becomes Iranian. Yet, an Iranian woman cannot transmit her nationality to a non-Iranian man by marriage. She will, nevertheless, retain her Iranian nationality unless, according to the law of the country of her husband, the latter's nationality is imposed on her through marriage.[42] In cases such as these, women may lose their Iranian nationality, as the Iranian civil code provides no protection in this regard.

Moreover, according to Iranian law, the nationality of women is not automatically assigned to their children. Article 976 (2) states that those born to an Iranian father in Iran or abroad are to be automatically considered Iranian.[43] However, children born to Iranian mothers are not granted automatic citizenship rights. This creates a complicated situation for Iranian women who marry non-Iranian citizens and subsequently have children. According to statistic released in 2011 by the Tehran governor's office of foreign nationality around 32,000 children in Iran do not have a birth certificate, due to the fact that their fathers are not Iranian citizens.[44] Additionally, there are many Iranians who live abroad and may want to marry non-Iranians, but are prevented by these regulations from freely choosing their future husbands. Mina and Marco, who were introduced earlier in the chapter, now have a child and are forced to obtain a visa for him every time they wish to travel to Iran.

Many Iranian women are married to foreign nationals. The example of Afghan nationals who have lived in Iran for many years and are married to Iranian women is a case in point. Due to the complications in registering such marriages, they have wed only in accordance with the Shari'a and obtained religious certificates for their marriages.[45] These unregistered marriages do not guarantee any rights to the Iranian wife and her children; they are not entitled to birth certificates and are therefore prevented from accessing many basic rights that the State is ordinarily obliged to provide citizens. In an interview with the Iran-based news outlet *Parsineh* in April 2015, an Iranian Baluchi woman shared some of the issues caused by Iran's current civil code. Born in a poor family, she said that she was forced to marry an Afghani man at the age of twelve. They had seven children together. However, after the birth of the seventh child, her husband returned to Afghanistan, leaving his family behind. As the law grants Iranian birth certificate based on the nationality of the father, all seven children now lack birth certificates. Fearing deportation, she is now staying in a remote cave in a mountain with no running water or electricity.[46]

Research indicates that children without birth certificates do not enjoy the same rights to education, are less educated than Iranian nationals and are more at risk of criminal behaviour.[47] On 24 September 2006, the Majles ratified a single-clause bill to determine the citizenship of children of Iranian women married to foreign men. According to this bill, these children, if born in Iran, can obtain Iranian nationality after turning eighteen.[48] On 2 August 2011, some deputies of the Majles proposed amendments to the bill to recognise Iranian nationality for children born to Iranian mothers. The legal and judiciary commission of the Majles, which was responsible for examining the proposed amendment, rejected it on the basis of 'security and political considerations'.[49] Nayereh Akhavan Bitaraf, a member of the commission, stated that the bill was rejected because of security concerns, explaining that children born to Iranian mothers could, upon acquiring Iranian citizenship, be entitled to work in government agencies.[50] Her analysis reiterates the argument discussed above in relation to a man's assumed power over his family.

Amendment of the bill was debated in the Majles on 6 May 2012; it was then decided that children born to Iranian mothers should obtain permanent residency in Iran and enjoy rights to education, health and social services.[51] On 16 May 2012, Mohammad Nazemi Ardekani, the head of the Sabt-e Ahvāl (Personal Status Registry Office), stated that children born to Iranian women would receive birth certificates and the same treatment as Iranian children whose fathers were Iranian.[52] This statement, however, is confusing, as the bill did not provide children born to Iranian women with Iranian nationality; it only granted them some social rights, including the right to education. Once again the bill to determine the citizenship of children of Iranian women married to foreign men was due to be discussed in the Majles in 2015. On 27 September 2015 the Majles rejected the bill.[53] Therefore, the issue of nationality is still unresolved. However, on 15 February 2017, the cabinet of ministers enacted a directive tasking the ministry of interior with the responsibility of cooperating with the ministry of education to issue 'supportive educational cards' for school-aged children who do not have birth certificates to be able to register in schools.

The marriage of a virgin girl[54]

To discuss the 'conditions of a father's consent', this section initially elaborates on the age of marriage. According to Article 1041 of the civil code, amended in the summer of 2002, marriage for girls younger than thirteen full solar years and for boys younger than fifteen full solar years requires the guardian's permission, but on the condition of expediency, as determined by a competent court.[55] This article has been reviewed several times for compatibility with the situation of women in contemporary Iranian society in an effort to provide greater support for parties to a marriage contract.

Before the amendment in 2002, Article 1041 of the civil code, ratified in 1935, prohibited the marriage of a girl before the age of fifteen and a boy before the age of eighteen. Although a prosecutor could ask the court to grant exemption from the age requirement, permission would not be given for a girl under thirteen or a boy under fifteen.[56] The Family Protection Law of 1975 increased the marriageable age for both parties; Article 23 of this law banned the marriage of a girl under eighteen or a boy under twenty. The prosecutor still had the power to ask the court to permit the union if it was necessary for a girl to marry, provided that she was mentally and physically ready for marriage and not younger than fifteen. A man or woman who married an individual under the legal age for marriage would be punished according to the law.[57] As previously mentioned, the Family Protection Law was abrogated after the 1979 Revolution. Three years later, in 1982, Article 1041 changed to the version below:

> Marriage before the age of majority is prohibited.
> Note – Marriage before puberty by the permission of the guardian and after considering the interest of the ward is valid.

The note to Article 1041 made permissible a situation that the article itself originally prohibits, that is, marriage before puberty. It is also important to note that the term 'permission' is used where the contract is finalised. This means that the note refers to the situation of a boy and girl who marry before reaching puberty with the permission of a guardian.[58] This clearly demonstrates the contradiction between the provisions of Article 1041 and the note appended to it. The article itself rightly prohibits marriage before puberty. It should also be mentioned that the competence of both parties is a necessary condition for the validity of the contract. In this regard, Article 210 of Iran's civil code states that both parties should be competent to transact the business.[59] According to Article 211, for a contract to be valid, both parties to it must have reached puberty and the required minimum age and must be in their proper senses.[60] Moreover, a transaction between people who are not of age, not in their proper senses and not mature is invalid because of their incompetence.[61]

Therefore, according to the above-mentioned provisions of Iran's civil code, immature boys or girls cannot be party to the marriage contract and, if they enter into it, the union would be considered null and void.

In addition, the meaning of the word *nekāh* is intercourse; according to jurists, intercourse with a girl who is not mature is forbidden. The person who marries a non-mature girl is held criminally and legally responsible. So, it seems that the term 'marriage' for the legislator in Article 1041 implies intercourse, while in the note to the article it means consummation of marriage. Therefore, the word 'marriage' is accompanied by the term 'contract' to make this clear and eradicate any doubt.[62]

Although marriage before the age of puberty is prohibited, the guardian is permitted to arrange a marriage for his ward before the latter reaches the age of puberty. Accordingly, the age of marriage could be even younger than the age of puberty. Because no outside authority has the right to monitor such marriages and permission is granted solely to the father, the opportunity to abuse this legal authority is high. As shown by the aforementioned article, girls are more at risk of early marriage than boys, as the law endorses a lower marriageable age for them. The most significant issue in the article above is the age given for puberty in Article 1210 of the civil code,[63] which prohibits marriage below the age of nine for girls and fifteen for boys. Naturally, one cannot imagine a girl marrying before the age of nine. For this reason, the clause has been highly criticised by many in society.

In 2000, the Majles passed legislation that raised the marital age limit for both sexes to eighteen solar years. However, girls who were at least fifteen years old could petition the court for permission to marry sooner. The Guardian Council rejected this legislation and sent it back to the Majles. As the Majles refused to change it, the legislation was forwarded to the Expediency Council. On 22 June 2002, the EC issued the following opinion: 'Marriage for girls younger than 13 full solar years and for boys younger than 15 full solar years requires the guardian's permission, but on the condition of expediency, as determined by a competent court.'[64]

With the passage of this law, the age of marriage was raised to thirteen for girls and fifteen for boys (solar years). The amended article might be seen as a positive step, because the supervision of a higher legal authority is required. Perhaps it suggests that the age of maturity is thirteen for girls and fifteen for boys, and not the ages stipulated in Article 1210. In other words, the age of maturity differs in accordance with religious interpretations of the age of puberty. This amended article still does not meet the needs of Iranian women; it should be amended to increase the age of marriage to eighteen for *both parties*. Some changes have spontaneously appeared within Iranian society regarding the role of women. Increasingly, families are willing to send their daughters to university to become more educated and independent. Even in smaller cities, girls already have access to education, consequently increasing the average age of marriage in the country. The One Million Signatures Campaign, launched in Iran in 2006 to raise awareness and promote reform of discriminatory laws against women, has been tackling the issue of the minimum marriage age as one of its priorities.[65]

A comprehensive study of prostitutes in Iran indicates that 88 per cent of these women marry before the age of seventeen, and that 36 per cent of their marriages are made without their personal consent and would be classified as forced marriages.[66] These statistics and the changes that have occurred in the status of Iranian women might be enough to justify increasing the age of marriage within Iranian legislation. The Committee on the Rights of the Child (CRC) – an international body of independent experts that monitors child rights – condemned Iran for the pre-defined ages of puberty for girls at nine and for boys at fifteen lunar years. The CRC stated that an increasing number of 'girls at the age of 10 years or younger' are 'subjected to child and forced marriages to much older men.' The committee urged the Iranian Government to 'increase the legal age of marriage to 18 years and criminalise marital rape.'[67]

As mentioned above, a girl and boy who have not reached puberty cannot marry without a guardian's permission. However, the guardian is free to make this decision and can act unilaterally, as one of the parties to the marriage contract. The guardian can say, 'I wed in the name of my daughter' or 'I accept the marriage on behalf of my son'. The guardian should, in principle, consider the interest of his ward and prove it before a competent court. If he does not do so, the child must affirm his or her approval once he/she reaches puberty.[68]

An important point that needs to be remembered is that a virgin girl who is marrying for the first time, regardless of age, legally needs her father or paternal grandfather's permission. In cases where the father or paternal grandfather withholds permission without justifiable reason, his authority can be voided, and the girl can marry with the permission of the court.[69] A girl needs the permission of her father or paternal grandfather to marry as long as she is a virgin. To justify this requirement, it is argued that girls reach puberty earlier than boys. They are more emotional and may make irrational decisions. Therefore, it is for their own benefit to require consultation with their fathers before marriage.[70] Reflecting on the new discourses on gender equality in Iranian society, one may reconsider these justifications.

There is no consensus among jurists on the matter of paternal consent. Some jurists, such as Mohaqeq Sani and Alameh Heli, believe that a mature girl should not need the permission of her guardian.[71] Other jurists, such as Ayatollah Makarem Shirazi, Ayatollah Safi, Ayatollah Nuri Hamedani and Ayatollah Khamenei, consider the father's consent necessary for a girl's marriage even after the age of maturity.[72] Others, such as Sanei, Golpayegani and Khoi, have chosen a moderate view and consider both elements – that is, free choice for the girl and her father's consent – to be necessary for a girl to marry.[73] According to the late Katuziyan, another jurist, Iran's civil code has adopted the moderate view, according to which both the girl's free choice and her father's consent are necessary requirements for the marriage of a virgin girl.[74]

According to Article 1043 of the civil code, if a father does not allow his daughter to marry a man, two different situations may result: the first occurs when the father or the paternal grandfather withholds permission without justification. In this case, the girl can appeal to a family court, giving full particulars of the man she wants to marry, the terms of marriage and the marriage portion payable to the wife agreed upon. Her father or paternal grandfather would then be notified of forgoing particulars through the court. The court can issue permission for marriage fifteen days after the date of notification to the guardian, if no response has been received from the guardian to justify refusal.[75] The second situation occurs when the father or paternal grandfather forbids her to marry for permissible reasons. For example, if a girl from an educated, economically well-off family marries a criminal without familial consent, her marriage is declared null and void.[76] According to Article 1044, if the girl has attained the legal age of marriage but her father or paternal grandfather are not physically available (or obtaining their permission is impossible), she may marry in any case. The registration of such a marriage is contingent upon proving the aforementioned conditions in court.[77]

In relation to Article 1043, it is important to note that the father's consent is necessary for the marriage of a virgin girl. If she marries and her marriage becomes null before sexual intercourse has taken place, or she loses her virginity by accident, her father's consent is still needed for her to remarry.[78] The only thing that removes the need for the father's consent is the loss of virginity through actual intercourse. Therefore, a girl does not need her father's consent to remarry if she marries a man without her father's consent and loses her virginity. A 1984 supreme court verdict declared that only intercourse removes the need for a father's consent.[79] The court's decision was issued approximately thirty years ago, when Iranian society was vastly different from today, which has some bearing on how we should read it. As Ayatollah Sanei argues:

> Today boys and girls choose on their own. It is only necessary for the girl to be of age and able to understand the terms of marriage; she is free [in Shari'a] to contract her own marriage. But this isn't incorporated in our laws at present [...] The recent law is based on the *fatwās* of many jurists who saw this permission as necessary, in line with the situation of society at that time. Today the situation is different, and that's why there is such a problem. Perhaps in future our legislators will reach the stage in which they will find a solution for this problem. A girl who has come of age and can understand the issues involved in marriage has the right to contract it herself; there's no barrier, from the viewpoint of Islam.[80]

This application of Article 1043 in practice could be complicated in some situations. In the case *F v M* the girl wedded in France without her father's consent. She wedded according to French law, and later presented the marriage certificate at a Sunni mosque and obtained written confirmation. She then went to the Iranian embassy to register her marriage, in accordance with Iranian law. The embassy rejected her file and asked for her father's consent. Due to a very controversial accusation that she made against her father, it was difficult to obtain his consent: she claimed that her father had raped her when she was thirteen years old, continuing to do so until she was twenty. She had also filed a case of *zenā* (adultery) against her father in the criminal court of Tehran. Because of this, she naturally did not want to ask for his permission. The only option was approval from the court, and for that she had to prove to the court that she was married. Therefore, she opened a case, introduced witnesses and presented evidence, such as a version of her French marriage certificate translated into Persian as well as photos from her wedding and her son's birth certificate. After seven months, she received approval from the court.[81]

Polygamy

It would be fair to say that polygamy constitutes the clearest violation of the principle of equality, although the question is contentious. The UN Human Rights Committee states: 'Polygamy violates the dignity of women. It is an inadmissible discrimination against women. Consequently, it should be definitely abolished wherever it continues to exist.'[82] The family structure and its function have changed in modern societies. It seems that polygamy was practiced in society at a time when the family prioritised reproduction and the satisfaction of the sexual needs of men.[83]

Polygamy in Iran has affected the lives of men and women negatively. Nushin Ahmadi Khorasani, a prominent women's rights activist, argues that polygamy makes women feel insecure in their marriages and also in their relationships with other women. In her analysis, every woman can be a potential threat in a society where polygamy is permitted. Married women unconsciously avoid making friends with unmarried women or widows, as they are afraid of losing their husbands. These apprehensions create an atmosphere that can even prevent women from working together. In most cases, polygamy also prevents the men from having stable relationships with their wives, and ultimately makes them more dependent on their mothers, as this tie seems to remain the only secure one.[84]

Although there is no explicit article regarding polygamy in Iran's civil code, polygamy is implicitly accepted in Iran due to its presence in Shari'a law. There are some articles in the code that address the question implicitly. Article 942 holds that, in the case of inheritance, if there is more than one wife, the fourth or eighth part of the inheritance of the husband's estate, depending on whether there are children, is divided equally among them.[85] Article 1048 forbids a man to marry two sisters simultaneously, even if both marriages are of temporary nature. According to Article 1049, no one can marry the daughter of his brother-in-law or the daughter of his sister-in-law unless his wife permits him to do so. Clearly, then the law recognises a right for men to have more than one wife at the same time. The Family Protection Law of 1975 states a man can marry a second wife only when one of the conditions stipulated in Article 16 of the law is met; in each case, his first wife always maintains the right to divorce him. A man who marries for the second time without the court's permission will be imprisoned for between six months and one year, according to Article 17 of the 1975 law.

Therefore, to some extent, Article 17 protects the rights of the first wife and discourages polygamy. However, after the 1979 Revolution, the Family Protection Law was abrogated, and the provision of the civil code prevailed. Despite the law's annulment at that time, its provisions remained valid after the revolution. This encouraged the Guardian Council to intervene to preserve Islamic principles. In 1984, it ruled that the punishment contained in Article 17 violates the provisions of the Shari'a, ruling it non-applicable.[86] In their view, there should be no punishment for a man who acts on his right to marry more than one wife. As aptly discussed by Katuziyan, the Guardian Council can only comment on laws enacted after the revolution; it is problematic and an expansion of its remit to include laws ratified before the revolution and prior to its existence.[87] It is important to note that, due to social and economic barriers and restrictions, polygamy is not very common in Iran.[88] There are no precise statistics, according to the head of the Sabt-e Ahvāl.[89] Polygamy has always been abhorred within Iranian society, and those who wish to practise it are not comfortable doing so explicitly. In most cases where a man marries more than one wife, the new wife(s) is (are) not aware of his previous marriages.[90]

In one case, a man who decided to take a second marriage told his first wife that he was going to work in Japan. However, in reality, he remained in Tehran, where he and the first wife lived, and moved in with his second wife in a different part of the city. The whole ruse fell apart when his first wife accidently ran into him in the city.[91] The cultural approbation against polygamy in Iranian society is corroborated by the stance of state institutions to it. Despite having been abrogated after the revolution, Iranian courts continue to apply the provisions of the Family Protection Law, requiring court permission for a man to take a second marriage. Moreover, the registry office has strictly policed that requirement, refusing to register second marriages without court permission.[92]

Recently, hard-liners have tried to reduce the opposition to polygamy and have encouraged men to marry more than one wife in response to certain societal problems such as the increasing rate of divorce as well as the issue of a growing number of unmarried women in the country, which has emerged as a result of modernisation and changing lifestyles.[93] A 2005 census indicated that the share of women of marriageable age was two per cent greater than the share of men. This was considered one justification for introducing a family protection bill in 2005.[94] Moreover, the divorce rate increased from 6.10 per cent in 2003 to approximately 18 per cent in 2009.[95] The bill contains an article similar to Article 16 of the 1975 Family Protection Law. Article 23 of the bill lists the conditions under which a man may marry for the second time.

Comparing Article 23 of the 2005 bill and Article 16 of the 1975 law shows the former omits the first wife's right to divorce her husband because of his second marriage. Moreover, the punishment stipulated in Article 17 of the 1975 law is excluded in the 2005 bill. When Article 23 was amended in parliament, the consent of the first wife was removed from the list of necessary conditions for the second marriage. The 2005 bill – which clearly promotes polygamy – faced opposition from different groups and leading women's rights activists while it was being debated in Majles. The bill was postponed, subject to parliamentary reviews, for several months. According to Zohreh Elahiyan, a Majles deputy, the provision on polygamy prevented the bill from being ratified for more than four years. Subsequently, on 6 March 2012, the bill was ratified in Majles but did not include any articles on polygamy.[96] Although the removal of Article 23 from the bill might be considered a progressive act, one should not forget that polygamy remains acceptable under Iran's civil code. In fact, in the absence of restrictions imposed by Article 17 of 1975 law, men are allowed by the civil code to freely marry more than one wife at the same time.

Therefore, without any explicit legal basis for polygamy, it is accepted that a man in Iran can have up to four *aqdi* (permanent) wives and an unlimited number of *siqehi* (temporary) wives. The existence of some provisions legitimising polygamy enables some men to take advantage of this given right. The limited grounds provided for women to file for divorce invite more violence and domestic crime. According to research on intra-marital homicide carried out in fifteen Iranian provinces, 67 per cent of women who murder their husbands do so because the husbands were unfaithful and had sexual intercourse with other women.[97] One woman explained that, while she was in custody at Evin prison in Tehran, her husband had contracted a *siqehi* wife without informing her.[98] She objected to this situation and asked her husband to agree to a divorce. He refused and suggested she refer to the courts. She went to court several times to request a divorce, but the judges refused her claim on the basis that she did not have any legal grounds for one. Life became unbearable; in the absence of proper laws to support her, she chose to kill her husband. The court denied her justice.[99] Polygamy, therefore, has some serious negative consequences, including intra-marital homicide.

Although polygamy is mentioned in the Qur'an, it should be noted that the reference is not unambiguous.[100] Referring to the Qur'an, some jurists and Muslim scholars have accepted polygamy under special circumstances, such as economic factors, or the wife's barrenness or chronic illness.[101] Other jurists argue that, although the Qur'an mentions polygamy, it also sets some preconditions.[102] In their view, the ability to treat co-wives justly, as mentioned in the Qur'an, is a prerequisite for polygamy.[103] As a result, due to the difficulty of treating co-wives justly, they conclude that monogamy is the rule while polygamy can only be an exception. Mohammad Abduh, the nineteenth-century jurist, advocated the idea that Islam prohibited polygamy according to the Qur'an verse 4:219, which explicitly states: 'You will never be able to do perfect justice between wives even if it is your ardent desire'.[104] Therefore, the progressive understanding of the Qur'an may be used to eradicate polygamy. According to Ayatollah Sanei, polygamy was accepted during a different time and was common in some Muslim societies; however, it is no longer accepted in most Muslim countries and most Muslim women cannot tolerate it.[105] Therefore, in his view, the first wife's permission is the major prerequisite for the second marriage. In his opinion, the condition of the first wife's permission may lead to justice in the case of polygamy.[106] Ayatollah Sanei therefore believes that Islam permits but does not encourage polygamy. It is important to understand the context that led to the above-mentioned verse. After the battle of the Uhud, where many men were killed, many widows and orphans were left in Muslim communities.[107] Polygamy might have been useful under those circumstances and in that time period, as its aim was to guarantee justice in a society that had experienced war, where women would have faced severe difficulties in the absence of their husbands. The 'occasion is past but the principle remains' to put women in inferior positions and humiliate them.[108]

Baderin proposes a solution for reaching a balance and limiting the practice of polygamy. He invokes the 'equalising up' and 'equalising down' approach. To redress the inequality of rights between men and women in the case of polygamy, the 'equalising down' approach means that right of men to polygamy should be prohibited to bring them into the same situation as women. Because the Qur'an recognises polygamy, this approach contradicts Islamic norms. Regarding the 'equalising up' approach, Islamic law prohibited polyandry by legal consensus. As a result, it is not possible to raise the rights of women to be equal with those of men. Nevertheless, it is possible to 'equalise up' the rights of women in other areas acceptable under Islamic law, for example, the rights of women to 'suspended repudiation' and/or 'delegated repudiation' of marriage. 'Suspended repudiation' means that the husband stipulates at the time of marriage that the marriage shall be repudiated if he participates in certain acts that are not in his wife's interest, which may include taking another wife. The other concept is 'delegated repudiation', which gives a woman the right to divorce her husband in the case of unjust circumstances. As a result, by providing other rights that are acceptable under Islamic law, the equality between men and women could be attained, while the rights of women who want to be co-wives in specific situations (as examined above) are protected under Islamic law.[109]

This statement on polygamy might be confusing. Why don't women enjoy equal rights in divorce? Why should polygamy be accepted to achieve the right of divorce for women? If both women and men had equal divorce rights, there would be little or no opportunity for men to marry more than one wife. To propose a suitable solution, the roots of a social disorder must be discovered. Polygamy does not meet the social needs of Iranian society and therefore without support from the public, its abolition would not be an insurmountable challenge. According to the aforementioned verse 4:219, perfect justice cannot be achieved between co-wives in the case of polygamy. This verse can be used as Qur'an-based evidence for the abolition of polygamy. Moreover, as argued by Ziba Mir-Hosseini, with the emergence of the new wave of reformists thought and feminist scholarship in Islam there is no need to look for all the new concepts like gender equality and human rights – which are the consequence of new relations in modern society – in religious texts, and to ground their origin within Islamic ones. As new thinkers believe, one might focus on 'how religion is understood and how religious knowledge is produced, how gender is constructed in Muslim legal tradition, and how interpretations of the Shari'a must be evaluated in their historical context'.[110]

The dissolution of marriage

According to the Iran's civil code, 'marriage may be dissolved by *faskh* (cancellation), by divorce, or by *bazl* (waiver) of the remaining period in the case of a temporary marriage'.[111] Divorce applies only to permanent marriages, the waiver is exclusive to temporary marriages, and the cancellation may occur in both kinds of marriages. The cancellation of marriage and divorce are different notions, and each has its own legal nature, terms and consequences. Their similarities and differences shall be examined to clarify the differences between these two independent legal concepts on dissolution of marriage.

1. Divorce is a legal act subject to the observance of specific procedures, for instance, it should be performed in the presence of two just men. However, the process of cancelling a marriage is not specific and the rightful claimant's will is sufficient to cancel the marriage.[112]
2. The observance of the arrangements stipulated in the case of divorce is not obligatory in the case of cancellation of marriage.[113] For instance, it is not proper to divorce a wife during her monthly period or during the convalescent period after childbirth.[114] However, it is not necessary to observe these conditions for the cancellation of marriage.
3. Divorce is a legal act that may only be executed by the husband or his legal representative, while either the husband or the wife may perform *faskh*.
4. Divorce is only relevant to permanent marriage, but cancellation is applied in cases of either permanent or temporary marriage.[115]

Therefore, the difference between divorce and the cancellation of marriage should be noted. This section will first examine the cancellation of marriage and will then analyse divorce under the Iranian Civil Code.

The annulment of marriage

The cancellation of marriage requires the spouses to obtain judicial termination of their marital status. The marriage might be cancelled in one of the following three circumstances: misrepresentation/trickery, violation of a stipulated qualification and defect.[116] Misrepresentation is not considered a cause for the cancellation of marriage under Iran's civil code. However, *feqh* names it as one of the causes. Misrepresentation happens when one of the parties intentionally deceives the other;[117] *actus reus* and *mens rea* are the two necessary elements for misrepresentation. In other words, one of the parties in the marriage contract must intentionally conduct an act either to demonstrate something that is not true or to conceal an existing problem and mislead the other party. If these two elements lead to the deception of the other party, he/she has the right to annul the marriage.

If a special qualification is mentioned as a condition of the marriage and it is later found out that the party concerned lacks the desired qualification, the other party has the right to cancel the marriage. The aforementioned is true irrespective of whether the qualification is mentioned explicitly in the marriage contract or whether the marriage has been performed with the qualification understood mutually by the parties involved.[118] For instance, if a man introduces himself as a doctor and a woman marries him on this condition but after marriage understands that he has lied to her, she has the right to cancel the marriage.

There are two kinds of 'defects', mental or physical disabilities specified by the law, according to which a marriage might be cancelled. One is a common defect, which is the permanent or temporary insanity of either spouse, provided that it is independently ascertained.[119] In the case of insanity, the wife has the right to cancel the marriage even if the insanity occurs after the date of marriage.[120] However, the man only has the right to cancel the marriage if the wife's madness existed at the time of the marriage.[121] It is important to note that if the madness of the wife or husband existed at the time of marriage and the other party was aware of it, he/she is not entitled to cancel the marriage.[122] Differences between men and women in the cancellation of marriage due to insanity are justified by the fact that divorce is the right of a man and he has a duty to maintain his wife. Therefore, if a woman becomes mad after marriage, her husband can work and support her and if it causes difficulties he can easily divorce his wife. However, if a man becomes mad after marriage, his wife would have difficulties in maintaining herself.

The specific 'defect' of a man or woman is the other reason, which entitles the parties to cancel the marriage. According to Article 1122 of the Iranian civil code, the following 'defects' in the man will give the woman the right to cancel the marriage: 1) impotency, provided he has not even once performed the matrimonial act; 2) amputation of the sexual organ to the extent that he is unable to perform his marital functions;[123] 3) insanity either at the time of marriage or after.[124]

It is accepted that sexual intercourse is one of the main purposes of a marriage.[125] Therefore, if a man is not able to perform his marital duties in this regard, his wife has the right to cancel the marriage provided that she was not aware of her husband's defect at the time of marriage.[126] Examining Article 1122 of Iran's civil code, one might realise that only a man's lack of ability to have intercourse gives a woman the right to cancel the marriage. However, the law provides more grounds for a man to cancel the marriage.

Article 1123 of Iran's civil code names the following 'defects' in a wife which give a man the right to cancel the marriage: *qaran* (protrusion of the womb), *juzām* (black leprosy), *baras* (leprosy), *efzā* (connection of the vaginal and anal passages) and being crippled or blind in both eyes. It is important to note that these defects of the wife entitle the man to cancel the marriage even if they existed at the time of the nuptial contract.[127] In addition to defects that make a sexual relationship impossible, the law considers being crippled or blind in both eyes as defects in a woman, and gives men the right to cancel their marriages because of these defects. The question that arises here concerns the legal reasons for allowing a woman to live with a blind man but granting a man the right to cancel his marriage if he lives with a blind spouse. It seems that the right to cancel a marriage is provided to prevent any harm to the parties. Therefore, it is necessary for the law to guarantee equal protection for both sexes.

There are specific conditions required to cancel a marriage. For instance, the option must be exercised immediately; if the party entitled to the option does not cancel the marriage after becoming cognisant of the legal grounds for doing so, he forfeits the option, provided also that he had full knowledge of the existence of the option and its urgent character.[128] According to Article 1131 of the code, the length of time during which the option remains valid depends on custom and usage.

Divorce (talāq)

Divorce is a unilateral act, which according to pre-modern Islamic jurists, gives a man the right to divorce his wife whenever he desires. Mere desire is not, however, enough for a woman to divorce her husband.[129] This view is reflected in Iran's civil code, Article 1133, which states that: 'A man can divorce his wife whenever he wishes to do so'. Divorce, therefore, is a legally unilateral act and the woman's consent is not needed. However, Iranian lawmakers have tried to amend the law to make it more compatible with the situation of women in modern society.

Prior to the enactment of the Family Protection Law of 1967 (amended in 1975), divorce was a man's right, and he could divorce his wife whenever he desired without court permission. The Family Protection Law stated that the court should decide all divorce cases. In the case of divorce, a *Gavāhi-ye Adam-e Emkān-e Sāze* (certificate of irreconcilable differences) is issued by the court to permit the ratification of the divorce. Article 8 of the 1975 law enumerates the grounds on which both men and women are allowed to file for a divorce.[130]

Although the 1975 law offered more rights to women, its deviation from Shari'a provisions in Iran's civil code have never been resolved. Even during that time, some Islamic jurists did not approve divorces that were decided under the provisions of the law.[131] The contradiction between the 1975 law and Islamic legal tradition appears in Article 1133 of the civil code.[132] Due to the abrogation of 1975 law after the 1979 Revolution, Article 1133 became applicable in the case of divorce. Both modern and traditional women were worried about the abrogation of laws which guaranteed some support for them. Women who supported the revolution asked Ayatollah Khomeini to react in their favour. In response to a group of women who visited him in Qom, Khomeini issued an opinion allowing women to make use of the law of divorce with the help of secondary contractual conditions.[133] According to Ayatollah Khomeini:

> If women concluding marriage set it as a condition that in matters of divorce they are the authorised representative [of the husband]

in absolute terms, i.e. that they may divorce him whenever they wish, or in relative terms, i.e. if he mistreats them or, for instance, takes another wife, then there are no other obstacles for them; they may obtain divorce.[134]

This *fatwā* did not satisfy women who were demanding their rights and they therefore continued their campaign to obtain the right to divorce. In 1982, the ministry of justice provided for twelve secondary contractual conditions to be printed in marriage contracts. The Sabt-e Ahvāl was instructed to invite people getting married to sign the conditions.[135] Ultimately the marriage contracts required two main conditions. The first required the husband to pass on to his wife, upon divorce, half the wealth or the equivalent thereof that he had acquired during that marriage, provided that the court decided that the divorce was not initiated or caused by any fault of the wife.[136] The second condition delegated the right to divorce to the wife, enabling her to instigate divorce after proving in court that one of the stipulated conditions in the marriage contract signed by her husband had been breached by him.[137]

Amendments to the Qānun-e Eslāh-e Moqararāt-e Marbut be Talāq (Law on Divorce Regulations) which required the spouse to obtain court permission for divorce, were passed in November 1982. Article 1133 retained validity even though both husband and wife, according to the latter provision, are obliged to file the divorce case in court. Article 1133 was amended in 2002 as follows: 'A man can file the divorce case in court in accordance with the prescribed conditions stated in the law'. According to the note on Article 1113, 'a woman can also file for a divorce in accordance with the prescribed terms and conditions inserted in articles 1119, 1129 and 1130'. Therefore, according to Iran's civil code, women are allowed to initiate a divorce under specific circumstances, such as when the husband refuses to pay his wife the cost of maintenance, assuming that it is not possible to enforce a judgment and induce him to pay the expenses.[138] Moreover, when it is proved to the court that the continuation of the marriage causes difficulties to the wife (in cases such as a criminal conviction that sentences the husband to more than five years in prison), the judge can compel the husband to grant a divorce to his wife.[139] It should be noted that the grounds for divorce are not explicitly stated in the law; they are at the discretion of the judge, thus making the court's decision entirely subjective. In the view of one judge, for example, a man beating his wife may constitute a valid reason for divorce. However, this may not be a sufficient reason for divorce in the view of a different judge.

I defended a case in which my client filed for divorce on the basis that she did not love her husband anymore and this made life unbearable for her. Her husband was an engineer with a good reputation and provided all of his family's material needs. I was not sure whether we had enough evidence for divorce and informed my client that her chances were very low and depended upon the decision of the judge. In court, she insisted on divorce, but her husband and his lawyer argued that she did not have any evidence and that her husband loved her and did not want to ruin their family life. I argued that the wife hated her husband and this placed her in an undesirable situation which was very harmful for her as well as for the rest of the family. I discussed the ruling on 'denial of harm' – which is acceptable in Islam and prevents hardship and harm – and asked the judge to refer the case to arbitration to determine whether they could bring about reconciliation between the spouses and if not, whether the judge would issue the divorce to avoid more harm to my client.[140] After two sessions, the arbiters decided that reconciliation between the spouses was not possible. Surprisingly, in the verdict the judges agreed to the divorce on the basis that the continuation of marriage would be harmful to the wife.[141] However, many similar cases are easily rejected by family court judges on the basis that there is not enough evidence to prove divorce. It is obvious that this uncertainty regarding divorce causes considerable damage to women who are seeking it, and who have to demonstrate that the continuation of the marriage is not feasible for them. If there is no clear definition of 'difficult and undesirable' conditions, or *osr va harag*, it becomes arduous for women to prove that they are indeed living under such circumstances. Due to the aforementioned problems, the Expediency Council added a note in 2002 to the said article to make clear what *osr va harag* is:

> Difficulty and hardship as provided in this article creates a condition in which continuation of the marriage is made difficult and intolerable for the wife. The following cases, if verified by the court, are examples of difficulty and hardship:

1. The husband deserting the family for at least six consecutive months or nine alternating months within a year without a justifiable reason;
2. The husband's addiction to any narcotic drug or alcohol in such as way so as to damage the foundation of family life or the impossibility of forcing him to give up the addiction during a period that a doctor deems necessary for him to give up the addiction. If the husband does not fulfil his obligation or, after quitting, becomes further addicted, the divorce shall be carried out upon the wife's request;
3. Final sentencing of the husband to five or more years in prison;
4. Violent behaviour or any continued misdemeanour by the husband which is not ordinarily bearable by the wife;
5. The husband's contraction of incurable mental diseases or rabies or any other contagious disease which harms marital life. The above cases in this article do not prevent the court from issuing the divorce in other cases in which difficulty and hardship is verified.[142]

Although the law tries to highlight the grounds upon which a woman may file for divorce, the woman must first provide concrete proof of hardship, which at times is difficult to supply. According to Article 1029 of Iran's civil code: 'If a man has been absent for four continuous years without making his location known, his wife can apply for a divorce. The judge will then grant the divorce subject to the stipulations of article 1023'. Therefore, the court can only issue a judgment on the presumed death of a continuously absent person when a notice has been published three consecutive times, at intervals of one month, in one of the local newspapers and one of the highly circulated papers published in Tehran, inviting anyone who may have news of the man to provide information to the court. The divorce is automatically granted one year after the first publication of this notice if it cannot still be proved that the man is indeed alive.[143] Therefore, it takes at least five years for a judge to grant a divorce to a woman whose husband is absent. If divorced by a judge, the wife of a continuously absent husband whose whereabouts are unknown must observe *eddeh*[144] (a legal period during which the wife is not allowed to remarry) for death starting from the date on which the divorce was granted.[145] If the continuously absent person returns after the divorce but before the expiry of the period of *eddeh*, he has the right to *ruju'* (cancel the divorce); if the *eddeh* period has already expired, his right will be terminated.[146] This seems to be a controversial issue due to the fact that there is no such provision for a man whose wife is absent. He does not need to wait for such a long time and, if he wishes, can divorce his wife or get permission from the court to marry for a second time without divorcing his first wife. It is very important to note that, if a woman has a sexual relationship with another man during the time that her husband is absent, she may face prosecution or punishment according to the nature of her relations with the other man. If she has any kind of relationship other than intercourse, she may be sentenced to ninety-nine lashes according to Article 637 of the Criminal Code of Iran (1996). In the case of intercourse, she may be stoned to death, based on Article 225 of Criminal Code of Iran (2013) and provided that the same conditions are fulfilled.[147]

To resolve the problems regarding divorce and to ensure equal rights for women, some legal scholars, such as Katuziyan, argue that, according to Article 1119, 'the parties to the marriage can stipulate any condition to the marriage which is not incompatible with the nature of the contract of marriage, either as part of the marriage contract or in another binding contract.'[148] Therefore, this provision is an instrument to aid Iranian women in obtaining equal rights within the family, as well as in regard to divorce. To support this idea, one may refer to Ayatollah Khomeini, who states that:

> For women, the religious legislator has provided an easy way so that they can take control of divorce, i.e. at the time of marriage they can stipulate that they shall represent the husband for divorce absolutely [...] and they can divorce themselves.[149]

However, most women cannot avail themselves of this article, as many men reject it. In addition, if a woman asks for the right to divorce in the marriage contract, according to the tradition and accepted moral norms in Iranian society, she will not be considered a person who really wants to create a family.[150] Since the law does not unequivocally grant women the right to divorce but leaves it to those involved to decide whether they would like to include a relevant clause in their contract, and given Iranian societal norms, it is, in practice, very difficult for women to file for divorce.

As mentioned previously, it is very difficult – in some cases impossible – to convince men to share their rights with women. But why do women need to ask men to give them their rights? Why doesn't the law itself provide equal rights for women? Ziba Mir-Hosseini had a very interesting discussion regarding divorce under Islamic law with Ayatollah Sanei and the clerical editors of *Payam-e Zan*, a women's magazine published in Qom.[151] While the clerics of *Payam-e Zan* viewed divorce as solely the right of men, Ayatollah Sanei provided a progressive view on divorce, which if implemented would put Iranian women in a better situation. Mir-Hosseini asked him, 'if it's a woman who cannot continue her marriage, how can she free herself?' He responded, 'it's very simple; she can free herself by annulment. If she realises that she cannot live with this man, and the marriage causes her harm, she can annul the contract.' One can argue that the legal form of this act is not defined in Iranian law. According to Sanei, Iranian laws are incomplete and therefore this form has not yet been defined in Iran's laws.[152]

Delegated repudiation, *tafviz-e talāq*, provided for by Article 1119 of the civil code was adopted to facilitate divorce for women. According to this article, it can be stipulated in the marriage contract that in certain situations, the wife has the power (which she can also transfer to a third party by power of attorney) to obtain a divorce after establishing the facts of the situation in court and receiving a final judgment.[153] Ayatollah Khomeini also recognised the above provision as a suitable way to make divorce more accessible to women.[154] It is necessary to note that a woman can obtain full power to initiate divorce in any circumstance; there is no need to specify the situations under which she can initiate divorce.[155] However, she should prove that her husband has violated one of the conditions mentioned in the marriage contract.[156] Therefore, Article 1119 only provides some examples of instances in which a man can delegate his right of divorce to his wife and it should not be considered as inclusive.[157]

The various forms of divorce

Article 1143 of the civil code identifies two forms of divorce: irrevocable and revocable. After an irrevocable divorce the husband does not have the right to renounce his intention of divorcing.[158] However, the husband has the right to renounce divorce in a revocable divorce provided that the period of *eddeh* has not expired.[159] Therefore, it is important to examine each kind of divorce and the conditions under which they are applied.

Irrevocable Divorce. A divorce is irrevocable in the following cases: if performed before matrimonial relations have occurred; where a wife is incapable of conception; where a wife provides *khul'* (financial compensation to her husband),[160] by *mobārāt* (mutual consent),[161] so long as the wife has not demanded the return of this compensation; and where, after three consecutive marriages (of the same parties), a fourth dissolution is sought, whether by mere declaration by the husband to return to the marriage (*ruju'*) or by a new marriage between the two parties.[162]

Due to the importance of *khul'*, it is crucial to elaborate more on this type of divorce by acknowledging that by applying *khul'*, women can divorce more easily, achieving equivalence with men under the provisions of Islamic law. Article 1146 of Iran's civil code, which provides for *khul'*, states: 'A *khul'* divorce occurs when the wife obtains a divorce because she dislikes her husband, against a payment which she needs to hand over to her husband. The property in question may consist of the *mahriyeh*, or the monetary equivalent thereof.'[163] Therefore, in the case of *khul'*, the wife gives the husband a certain sum in return for the husband agreeing to release her from the bond of marriage. In the case of *khul'*, the Qur'an provides that:

> And it is not lawful for you that ye take from women aught of that which ye have given them except in the case when both fear that they may not be able to keep within the limits imposed by God. And if ye fear that they may not be able to keep the limits of God, it is not sin for either of them if the woman ransoms herself.[164]

Although the Qur'an provides for mutual divorce, or *khul'*, to balance the rights of the spouses in the case of divorce, this kind of divorce is not implemented properly. Although *khul'* gives a wife the right to ask for divorce, by giving her marriage portion or some other compensation to the husband, the husband's consent is still necessary, even in this case.[165] In the M v L case, where the wife filed for a *khul'* divorce, the husband asked for a large amount of money before giving his consent. In the court, he argued that he loves his wife and does not want to divorce her. However, outside the courtroom he put pressure on my client, a wealthy woman, to pay him some amount of money equivalent to $500,000 to agree to the divorce. The legal department of the judiciary declared that the court couldn't compel the husband to accept the compensation and divorce his wife.[166] It may be argued that the way in which *khul'* is applied in Iran runs against the provisions of the Qur'an. The adoption of *khul'* can, in some cases, facilitate divorce for women who do not have financial difficulties. However, in general, specifying the grounds for divorce for women in Iran's civil code would provide a better solution, rather than insisting on *khul'*, because of the financial constraints involved in achieving the latter.

Revocable divorce (*Talāq-e Raj'i*). The husband has the right to renounce divorce in a revocable divorce provided the period of *eddeh* has not expired. Return to the wife after divorce can be affected by any word or deed, which may convey the idea, provided that it is based on an intention to do so.[167] According to Katuziyan, revocable divorce is a unilateral act restricted to men.[168] In the case of revocable divorce, the husband and the wife should legally live together in the same house for almost three months after the divorce; if they decide to resume marriage and become man and wife, their divorce will be cancelled and there is no need to remarry.[169] However, it is not acceptable in Iranian society for a divorced wife to continue living with her previous husband during the *eddeh*: in fact, revocable divorce concludes the marital relationship.[170] However, the law is different from social norms and for almost three months after divorce, a woman remains married and her husband has the right to revoke the divorce. It is difficult to imagine how stressful it is for a woman to pass the *eddeh*. It is said that keeping *eddeh* (except in the case of the husband's death) shows whether a wife is pregnant and reveals who the father of her child is.[171] However, one might criticise this justification and argue that it would be very easy to discover the child's father through genetic testing. Therefore, it is not necessary for the wife to wait for three months before divorcing her husband.[172]

Temporary marriage and its dissolution[173]

The Twelver Imami is the only school of Muslim law to recognise temporary marriage as a valid contract.[174] Although the practice pre-dates Islam in both Arabia and Iran, Shi'a Muslims maintained the custom as a form of a legitimate marriage. The sixth Shi'a Imam, Imam

Ja'far Sadeq was a proponent of such marriage.[175] The other branches of Islam believe that Omar Ibn Al-Khattab, the second caliph, forbade temporary marriage.[176] Motahhari argued during the 1970s that the second caliph had assumed that the issue of temporary marriage comes under the authority of the Vali-ye Amr-e Moslemin (the guardian of the Muslims), and therefore prohibited it on a political basis, not on a religious or legal one.[177]

To state the case for temporary marriage, reference is made to Qur'an verse 4:24, which states: 'for whatever you enjoy [of marriage] from them, give them their due compensation as an obligation'. The supporters of temporary marriage propose different reasons to justify and accommodate it within the modern social context. They argue that it provides for a healthy relationship between people who cannot marry permanently for acceptable reasons, such as financial hardship. In Iran, 2 million of the 3 million people of both sexes who have reached the age of marriage remain unmarried each year. Divorce rates have increased by 29 per cent while marriage rates have risen only 7 per cent.[178] Temporary marriage also regulates the relationships between men and women and provides support for children.[179] Those who oppose it, on the other hand, argue that temporary marriage humiliates women and ignores their rights. Temporary marriage does not, in their view, promote healthy relationships, but leads to prostitution.[180] Motahhari recognised temporary marriage as a cure for social disorders resulting from the absence of proper relationships between unmarried men and women within the society.[181] Makarem Shirazi responded with anger to those who assume that women are treated as slaves in temporary marriages, calling those critics bereft of sufficient knowledge about the concept and nature of this 'socially helpful' contract.[182]

Temporary marriage is accepted under Iran's civil code and six articles are devoted to it.[183] It is defined as a marriage that is for a limited period of time.[184] Temporary marriage is called *siqeh*, and a *siqeh-i* wife means a temporary spouse. There are some specific conditions for this kind of marriage. For instance, during temporary marriage, the amount of the woman's *mahriyeh* or *mahr*, say £1,200, and the duration of the marriage – thirty days, as an example – must be indicated.[185] The reason for the law's sensitivity to a precise and clear time period and amount of *mahriyeh* is that, contrary to permanent marriage, temporary marriage is not for the purpose of creating a family. It is a temporary action and women are entitled to a *mahriyeh* in exchange for men's sexual pleasure.[186] Therefore, both parties must be aware of their legal positions and a woman must know the amount to which she is entitled for the time spent at her husband's disposal. Ziba Mir-Hosseini in her book *Marriage on Trial* explains that Shi'ite jurists discussing the legal concept of the temporary marriage 'employ the analogy of rent as opposed to the analogy of sale which they used for permanent marriage'.[187]

In temporary marriage, if the man does not consummate the marriage, he must still pay the *mahriyeh* because he chose not to exercise his right. *Mahriyeh* is the only financial right that the woman is entitled to in temporary marriage. A woman can, however, stipulate the right to maintenance or other financial support in the contract, such as *ojrat-ol-mesl*, payment for household services rendered to her husband during marriage.[188] Moreover, in temporary marriage, as opposed to permanent marriage, the couple is not entitled to each other's inheritance.[189] Therefore, a temporary wife, even if she stipulated the right to inherit in the marriage contract, would not inherit from her husband. A child who is conceived in a temporary marriage is exactly like a child born from a permanent marriage and in this respect there is no difference. It is not necessary for spouses to register their temporary marriage.

The issue of registration of temporary marriages was taken up at the same time as amendments to the Family Protection Law were being debated in the Majles in 2006. Sattar Hedayat Khah, the representative for Boyer-Ahmad and the spokesman of the Majles' legal and judicial commission, proposed the registration of temporary marriages to prevent misuse and the potential harm it could cause women.[190] In his view, if the registration of temporary marriages did not become mandatory, no woman could be sure that her husband was not in a sexual relationship with another woman. Therefore, there is now no difference between here [Iran] and the West. Anyone can have a sexual relationship with another person without the need to prove that there has been a 'temporary marriage' agreement.[191]

Speaking in opposition to the Hedayat Khah proposal, Mohammad Dehqan, the representative for Torqabeh, stated that requiring individuals to register their temporary marriages would be contrary to people's personal relationship issues; if someone does not practice the law, he cannot protest.¹⁹² Despite all efforts made by some MPs to avoid mandatory registration for temporary marriages, Article 22 of the Family Protection Law, which was ratified on 5 March 2012, requires such registration in three cases: where the wife is pregnant, or parties have agreed to register their marriage, or when the registration of the temporary marriage is stipulated in the marriage contract.

Divorce is linked to permanent marriage and a temporary marriage will be dissolved when its specified time expires or the husband waives his right to the remaining period of time.¹⁹³ In case of distress and hardship, the wife known as *zan-e siqeh-i* can ask the court to force the husband to waive his right to the remaining period. After the predetermined time has expired, the temporary marriage is automatically dissolved; no legal provisions are necessary. During temporary marriage, the man can give up any remaining time to the woman. For instance, if a marriage was for three months, at the end of the first month, the husband can waive the next two months and declare the marriage over. If the husband waives the marriage at the outset, before consummation, he is obligated to pay half the woman's *mahriyeh*.¹⁹⁴ However, if the marriage was consummated, then the wife is entitled to the full amount. As Mir-Hosseini stated '*mahr* plays such an important role in this union that any ambiguity surrounding it can render the contract void'.¹⁹⁵

After the marriage has expired or been waived, the woman may not immediately marry someone else, but the man may do so. In temporary marriage, the period of *eddeh* (waiting period) is two 'purity' cycles, meaning that a woman must complete two menstrual cycles and be purified twice. If, for some reason, a woman does not menstruate, then her period of *eddeh* is forty-five days.¹⁹⁶ If a woman has reached menopause, there is no *eddeh* and she may immediately remarry. If the marriage partners had no sexual relations, then the woman has no *eddeh* either. If a woman is pregnant, her *eddeh* will last until childbirth.¹⁹⁷ Therefore, if a man marries a woman for a period of one month and the *mahriyeh* is set at £180 and, after twenty days, he forgives the remaining time and the woman becomes pregnant, for the next nine months, until childbirth, she must not remarry. During this period, she is not entitled to any support of *nafaqeh*, or maintenance. In the absence of any other social support and care for such a woman, the condition under which she must give birth to her child is unbearable. Those who support temporary marriage and consider it protective legislation for women should bear in mind that, in this case, the life of another innocent person that is, a child, is also involved. It seems that the new law requiring the registration of temporary marriages when the wife is pregnant is not useful, as there are no adequate legal and social procedures to support *zan-e siqeh-i* and her child.

As a temporary marriage is only for a limited time, only permanent marriages can serve as the foundation of a family. Although *siqeh* is recognised by Iran's civil code, according to Mir-Hosseini, 'its transient nature violates the social construction of marriage.'[198] In addition to legalising temporary marriage, a great number of websites were created to advocate and promote temporary marriages amongst the younger generation and those who were not able to enter into permanent marriages. However, it seems that these efforts did not help to legitimise temporary marriage within Iranian society and still it is considered unacceptable.

Inheritance

The Qur'an in verse 4:12 illustrates the share each spouse is entitled to in the case of inheritance; the woman's share is half of the man.[199] Given Shari'a law allow a Muslim man up to four wives, if he leaves an inheritance, his wives should divide it into one-fourth or one-eighth shares.[200] These provisions have been reflected in Iran's civil code. According to Article 907 of the civil code, sons receive twice as much inheritance as daughters.[201] Regarding spousal inheritance, the husband is entitled to take half of his deceased wife's estate (on condition that there are no children) regardless of whether it originally came from himself or from another husband. He is entitled to one-quarter of the estate as his share if the woman dies with children. A woman is entitled to take one-quarter of the estate as her share if the husband has died without offspring. A wife or wives are entitled to one-eighth, provided the husband has died leaving children.[202] As it was discussed previously, Iran's civil code recognises two kinds of marriages: permanent and temporary. According to Article 940, spouses who are married permanently and are not prohibited from receiving an inheritance, inherit from one another.

These provisions of the civil code are based on the Qur'an and therefore cannot be challenged easily. However, it should be noted that

Islam introduced the right to a fixed share of inheritance for women, at a time when no such system was in place in Iran. In fact, some scholars argue Islam brought about a massive change in Arab societies.[203] The Qur'anic verse explicitly states that:

> From what is left by parents and those related the closest, there is a share for men and a share for women – whether the property be small or large – a determinate share.[204]

According to Baderin, prior to Islam only men had the right to inherit, while women were considered objects that could be inherited. As a result, inheritance rights improved the status of women. He explains that in some cases women and men even get the same share. For example, a mother and father receive the same share from their deceased children. He argues that the provisions of Islamic law should be seen in the context and the time in which they were applied.[205] The question that remains is why there should be this inequality now? If one believes that Islam improves the situation of women, why doesn't the Qur'an grant equal rights to women? What is the justification for this inequality?[206]

According to Baderin, the man is responsible for meeting the financial needs of the family and the wife has no such responsibility; it can therefore be concluded that, in reality, considering inheritance rights as part of the family structure, both partners have the same rights with regards to inheritance. To make these provisions more compatible with modern life, he proposes that everyone use the mechanism of *hebe* (gift) which exists in Islamic law to provide equal rights for women. For example, a brother can *hebe* his extra share to his sister.[207] This solution is arguably not binding, as *hebe* is not compulsory. Therefore, its application in real life faces problems; it is not useful in all Muslim societies. It is important to bear in mind that tradition still plays a very important role in Muslim countries and that the principle of patriarchy remains very strong. However, one might argue that this rule should be examined together with other rules set by Islam in relation to other issues to find the balance that Islam attempts to provide in family life.

According to Article 946 of Iran's civil code, the husband inherits a portion of the whole of his wife's effects, while the wife inherits a portion of his movable property only (of whatever kind) and of buildings and trees. Moreover, if there be no heir, the husband takes the whole of the estate of his late wife, but the wife takes only her portion; the rest of the husband's estate is considered the estate of a man without any heir.[208] Some reformist jurists, namely Ayatollah Sanei, have observed that there are no provisions in Islam that prohibit women from inheriting land. In 2008, he issued a *fatwā* regarding the inheritance that women receive from their deceased husbands. He explained that when a man with no heirs apart from his wife passes away, his wife should become the sole heir.[209] Iranian women, with support from reformist jurists, have asked to abolish the discriminatory provision. In 2003, the Iranian Parliament passed legislation making it possible for women to inherit up to a quarter of the land and standing property their husbands owned while alive. The Guardian Council kept silent over the issue and, in 2009, the president ordered the legislation into implementation. As mentioned before, all parliamentary bills require the approval of the Guardian Council before they are written into the law; the Guardian Council is expected to declare its opinion within a set period of time. The speaker of the parliament, Ali Larijani, stated that parliament passed the law after receiving approval from the Supreme Leader. He explained that, 'the Guardian Council asked the Leader for a *fatwā* (religious ruling) on the matter and parliament passed the Leader's exact *fatwā*.'[210]

Conclusion

Through the analysis of some articles of Iran's Civil Code, it can be concluded that there is substantially less protection applied to women than to men. The reason for this difference may be attributed to the fact that the civil code is based partly on the Qur'an and the *feqh* (Islamic jurisprudence). Islamic jurists have different interpretations of Islamic principles, and Qur'anic verses have often been interpreted to prove that men are superior to women and the latter should remain dependent on the former. As Mir-Hosseini wisely stated, 'the *olamā* placed a big stick in men's hands and then told them it was not morally correct to beat their wives'. She argues that as long as men are not disarmed, they will use the stick to get their way, either by 'exerting violence or threatening to do so'.[211] Therefore, to bring about a balance between men and women's duties and responsibilities in the family, similar protection should be allocated for both genders. As happened in the case of Iranian women's inheritance rights, the jurists can issue a *fatwā* in favour of women. The question, then, is why do jurists keep silent over other controversial issues regarding women's rights? It is argued that the jurists' involvement in issues related to women's rights depends on the efforts that women undertake to advance their own cause. Women should continue to challenge their treatment under discriminatory laws and practices, so that jurists have no option but to hear their voices and respond to their needs.

CHAPTER 5

IRANIAN WOMEN DEMANDING EQUAL RIGHTS: THE CASE OF IRAN'S CRIMINAL CODE

Introduction

Reza Shah and his son, Mohammad Reza Shah, fell short of introducing comprehensive legal rights for women. This was not 'because they feared the clergy, but because they faced consensus in preserving the fundamental aspects of patriarchy, rather than its overthrow'.[1]

The first criminal code of Iran, which to a large extent was modelled on French criminal law, came into existence in 1926 and was extensively amended in 1974. Article 179 of this code permitted a man to kill his wife as well as her lover at the moment in which they were caught *in flagrante delicto*.[2] To proceed with the modernisation and secularisation of laws, some Islamic provisions of the criminal code, including Article 207 concerning *zenā* and *lavāt*, were removed from the code on 28 April 1931 and 20 September 1933. Although Reza Shah aimed to facilitate women's involvement in the nation's social life through his compulsory unveiling policy,[3] this in effect further violated the rights of Iranian women. It attracted opposition from religious and traditional groups in society, thus limiting the reforms of law pertaining to women during the Pahlavi era. Despite all efforts made by Iranian women's rights activists, the new Islamic criminal code, ratified in 2013, has not changed dramatically to accommodate more rights for Iranian women.

Iranian Women Demanding Equal Rights

The aim of this chapter to analyse the situation of women under the current Iranian criminal code with a view to demonstrating that the latter is not gender-balanced. In some circumstances, it even disregards the humanity of women. This chapter explores the reasons behind such an unequal treatment of genders in Iran's criminal code to find possible ways for changing and improving the situation of Iranian women.

An overview of Iran's criminal code

The Islamic criminal code, which defines criminal acts and imposes punishments, was completed in stages after the 1979 Revolution, with the goal of full Islamisation of legal regulations. A temporary law covering *hudud* (fixed punishments) and *qesās* (retaliation) consisting of 218 articles was ratified in two parts in 1982 and was applicable for ten years.[4] *Tahrir Al-Vasileh*, a book on *feqh* (Shi'ite jurisprudence) written by Ayatollah Khomeini, was the main source on which the code was developed. On 31 October 1982, another part consisting of forty-one articles dealing with the general principles of criminal law was ratified. The law covering *diyeh* or monetary punishments, inclusive of 211 articles, acquired validity on 29 December 1982. *Ta'zirāt* or discretionary punishments, which included 159 articles, was codified on 9 August 1983. In 1991, all these disparate elements were rationalised in a single Islamic criminal code, valid for a period of five years. In 1996, after the end of the set five-year period, another part of the Islamic criminal code was ratified and added, and the whole code was extended for another ten years.[5]

In 2007, the judiciary proposed a new bill to the Majles, which was ratified in September 2008 and, after several revisions, approved by the Guardian Council on 18 January 2012. While awaiting president's signature,[6] for the first time in the history of law-making after the 1979 Revolution, the bill was returned to the GC for a second examination. Since the GC wanted to reconsider the bill with more attention, the Supreme Leader was asked to intervene and to announce that the previous law would remain in place until the Council made its final decision.[7] Finally in May 2013, a new code was ratified, replacing the 1991 code. The *ta'zirāt* section added in 1996 mostly retained validity.

The Islamic criminal code provides four categories of punishments: retaliation (*qesās*), compensation (*diyāt*), fixed punishments (*hudud*) and discretionary punishments (*ta'zirāt*).[8] *Qesās* is a punishment that should be equal to the crime.[9] *Diyeh* or blood money is a financial punishment determined by a judge during sentencing.[10] *Hadd* is a punishment that has been specified in the Shari'a.[11] *Ta'azir*, on the other hand, has not been specified in the Shari'a but has been codified in the Iranian legal system. *Ta'azir* can assume the form of imprisonment, fines or flogging less severe than *hadd*.[12]

Under each category, there are several provisions that are discriminatory towards women. Since it is not possible to deal with all these discriminatory aspects, this chapter focuses on the most contentious provisions – those laws that stipulate different procedures and punishments for men and women who commit the same act and offence. These include the age of criminal responsibility, the evidential capacity of women, the laws that support honour killing and the controversial issue of blood money.

The age of criminal responsibility

The important question that needs to be answered here relates to the legal classification of children. Under the 1926 code, the age of criminal responsibility for minors ranged from twelve to eighteen. According to Article 34 of the aforementioned law, a child younger than twelve could not be held criminally liable, because she/he is considered to be undiscerning (*saqir-e qeir-e momayez*) and has no criminal responsibility. However, minors aged between twelve and fifteen who committed a crime were held responsible to some extent and were either handed over to their parents' custody with due discipline and commitment to moral education and care or were assigned to a juvenile detention facility. Article 36 of the 1926 code considered a gradual scale of criminal responsibility for non-adult discerning minors between the ages of fifteen and eighteen. These individuals were imprisoned in a house of correction for no more than five years.

The revised 1974 code adopted the same age brackets for criminal responsibility, that is, 12–15 years and 15–18 years. Children younger than twelve were acquitted from criminal responsibility. Between fifteen and eighteen, the children were entitled to a special criminal investigations regime if they were suspected of having committed a crime.

After the 1979 Revolution, the 1974 code was revoked, with the new Islamic code defining a minor as 'a person who has not reached the age of maturity as stipulated by Islamic jurisprudence'.[13] However, no clear definition of maturity actually exists under Islamic law. According to Islamic jurisprudence, it is a child's puberty (*buluq*) that constitutes the criterion for adulthood, rather than age. As a result, the age of maturity differs from country to country. Some jurists believe that, according to Islamic jurisprudence, 'a minor child is a person who has not attained puberty and maturity (*roshd*)'.[14] In their view, both of these conditions, one of which, *buluq*, involves physical growth while the other, *roshd*, relates to mental development, are necessary in considering a child as a mature individual.[15] Iranian legislation adopts the ideas of those Islamic jurists who set the threshold for maturity at fifteen for boys and nine for girls. Article 1210 (1) of Iran's civil code stipulates that:

> The age of maturity for a male is 15 complete lunar years and 9 complete lunar years for a female.[16]

In relation to the issue of the child's criminal responsibility, Article 49 of the 1991 Islamic criminal code stated: '[Minors], if committing an offence, are exempt from criminal responsibility. Their correction is the responsibility of their guardians or, if the court decides, by a centre for correction of minors.'[17]

It is clear from the aforementioned articles that the age of criminal responsibility for girls is nine, and for boys fifteen. Therefore, according to the post-revolutionary laws, a girl is actually regarded as an adult woman at the age of nine. Hence, if a girl of that age is accused of any crimes, she will be sentenced to charges as an adult. It is interesting to note that a virgin woman needs the consent of her father to marry even if she is of adult age and professionally independent such as a university professor. However, in comparison, if a girl commits a crime at the age of ten, she is considered an adult before the law. The related provisions under the civil and criminal codes are thus in contrast with each other.

Despite accepting, as in the past, the ages of nine and fifteen as the start of criminal responsibility for girls and boys respectively, the 2013 code has attempted to create a practical solution to avoid problems associated with the accepted current age of criminal responsibility. It has therefore adopted a dual system that accepts eighteen and a gradual scale of criminal responsibility for *ta'zir* crimes and nine and fifteen as the ages of criminal responsibility for *hudud* and *qesās*.[18] Through the requirement of maturity in addition to the accepted age of criminal responsibility, legislators have attempted to provide a practical solution so that judges can avoid issuing capital punishments in the case of *hudud* and *qesās*. Article 91 in this regard states that:

> In respect to crimes punishable by *hudud* and *qesās*, if the offenders, who are under 18 years old but who have attained the age of maturity, do not understand the nature of the committed crime or its prohibition, or if there are doubts about their mental development and perfection, then, according to their age, they shall receive one of the punishments provided in this chapter.
>
> Note – In recognising the mental development and perfection, the court may ask for the opinion of forensic medicine or employ other means that it deems appropriate.[19]

Although this provision may be thought of as a positive step towards rescuing children from harsh punishments, the ambiguity of the term 'mental development and perfection' and the means for its recognition may still put children at risk of being held criminally responsible for crimes committed under the age of eighteen. It is important to note that the sexual discrimination embedded in this law is not derived from the Qur'an, the words of the Prophet or his tradition.

One should take into consideration that, as the Shari'a does not set a particular age for maturity, the Iranian judicial system could easily follow the view of those jurists who consider both *buluq* and *roshd* as conditions for maturity and set eighteen as the age of criminal responsibility. Iran has ratified the UN Convention on the Rights of the Child, according to which 'a child means every human being below the age of eighteen years.'[20] It can therefore be argued that Iran has an international obligation to set a common minimum age of criminal responsibility for girls and boys alike. Moreover, it is necessary for Iranian legislation to distinguish between the age of criminal responsibility and the age of criminal maturity and therefore to consider an intermediate step between these two important stages during which a child or child offender may be prosecuted under special criminal procedures for juveniles.

Testimony

Testimony is proof that can be used as a claim in both civil and criminal affairs. The views of some Shi'ite jurists have had an impact on Iranian laws concerning women's testimony.[21] Consequently, the evidential capacity of women under Iran's law is a controversial issue that involves women's equal right to a fair hearing and due process. The 1991 Islamic criminal code clearly addressed the issue of testimony and listed the articles according to which women enjoyed less protection than men. The code stipulated the testimony of two women as equivalent to that of a single man. For example, Article 237 stated that: '(1) First degree murder shall be proven by testimony of two *ādel* (just) men;[22] (2) Evidence for second-degree murder or manslaughter shall consist of the testimony of two just men or that of one just man and two just women, or the testimony of one just man and the sworn testimony of the accuser'.[23] Another example is Article 74, which stated 'Whether *zenā* leads to *hadd* or *rajm* can be determined through the testimony of four *ādel* men, or three *ādel* men and two *ādel* women'. Article 75 stipulated: 'In cases in which *zenā* carries only *hadd-e jald* (punishment by lashes), the testimony of two *ādel* men and four *ādel* women can substantiate it'.

The 1999 code also stipulated cases in which women's testimony was not accepted at all. These include sodomy,[24] homosexuality,[25] *qazf* (slanderous accusation of fornication),[26] *qavvādi* (pandering),[27] felonious theft,[28] *mohārebeh* (sedition),[29] *efsād-e fel arz* (spreading corruption on earth)[30] and drinking alcohol.[31] More controversial issues arise in cases in which the opinion of an expert woman is worth half that of a man in terms of delivering an opinion. For example, the blinding of both of a victim's eyes is subject to full blood money and the blinding of a single one is subject to half that amount. If the perpetrator and the victim disagree, the testimony of two just male experts or that of one male expert and two just female experts asserting an unrecoverable loss of sight or loss of sight for an indeterminate period shall entitle the victim to blood money.[32] As Shirin Ebadi argues, this matter is completely dependent on specialised knowledge and it is clear that there are no differences between a male and a female ophthalmologist.[33] However, the 1991 code was not of this view and did not recognise that the opinion of male and female ophthalmologists had the same value on the aforementioned issue. The removal of this article from the 2013 code is a positive development towards equal rights for Iranian women, as it would remove a provision that expressly discriminates against them by enforcing gender requirements for delivering an expert opinion.

The 2013 code removed specified articles dealing with testimony attached to each issue. Therefore, at first glance, one might think that it provides same rights for men and women in relation to testimony. Article 199 of the 2013 code nevertheless adopts the same vision as the 1991 code had and considers the value of a woman's testimony half that of a man's. According to this article 'all crimes would be established by the testimony of two men'.[34] According to Article 199, *zenā*, *lavāt* and lesbianism would be proved by the testimony of four men. Testimony of two men and four women would be sufficient to prove *zenā* unless *zenā* leads to *hadd* or *rajm*; that can be determined through the testimony of three *ādel* men and two *ādel* women. In case of crimes that are punishable by *diyeh* the testimony of one man and two women would be sufficient to establish the crime.[35] Therefore, the 2013 code also values the testimony of women less than that of men. There are no differences between the testimonies of men and women according to the Procedure of the General and Revolutionary Courts in Criminal Matters Act (passed 1999).[36]

To justify why the testimony of women is not as valid as that of men, it is claimed that this provision is based on the Qur'an, and hence one cannot change it. Advocates of this approach refer to verse 2:282 of the Qur'an, which states that:

> O you who believe! When you contract a debt for a fixed period, write it down. And get two witnesses out of your own men, and if there are not two men [available] then a man and two women, such as you agree for witnesses, so that if one of them [two women] errs, the other can remind her.

Relying on this verse, Ayatollah Khamenei argued:

> Women could not be relied on to be good witnesses. The truth is often coloured by the circumstances and experiences of the witness who may well see something quite different from the reality. It is in women's nature to be more swayed by circumstances.[37]

Referring to verse 2:282, some jurists, on the other hand, argue that the difference in testimony between men and women does not apply in all cases; it is only applicable to business transactions, civil debts and contracts.[38] Therefore, it is not the case that one can easily deduce the general rule from this verse and apply it in all circumstances to assign an inferior position to testimony of women. For instance, Shah argues that: 'the verse does not consider women to be mentally deficient or weak, which is why they are allowed to act as witnesses. If a person is mentally deficient, neither he nor she can conduct transactions or bear witness.'[39] He believes that the Qur'an aims at establishing the truth to avoid injustice, and that this may be achieved through the evidence provided by a man or woman.[40] El-Bahnassawi rightly emphasises that this differentiation between the sexes does not indicate women's inferiority but touches directly on people's interests and the safeguarding of justice.[41] Some jurists argue that, in other issues, apart from business and financial transactions, the Qur'an does not differentiate between male and female witnesses.[42] For example, in provisions related to divorce, the Qur'an provides that:

> When you divorce women [...] either take them back on equitable terms or part with them on equitable terms; and take for witnesses two persons from among you, endued with justice.[43]

As discussed in the previous chapter, according to Iranian law, *talāq* only acquires legal validity following the testimony of two men. Therefore, in this case the Iranian law arguably violates the provisions which are mentioned in the Qur'an. In other cases – including bequest matters[44] and fornication/adultery[45] – the term 'two persons' or witnesses is mentioned in the Qur'an. One might agree with Baderin who argues that the transposing of the provision concerning business transactions upon all other types of testamentary evidence arose from the traditional position of women in society and not from a direct Qur'anic provision.[46] Therefore, the hard-line traditional approach to the issue of women's testimony is not compatible with the status of women who nowadays are active in commercial transactions. Subsequently, a liberal interpretation of the Shari'a might be adopted to eliminate this discrimination in Iranian laws.

Laws that support honour killings

Iran is a male-dominated country in which the family structure is based on the patriarchal system. There are different ethnic minorities living in Iran.[47] Honour killing, which is here taken to mean 'the murder, or attempted murder, of a woman by members of her family who do not approve of her sexual behaviour',[48] has been carried out in different areas in the country. According to a report produced by Asia-Pacific Women's Watch in 2004, honour killings are particularly prevalent in the provinces of Khuzestan and Ilam.[49] Yakin Ertürk, the UN special rapporteur on violence against women, has also declared that honour killings are most prevalent in Ilam and Khuzestan.[50] However, Iranian authorities have never provided any official statistics on this important issue.[51]

According to the data provided by a consultant to the governor of Khuzestan in 2003, 565 women lost their lives due to honour-related violence in the region throughout 2001. Of these, 375 women were said to have committed suicide (self-immolation).[52] Due to the fact that the suicide figure was very high in the province of Ilam, the UN special rapporteur visited Ilam in 2005. In her report, she categorised the possible reasons for suicide as the following: social pressure, lack of legal protection for women who are victims of violence, the lack of shelters, family legislation which favours men in divorce and child custody cases and widespread discrimination against women in society. While declaring that some of the suicides appeared to be honour-related, she acknowledged 'in Ilam women feel compelled to tolerate violence, inflicted not only by their husbands but also by other family members, for fear of shame, of being ostracized, or of being divorced and for lack of alternatives to the abusive environment'.[53]

A study of honour-related crimes in Khuzestan indicates that forced marriage is one of the main causes of honour killings in the region. If a girl does not agree to an arranged marriage, she will be either killed or will be denied marriage to any other man for the rest of her life. In one case, a twenty-five-year-old girl refused to marry her thirty-five-year-old cousin. Her cousin married but she was forbidden to marry anyone else until her cousin's wife died, when she, at the age of fifty, married him.[54] Another example is the case of an eighteen-year-old girl who refused to marry her cousin. Not only was she forbidden to marry again, she was killed ten years later. There is a certain arrangement made to choose the killer of a girl or a woman who, in the opinion of the men of her tribe, has dishonoured her family. The killer is selected from amongst the following people: her brothers, cousins, father, uncles, the children of the accused woman and the youth of the tribe who are between the age of seventeen and twenty-five. The task is to kill the accused girl or woman, wherever she may be. In some instances the victim is killed in a hospital or even in a police station or a court.[55] In addition to the strong traditions that provoke this harsh violence against women, the law that puts the responsibility for punishment into the hands of private parties also facilitates such crimes. The punishment for intentional murder is *qesās* – retaliation – which by law is the right of the family of the victim; they can either ask for *qesās* or forgive the killer.[56] In most cases of honour killing, therefore, the perpetrator escapes punishment as he himself is among those who hold the right of *qesās*.

In another case, a twenty-one-year-old girl named Marjan was killed by her brother because she wanted to marry a man who had yet to obtain the approval of her family.[57] The family of the victim (who are the father and mother of the killer as well) did not produce any formal complaint. Therefore, the killer was not classified as a murderer and may face a limited prison sentence of three to ten years.

According to Article 301 of the Islamic criminal code, if a father or grandfather (on father's side) kills his child or grandchild, he will not be convicted or punished for murder.[58] Maryam, a fourteen-year-old girl, was found dead in her bedroom. Her father confessed that he strangled her with her headscarf because of 'her suspicious behaviour'.[59] Some Iranian lawyers have repeatedly argued that this provision is one of the reasons for the increasing number of so-called 'honour killings' in Iran.[60]

In relation to honour-related crimes, Article 630 of the 1996 Islamic criminal code states that if a woman commits adultery and her husband catches her while she is sexually intimate with another man, he can kill her on the spot and be acquitted of any wrongdoing.[61] Hence, it is legal for a man to kill his wife in certain circumstances; some statistics have shown that 20 per cent of murders in Iran have been such cases. In 90 per cent of those cases, the wife was not cheating, and the husband was simply suspicious.[62] This provision, therefore, may encourage more violence against women. It should be noted that punishment for *zenā* (adultery) by a married woman, even if in need of no further proof, has legal conditions that must first be met for the woman to be *mahdur-o dam* (deserving death). She must have a permanent husband (not a temporary one), be *āqel* (cognisant and aware) while having intercourse with her husband and she must have access to her husband (he must not be away or suffering from impotence).[63] The 2013 Islamic criminal code removed articles which detail legal conditions necessary to prove *zenā*. However, the application of these provisions will remain unchanged as they are derived from *feqh*.[64]

The previous conditions must be corroborated in a court of law before the sentence of stoning can be issued.[65] Article 630 of the 1996 code deprived women of the right of defence before the law. There are different justifications for this provision. Some jurists attempt to justify it by arguing that if a man witnesses his wife's infidelity, he will commit acts based on raw emotion.[66] This reasoning is unacceptable because a husband may be able to take control of his emotions, while Article 630 encourages him to do otherwise. But the law does not allow women to let their emotions 'take over'. More importantly, the philosophy behind establishing the courts of law is that of minimising instances of personal vengeance. No single person can take the law in their own hands, because that would create unruliness and anarchy within society.

The history of this provision goes back to the 1920s. Article 179 of the Criminal Code of Iran (1926) permitted a man to kill his wife as well as her lover, at the moment in which they were caught *in flagrante delicto*.[67] Mohammad Jafar Habibzadeh, a university professor, argues that this article was modelled after the French penal code of 1810. Since Article 1 of Iran's 1926 criminal code clearly stated that its purpose was not to apply Shari'a provisions, it would be more accurate to claim that Article 179 was actually modelled on Article 324 of the French code, which states:

> Murder, committed by the husband, upon his wife, or by the wife, upon her husband, is not excusable, if the life of the husband or wife, who has committed such murder, has not been put in peril, at the very moment when the murder has taken place. Nevertheless, in the case of adultery, provide for by Article 336, murder committed upon the wife as well as upon her accomplice, at the moment when the husband shall have caught them in the fact, in the house where the husband and wife dwell, is excusable.[68]

Jafar Habibzadeh also acknowledges the foqahā debate on the admissibility of a husband killing his wife and her accomplice. Although some foqahā like Shaykh Tusi, Mohaghegh Heli and Shahid Sani discuss the issue of honour killing, the first three versions of the post-revolutionary Islamic criminal code did not cover this subject.[69] In fact, seventeen years after the revolution, lawmakers legalised the act of a husband killing his wife and her accomplice if he encounters them in the midst of sexual intercourse. Unfortunately, there are no statistics that enable researchers to track the number of such killings during the time in which the law was silent on this issue, between 1979–96.

Since there is no discussion of honour killings in the Qur'an, in the absence of a Shari'a-based justification for this inhumane treatment, the reason for giving such authority to the man and presuming him above the law is vaguely defined. Even if a woman is found guilty, her husband should not be entitled to punish her. Although Iranian women have lobbied to have this obtuse article removed, it remains unchanged in the 2013 code.

Blood money (*diyeh*)

Diyeh[70] is a 'monetary compensation given to the surviving victim or his next of kin because of a crime against a life or bodily harm.'[71] As noted in Article 448 of Iran's criminal code, there are two types of *diyeh*. First, it is applied in cases in which the victim has died, and compensation is to be paid to the next of kin; second, *diyeh* for bodily harm requires the defendant to pay compensation to the surviving victim. Therefore, homicide, bodily injury or other forms of harm committed against the physical security of the person constitute crimes of retaliation and compensation known as *diyeh*.[72] Retaliation is imposed in murder cases, although a death sentence might be changed to compensation where it is proved that the killing was unintentional. Therefore, in the case of murder, the family of the victim can make a remission and ask for *diyeh* instead.[73] According to the 2013 code, a woman's life is worth half of a man's life in terms of blood money: 'The blood money for the murder of a woman is half of that of a man'.[74] According to Article 554 of the 2013 code, based on the *hokm-e hukumati* there are no differences between the blood money of Muslims and non-Muslims belonging to religious minorities recognised by the constitution. Article 382 of Iran's criminal code states that:

> when a Muslim woman is murdered, the right to *qesās* (retaliation) is created;[75] however, if the murderer is a Muslim man, prior to *qesās*, the heir(s) of the victim should pay the murderer half of the *diyeh* of a man.[76]

If the murderer is a non-Muslim man, the latter are not mandated to pay the difference. In the case where both murderer and victim are non-Muslim, the payment of differences in blood money becomes necessary.[77] As discussed above, blood money is the amount of money paid as compensation to the family of a murdered person.[78] If, for example, a woman and a man died in an accident, the compensation given to the woman's family would be half that given to the man's family. It is claimed that this discrimination is because men are the breadwinners of the family and provide for the family's living expenses.[79] Therefore, the man's absence can cause more harm to a family and put it in a more difficult economic position. Mohammad Musavi Bojnurdi has stated:

> Of course, when a woman is killed it is a major crime, a real crime. But when we think about it rationally if we execute the man then we have made two families miserable; especially the second family who, with this execution, lose their breadwinner and are reduced to poverty. We have to ask whether executing the man solves any problems.[80]

The application of this discriminatory law has produced many problems for the families of victims, who seek justice, and also for perpetrators, who may face additional punishment in some cases.

It is worth mentioning Leila Fathi's case. This is an outstanding case in relation to blood money. An eleven-year-old girl was raped by three men and later killed. One day Leila left her village in the predominantly Kurdish region of Saqez to pick wild flowers and never came back home. Three men, Hadi, Mohammadsafar and Hasan, were arrested and charged with murder. Hadi accepted the charge and confessed; he later hanged himself in prison. The other two denied the charge but were found guilty after the trial. As discussed earlier, a woman's life is worth half of that of a man with regards to blood money calculations. Therefore, Leila's family needed to pay the balance of the compensation if they wanted to punish the killers. Her poor family was not able to provide the compensation and tried different means to raise the money. They sold their house and all their assets but were still unable to provide the needed money to pay the compensation. Her father and disabled brother each tried to sell one of their kidneys to raise more money. Although the compensation was prepared, and the sentence was approved by the high court, it took a very long time for the punishment to be applied. Mohammadsafar was executed in 2007, while Hadi hid himself in an unknown place; he is married now and has a child.[81] Leila's family discovered Hadi's whereabouts in 2011 and asked the court for the execution of the verdict. As is clear from this case, one should note that these discriminatory provisions result in a double injustice. On the one hand, the family of the victim, having already lost a child, must pay compensation to the killer to have the law applied. On the other hand, an additional punishment is imposed on the person who will be executed. It might be argued that it is unfair that the murderer should be punished by retaliation after several years in limbo, expecting to die. Moreover, Leila's case disproved the justification of those who believe that paying half of the *diyeh* is a check to prevent *qesās*. In the view of Bojnurdi:

> To forgive is a moral issue and carries the implication that when dealing with half of the diyeh the parents of the murdered woman would come to make peace and not insist on the execution and accept that it is bad enough for a family to be headed by a criminal and a murderer and they should not be punished further and become unprotected.[82]

Ebadi rightly examines the inferior status of women in the Iran's criminal code in the following passage:

> The section of the code devoted to blood money, *diyeh*, and holds that if a man suffers an injury that damages his testicles, he is entitled to compensation equal to a woman's life. I put it this way in my article: if a professional woman with a PhD is run over in the

street and killed and an illiterate thug gets one of his testicles injured in a fight, the value of her life and his damaged testicle are equal.[83]

She further explains:

There is a vulgar expression in Persian that conveys the sense of deep contempt, it is: 'you are not even worth one of my testicles.' I politely invoke this in my article, to explain that no Iranian could mistake just how outrageous these laws are and how they treat women as non-people.[84]

Ebadi has also written some articles questioning the justice of laws that discriminate against women, and for this she has been accused of treating complex issues emotionally rather than logically.[85] It has been argued that her view of blood money, for instance, is gendered and gives the wrong impression. Blood money has 'nothing to do with putting value on human life, nor with gender; if understood properly, the difference revealed Islam's compassion for women as a class.'[86]

Unequal treatment also exists between male and female embryos in Iran's criminal code.[87] It should be noted that if a pregnant woman dies in an accident, the amount of blood money received for the male embryo would be twice that of the mother.[88] Consequently, under Iranian law, provisions for compensation for death consider the value of a man's life as being twice that of a woman. The point that should be made here is that men and women ought to be treated equally in retribution for injury to, or loss of, bodily organs. Thus, a male culprit who has maimed a woman or caused her other bodily injuries is subject to commensurate retribution unless the blood money for the lost organ is a third or more than a third of the full blood money, in which case the female victim pays the culprit half of the blood money for said organ.[89]

The Iranian Government is aware of the brutality of this provision and has tried to make some improvements to its law regarding blood money. For instance, under legislation passed by parliament, the same insurance company compensation is provided for both men and women who suffer injury or death in a car accident.[90] In supporting this provision, the judiciary spokesman Alireza Jamshidi stated that: 'Since a person's agreement with an insurance company has contractual basis and both sexes pay equal premiums, the compensation should also be equal and the law is not in contravention of the Shariʻa.'[91] Furthermore, he explained that the law would only apply to insurance claims for people involved in traffic accidents, and not to compensation in other areas, for example, murder cases. This law was approved by the Guardian Council on 14 March 2016.

One should bear in mind that, in Iran, where all laws must be compatible with the principles of the Shariʻa, the existing Shariʻa-based laws might be challenged using the same tool, that is, Shariʻa and Islamic principles. For this reason, it is crucial to take advantage of the following verse, which deals with *diyeh*, to challenge the gender-based approach to *diyeh*. On the issue of *diyeh* the Qur'an states that:

> Never should a believer kill a believer, except by mistake, and whoever kills a believer by mistake, it is ordained that he should free a believing slave. And pay blood money to the deceased's family, unless they remit it freely. If the deceased belonged to an army at war with you, and he was a believer, to freeing of a believing slave. If he belonged to people with whom you have a treaty of mutual alliance, blood money should be paid to his family and the believing slave be freed.[92]

Because the Qur'an only describes the principle of *diyeh* in reference to accidental killing and does not discuss procedural issues such as the amount of *diyeh* or differences between men and women, some reformist *mojtahed*s believe that blood money should follow the same principles in all cases. For example, Sanei is of the view that the blood money for a man and a woman should be considered equal in Islamic law. He criticises those Islamic jurists who do not treat men and women equally in terms of blood money. He believes that the *ahadith* they cite should not be invoked because they contradict the Qur'an, and the Sunna, the philosophy and conclusive rules and principles of Islam.[93] He refers to other verses of the Qur'an to prove that God does not do injustice to his servants.[94] Invoking these verses and the religious traditions, he states that the difference is undoubtedly an injustice according to the logic of the Qur'an and Sunna, social conventions and philosophy. According to Grand Ayatollah Yusef Sanei, retaliation against a man for a woman on condition of the payment of half of blood money contradicts the principle of a life for a life in the Qur'an which says: 'Life for life, eye for eye, nose for nose, ear for ear, tooth for tooth, and wounds equal for equal.'[95] In his view, blood money is the price of a human life. Furthermore, he argues, death occurs when the soul departs the body. As men and women have an equal soul, they should have equal *diyeh*.[96] Therefore, according to the Qur'anic verses in which women and men are of equal value before God, how can one differentiate between them in the case of retaliation? It is therefore possible for Iran to use *fatwā* to abolish its discriminatory laws against women in cases in which blood money is concerned. Shirin Ebadi argues that:

> Given what the Holy Qur'an says in Verse 32 of Sura 5, 'whoever slays a soul, unless it be for manslaughter or mischief in the land, it is as though he slew all men', can we not amend Article 209 of the Law of Islamic Punishments? Given the Holy verse 'We have created you of a male and female, and made you into tribes and families that you may know each other, surely the most honourable of you with Allah is the one among you most careful (of his duties)',[97] how do we explain article 209 of the Law of Islamic Punishments? Are women not God's creatures, that they can be killed so mercilessly?[98]

Taking into consideration these facts and arguments, the Iranian Government has now accepted to pay the difference between the *diyeh* for men and women. According to the note to Article 551 of the criminal code, in all crimes where the victim is not male, the difference between men and women blood money will be paid by the government's physical damages fund. This is an interesting compromise, and perhaps acknowledges the gap between religious codes and socio-political norms in today's Iran. The struggle and discrepancy between religion and modernity have been omnipresent in not only Iran but also throughout the Islamic world. This new development in Iran is proof that although the Islamic Government cannot change, amend or even reinterpret, the context of the Qur'an, it can work around religion, politics and the law to find solutions that produce compromises rather than upending the law when dealing with modern issues that arise.

Conclusion

Iranian women's rights activists have employed different strategies for overcoming the gendered perspective of *feqh* reflected in the Islamic criminal code in Iran. Through the method of referencing the Qur'an in criticising *feqh* rulings, women's rights activists have urged some religious figures to admit 'that *feqh* laws can accommodate change, and that the Islamic Ruler is in a position to put aside or legislate new ones when necessary'.[99] According to these religious men, 'the hand of the Islamic Ruler, the judge, will be freed if they see that enforcing a law or a right results in corruption; then it can be stopped by means of the ruling Principles'.[100] The activists believe that 'there's no problem that can't be solved'. However, they contradict themselves when arguing that the 'hegemony of *feqh* rulings in family and society must be maintained, regardless of changes over time in economic and social roles'.[101] In addition to this contradiction, the discussion about changing outdated laws to a large extent remains at the level of discussion and has not gone far enough to involve deputies for the aim of amending those laws currently considered to be discriminatory towards women. Although the 2013 Islamic criminal code may be considered more progressive in comparison to previous Islamic criminal laws adopted after the revolution, its gendered approach to criminal responsibility and some punishments remains unchanged. It seems that as long as gender equality has no place in the Iranian Government's policies, all efforts made by women's rights activists can have only a limited impact on the status of women.

All this being said, the method of challenging discriminatory laws through a Shari'a-based mechanism – used by Iranian women and those who believe in gender equality – could be an effective strategy in tackling discriminatory laws against women not only within society but also amongst decision makers. As discussed in the previous chapter, through the adoption of aforementioned strategy, women have gained some success in bringing change to the civil code, for instance in regulations relating to inheritance. As mentioned in the previous chapter, the engagement of women activists with high-ranking clerical figures has led to the issuance of *fatwās* which became an important factor in the legislators' response to activists' demands. The same can be stated in the case of criminal matters, and for the engagement of both public opinion and the political sphere in this realm. To be effective and gain public support, the process of law reform should comply with the norms of the society in which it is to be implemented. It is generally accepted that secular laws based on Western systems of legislation are insufficient and at times dysfunctional within Muslim societies.[102]

CHAPTER 6

THE ONE MILLION SIGNATURES CAMPAIGN: DOMESTIC DISCOURSE ON GENDER EQUALITY

Introduction

Iran's failure to ratify the CEDAW has not prevented Iranian women from demanding equality. Inspired by their counterparts in Morocco, Iranian women's rights activists campaigned for gender equality by challenging the government on the streets.[1] Women who had won some initial successes during the reformist period (1997–2005) decided to broaden their activities to unify all possible forces to demand gender equality. The One Million Signatures Campaign was launched in Iran on 27 August 2006 and has quickly become the most visible collective action on the legal status of women, involving women's rights activists of both secular and religious orientations. These women realised that their demands and desire to eliminate discrimination against women and to guarantee equality of rights have been their central concern for the past 100 years. Therefore, they decided to give priority to legal equality in their struggle to combat discrimination against women. This effort led to the creation of the One Million Signatures Campaign, which aimed to raise awareness among the Iranian public and to collect one million signatures to demand changes to discriminatory laws against women. Women's rights activists hope that the next step will be to draft a bill guaranteeing equal rights for women, to present to the Majles for its consideration.[2]

The present chapter will examine the campaign, its goals, strategies, methods, achievements and the challenges it has encountered since its inception. The aim is to show how Iranian women have attempted to use domestic discourse and options to reform discriminatory laws, instead of relying only on the CEDAW. The campaign aims to make gender equality a dominant discourse by expanding its membership to include women from all levels of society. The long historical process of struggle for gender equality has equipped the present-day women's movement in Iran with a profound understanding of Iranian society. Women's rights activists, therefore, have taken to the streets to share their knowledge with people and engage them in discussions and debates on gender equality. They have attempted to contextualise the concept of equality in the everyday life of those who have experienced discrimination.

Given the closed nature of the state and the major restrictions placed on political and social activism, especially by independent groups, the campaign's goal of creating a mass movement was seen as direct threat from the outset. Like any other civil movement, the campaign has faced many difficulties since its creation, including the arrest and imprisonment of its members. Membership in the campaign has been a pretext for the arrest of many women activists. Newspapers and magazines which promote equality have been banned, and the campaign's website has been blocked by the authorities several times.

This chapter will highlight some individual cases of women's rights activists who have been involved in the creation process of the campaign and its subsequent development. The main purpose of this analysis is to demonstrate that, despite the realisation by Iranian women's rights activists that they need to work together without considering ideology or differences in beliefs, they have not yet reached their common main goal, namely legal equality. This is because the current ruling elite does not have the political will to end discrimination against women and still considers women a threat to national security.

The birth of the campaign

In the words of Nushin Ahmadi Khorasani, a prominent feminist, 'the One Million Signatures Campaign was born from womanly imagination to resist the violence imposed on us by the riot police when they attacked our peaceful rally for equal legal rights on June 12, 2006 in Haft-e Tir Square'.[3]

The issues pertaining to the rights of women have concerned women's rights activists throughout Iran's contemporary history. Scant attention was paid to women's legal status.[4] In early June 2005, Iranian women gathered in front of the University of Tehran to demand equal rights in line with the rights of their male counterparts and to ask the authorities to recognise their basic human rights. At this time the political situation was hostile to the women's struggle for equality. Hardliners were actively campaigning to take control over the country. Therefore, any kind of public demand or demonstration was deemed a threat against national security and attacked by the security forces. Mahmud Ahmadinejad's campaign, supported by the Alliance of Builders of Islamic Iran,[5] collected 62 per cent of the run-off election votes; he became president on 3 August 2005.[6] Despite the fact that women activists were under considerable pressure, this did not prevent them from taking further action to ensure equal rights. As Parvin Ardalan, a prominent feminist, rightly stated, 'women's groups and organisations were determined more than ever to overcome the atmosphere of fear and militarisation'.[7] Ardalan explained how women became more determined to collaborate to combat discrimination. For instance, both the Intellectual Partnership of Women[8] and the Global Women's Movement[9] decided to collaboratively organise a public protest in Park-e-Daneshjoo on the occasion of International Women's Day on 8 March 2006. News of this event was published a few days prior to the date on multiple websites, inviting people who supported women in their quest for equal rights, to take part.[10] More than 200 individuals, both men and women, participated in the celebration of International Women's Day, which descended into violence due to the intervention of the security forces. Participants in a peaceful demonstration were suppressed and beaten by the so-called plain-clothes and security forces. Simin Behbahani, a prominent poet, was among those attacked by the security forces. Women's activists who were beaten or arrested went to court and filed a petition against the police. They knew that their complaint would not be taken seriously, but they wanted to demonstrate that women were no longer second-class citizens and would not tolerate any kind of oppression imposed on them because of their gender.[11] After several months, the court closed the case against the police.

After 8 March 2006, there was disagreement among different groups of women activists, including the Intellectual Partnership of Women and the Global Women's Movement, about which strategies to adopt to move forward their struggle to achieve gender equality. There was no solid agreement amongst women's groups about methods or approaches.[12] Some wanted to ask for fundamental changes in the constitution while others hoped to start by reforming civil laws. Some believed that women's demands should be demonstrated publicly – women should come out and take their demands to the streets to demonstrate the fact that they would not keep silent unless they obtained legal equality. Others, on the other hand, argued for an approach that would involve less risk for women's rights activists. They believed that publishing women's demands would be sufficient. In their view the peaceful street style was actually a radical and revolutionary approach that could jeopardize the whole movement. Shahla Sherkat, an Islamic feminist, argued that public gatherings were 'futile and furthermore, radical and revolutionary'.[13]

Those who supported public demonstrations argued that social movements of all kinds need to increase their capacity and tolerance for enduring the cost associated with action, to push for their objectives. In the end, a small group proceeded to organise for a street action. To support this idea Ardalan argued that:

> Political change and social demands occur in real life not in an abstraction. Therefore, our demands for change become meaningful with respect to specific conditions and in correspondence with the actual social political environment of the time. In other words, a demand that may be deemed as liberal in one situation can be and may be quite radical in another atmosphere. In a time when the majority of our very basic rights such as the marriage rights, the divorce legal codes, polygamy and so on are still a major challenge in our lives, a public protest to change these legal measures is quite radical.[14]

A demonstration took place in Haft-e Tir Square on 12 June 2006. At this time, women's rights activists, despite being more at risk, decided to take part as individuals, bypassing the limitations imposed by their organisations. Acting individually gave them support from members of other social movements, including journalists, students, writers and lawyers. The demonstration attracted the participation of many individuals, a factor which could not be tolerated by the security forces. The peaceful demonstration therefore turned to violence. Some demonstrators were arrested and charged with threatening national security. Despite all the brutalities, arrests, prosecutions and even long-term imprisonment for some women's rights activists, public gatherings strengthened the women's movement. Women's rights activists learned from their public experiences that they should come out from their own networks and start to work with other groups and the population of the country, not focusing solely on groups and individuals with whom they are familiar.[15] Therefore, the experience of Haft-e Tir Square encouraged women's rights activists from different backgrounds to come together and design a new strategy to move their struggle forward toward the common goal of gender equality.

During the period between the Hafte-Tir protest on 12 June 2006 and the launch of the campaign on 27 August 2006, more than fifty women activists from Tehran and other cities across the country gathered and collaborated. They focused on preparing documents to guide them in their common work to achieve legal equality. As a result, three documents were prepared: a 'campaign petition' which Iranian citizens were asked to sign if they wanted to be involved in the process of legal reform of discriminatory laws against women, a 'campaign plan,' which contained goals, procedures and the work of its executive committees and 'pamphlets', which highlighted discriminatory provisions against women in Iranian legislation, including in the civil and criminal codes.[16]

A seminar on the impact of laws on women's lives was scheduled to be held in Tehran on 27 August 2006. The location chosen for the conference was sealed off by the security forces prior to the event; participants faced closed doors. Nevertheless, they decided to stay in front of the closed doors and once again to voice their demands loudly in public. Some small booklets, which had been prepared for the conference, were distributed among people in the street. The booklets described in very simple language the discriminatory laws against women in the legislation of the country. They also explained the position of women's activists. Shirin Ebadi took the floor in the street and talked to the crowd. The campaign was born on this day, giving new energy to the Iranian women's movement.[17]

The major goals of the campaign

The message of the Iranian women's rights activists who initiated the campaign was clear: put an end to legal discrimination against women in Iran.[18] To reach this goal, the campaign bypassed the CEDAW, instead reminding the Iranian Government of its existing commitments. Its petition stated that:

> The Iranian government is a signatory to several international human rights conventions, and accordingly is required to bring its legal code in line with international standards. The most important international human rights standard calls for elimination of discrimination based on gender, ethnicity, religion, etc. The undersigned ask for the elimination of all forms of legal discrimination against women in Iranian law and ask legislators to review and reform existing laws based on the government's commitments to international human rights conventions.[19]

For several reasons, the campaign focused on upholding the Iranian Government's existing international commitments to guarantee equality of rights for women. The main reason for this, according to Shirin Ebadi, the Nobel Peace Prize laureate, was the issue of time and the immediate need for Iranian women to acquire equal rights with their male counterparts. In her view, although the CEDAW is a comprehensive instrument regarding women's rights, it is not the only international treaty that contains gender equality provisions. Moreover, the Iranian Government has not yet ratified it. Therefore, she believes that Iranian women should, at the moment, pay more attention to the Iranian Government's existing international obligations, and ask that these be honoured. In a longer timeframe, this strategy will pave the way for ratification of the CEDAW by the Iranian Government.[20]

As discussed in Chapter 1, the Universal Declaration of Human Rights in its preamble urges states to affirm 'faith in fundamental human rights, in the dignity and worth of the human person and in the equal rights of men and women'. Furthermore, its Article 2 states that 'everyone is entitled to all rights and freedoms set forth in this Declaration, without distinction of any kind'. This includes gender. Moreover, Iran is signatory to both the ICCPR and the ICESCR. According to joint Article 3 of these two international covenants on human rights, Iran should 'ensure the equal rights of men and women to the enjoyment of all civil and political rights set forth' in both treaties. Iran also adopted the Beijing Declaration and platform for action in 1995, according to which it should 'take all necessary measures to eliminate all forms of discrimination against women and the girl child and remove all obstacles to gender equality and the advancement and empowerment of women'.[21]

> From the outset, the campaign targeted the legal status of Iranian women; however, there was no consensus among women's rights activists over assigning priority to any specific existing discriminatory law. Due to the large quantity of such laws, the campaign stressed the need and necessity to change all discriminatory laws in general, allowing the 'collective intellect' of the signers to decide what the 'legal preference' of the campaign should be, in its approach to Parliament and other assemblies.[22]

The campaign also promotes collaboration and cooperation between activists from different backgrounds and social classes to facilitate the process of change and reform in the country.[23] Moreover, the campaign aims to raise awareness and understanding amongst Iranians in relation to the rights of women, through dialogue, collaboration and democratic action. The campaign believed that changes should happen within society and from the bottom up. Therefore, it attempted to work with civil society and grassroots initiatives to achieve sustainable changes and to empower women. Through cooperation with civil society and connections with different women's rights groups, the campaign was rooted in society and could therefore be the voice of marginalised women.

The methods and strategies of the campaign

The campaign opened a new door for women's rights activists to continue their struggle for gender equality. Iranian society, according to Ardalan, is patriarchal and has no room for women to manoeuvre. In her view, Iranian society's male-oriented mentality is such that it continuously keeps women within an ever-increasing segregated circle. There are no opportunities for women unless they create an atmosphere that enables them to highlight their presence and ideas within society. Interestingly, women activists have learned from their experience to create a new plan and thus follow a peaceful public approach to taking control of every aspect of their lives.[24]

To raise awareness about discriminatory laws against women to gain the public's support for reforming these laws, the campaign employed the method of collecting signatures. Collecting signatures can be defined as the first phase of the campaign. The second phase consisted of preparing a draft law to be presented to the Majles; this was never carried out, owing to a failure to complete the first phase. Collecting signatures enabled activists to speak directly with people and hold face-to-face dialogues.[25] In the view of Ardalan, 'through face-to-face dialogue with women we would be able to internalise the need for change through a horizontal network that runs from one city to another, from one neighbourhood to the next, through alleys, households, and in face-to-face interactions'.[26]

To collect the signatures, the campaign designed a series of workshops for those interested in being involved with the campaign's activities. The workshops were designed to be held every two weeks to provide training for the participants. Each workshop consisted of three different sections. The first part provided a general introduction to the campaign and its activities. A member of the campaign led this session and also provided some information about the need for a campaign and the reasons behind its creation. The second section provided legal training for the participants. A legal expert explained discriminatory laws against women and analysed the current situation of women in Iran. In addition, the expert presented an overview of international standards on women's rights, including the CEDAW. During the third section, participants were introduced to the collecting signatures method to be able to present the campaign to other individuals in society. It is important to note that each of the participants, if interested, would be trained to teach future participants. This was not, however, applicable in the case of legal training, as this part could only be taught by a legal expert.[27]

To collect the signatures, volunteers who had participated in the training sessions introduced the campaign to the individuals and then asked them to sign the petition. This method has proved to be a useful tool for women's rights activists, enabling them to take their demands into the streets and to gather support from the working class. Face-to-face dialogue created a network that included women's rights activists and other people who were not necessary struggling for the rights of women. It gave activists an opportunity to challenge the existing justifications for discriminatory laws alleged to be based on Islamic principles and therefore not open to new or objective interpretations. Through dialogue, women's rights activists explained to ordinary people that such justifications are not necessarily based on Islam and can be challenged. Some senior religious scholars within the country and even within the current establishment agreed that there could be other objective interpretations of these laws.[28] Therefore, in the absence of a public platform for women activists to present their views, this face-to-face method provided them with a valuable alternative option. At the same time, the women's rights activists were able to hear the real needs and demands of women from the society and update their knowledge. This is a crucial development that will, according to Ebadi, eventually lead to sustainable change in Iran. She has explained that so many women in Iran are not aware of the discriminatory laws until they are in distress, as is often the case with divorce or inheritance.[29]

Due to the severe suppression of civil activities after the 2009 presidential election, the collecting of signatures by campaign members has been stopped.

In relation to the strategy adopted by the campaign to reach its main goal, it should be noted that there were two strands of thought within the campaign from the beginning: those who thought that campaign activists should reach out to officials[30] and try to lobby them, and those who thought that reaching out to politicians would be useless and that the focus should remain on educating the public and collecting signatures, as a means of eventually pressuring the government to concede to their demands. Several public meetings were organised to discuss this issue. Kaveh Mozafari, a young male member of the campaign, believes that 'social activists ought to focus on social demands, preserving their independence from political games and deception.'[31] He provided an analysis of the relationship between the campaign and political parties, as well as other social movements, in one of the campaign's public meetings. He argued that:

> If there is to be any kind of interaction between the One Million Signatures Campaign and a particular political movement, that

interaction would be successful only if it is 'short-term, partial and with a social goal'. In that way, it safeguards the campaign's independence while managing to promote it by observing the minimum standards. In other words, political opportunities and certain political levers could be used for the realisation of social goals (such as further advancement of the campaign) only if these political opportunities/tools do not themselves become goals in the long term.[32]

Bahareh Hedayat, a member of the campaign as well as a member of the Shoraye Markazi Daftar-e Tahkim-e Vahdat (Central Council of the Office to Foster Unity), while entertaining no hope of cooperation with the authorities currently in power, argued that:

> The promotion of a specific slogan and clear demand, that is the demand for equality and the change of laws, is potent enough to shatter the patriarchal structure (to use feminist rhetoric) in our society for the promise of a brighter future. It is our duty to spread the news about our demands for change and our proposals for reform to all, including the politically active and among political factions [...] Regardless of our personal preferences, this minority group is especially powerful in effectively demanding a radicalisation of the law. In a more stable political and economic condition, whose existence is neither the aim nor the responsibility of this Campaign, one can benefit from the increased awareness among those with power to change the law.[33]

She further suggested that collaboration and cooperation with political groups could be beneficial to the campaign if its members mobilised their resources in line with the campaign's objectives, considering this possible relationship as an opportunity for furthering their own aims and goals.[34]

The group opposing contact with the politicians was certainly more forceful and aggressive, despite not representing a majority of campaign members. As such, those members of the campaign who believed that they should reach out to officials were at a loss what to do. As Tahmasebi states, the latter did not want to harm the alliances which had formed within the campaign between people of different backgrounds and perspectives; at the same time, they believed that the public and grassroots education and outreach effort would only prove effective if the campaign also focused on educating and reaching out to state officials and policymakers.[35] In Tahmasebi's view:

> Since the campaign is ultimately asking for the power structure, namely the legislature, to address its demands, efforts to build alliances and create connections with political groups and parties, and those currently in office, is a necessary step forward toward the eventual success of this effort.[36]

Tohidi agrees, arguing that although the 'bottom-up approach from people's homes to the streets, and from streets to homes, from virtual spaces to actual spaces, is certainly a strength of the campaign, it can be much more effective if combined with the participation and support of members of the elites and experts as well.'[37] In her view, cooperation, coordination and dialectic interaction between the streets and the elite is most likely to bring about substantive changes in Iranian law and society.[38]

Although some of the members of the campaign agreed to lobby officials, there did not seem to be any sort of majority consensus on reaching out to officials until about five or six months into the campaign, when activists started getting arrested and the campaign was under attack. To support the idea of reaching out to the officials, Tahmasebi argues that activists began to recognise the value of introducing the campaign to officials, instead of being introduced by groups opposed to the campaign, who wished to see a crackdown. She further explained that newspapers had been ordered to stop writing about the campaign or reporting its news, both relating to the efforts of its members and to their arrests. Although newspapers never covered the campaign extensively, this ban deprived the activists of a medium for communicating their message broadly to the public and to officials. The campaign lost an opportunity to introduce its efforts and intentions and to defend itself against accusations, often made by leading conservative papers, that its members were out to undermine the state and national security, or to promote immorality and do away with the *hejāb* (mandatory veiling).

For this reason, the public relations committee of the campaign decided to reach out to a group of women associated with the state.

It started its efforts with reformists.[39] According to Tahmasebi, the campaign tried to attract support from the reformists because some campaign members had withdrawn support from the reformists during the previous presidential elections, a full year before the start of the campaign. Tahmasebi explained that 'the reformist women who came to the meeting were very receptive of the campaign's agenda and for the most part they promoted its demands among their own circles.'[40] However, this support began to vanish when thirty-three women's rights activists were arrested outside a courtroom in which women's rights activists were on trial. The campaign became in this way too dangerous and was deemed a security concern, so that was no longer worth the risk of association. As propaganda against the campaign increased – and its members were arrested more often and in greater numbers and their efforts increasingly thwarted – the support it had received from both reformists and conservatives decreased. As the press, both the international press and Persian-language press based outside Iran (including Voice of America), began to cover news about the arrests of campaign members, open support from state officials essentially disappeared.

It is interesting to note that, at the same time, some officials began to pay more attention to the campaign's demands, even adopting them as their own. For example, conservative women began to advocate more openly for changes in the laws they had problems with. One group of conservative women lamented, during a visit to Ayatollah Khamenei, the fact that women could not inherit land from their husbands, a demand the campaign had put pressure on the government about. This ultimately resulted in a legal change in land inheritance for women, resulting, in large part, from the meeting of conservative women with the Supreme Leader of Iran.[41] Perhaps these women felt that they should be the ones pushing for such changes. Furthermore, they probably thought that the campaign members were not appropriate figures to bring about this change – or perhaps their outward efforts and the voicing of their demands carried a high cost and they were consequently paying a high price for it. This elevated the general discourse on women's rights both among the elites and the public, to the extent that disparities in the social and legal status of women not only became more noticeable, but acceptable to address and redress in light of such increased attention.[42] It should also be noted that, during this time, the family protection bill was introduced and a varied group of citizens began to oppose it, as will be discussed in further detail below. This constituted a very conservative response, but nonetheless a wide spectrum of women, from extreme conservative groups to campaign activists, began to oppose this bill, offering some opportunities for collaboration between state officials and activists.

It is also important to note that the campaign was accused of pressing for regime change in Iran, rather than advocating, as the political reformists were doing, for legal reform within the current political structure.[43] However, women's rights activists and members of the campaign have repeatedly stated that they are not 'engaged in anti-governmental activities and their entire objective is to raise awareness of their goal in a transparent manner.'[44]

Disagreement amongst the members of the campaign as to the adoption of a common strategy to reach the agreed goal is a very important issue, which has caused a lack of cohesion. It can be seen as one of the weaknesses of the campaign; it has affected its activities and led to a very complicated dispute between the members.

The campaign's successes and achievements

Although the campaign was not completely successful in reaching its primary goal of putting an end to discriminatory laws against women, its efforts led to some tangible changes in the legal status of Iranian women. The campaign involved religious figures in the process of reforming discriminatory laws, to gain legitimacy and protect itself from accusations of being anti-Islamic. The campaign to a large extent helped Iranian society to become more aware of the gender disparity of Iran's legal system.

The impact of the campaign on changing legislation
The extent to which the campaign was effective in changing or amending discriminatory laws against women or preventing the legislature from adopting further discriminatory laws is an important issue that needs to be discussed in light of the context in which the campaign came into being. Since launching in August 2006, some of the discriminatory laws it challenged have been brought to the attention of politicians and parliamentarians, who subsequently brought about positive changes in *diyeh*[45] and inheritance. The campaign has also

helped to prevent the Majles from enacting more discriminatory laws against women by challenging the family protection bill.

In May 2007, Elham Aminzadeh, an MP, explained in an interview that the *ferāksiun-e zanān* (women's caucus) in Parliament had internally discussed the possibility of introducing legislation to address the inequality of *diyeh* or blood money for men and women. She further expressed her hope that 'even if this legislation is vetoed by the Guardian Council, the Expediency Council will take steps to support it'.[46] She announced that the head of the Expediency Council, Hashemi Rafsanjani, had voiced support for taking steps toward equalising *diyeh* for men and women, during a meeting with conservative women. He pointed out that 'if the Seventh Majles passes this legislation, it will be a source of pride for us, but if they fail to pass the legislation or if it is blocked by the Guardian Council, we can take steps to ensure its passage into law within the Expediency Council.'[47] His statement might be considered a warning to both the Majles and the Guardian Council to take the issue seriously and legislate in favour of equal rights of *diyeh* for both men and women. Hashemi's positive reaction to the issue of *diyeh* was welcomed by some representatives of the Majles.[48] Maryam Behroozi, the director of the conservative women's Zeinab Society, and MPs in the seventh parliament announced their plans to address the issue of equal *diyeh* on the Majles floor.

Golam-Hossein Elham, the official government spokesperson and the minister of justice at the time, emphasised equal rights for women in relation to *diyeh* during a seminar on managing the challenges faced by the insurance industry which was held on June 2007.[49] A number of women's associations, including the Association of Islamic Scholars, the Society for the Protection of Women's Human Rights, the Society of Modern-Thinking Women, the Association of Women Journalists of Iran, the Islamic Association of Women and Active Women in Reformist Parties issued an open letter to the Majles on 31 July 2007, on the occasion of the celebration of the birth of Fatemeh, the daughter of the Prophet. In this letter they urged the Majles to eradicate discriminatory laws in relation to blood money.[50] They questioned the current situation of Iranian women and asked, 'Where is the Iranian woman standing? Is her current status commensurate with her dignity and human personality?'[51] On 2 May 2008, the Majles passed a bill which entitled women victims of road accidents to receive the same amount of blood money as men.[52] To respond to the claim that the bill ran counter to the Shari'a, the judiciary spokesman Alireza Jamshidi declared that the new bill 'does not contradict the Shari'a because the insurance policy is based on a contract, whereas men and women pay equal premiums. They therefore have to be compensated in equal amounts'.[53] The Guardian Council approved the bill on 14 March 2016.

Another legal document that was debated in the parliament after the launch of the campaign was the family protection bill. In 2007, the judiciary prepared a legal bill proposing amendments to the procedures applicable in family courts and presented it to the executive for the same to be sent to the Majles. On 24 June 2007, the cabinet ratified the family protection bill proposed by the judiciary. On 23 July 2007, Ahmadinejad's government sent the bill to the Majles while adding a controversial provision to it, legitimising polygamy.[54] This act provoked the judiciary's objection. Alireza Jamshidi, the judiciary spokesperson at the time, considered the action of the government as illegal and in breach of current legislation.[55]

The legal and judicial commission of the Majles examined the bill and approved it on 28 July 2008.[56] Subsequently, the bill was sent to the Majles floor to be debated article by article. The most controversial articles included Articles 22, 23 and 25. Article 22 involves the obligation to register temporary marriages in case of pregnancy;[57] Article 23 involves changes in the conditions men must meet to take a second wife;[58] and Article 25 describes the tax that a woman should pay on her marriage portion.[59] Prior to the bill, polygamy did not have its own standing as a single article within Iran's codified laws. It was mentioned in other provisions, for instance, those concerning inheritance. Although the Majles was under the control of conservatives, women belonging both to the conservative and reformist camps raised their concerns about the bill. On 27 August 2007, the Majles social and cultural commission discussed the bill in its session and urged MPs to take women's interests into account while considering the family protection bill. The commission raised its concern about Article 23 in particular, which allowed polygamy.[60] Rafat Bayat, one of the women MPs, said: 'Women MPs are against the family protection bill.' She further explained that the bill not only failed to guarantee any new rights for Iranian women, but in fact it took away their rights in some areas. While emphasising the compatibility of laws with the norms of society, she said: 'Our families are normally monogamous, and the laws should make sure that the common rules are maintained. The authors of the bill must be asked how the court can only consider the condition of the husband should enjoy the financial ability to guarantee justice for his wife? What are the tools that can measure this justice? Which institution possesses the ability to monitor it?'[61]

Women from the reformist camp also raised their concerns about the bill. Soheila Jolodarzadeh, a member of women's parliamentary caucus, was one of the opponents of the bill. In particular, she objected to the article legitimising polygamy. In August 2007, she expressly criticised this provision for undermining families.[62] Farideh Mashini, the president of the Participation Front's Women Commission, criticised the bill and urged the authorities to support families, where men and women should enjoy equal rights.[63] The wave of disapproval of the bill subsequently spread to a great extent to include high-ranking politicians and the religious establishment. Former President Khatami, in an interview with *Sarmayeh* newspaper on 28 August 2007, condemned polygamy and called it a great violation of the rights of women.[64] In the same month, Ayatollah Yousef Sanei issued a *fatwā* forbidding a husband's second marriage without the consent of his first wife.[65]

In September 2007, the Zeynab Society hosted a gathering of conservative women to review and analyse the family protection bill. Maryam Mahmoodzadeh, a member of the Society of Devotees of the Islamic Revolution or Jamiyat-e Isārgarān-e Enghelāb-e Eslāmi, and Maryam Behroozi, the head of the Zeynab Society, were amongst those who spoke against the bill on that day. Mahmoodzadeh questioned Article 23 of the bill, claiming it gave consideration only to the financial ability of a man to apply justice equally amongst his wives as the necessary prerequisite to polygamy. But in her view, money has nothing to do with guaranteeing justice for the multiple wives of a single husband. Maryam Behroozi said: 'The family protection bill destroys families and challenges our society. The bill undermines the security of families and, we therefore urge MPs not to allow the ratification of the bill'.[66] The Zeynab Society sent several letters to the Majles to prevent MPs from ratifying the bill.[67]

On 4 September 2007, women from the reformist camp organised a gathering to express their collective objection to the bill. Shahindokht

Molaverdi, who became vice president in 2013, chaired a panel discussion on the legal aspects of the bill in the presence of Farideh Gheyrat, Mohsen Kadivar and Ashraf Geramizadegan. At the end of the gathering, the participants issued a statement declaring the bill to be in contradiction of Articles 10 and 21 of the constitution.[68] The Participation Front's Women Commission, the Association for the Support of Human Rights of Women, the Iranian Women Journalists Association, the Reformist Muslim Women Association and the Association of Women Researchers in Islamic Science were among those who signed the statement. The next day, on 5 September 2007, the women committee of Khāneh Ahzāb (the House of Parties), headed by Fatemeh Rākei, held a gathering to discuss the bill. Rākei expressed the concerns of women related to both reformist and fundamentalist groups and urged the Majles not to consider such a bill. Several gatherings were organised to address the challenges women would further face in case the bill was ratified. In addition to the 4 September declaration, women from the reformist camp issued another statement in November 2007, warning the Majles about the shortcomings of the bill. More women and organisations signed the statement, which was an indication of the emergence of collective action by different women's groups and organisations. This in fact led to the creation of an 'Islamic coalition of women' in 2008, which included many reformist and conservative women groups.

Iranian women's rights activists had also been following developments in the Majles regarding this bill and objected to some of its articles, which they believed would undermine their rights. They had started challenging the bill since the early days of its public announcement. Women activists argued that this bill would pave the way for polygamy and therefore harm traditional family structures. They believed that the bill gave men a free hand to take advantage of their granted rights and to deprive women of any rights within the family. Shirin Ebadi, for example, stated that 'the bill reinforces the unequal divorce law and encourages polygamy, as it forces a woman to share her marriage and her feelings with another woman without even being granted the chance to divorce her husband'.[69] In the view of the prominent human rights lawyer, Nasrin Sotoudeh, Iranian women both inside and outside the country would not remain silent about the bill, which would be detrimental for them. She further added 'If the Iranian government would adopt a more intelligent posture, they would never cause an increase in the anger that has been accumulating in Iranian women's hearts for years'.[70] *Zanestān, Change for Equality, Miydān-e Zanān* and *Kānoon-e Zanān-e Irani* were four main websites that highlighted the objections of women rights activists and women groups to the bill. Members of the One Million Signatures Campaign wanted to organise the first anniversary of the campaign. Although they were not able to secure a public place for their gathering, they were able to organise a press conference in the car park of the building of *Nāmeh*, a monthly publication, which was previously banned. In this press conference Shirin Ebadi, while criticising the bill, described it as a step backward for women's rights in Iran. She asked parliamentarian not to approve the bill, as it contained legal flaws and was against Iran's international commitments. She further explained that the bill was also against the Islamic Shari'a. She warned the Majles about more protests and public rallies and events held by women in front of the Majles building, should the bill receive parliamentary approval.[71] After that press conference, the One Million Signatures Campaign organised a public gathering in which Nasrin Sotoudeh, Farideh Gheyrat, Shahla Ezazi and Shiva Dolatabadi assessed the bill from different angles. The outcome of this gathering was a statement addressed to the Majles deputies and urging them to remove the consideration of the bill from their agenda. The statement was published later after 2000 individuals signed it.

On 23 September 2007, the Women's Cultural Centre published a special edition challenging the discriminatory provisions of the bill. Meydān-e Zanān was another women's group that worked extensively to deter the Majles from ratifying the bill. It allocated a section of its website to issues concerning the bill. This section was called 'No to Family Protection Bill'. They published materials about the bill as well as letters that women wrote to the Majles' deputies to dissuade them from ratifying the bill. In October 2007, some members of the campaign's public relations office went to the Majles to hold a meeting with the deputies. On 4 December 2007, the campaign issued another statement inviting parliamentarians to a public and transparent discussion. On 24 December 2007, some women deputies responded to the request. However, the meeting was postponed to the next year because no further debates about the bill took place in the seventh Majles.

The activities regarding the family protection bill also attracted the attention of foreign politicians. In December 2007, several deputies from the European Parliament visited Iran. Angelika Beer, who was the head of the delegation for relations with Iran, told her Iranian counterparts that the bill is a clear violation of the rights of Iranian women, and hence therefore urged the Majles not to ratify it.[72]

The seventh Majles ended its tenure without ratifying the bill. Therefore, those who were opposing the bill could not afford to rest, given that the decision about the bill had been transferred to the eighth Majles, which featured the majority of seats being controlled by conservatives. The women's movement created a coalition against the family protection bill. Although this coalition only lived for one month, its results were great for the Iranian women's movement. The coalition came to existence in June 2008 with twelve initial groups and another thirty groups joined it later. The coalition prepared booklets explaining the family protection bill and its challenges in a simple language. Owing to the great network of the coalition, the booklets were distributed around the country. Due the fact that the coalition had attracted many young journalists, the media played a very important role in raising awareness throughout the country about the coalition and its aims. These journalists were successful in reaching politicians and MPs as well. Apart from journalists, many women's groups in Tehran and other cities also met with the MPs and encouraged them not to vote in favour of the bill.

Another positive aspect of the coalition was to engage different political groups. On 4 August 2008, the Centre for the Defenders of Human Rights, spearheaded by Shirin Ebadi, organised a gathering to discuss the bill. Ebrahim Yazdi, Hasan Yousefi Eshkevari, Abbas Abdi, and Ahmad Zeydabadi, were amongst the political figures who shared their views about the bill, alongside women rights defenders such as Shirin Ebadi, Mansoureh Shojaei, Simin Behbahani and Rakhshan Bani-Etemad.[73] On 6 August 2008, the Islamic Iran Participation Front organised a gathering during which Farideh Mashini, Sedigheh Vasmaghi and Shahindokht Molaverdi shed light on the provisions of the bill that were in clear violation of women's rights. On 7 August 2008, the women's committee of the Shoraye Markazi Daftar-e Tahkim-e Vahdat issued a statement indicating its concerns about the bill. On 9 August 2008, the women's committee of Khaneh Ahzab also organised a gathering in which Fatemeh Rakei talked about the bill.

On 29 August 2008, female members of Tehran's city council sent a letter to female MPs, in which their objection to the bill was emphasised.

Meanwhile there was no serious reaction from the male MPs to the family protection bill and its controversial article legitimising polygamy. On 11 August 2008, a group of reformist women had a meeting with the minority caucus in the Majles. Zahra Shojaei, the head of Women's Participation Centre during Khatami's presidency, informed deputies about the news published in Mohtashamipur's weblog. It was claimed there that sixty-five male deputies of the Majles had a second wife.[74] Women rights activists used this situation to put pressure on the Majles to reject the family protection bill. To name and shame the male deputies practising polygamy, a weblog was established to identify those MPs. This weblog was called Shalvārhā-ye Nāzok-e Ehsās dar Khāneh-ye Mellat, which translates as 'Sensitive Thin Trousers in the House of the Nation' (i.e., the Majles).[75]

On 19 August 2008, Zahra Rahnavard, the head of Al-Zahra University and wife of the former prime minister and prominent member of the Islamic Republic's political elite, Mir Hossein Musavi, called upon parliament to remove the bill from its agenda for the sake of the '"durability" of Iranian families'.[76] To involve MPs in a more concerted way and encourage them to respond to the demands of women rights activists, all women groups working on the bill were planning to secure a meeting with MPs. However, it was a difficult task to select a smaller group of women within the larger group encompassing the entire women's movement. To make this meeting possible, Shirin Ebadi decided to choose a number of women rights activists and invited them to her office to plan for the meeting. On 31 August 2008, approximately 100 activists from various women's groups such as the One Million Signatures Campaign, *Meydān-e Zanān* and *Kānoon Zanān-e Irani* met with some representatives of the Majles to express their opposition to the bill.[77] Ebadi called it 'a sign of the Iranian government's regression to many centuries ago' and emphasised that she and her colleagues would stage a sit-in at the parliament if the bill was discussed on the Majles floor.'[78] Simin Behbahani declared that a women's meeting with Tajri, the MP for Tehran, was fruitful.[79]

On the same day, Ali Larijani, the speaker of the parliament, declared that the bill had been removed from the Majles' working agenda. This was undoubtedly the result of the efforts of women rights activists and members of the women's movement. However, this decision by parliament led to objections by the supporters of the bill within the establishment. Some deputies declared that the Majles' decision was illegal. A roundtable discussion was organised and broadcasted by state TV. Zahra Ayatollahi, a member of the Women's Cultural and Social Council, Zohreh Tabibzadeh, the president of the Centre for Women and Family Affairs, and Gholam-Hossein Elham, the minister of justice, featured in the roundtable discussion to support the bill. The strong objection to the Majles' decision caused the latter to reconsider its first decision and only remove more controversial articles from the bill, instead of ignoring the whole document altogether.

In response to the efforts of this informal female coalition, the Majles removed some of the most controversial parts of the bill. According to Speaker Larijani: 'In view of the warnings by the deputies and discussions with the judiciary, articles 22, 23 and 25 bear some religious and legal problems, therefore, these articles have been sent to the legal and judicial commission to be rectified'.[80] On 12 May 2010, ten conditions were added to Article 23, which made it even more discriminatory. This led to more objections by women's activists, which forced in turn the authorities to review the bill.[81] Finally, on 27 July 2011, Ali Shahrokhi, the head of the Majles's legal and judicial commission, sent back the amended bill to the Majles for its consideration.[82] Due to the resistance of women's rights activists and the active presence of women in society, the Majles could not easily make a decision without considering the real needs and concerns of women within the current context of Iranian society. The bill was finally approved on 27 February 2013 without Articles 23 and 25. This could be seen as a result of the campaign's engagement with the government on issues pertaining to women. In fact, the campaign has promoted open discussion amongst political groups and power brokers about women's rights issues. In the words of Tahmasebi:

> Since the creation of the campaign, Iranian society has witnessed the emergence of a discourse centred on women's rights that has managed to seep into even the most conservative of sectors, and spans a broad segment of society, such as women's rights activists,

NGOs and civil society, academia, government, religious leaders, and the general public.[83]

The involvement of Islamic scholars in reforming women's rights

The main justification given by statesman in the Islamic Republic for discriminatory laws against women is that they are based on the Shari'a and therefore cannot and should not be challenged. For decades, Iranian women have struggled to prove that the Shari'a does not discriminate against women *per se*.[84] Other factors, such as the patriarchal structure of society, should also be taken into consideration to tackle the issue of inequality of rights for women.

In all of this, as discussed, women's rights advocates and lawyers continuously searched for ways to demand women's rights within the existing legal structure of the Islamic Republic, which is entirely based on Islamic principles. As such, examining the role of Islamic discourse in the formation and evolution of struggles for gender equality in the Islamic Republic is key to better understand the local and international nuances of the Iranian example. Iranian women have used Islamic discourse as a key strategy for challenging Shari'a-based discriminatory laws in Iran. Regardless of whether women's rights advocates in Iran were religious or secular, they all made use of Islamic discourse as a strategy to voice their demands and their concerns within the frameworks and limitations of the Islamic Republic. Women's rights advocates in Iran did not necessarily contrast existing concepts of Islamic feminisms versus secular feminism as a defining categorisation for their approach. This was arguably because defending women's rights in Iran must happen within the Islamic-oriented frameworks of laws already in place, thus forcing an Islamic narrative even on feminists who were critical of these laws. Given that using Islamic discourse proved to be a rather effective strategy used by Iranian feminists, scholars of gender and women's studies focused on Iran began to examine this strategy, and to contextualise it within feminist discourses that are particularly prevalent in other Islamic contexts. This contextualisation in turn provided a more theoretic and comparative outlook for Iranian feminists to further define their approach and strategies. However, we should not ignore that some writers on women's issues have set the division between Islamic feminists and secular ones. In the late 1990s and early 2000s, a considerable number of books on women's issues were published as a result of debates and intellectual confrontation between influential writers inside and outside Iran.[85] In line with these debates and academic writings, some women academics inside Iran such as Shahla Ezazi and Nayereh Tavakoli organised some seminars at universities to discuss discriminatory laws against women and the possibility of reforming them.

Meanwhile, a considerable literature on the issue of feminists and women's rights in Iran was published in English. The newly published thoughts presented two different methodological approaches towards the women question in the Islamic world in general and Iran in particular; the first group, called the 'Islamic feminists', challenge discriminatory laws against women and aim to establish women's rights within the Islamic framework by reinterpreting Islamic sources. Haleh Afshar, Ziba Mir-Hosseini, Nayereh Tohidi and Afsaneh Najmabadi are amongst the leading scholars who have done extensive research in this regard.[86] According to Afshar, 'without doubt the most successful groups fighting for women's human rights in Iran have been those who have located their political action in the context of Islam and its teaching'.[87] Mir-Hosseini in her writings focuses 'on new discourses on gender among Islamic theologians, the challenging of Islamic family laws by ordinary women, and the emergence of reform-minded Islamic feminists'.[88] Najmabadi describes 'how Islamic feminists have come to insist that gender discrimination has a social rather than a natural (or divine) basis and how this could open the door to new possibilities for gender equality'.[89] Nayereh Tohidi discusses how women in the Muslim world are deploying Islamic feminism as a strategy to fight for women's rights.[90] In the view of this new wave of feminist scholarship women interest have not been considered in the reading of Qur'an and application of Islamic Shari'a and in fact women have been marginalised throughout Islamic history. They believe that gender equality can be achieved within an Islamic framework when women themselves read the text, which – according to Zainah Anwar, the prominent Malaysian Muslim feminist – leads women to '[discover] words, messages and meanings that we were never exposed to in all the traditional education on Islam that we went through in our lives'.[91] She further explains that:

We felt the urgent need to read the Qur'an for ourselves and to find out if the text actually supported the oppression and ill-treatment of women. This process Sisters went through was the most liberating and spiritually uplifting experience for all of us. We took the path of Iqraq ('Read', the first word revealed to Prophet Muhammad) and it opened a world of Islam that we could recognise, a world for women that was filled with love and mercy and with equality and justice. We need not look any further to validate our struggle. Women's rights were rooted in our tradition, in our faith. We were more convinced than ever that it is not Islam that oppresses women, but interpretations of the Quran influenced by cultural practices and values of patriarchal society which regard women as inferior and subordinate to men.[92]

In contrast, the second group, 'secular feminists', believe that one cannot seek equality for women within the Islamic framework and advocate the application of a set of universal rights for all women. Haideh Moghissi argues that Islamic feminism is a problematic issue that has become fashionable in the Muslim world. Seeing Islamic feminism as an oxymoron, she argues:

> The Shari'a distinguishes between the rights of human beings on the basis of sex (and religion). The Shari'a unapologetically discriminates against women and religious minorities. If the principles of the Shari'a are to be maintained, women cannot be treated any better. Women cannot enjoy equality before the law and within it. The Shari'a is not compatible with the principles of equality of human beings.[93]

In her view 'the emphasis on the achievements of those believing women who reinterpret the Qur'an obscure the political, ideological, and religious differences among Iranian women and mask the valiant efforts of socialists, democrats, and feminists to work toward secularism.'[94] Like Moghissi, the late Hammed Shahidian argues that the politics of Islamic feminism are problematic as there are a certain links between Islam and patriarchy:

> If feminism is taken to mean easing patriarchal pressures on women and making patriarchy less appalling, Islamic women's

reformism is certainly a feminist trend. But if I understand feminism as a movement to abolish patriarchy, to protect human beings from being prisoners of fixed identities, to contribute towards a society in which individuals can fashion their lives free from economic, political, social, and cultural constraints, then Islamist women's reformism proves considerably inadequate. I define feminism in these latter terms, and for that reason, I consider Islamic women's reformism a weak alternative to what exists in the Islamic Republic of Iran.[95]

By contrast, Ziba Mir-Hosseini contends:

[G]iven the current realities of the Muslim world, in which the Islamists have the upper hand in defining the terms of reference of political and gender discourses, I would maintain that only those who are prepared to engage with Islam's sacred texts and its legal tradition can bring change from within. Otherwise, Muslim women's quest for equality will remain a hostage to the fortunes of various political forces and tendencies, as was the case in the twentieth century.[96]

After having observed the Iranian women's movement for many years, I have reached the conclusion that in recent years, Iranian women's rights activists have shifted away from the conventional Islamic feminist/ secular feminist approach. In fact, they have responded to the political context by shifting their strategies. Prior to the reform era, or *eslāhāt*, there was no room for manoeuvres by secular feminists. It was only after the start of the presidency of Mohammad Khatami that secular feminists could present their views and, as a result, women's rights activists were divided in strategy. The closure of the political space which followed the start of the Ahmadinejad presidency brought no possibility for secular feminists to act. With the launch of the One Million Signatures Campaign in August 2006, both secular and religious women's rights activists came together using the discourse of universal human rights to take joint steps forward in their demands for equal rights.[97]

Through the adoption of Islamic discourse strategy, the campaign was to a very large extent successful in involving Islamic clerics in the discussion regarding gender equality.[98] Ayatollah Mousavi Tabrizi, a senior cleric, believed that discriminatory laws against women could be reformed and he proclaimed that:

> We have many laws that address the status of women or even that of men [in the Iranian legal code], which have to be reformed in accordance to current needs to come in line with and meet the needs of citizens. Concerning women, laws such as *diyeh*, inheritance, child custody, divorce and [...] can in fact be changed, and these reforms and changes are in no way in contradiction to Shari'a law.[99]

After the launch of the campaign, in fact, many religious leaders and Grand Ayatollahs have issued *fatwā*s which seek to reform current discriminatory laws against women. In January 2008, Grand Ayatollah Mazaheri, a renowned religious scholar based in Isfahan, issued a *fatwā* to legitimise abortion for women who became pregnant out of wedlock.[100] In February 2008, Ayatollah Sanei issued a *fatwā* regarding the inheritance women receive from their deceased husbands.[101] The support of these high-profile clerics for the campaign is an important achievement that has enabled its members to respond to the government's claim that the campaign's activities are against the Shari'a and therefore 'un-Islamic'.[102] Some Islamic scholars have expressly stated that women's demands and challenges do not contravene Islamic principles and that the old laws should be changed in light of the current situation of women. For instance, Ayatollah Fazel Meybodi, a senior cleric, proclaimed that 'the principles related to Civil and Criminal Codes can be reformed through *ejtehād*, as well as the principles related to traditional jurisprudence'.[103] He added that 'If thirteen centuries ago polygamy was customary or the marriage of girls at 9 years old was recommended, in this day and age, given the principles of justice and current social conditions, we have to acknowledge that these practices are no longer acceptable'.[104] These jurists have argued that equality may be achieved through an objective interpretation of the Shari'a. For example, Ayatollah Bojnurdi has stated that 'changes can be made in many of the laws that are considered discriminatory and I believe that the rights that currently exist for women in Shi'ite jurisprudence are not fixed, and can be changed.'[105] On the question of joining the CEDAW, Bojnurdi said: 'I don't believe that Iran should join with reservations, because in this respect, many of our domestic laws are in the process of changing.'[106]

The important question that arises here involves the campaign's reliance on Islam to bring about changes in the current legal status of women. According to Ebadi, Muslims will not allow Islamic governments to discriminate against them in the name of Islam if they are made aware of and gain an adequate knowledge of the faith itself. To elaborate on this issue, she points out that Muslims find proper solutions to their problems from Islamic paradigms.[107] She mentions an example to make this argument clearer:

> When I was studying at law school during the Pahlavi era, Islamic courses were considered to be an important subject that we should take every semester. At that time, we were encouraged to go in depth to the Islamic principles to be able to understand the background and roots of those parts of our laws which are based on the Sharia. My daughter went to Law school after the revolution, during the era in which the State was considered to be an Islamic one. I have noticed that she only had a few Islamic courses which would not enable her to understand the Islamic principles behind the Iranian laws in depth.[108]

Ebadi therefore realised that an Islamic State is not interested in its citizens obtaining detailed information about the Shari'a, as they could use it to challenge those who claim to apply the principles of the Shari'a to rule the country. Over 90 per cent of Iran's population is Muslim. This demographic reality makes it essential to use religious discourse to tackle the gendered nature of Iranian laws. Iran is a society with rapidly changing norms in relation to women's social status. Yet the discourse with respect to women's rights has its place in Islam. It is a discourse that challenges hard-line Muslims who oppose women's rights claiming they are not Islamic, and also speaks to a government and legal system that claims it is based on Islamic law. But Islamic discourse is important for the average person who wants to marry his or her religious beliefs with a belief in human rights, equality and dignity. These people are empowered to stand behind their human rights principles, without abandoning their religious beliefs. So to build a broad movement and unite like-minded people, it is important to be able to argue that Islam and human rights are not mutually exclusive and that Islam supports human rights.

With support from unlikely sources, and by using methods such as the ones discussed earlier which involve utilising the country's existing laws and recognising and exploiting their potential, Islamic rules can be revised. In this regard, one could agree with Mir-Hosseini, who believes that this revision should be done through *ejtehād*. Mir-Hosseini also challenges the discriminatory rules regarding women's rights at the level of *feqh* and believes that the problem of inequality lies in the tradition and inner contradiction between the ideals of the Shari'a and the norms of Muslim societies. Therefore, the tactic of involving reformist religion scholars to provide alternative interpretations has been effective to a large extent in raising public awareness of the origin of these discriminatory laws. However, the unwillingness of the Iranian Government to change the discriminatory situation of women has imposed restrictions on the use of *ejtehād*. In the words of Shirin Ebadi:

> *Ejtehād* frees us by removing the burden of definitiveness – we can interpret and reinterpret Qur'anic teachings forever; but it also means clerics can take the Universal Declaration of Human Rights home and argue richly about it for centuries. It means it is possible for everyone, always, to have a point. It means that patriarchal men and powerful authoritarian regimes who repress in the name of Islam can exploit *ejtehād* to interpret Islam in the regressive, unforgiving manner that suits their sensibilities and political agenda [...] This does not means that invoking Islam in a theocracy refracts the religion through a kaleidoscope, with interpretations perpetually shifting and mingling and the vantage of the most powerful prevailing.[109]

Ebadi's insight suggests that within the legal and political system of an Islamic republic women's rights is a contested issue which cannot be changed even within an Islamic framework. This was also a lesson from the *eslāhāt*, or reform era, during which women's rights activists and reformist politicians' efforts were unsuccessful in bringing about Iran's accession to the CEDAW. The coexistence between Islamic provisions safeguarding gender discrimination and articles that potentially pave the way for full societal equality within Iran's constitution hinders the reform of Iran's legal system. Although adopting a Shari'a-based strategy supported by well-known clerics to combat discriminatory laws — justified by the government's interpretation of Shari'a — has proven to be an effective way to gain the support of the public. Naturally, this is not a matter that can be resolved overnight but requires a steady and systematic approach.

Awareness-raising by the campaign

The campaign played an important role in raising awareness. While Iranian society was already fairly advanced in this respect, women's rights activists believed that raising awareness was important. The campaign succeeded in easily gaining notoriety within different social groups and families. In other words, 'The campaign has been able to accomplish a goal which women's rights activists have been aiming at for a long time: transferring the sense of commitment to gender issues and social resistance from among women's rights activists to the general public'.[110] To a large extent, this latter goal has been achieved through the adoption of the 'face to face' and social networking strategies. The stern reaction by government authorities, which has resulted in the arrest of campaign member during their awareness-raising activities in public places, the extensive coverage accorded to the campaign by Iranian mainstream media, satellite television channels operating from abroad, such as Voice of America, and the considerable focus given to it by Iranian Internet users all contribute to validating the claim that the campaign has gone beyond being a topic of discussion and debate within the activist circles and has achieved a non-negligible level of penetration, which remains arduous to ascertain precisely, within society at large. The Campaign reached out to two groups with particular intensity. One was the younger generation and the other was politicians and policy-makers. In the words of Tahmasebi:

> While our intent was to reach out to the public, the policy makers took note of us more quickly as a potential source of grassroots pressure and responded to some degree. Namely the change in laws with respect to inheritance and the *diyeh* were a result of this indirect pressure. Also, the adoption of agendas by Mousavi, Karroubi and Rezaei for the presidential elections of 2009,

demonstrates that we had a significant impact on presidential candidates during the three to four years of the campaign. Rezaie, while not committing to all the demands of the campaign, like Mousavi and Karroubi, used the term equality which is the women's movements' and especially the campaign's term.[111]

One of the reformist candidates for the presidential elections of 2009, Mehdi Karroubi, had pledged to put forward a bill to the Majles for the ratification of the CEDAW if elected to office.[112] For the first time since the 1979 Revolution, presidential candidates appeared with their wives at rallies. Karroubi's wife, a strong-willed woman who was herself an experienced political activist, was actively involved in the management of his campaign. Mousavi's wife, Zahra Rahnavard, accompanied him to all his rallies and made some speeches herself in support of women's rights.[113] Rahnavard is a prominent Muslim woman activist, and an accomplished writer, academic and artist. She is the first woman to have become a university president in Iran. According to Tohidi: 'Her stature, strong personality, outspokenness about human/women's rights and colourful headscarf were among the traits that added to the appeal of this couple as a promising choice for change'.[114]

Mohsen Rezaei, a conservative candidate, issued a statement outlining his views on women. In this statement he promised to take necessary steps to ensure the 'equality' of women in society: to adopt adequate policies to bring about a balance in the rights and responsibilities of men and women within the family and society; to promote women's organisations; to fairly distribute opportunities and resources for women in sports, education, professions and jobs and production and business.[115] The progress in terms of the candidates' agendas can be seen as the result of years of slow but persistent efforts by women's rights activists, including the members of the campaign, to publicise issues pertaining to women and to hold the politicians accountable for the concerns of women.

The campaign was successful in attracting the younger generation to work together, side by side, demanding their rights to build their own future. The large number of articles published on the campaign's website indicates the level of engagement of the younger generation. Through involvement in the campaign's activities, young women would feel strong enough to express their views loudly in public and could therefore strengthen their personal identity. Javaheri explained that:

Before joining the women's movement, I wasn't very optimistic about my future. But now I am someone who thinks for herself and independently makes choices about my friends, who to love, how to live my life. More importantly, I have been able to make a difference in the lives of people around me. Feminism has given me a distinct and reaffirming identity.[116]

Iranian men have also actively participated in the campaign to demonstrate that they have realised the importance of recognising the rights of their female counterparts. The involvement of men in the campaign is an important factor that indicates the high level of women's participation in the social life of the country. As Javaheri explains, the younger men who join the women's movement are different from the older generation, as they have internalised the discourse of equality more seriously.[117] This is a very important factor in acquiring men's support for the campaign to promote gender equality. Some discriminatory behaviour towards women resulted from a lack of knowledge of women's issues, and even from misinformation publicised through incompetent sources. Talking with men in a language that does not spread hate and does not consider them the cause of discrimination against women is vital to engaging them in the discourse of gender equality. Men are themselves victims of a patriarchal culture that promotes discrimination against women. The men's committee of the campaign successfully worked to raise the awareness of the public and to promote the idea that women are not alien to society and should benefit from the same rights as men.[118]

Challenges faced by the campaign

The severe challenges and difficulties imposed on the campaign by a variety of different factors, including State repression, attributes increased importance to its work. While pursuing its activities through the application of a narrow interpretation of the Shari'a, the Iranian Government has prevented women's rights activists from freely practising their human rights. State repression may represent the main obstacle to the campaign's activities. However, traditional and patriarchal practices are another barrier to the activities of the campaign.

State repression

In line with the theory of the 'Velvet Revolution', all social and human rights activists, including the campaign's members, are seen as a threat to national security by attempting to bring about a velvet revolution and the overthrow of the government. According to Ardalan:

> This theory, in reality, revolves around the large, more encompassing theory of conspiracy, which sees social movements as the breeding ground for soft revolutions, intent on toppling the government. The summons, interrogation and arrests of these social activists, demonstrates once again, that security forces have chosen to look from the outside in, and search for the footprints of the 'enemy' in explaining the demands of these groups, rather than choosing to ensure national security by facilitating conditions which bring about appropriate responses to the just demands of social activists.[119]

Since the creation of the campaign, its activities have been seen as a threat to national security; the greatest opposition, according to Javaheri, comes from the security and intelligence forces that fear the growing connections between women.[120] However, the security forces' lack of knowledge about social movements, which are indeed national and come from the society itself, may be the main reason for their fear. To silence women's rights activists and to prevent them from working together, the State has employed different methods. Gatherings, criticising discriminatory laws, writing articles, giving interviews to the media and participating in seminars, despite not being illegal, have been pretexts for threats, interrogations, arrests and jail terms for tens of women activists in Iran. A number of these individuals have been acquitted, and others have been handed suspended jail sentences; some have received heavy sentences.[121]

It is worth mentioning two cases here, by way of example. Aliyeh Eghdam Doost was sentenced to three years and four months imprisonment and ten lashes because of allegedly acting against 'national security' and disrupting the public order. The court of appeal reduced her sentence to three years and she was released on 8 January 2012 after serving her prison term. Mahbubeh Karami was initially sentenced to four years in prison on charges of 'membership in the Human Rights Activists'

Organisation', 'spreading propaganda', 'gathering and collusion with the intent to commit crimes against national security' and 'publication of lies.' The court of appeal acquitted her on the charge of publication of lies but upheld three years of the initial sentence.[122]

On what legal basis could challenging discriminatory laws against women be seen as a threat to national security? It is obvious from the provisions of Iran's constitution and the criminal code that for a crime to be proved, the criminal act must be defined as such in the existing law.[123] There is hence no legal basis for convicting human rights activists merely on the basis of their activities.

According to Ebadi, the looming threat that women in general have faced in their challenge to Shari'a-based laws has been the risk of being charged with apostasy. References to the opinions of Islamic jurists who believe it is possible to change these discriminatory laws have provided the only protection from the accusation of apostasy.[124] Therefore, campaign members have never been accused of apostasy and as the criteria of legal issues to be addressed by the latter was determined, the campaign has not become involved in challenging the charge of apostasy. They have always declared that their activities fall within the framework of Islam and do not aim to challenge it. The cases of women's rights activists and members of the campaign were considered to be political ones and therefore came under the jurisdiction of the revolutionary courts.[125] Despite the constitutional and legal requirement for courts to conduct hearings in the presence of a defence lawyer, in practice many women's rights activists were denied this right and placed on trial without access to a lawyer.[126] Moreover, they were tried behind closed doors.[127] A member of the security forces who is called a 'case expert' typically observes proceedings. The behaviour of the judge, the prosecutor and the security expert create an atmosphere of fear for the accused and his/her lawyer. The lawyers are also at risk of being arrested simply because of their activities and defence of those whose civil and political rights have been violated. One example is the case of Nasrin Sotoudeh, a lawyer who has been working in Iran for many years defending human rights and women's rights activists through the normal legal channels. She was arrested on 4 September 2010 and charged with 'acting against national security', 'congregation and collusion with intent to disrupt national security' and 'cooperation with the Centre for Human Rights Defenders.' She was subsequently sentenced to eleven years in jail and banned from practicing law and traveling for twenty years. The appeals court has reduced her prison term to six years and Nasrin was released on 18 September 2013, after serving three years imprisonment. The UN Working Group on Arbitrary Detention has raised its concern about Nasrin's case and declared that her detention in retaliation for her work as a human rights defender resulted from her exercise of fundamental rights as protected by the ICPR, to which Iran is a party. Specifically, it found that her detention violates Articles 18 (freedom of thought), 19 (freedom of opinion and expression), 21 (peaceful assembly) and 22 (freedom of association). In addition, the working group found that Sotoudeh's trial violated minimum international standards for due process contained in Article 14 of the ICPR, to such an extent as to render her detention arbitrary. In doing so, the working group noted that the government had denied Sotoudeh the right to effective legal assistance as guaranteed by international law.[128]

The case presented above underscores the harsh response from the government to any civil activity including the campaign, which was considered to have undermined 'national security' through its activities, strategies and methods. In fact, the hardliners within the government mistakenly assumed that the campaign was their political opponent and have done their best to control, confront and repress it.[129] Yet the campaign explicitly announced its major aim: to change the laws that discriminate against women in Iran. These do not include constitutional provisions, but rather focus on provisions in civil and criminal codes.

The campaign's members have repeatedly declared that they do not want to bring down the regime in Iran.[130] On the contrary, the members of the campaign are challenging these laws because they are passionate about their country and their Iranian identity. Despite all of the limitations and obstacles, the women's rights movement has become stronger and, according to Javaheri, it is not possible to stifle women's discourse on gender equality. In her view:

> Arrests of women's rights activists have kept the campaign alive and high on the public's consciousness [...] On the one hand, people are arrested, but on the other, people are still going out and collecting signatures. This has a positive impact on people who see that the campaign and its activists are serious and committed about reforming discriminatory laws.[131]

THE ONE MILLION SIGNATURES CAMPAIGN 193

It is very important to note that those members of the campaign, who have been arrested and imprisoned for more than a few days, have taken their activism inside women's prisons. According to Tahmasebi:

> These activists have taken it upon themselves to tell the stories of these women and to initiate efforts designed to improve their circumstances in prison. It is very interesting to note that the female prisoners in Evin's public ward, where most activists who have been incarcerated for any length of time have been held, as well as guards, have come to know and respect the activists involved in the campaign as well as the aims of the campaign, and treat activists well during their stay in prison.[132]

However, the state's repression has had, in fact, some negative impact on the campaign's activities, including the process of collecting signatures, which has turned out to be much slower than expected. The campaign's activists initially assumed that it would take two to three years to collect the signatures. The prosecution and arrests of women's rights activists has become more serious after the presidential elections of 2009, the aftermath of which forced some prominent women's rights activists to leave the country and reside in Europe and the United States. Among these are Asieh Amini, Parvin Ardalan, Mansoureh Shojaei, Khadijeh Moqadam, Maryam Hosseinkhah, Susan Tahmasebi, Shirin Ebadi and many others. Those who prefer to stay in the country and continue their struggles under the current political situation, unfortunately, have no platform to voice their demands from and no space to freely carry out their peaceful activities.[133] Therefore, 'It is indeed true that since the disputed presidential elections in June 2009, the accomplishments of the women's movement and the campaign have not been reflected fully in the media but this lack of reporting should not be viewed as a sign of dormancy'.[134]

Nevertheless, the fact that campaign activists have reorganised and changed strategies to be able to continue their tasks drives the message home that both the Iranian women's movement and the campaign are still alive. According to Tahmasebi:

Re-strategising for an even more difficult and challenging political climate but maintaining a focus on women's rights and awareness-raising is only a testament to the innovation of the campaign and the resolve of its activists. So on the fourth anniversary of the campaign, despite not having reached its goals of signature collection or sweeping changes in the law, the campaign continues along its path with lesser known and younger activists at the helm, who through four years of activism and experience have learned that a movement can stay alive only if it is decentralised and its structure participatory. In fact, these developments and accomplishments do much to demonstrate that the campaign and the Iranian women's movement are an active part of Iranian society, creating and promoting change – often with ebbs and flows, but nevertheless moving forward steadfastly.[135]

Despite the threats against women's rights activists, Nadya Khalife, women's rights researcher at Human Rights Watch, believes that: 'Iranian feminists and activists are still fighting for equality and demanding their rights to gender equality and democratic reforms'.[136] She urged the Iranian Government to heed these calls and refrain from using violence against those calling for change.

Traditional and patriarchal practices

Patriarchal values and attitudes based on male supremacy are one of the main reasons for gender inequality in Iran. It may be claimed that Iranian society is male-dominated with male-empowering values, laws and practices that make it difficult for women to amend or abolish discriminatory laws.[137] The members of the campaign were well aware that the latter is one of the key obstacles in implementing the 'change for equality' agenda. Some people avoid signing the campaign's petition for several reasons. In the view of some people, traditional forms of family unity are more 'natural' and provide fewer complications than the model introduced by the campaign. Lida, a twenty-eight-year-old girl from Tehran, explained how tradition controls the life of even some younger generation Iranians and prevents them from freely making decisions about their own lives without considering the implications of tradition. She pointed out that even some boys who seem modern in appearance are very traditional when it comes to the issue of women's rights.

She mentioned her own brother, who is a thirty-five-year-old businessman. He decided to marry a girl who is sixteen and not yet out of school. He chose her because, in his view, education is one of the factors that compel a woman to be disloyal to her husband. Lida asked her brother to sign the campaign petition but he refused to do so, arguing that, according to our tradition, women should have lesser rights than men. He added that if women gained equal rights, the status of men would decrease. When Lida told him that this was not our tradition, he insisted that it was both our tradition and our religion.[138]

Although this view cannot be taken as representative of the views of Iranian men in general, it nevertheless answers the question why some members of Iranian society might resist a petition that proposes laws to provide more rights for women, recognising their roles and responsibilities in both the domestic and social spheres. In Lida's discussion with her brother, religion was also mentioned as a reason why some people might refuse to sign the campaign's petition. Some people argue that the campaign goes against the Shari'a and that signing the petition might cause them to be accused of acting against their faith. Yet the campaign's members believe that the demands of the campaign are not in opposition to Islam; in fact, activists welcome progressive interpretations of Islam regarding women's rights. Tahmasebi argued that:

> Iranian law is based on interpretations of Shari'a law, but these interpretations have been up for debate by religious scholars for some time, not only in Iran but also around the Islamic world. Shi'ite Islam, on which the interpretations of Shari'a rely with respect to Iranian law, claims to be dynamic and responsive to the specific needs of people and time. Iranian society has changed much since 1400 years ago, but the interpretations of Shari'a on which the Iranian law is based remain rather conservative.[139]

One may agree with Ebadi, who pointed out that Islam does not cause the problems of Iranian women; rather they are due to patriarchal practices that are rooted in Iranian culture and transferred from one generation to another. She suggested that women themselves have played an essential role in keeping this practice alive. Therefore, one should tackle the issue of gender inequality in Iran from different angles, including patriarchal practices.[140]

This account may lead us to the question of whether the campaign is relevant to non-Muslims. The response of the campaign is that the discriminatory laws affect all women of every social extraction, education, age, ethnicity and religion across Iran. Legal discrimination, according to compilation of answers to common questions faced by the campaign, is a common ailment of all Iranian women and demand for change in these discriminatory laws is considered to be the desire of the majority of these women.[141] However, as mentioned in the introduction of the book, it should be borne in mind that religious minorities recognised within the constitution are covered by their own Personal Status Law, and only non-recognised religious minorities, such as the Baha'is, fall under Iranian state law.

Women's rights activists beyond the campaign: The coalition of women before the 2009 presidential election

A relative openness of the political atmosphere in the months preceding the 2009 presidential elections created a unique opportunity for civil society to express itself to a greater extent. Iranian women's rights activists, including the campaign's members, succeeded for the first time since the revolution in becoming involved in an election in an autonomous manner during the 2009 presidential elections. Instead of aligning itself with one of the main political factions, the women's movement took advantage of a relatively open atmosphere, which came about in the run-up to the 2009 elections, to press all political sides for a resolution to its unanswered demands, and to persuade the presidential candidates to advocate and defer to women's rights. A diverse coalition called the Hamgerāi-ye Zanān (Convergence of Women), which represented forty-two women's groups and 700 individual activists, came into existence on 25 April 2009, less than two months before the presidential elections of 12 June 2009.[142] In fact, the independent presence of the women's movement in the 2009 election was the result of a long journey through which women's rights activists experienced extensive challenges. This arduous path enabled these women to strengthen their position and their capacities. As a result, it took nearly twelve years before women could again claim their own demands during the 2009 presidential elections. Therefore, prior to assessing the 2009 collective action of the women's movement, it is essential to shed light on the chain of interlinked events that led to this critical women's awakening and its consequences. The fifth Majles election in 1996 was arguably the first one that cast the spotlight on women challenges and brought them to public attention. The Kārgozārān-e Sāzandegi (Executives of Construction) party and its female committee, thus, with the presence of Faezeh Hashemi, became active in the election, seeking to win a majority of seats in the Majles. To that end, the said party called for the active presence of women in the election and gained support from the prominent civil society group.[143]

This action of the Kārgozārān-e Sāzandegi party provoked reaction from conservative groups. In this regard, some conservative women organisations, such as the Zeynab Society, spearheaded by Maryam Behroozi, raised concerns about the 'liberal' views of women promoted by reformist minded women like Faezeh Hashemi, Jamileh Kadivar and Soheila Jolodarzadeh. Their disagreements generated a heated debate within Iranian society. Maryam Behroozi was critical of Faezeh Hashemi's agenda to promote women's status in sport. She believed that Faezeh Hashemi's view of prompting women's presence in public spheres by encouraging more women into sports such as horse-riding, skiing and cycling was the most 'ridiculous and insulting' idea concerning the presence of women in Iranian society.[144] Conservative groups have done their utmost to diminish the credibility of female candidates for the Majles who were not in their camp. Jamileh Kadivar was a candidate from Shiraz. She was accused by conservative groups of being pro Iran–US and Iran–Israeli relations, something that considered by them as being in betrayal of core revolutionary values. In the end, Kadivar failed to win a seat in the Majles.[145] However, the propaganda against Faezeh Hashemi was conducive in encouraging people to vote for her. She did, however, receive the second-highest vote in the Tehran electoral zone.

But for the women's right movement at that time, the presence of women in the Majles was not a priority. They focused on changes within the society and made advantage of the relatively politically eased atmosphere to establish independent women organisations. In the view of these women, the ground was not ready for those MPs to lobby for the advancement of women's rights within the legislative body. Therefore, in their view it was essential to work towards establishing a robust civil society, to bring women's demands to the attention of public affairs and also to priorities women rights as part of the state's social policies.

In 1997, only a year after the fifth Majles elections, Iranians were readying for the upcoming presidential elections. For the women's movement, the formation, establishment and expansion of women organisations remained the most important challenge. In fact, the women's movement did not have any concrete and clear agenda to demand from their presidential candidates for the advancement of women's rights. Therefore, women only took part in the election in their personal capacity as Iranian citizens. Yet, their active presence brought Mohammad Khatami to office, leading to the start of eight years of the reform or the *eslāhāt* era. The newly formed women's movement could not fully benefit from the relatively eased political climate of the 1997 presidential elections. However, it was one of the few social movements in Iran that rose up rapidly after the elections and during the eight years of administration of Mohamamad Khatami. In fact, the women's rights movement was successful in using the relative political openness during the reform era to expand its discourse within the Iranian society and polity. By expanding its activities and acquiring a reputable standing among the civil societies, the women's rights movement succeeding in carving out a media presence, which it used to highlight the status of women and bring the women question from the margin to the heart of social and civil demands.

One of the achievements of the newly established reformist government was to hold the municipal elections for village and city councils. Even though the constitution allows the municipal elections, none of the previous governments paid attention to this important provision to safeguard the rights of all citizens to participate in the public and local affairs of the country. Therefore, 1998 was the first year in which government was prepared to organise the councils' elections. Following the start of debates surrounding the municipal elections, women-related entities within the government began their work to encourage women to run for office. The Centre for Women's Participation, the women's section of the interior ministry, the ministry of education and some other organisations encouraged women to take part in the elections. The Women's Participation Centre named, for instance, 10 December 1998 as the 'National Women Day: Participation and Councils'. On 13 December 1998, the Women's Participation

Centre invited representatives of several non-governmental organisations working on women's issues to attend a meeting during which the centre urged them to spread the word in a bid to boost women's participation. The Islamic Republic Women's Association, spearheaded by Zahra Mostafavi, the daughter of the late Ayatollah Khomeini, the Society of Islamic Revolution Women, led by Azam Taleghani, and the ministry of agriculture's office for the promotion women's activities were among those organisations that responded to the centre's call. To promote women's participation even further, a number of gatherings were organised and held across the country. Special registration forms were designed and distributed during each gathering to help women declare their candidacy. After the end of the registration period, the Women's Participation Centre facilitated training for the candidates on the work of the councils. Despite all these activities, women only constituted two per cent of the candidates.[146] There were still some groups who were against the councils, as well as women's participation in such elections. The most important challenge for women's participation consisted of the disqualification of candidates by the committee supervising elections. Azam Taleghani, Jamileh Kadivar, Fatemeh Jalaeipuor and Nahid Shid were among those women disqualified by the committee. Two-hundred and ninety-seven women in major cities and 484 women in villages finally took part in the 26 February 1998 council elections. In general, the result was a satisfactory one for the women's movement in Iran. Female candidates received the highest votes in fifty-six cities. At least one woman in each council in either city or village occupied a seat. In some areas four women entered the councils.[147] Therefore, it can be seen how women made use of all the socio-political opportunities to present themselves to contribute to the process of democratisation of the Iranian polity and society.

The presence of women in the sixth Majles was also very important. The events prior to and after the elections added to the importance of this reformist-oriented Majles, in particular, and to the whole reform movement, in general. In fact, the elections of the sixth Majles occurred between two critical events. The first was the Kuye Daneshgah incident in July 1999 (a fatal attack on Tehran university dormitories) and the second was a conference in Berlin in April 2000, which was attended by several reformist thinkers. Some of the attendees were prosecuted upon return to Iran. As a law student at the University of Tehran when the

Kuye Daneshgah incident occurred, I personally observed how the authorities confronted the students in a severe manner, to further weaken the reformists' position, particularly amongst the youth and women. The oppression of this protest in fact was designed to exhaust the democracy movement in Iran. These events reduced the power of reformists' government, and created a sense of dismay and hopelessness amongst advocate of the reformist movement.[148]

The sixth Majles election in February 2000 was an important event for the reform process as well as the women's movement. Although women participation was greater compare to other Majles elections, women's movement was still not recognised as an independent movement with its own voice and candidates. The fact was that women participated as individuals not as part of an organised movement. The Women's Participation Centre released a statement inviting eligible women to put themselves forward as candidates in the election. For the first time, women from different groups, and not necessarily from within state-linked bodies, put themselves forward as candidates in the election. Minoo Mortazi Langarudi, Jaleh Shaditalab, Azam Taleqani, Fariba Davoodi Mohajer and Fatemeh Haghighatjoo from the student movement were amongst those candidates. Although the competency of most of these women was rejected, their participation was important as it served to encourage women to take part in public life. For the first time, on 5 February 2000, Rooshangaran publishing house presided by Shahla Lahiji with the collaboration of *Zanān* magazine spearheaded by Shahla Sherkat organised a gathering with women MPs and candidates standing for the sixth Majles. Soheila Jelodarzadeh, Faezeh Hashemi and Fatemeh Ramezanzadeh participated in the gathering out of a total of fourteen women deputies of the fifth Majles. It was a dynamic gathering. Mehrangiz Kar, Shirin Ebadi and Shahla Lahiji criticised the work of female MPs who were not able to advance women's situation during their term in parliament. However, the women's movement was not in a position to introduce and support its own candidates. It was only a start for the women's movement to discuss its existence and introduce itself. It was from 2003 onwards that the movement itself was officially recognised as such, mainly in the media and among intellectual networks.

In December 2003, the women's caucus in the sixth Majles invited a considerable number of women's organisations and women activists to analyse women's participations in the election. They proposed a

30 per cent quota for women to secure their seats in the Majles. Around 120 women were invited to the session, but only thirty attended. Nevertheless, the meeting was not well organised and in fact had little impact. Several women's organisations which were working under the umbrella of the Islamic Republic of Iran Non-Governmental Organisations Network released a statement in February 2004 addressing women's demands from the Majles. But the general atmosphere was not in favour of the women's movement as to help it to encourage more women to take part in the elections. The sixth Majles was not successful in enacting laws concerning women's rights.[149]

The women's movement has witnessed its toughest time during Ahmadinejad's first presidential term, 2005–9. The restrictions and the limitations of the political atmosphere restricted peaceful activities by every social and/or political movement in the country, including the women's movement. Social and economic crisis, stemming from the perceived hostile foreign policy of Ahmadinejad's government, also took their toll on civil society. Every day, a new policy was put into place to control women. For instance, the policy of 'sex segregation' in universities came to existence to prohibit women from studying in certain higher education fields and subjects at universities. The confrontation of Ahmadinejad's policies against the West created an unstable situation in the country. It was during this time, mainly in 2007–8, that a new wave of brain drain among the urban middle class started. This also included political and civil rights activists, journalists, lawyers and human rights defenders. The extensive political pressures on activists led to a greater number of individuals to leave the country.

The 12 June 2005 gathering in front of the University of Tehran, as well as the 12 June 2006 gathering in Haft-e Tir Square and its coverage by the media, were conducive to the recognition of the women's movement. All efforts eventually assisted reformist women in their quest to secure their seats in the sixth Majles, which in fact was a turning point in the advancement of women's rights. But this was the beginning of a complex struggle between reformists and conservatives. The latter created many challenges for the sixth Majles as a result of which reformists lost their credibility within the society. Fewer people participated as a consequence in the elections of the seventh Majles, which resulted in a win by the conservatives. The level of people's participation was reduced from 70 per cent in the fifth and sixth Majleses to 50 per cent in the seventh.

For reformists, the question that remained to be answered was how in such a political climate can people be encouraged to vote? According to electoral practice in Iran, the main political associations prepare lists of endorsed parliamentary candidates once these are formally cleared for competing in the race by the Guardian Council. Women's political groups, which had their own list of candidates for the sixth Majles, did not introduce any separate lists of female candidates. In fact, they collaborated with their male politician allies. For instance, the Islamic Association of Women, spearheaded by Fatemeh Karoobi, did not present any list of their female candidates for the Seventh Majles despite doing so for the sixth. They joined instead their male allies in a new formation, the Coalition for Iran. The Zeynab Society led by Maryam Behroozi worked with the Abadgaran-e Iran Coalition. And some women political entities, like the Women Association of Islamic Republic, did not present any list at all. Therefore, during that election women took no serious action. Finally, five women from the conservative camps went to the Majles. Only one woman, Mehrangiz Moravati, from the sixth Majles was confirmed in the seventh. No women from the reformist camp succeeded in gaining a seat in the seventh Majles.

Hamandishi-ye Zanān, which was established in 2003, only started to engage with the discussion regarding the elections and women's participation in 2005, at the time of the presidential campaign of that year. The election's atmosphere was different from the previous two terms under President Khatami, who was unable, by law, to run for a third term. The reformists failed to meet people's expectations during their two consecutive years in office and people had lost their faith in them. Consequently, the civil society, social and political groups, intellectuals and scholars were confused and dismayed with regards to the upcoming elections. Moreover, the failure of the reformists to introduce a powerful candidate further disappointed people and, as a result, paved the ground in favour of the opposite camps, that is, the conservatives.

During 1995–2005, the feminist movement only succeeded in paving the way for a greater visibility of the collective action of women. But it failed to establish its own standing as an independent movement. Therefore, the only possible act that the women's movement could do at that time was attempting to gain more visibility. There were two trends of thoughts within the Hamandishi-ye-Zanān on the elections and women's participation. Some were in favour of supporting the reformists' candidates. Another group wanted to take advantage of the openness of the political atmosphere to advocate women's rights. Those who sought to support reformists' candidates became active in elections camps. Within this group some like Jila Baniyaghoob and Shadi Sadr acted individually not as part of the women's movement. Some other women related to Meli-Mazhabi group, including Nahid Tavasoli, Fatemeh Farhangkhah and Azam Taleqani, were active in their own election's camp to provide support for Mustafa Moin, who was part of the reformist front.

Hamandishi-ye-Zanān organised a gathering in front of the the University of Tehran in 2005. Different groups of women represented the feminist movement in this event. In fact, this gathering shed more light on women's demands and gave them greater visibility. But what happened after the defeat of the reformists in the election caused the feminist movement to think about new strategies to cope with the new situation. Right after the election in August 2005, twelve non-governmental organisations were shut down only in the city of Khodabandeh. Therefore, acting through campaigns and smaller coalitions and forums became the new strategy favoured by women's rights activists.

Aware that gender equality was a pre-condition for democracy, sustainable development and the creation of a society without violence, poverty or injustice, the coalition focused on two specific sets of women's demands: the ratification of the CEDAW and the revision of four articles (19, 20, 21 and 115) of the constitution which enshrined gender-based discrimination.[150] The coalition was a demand-centred or *motālebeh-mehvar* campaign and avoided endorsing any particular candidate. As Tohidi explained, 'It rather put each candidate on the spot to address women's issues and respond to the demands specified by the coalition'.[151]

It is very interesting to note that the issue of Iran's accession to the CEDAW, after being rejected by the Guardian Council, became a taboo; there was therefore not much discussion of this issue prior to the creation of the Coalition in April 2009. The coalition once again highlighted this important matter and urged the presidential candidates to devote particular attention to Iran's accession to the CEDAW. Azam Taleqani, Farideh Mashini, Elaheh Kulaei, Shirin Ebadi and Mehrangiz Kar were among those members of the coalition who explicitly asked presidential candidates to include joining the CEDAW in their main agenda and give priority to it.[152] As discussed previously, Karubi and Mousavi, the two reformist candidates, expressly talked about the convention and the need for Iran to adhere to it. Soon after the creation of the coalition, some workshops on the CEDAW were designed and held in different cities around the country. Shiraz was the first city in which women's rights activists held a workshop, on 20 May 2009.[153] On 21 May, the workshop was held in Isfahan and after that the coalition continued these workshops in other cities.

The last meeting of the coalition took place on 6 June 2009 with the presence of two representatives of the aforementioned reformist candidates and approximately 200 participants. Zahra Shojaei, who represented Mousavi at this meeting, stated that progress had been made in the status of women during the past few years. At the same time, there were challenges that remained problematic. If we were to depict the status of women in a drawing, one would have to depict beauty as well as 'ugly' intolerable difficulties. She emphasised that women's issues and concerns should be fully considered. In her view, the coalition of women was a way to demonstrate the progress being made on women's issues. Kadivar, the representative of Karroubi, elaborated on the issue of the revision of the constitution through a reference to Article 177[154] and the role that the president can play in this process. She mentioned that the circumstances of the country need to be kept in mind and reasonable expectations need to be formulated with respect to the future president. She emphasised that Iran would join the CEDAW with reservation if Karoubi became president.[155]

Some participants insisted that the candidates should make clear their position on women's issues. Mahbubeh Abbasqolisadeh, for instance, argued that gender-based structural reforms should be carried out to improve the status of women. She criticised the reformist candidates, because they did not, in her view, bring the issue of gender equality clearly into their agendas, preferring to talk instead about justice, a term which has been used by the Iranian Government over the past thirty years.

The re-election of Ahmadinejad, who made no mention of women's issues during his second presidential campaign, was a big shock for women activists. However, they chose a peaceful way to overcome this negative outcome and pursue their aims for equality. The women's movement is now intertwined with the Iranian quest for democracy and women's rights activists are considering how to integrate women's demands with the broader quest for reform and democracy, in the face of increasing repression. In the words of Tohidi:

> The advocates for women's rights are seeking ways to continue rendering a feminist intervention in the current democracy movement to assure its direction is toward a nonviolent, non-sectarian, pluralistic, and egalitarian future. This is a daunting struggle, yet also an exciting and inspiring process, from which global feminism, especially women activists in Muslim communities, can learn many new lessons.[156]

After four years of silence and in the absence of many of its members, the Hamgarāi-ye Zanān held two meetings both before and after the 2013 presidential elections, to convince the new president to listen to women's demands and prepare the ground for them to continue their activities.[157] Hassan Rowhani, who was elected in mid-2013, has promised to 'de-securitise' the general 'atmosphere' and to promote 'justice' and 'civil rights.'[158] Rowhani, a moderate conservative cleric, was the only candidate to promise the establishment of a 'Women's Ministry' to push the implementation of strategies and programs designed to advance women's status forward in a structured and consistent manner. He also addressed the issue of Iran's accession to the CEDAW. The spokesperson for the women's affairs committee of Rowhani's campaign stated before the elections that the President-elect would present 'adequate proposals' for ratifying the CEDAW.[159] The position of the Rowhani campaign team stands in contrast to the more detailed promises made by both Mousavi and Karroubi four years earlier.[160] Nevertheless, Rowhani's victory in the 2013 presidential race raised initial hopes that the ratification of the CEDAW would be finally reinserted into the government's agenda, albeit not necessarily with a priority status. However, during the past four years, this prospect did not materialise and accession to the CEDAW remained mothballed, just like during the previous Ahmadinejad era.

Within government, Iran's vice president for women and family affairs, Shahindokht Molaverdi, seems genuinely concerned about the situation. In several instances she issued harsh criticism of mistreatment for Iranian women. In 2015 she clearly condemned bans on women attending live sporting events. Molaverdi announced, on 6 April 2015, that the government had approved the presence of women in arenas for volleyball matches. Three months later she reiterated the new policy during a meeting with police officials and representatives from the interior ministry and the sports ministry. She stated that some female supporters would be allowed to watch volleyball matches, but security officials later contradicted her and stated that no attendance policies had been modified. Religious hardliners threatened violent reaction if women were allowed into the stadium. They called female volleyball fans 'prostitutes' and 'sluts' on online forums and on posters allegedly distributed in downtown Tehran. Morover, Ansar-e Hezbollah, a religious vigilante group, stated that: 'We are taking a stand against legalising the presence of prostitutes [...] in stadiums'.[161] A number of senior clerics have also denounced the move. Ayatollah Mohammad Ali Alavi Gorgani said 'We didn't rise up in an Islamic Revolution for the right of women to enter sports stadiums.'[162]

Molaverdi responded to these allegations by stating that such opposition came 'from those who were denounced two years ago by voters, and who had crawled into their cave of oblivion for eight years'.[163] She further explained that the publication of such notices by 'those who call themselves followers of God [...] and used words that one loathes to repeat, clearly constitute several offences under the law'.[164] She also wrote on Facebook that:

> [A] crowd of sanctimonious people who published one notice after another denouncing the modest and decent girls and women of this land [who] talked of confrontation used obscene and disgusting insults that only befit themselves. Even if one day our beloved girls and women forgive this crowd, they will never forget them and keep these days in their historical memory.[165]

Molaverdi invited Iranian women to become candidates for the Assembly of Experts, which is tasked to appoint and supervise the Spreme Leader. The assembly has eighty-eight members elected for eight years. No woman has ever been a member, and this remains in place following the election in March 2016. However, a positive development for the new government could be marked by the fact that the highest ever number of women was elected for the Majles. Fourteen women have entered the

290-seat eleventh Majles. This figure will not change the nature of the Iranian parliament, which will remain male-dominated. Nevertheless, the main question is: are these women deputies and reformists in general going to bring changes in laws, in favour of women?

'We are here to fight against discrimination', Parvaneh Salahshouri, one of the elected members of Majles during the 2016 Iranian parliamentary elections, said in an interview. She expressed her views regarding economic growth, sustainable development, the eradication of violence against women at home and within society, women's unemployment, the growing number of divorces and more. In her view, women deputies belonging to the conservative party are mostly against women's rights. Salahshouri named them female only because of their gender. One of these conservative deputies that Salahshouri referred to is Fatemeh Rahbar, who in response to the well-known journalist Masih Alinejad's question about discriminatory laws in Iran had ignored the existence of any such discriminatory norms. She was not elected to the new Majles. Therefore, the presence of deputies who are pro-women's rights could be conducive to addressing discriminatory laws and making amendments.

Salahshouri was the first women politician in the history of the Islamic Republic of Iran to suggest publicly that *hejab* should not be compulsory, arguing that it is a primary right of women to choose whether they want to wear *hejab* or not. But a day after her interview, she corrected her view about *hejāb* and made it clear that Islamic *chādor* is more appropriate cover for Iranian women. However, it is very important to note that the only concern was *hejāb*, not other important issues that she covered in her interview. This means that the *hejāb* is the most critical issue for the Iranian Government and therefore women's rights activists may not gain any success to guarantee free choice for women, at least in coming years.

During the 2017 presidential elections, Hassan Rowhani's campaign – as it had four years prior, and perhaps even more so – talked about creating equal opportunities for women. One of the most important promises of Rowhani's campaign, according to Shahindokht Molaverdi, the vice president for women and family affairs, was to have more women ministers in the cabinet. Although Molaverdi herself has tried to advance the situation of women during the past four years, a simple evaluation of the government's programs concerning women shows Rowhani's administrative failure to meet the 2013 campaign's promises.

In terms of gender equality in law, no significant changes have happened during the past four years of Rowhani's administration. Despite some efforts to improve women participation in the economy, Rowhani administration has failed to increase the level of female participation in the job market. Therefore, based on the official statistics, women's participation in the economy is only 13–15 per cent, which in fact has led to the feminisation of poverty. As a result, a high percentage of people below the poverty line are women and children. In other areas, such as providing social insurance for housewives, adequate wages for female-headed households and maternity leave, Rowhani's promises have yet to bear fruits. In 2013, Rowhani has promised to establish a ministry for women as well as to appoint women ministers. But he only succeeded to appoint four female vice presidents: Masoumeh Ebtekar, the head of the environmental protection organisation, Zahra Ahmadi Pour, the head of cultural heritage, Shahindokht Molaverdi, vice president for women and family affairs, and Elham Amin-Zadeh, legal advisor to the president on the citizen rights charter. He also failed to appoint any women ministers in the 2017 cabinet. Molaverdi was replaced by Masoomeh Ebtekar.

Rowhani's administration has also failed to de-securitise the atmosphere and reduce the presence of security forces. As a result, many women's rights activists who have tried to raise their voice in this regard, including during the Majles elections, have been summoned and interrogated. Therefore, no serious meetings and gatherings were organised prior to the presidential elections. In the few days prior to the 19 May election, women's rights activists only issued a statement outlining their demands from the future president. Some of their demands listed in the statement include equal access for women to the labour market and equal pay, elimination of gender discrimination in the choice of the fields of study, suspension of moral police in urban areas, removal of the ban of women entry into stadiums, amending some discriminatory civil and criminal laws concerning women, developing a comprehensive bill to protect women against violence and allocating at least 30 per cent of seats in the ministerial team for women.

It is crucial to continue to scrutinise the women's movement in the current political environment to assess whether they are able to achieve their goals. The peaceful strategy of advocating for both women's rights and democracy may prove successful in the coming years.

Conclusion

A large number of women's rights activists with diverse ideological backgrounds have come together and initiated the campaign to work towards their common goal, achieving gender equality. This is considered to be an important achievement for the women's movement in Iran after a century of struggle for gender equality.

Although this new initiative has attracted considerable support from Iranians within and outside the country, State repression and social limitations predating the present political atmosphere have acted as a restriction to its activities. However, members and supporters of the campaign have continued their quest for gender equality and have urged the Iranian Government to put an end to legal discrimination against women. The campaign's strategies have mobilised women's rights activists and provided them with an efficient and practical way to take steps forward in their struggle to reform discriminatory laws in Iran. The awareness-raising strategy employed by the campaign is an essential factor in this regard and has proven to be successful for engaging many Iranians, both men and women, to work towards the campaign's goals.

Moreover, this strategy has made politicians and officials realise that some of the laws should be reformed better address the current plight of Iranian women. Some minor legal reforms have occurred since the creation of the campaign, as seen below. The campaign has also been effective in involving clerics in the process of legal reform in favour of gender equality. In recent years, senior religious figures such as Grand Ayatollah Sanei have produced *fatwā*s upon interpellation from campaign members, undermining the claim that the current state legislation concerning female inheritance and blood money correctly adheres to Islamic principles. These religious decrees have put pressure on the political system to change its stance regarding inheritance. In 2009, the Majles finally approved a law which allowed women to inherit land holdings from their male ancestors, thereby marking an accomplishment for the campaign itself.

The campaign has faced many obstacles since it came into existence. State apparatuses have spared little effort in stymying the campaign's activities. Access to its main website was blocked by state censorship systems several times and its members were arrested and charged with acting against national security. State propaganda against the campaign and its members was to some degree successful in delivering the message that the campaign would undermine the structure of the family and Islamic values. Severe restrictions imposed by the state on campaign members prevented them from collecting the one million signatures they set out to gather in the course of two years. However, the campaign in particular and the women's rights movement in Iran in general have become more resilient and more capable of withstanding the state's attempts at repression.

Contrary to previous feminist movements across twentieth-century Iran, the contemporary women's rights movement has succeded in articulating its own set of cogent universal demands, which in turn is a crucial factor in the continuation of the struggle for gender equality. In conclusion, the analysis proferred by Noushin Ahmadi Khorasani, a prominent women's rights activist, in the immediate aftermath of the contested elections of 2009 is still valid today:

> Moving forward, we need to keep our message alive. We want true democracy in Iran. We need to continue educating the masses so they will peacefully resist the violence of the state. We must teach our children, the young generation, to never forget the history of our struggle, and we must explain to them that justice and equality can best be achieved through patience and tolerance.[166]

CONCLUSION

Iranian women have confonted an enduring paradox after the 1979 Revolution. On the one hand, the gradual Islamisation of the State was conducive to the enactment of legislation that consolidated gender discrimination. While there were some attempts to legally enhance women's status in Iran before the revolution, this has taken an opposing direction since 1979. Due to Islamisation policies adopted by the new legal system, women further lost their legal rights, and lagged far behind their counterparts in white-collar jobs, top-level estate management and in institutions that in principle allow female incumbency, such as the Parliament and the government. On the other hand, women's participation in general social and public life has surprisingly increased since the revolution. For instance, the proportion of university places, industrial jobs and economic roles held by women has increased significantly, thus providing an indicator of the socio-legal division between how women perceive themselves and how their societal role is presented within Islamic and Shari'a law. This book has thus delved into such socio-legal dynamics to explore continuity and change encountered by women vis-à-vis the underlying social and legal frameworks since the 1979 Revolution.

Although the revolution has been described by some as nonemancipatory for women, this book suggests that the socio-economic activism and militancy of women markedly increased from 1979 onwards. The severe restrictions on women's participation in public life which came into being in the early stages of the Islamic Republic pushed them to coalesce to improve their social status to minimise the impact of legal discrimination and to maximise their influence within society. I experienced deep discrimination as an adolescent in Iran. However, it was not until I started to study law that I began to understand and analyse the extent of this discrimination. My legal studies made me aware of the extent to which systematic gender discrimination is still present in Iran, but also opened my eyes to the opportunities that were available to women to strive for equality.

Despite legal restrictions on the extent to which women could engage in lobbying activities to improve their condition, there has been an ongoing effort to ratify international conventions safeguarding gender equality. This book has mainly focused on such socio-legal dynamics, and on how women sought to solidify their rights legally and politically. It has chosen to focus on one key aspect of this process, the efforts to secure the full accession of Iran to the CEDAW. One key result of this analysis has been that, despite some improvements, the legal status of Iranian women after the 1979 Revolution remains to this day one in which discrimination prevails. As an attorney and lawyer, my priority has always been that of to assisting women in seeking and finding creative avenues, particularly when the government and existing legislation have come short in protecting them. Nevertheless, my experience also shows that law and culture can work hand-in-hand to advance the plight of women. Through an examination of the discriminatory situation of Iranian women under the Islamic criminal and civil codes, I demonstrate the law's negative effect on both; women as *direct* victims and men as *indirect* victims of discrimination. In every family case, I have made joint use of Islamic law and international law and have demonstrated how this *corpus* together could promote gender equality and universal rights. Indeed, I rely heavily on international norms and the work of UN bodies to bolster my day-to-day efforts, whether advocating in the media for legislative reforms or pressing for my client's right to divorce an abusive husband.

The Iranian women's struggle to bring civil laws into line with social realities is an on-going process. Despite periods of intense bargaining, which received support, even from within the complex echelons of the Islamic Republic's political elite, large-scale campaigns, such as the one undertaken by the One Million Signatures Campaign or by feminist activists supported by some of the female MPs of the sixth Majles, the underlying political-legal framework has resisted this round of efforts to bring about tangible change. As argued throughout this book, this is due to women's own lack of awareness regarding the origin of these laws, religious sanctity, tradition, custom, various interpretations of Shari'a law and, more importantly, the resistance of the conservative establishment to significant improvements in the status of women.

The struggle to augment women's rights went through several phases and was subject to continuous and strong change. Due to the exceptional circumstances of the early revolutionary era and the exigencies of the Iran–Iraq War, women rights were not given priority by the state. This phase of the early revolutionary Iran can be termed the *silent* era, when women's rights were widely ignored. The second decade of the revolution, however, can be termed the *recognition* period, when women's rights activists gradually brought the issue of gender equality further to the attention of the public and government. The reformist government in 1997 accelerated such demands and led to the growth of civil society, and women's rights activities. As a result, women found the courage to urge the government to become a party to the CEDAW. The reasons for such a turn towards CEDAW reflect the fact that human rights are a universal standard that can be applied in any country.

Due to the relative openness of the political atmosphere during the reform era (1997–2005), Iranian women initially succeeded in realising their demands. The sixth Majles (2000–04) ratified Iran's accession to the CEDAW, although the ratification was vetoed by the Guardian Council on the grounds that it contradicted the Shari'a law and the Iranian constitution. The extent of opposition to the GC's decision from members of the clergy and experts on religious law highlights the lack of a uniform view on the CEDAW's compatibility with Islamic principles. This underscores once again the multiplicity and complexity of the hurdles faced by women activists in their struggle for equality.

The circumstances surrounding the rejection of the bill of accession to the CEDAW by the GC in August 2003 suggest that influential state bodies, including the council itself – responsible for vetting all laws approved by parliament to ensure their adherence to its own interpretation of the Shari'a – still favour a conservative interpretation of Islamic principles. It can therefore be argued that religious principles, as interpreted by conservative institutions, and the wider political environment that informs decisions about the compatibility of legislation with the Shari'a, are two hindering factors, which augment the challenges faced by Iranian women in their quest for equality.

Despite severe pressure imposed by the succeeding right-wing governments between 2005 and 2013, the women's movement in Iran has been largely successful by taking its demands into the street and contextualising the concept of equality in everyday life of those who have experienced discrimination. Because of the activities of women's rights defenders in general and the One Million Signatures Campaign in particular, some changes have now occurred from the bottom up in Iranian society.

This book has further studied the interplay between women struggle for equal rights and the political changes in Iran by looking at the 2009 presidential election, the formation of the 2013 Rowhani government and its re-election in 2017. Prior to the presidential elections of 2009, a coalition of women's movements to advocate electoral demands proved that Iranian women have their own requests and can play their own roles in the public affairs of the country. Women's presence in the election and during the unrest that followed shows that women are now aware of the importance of participating in public life to prepare the ground for reform.

Despite such dramatic socio-political changes, nevertheless, obstacles remained for women in achieving their goals. The findings of this study therefore suggest that such strong opposition shown by the religious/conservative establishment to change or amendment of the law decreases the likelihood of any *substantial* reform favouring women in the foreseeable future. Such arguments, however, do not suggest that hope for gradual reform is lost. The victory of Rowhani in the 2013 and 2017 presidential elections highlighted the fact that the women remained vibrant and continued seeking gradual changes to improve their status.

The eventual ratification of the CEDAW through the efforts of a moderate government would be considered as a great legal victory for women in Iran. This task, nevertheless, cannot be achieved unless other influential segments of the religio-political institutions would ratify the ratification, including the Supreme Leader's view, as the most powerful figure in Iran's political configuration of forces. Irrespective of whether Rowhani or a president of another persuasion becomes involved in the advancement of women's rights, the main objective of the women's movement should be that of securing the government's support, and making use of the latter to lobby more senior figures, such as the Supreme Leader, towards relenting on restrictions on women's rights and the refusal to fully ratify the CEDAW.

The issue of women and women rights is not new and has a complexity of its own when it comes to Iran. Addressing such a problem requires a multifaceted/multidisciplinary and multidimensional/multiinstitutional efforts. Issues surrounding women in Iran are social, religious, political and also economic. Besides, the issue cannot be dealt with properly unless different establishments, institutions and figures seriously engage with the matter to offer substantial change to the women situation in Iran. Iranian women, informally, were capable, since the advent of the twentieth century, to be more active than passive in the socio-political domains. This is despite the fact that structural and legal obstacles have prevented women from acquiring their deserved position in not only societal but also political life. I believe gender equality to be an innate right – no matter what culture or religion one is born into – and avenues exist for bringing Islamic law into harmony with international women's rights norms, despite the current and ongoing discriminatory practices in Iran.

NOTES

Introduction and Theoretical Framework

1. Interview with the author, London, January 2017.
2. The definition of Shari'a adopted throughout this book refers to the revealed law as contained in the Qur'an and in the authentic traditions (Sunna) of the Prophet Mohammad.
3. The late Ayatollah Khomeini, the founder of the Islamic Republic of Iran, expressed his view about Iranian women on various occasions. These can be consulted on his official website: http://en.imam-khomeini.ir/en/page/137/Result-Search/?action=qs&txt=women (accessed 5 January 2017).
4. A. An-Na'im, 'State Responsibility Under International Human Rights Law to Change Religious and Customary Laws', in R.J. Cook (ed.), *Human Rights of Women: National and International Perspectives* (Pennsylvania: University of Pennsylvania Press, 1994), pp. 167–88 at p. 181.
5. The metholodgy employed by this book warrants brief attention to the scientific method of deduction, according to which both reached hypothesis and researched question(s) are deduced as the product of a process of surveying and analysis, is used for this research's methodology. See Charles Ragin, *Constructing Social Research: The Unity and Diversity of Method* (Thousand Oaks, California and London: Pine Forge Press, 1994). Ragin states: '[The scientific method dictates that a] hypothesis is derived from theory and from existing knowledge about the research subject. Data relevant to the hypothesis are assembled and the correctness of the hypothesis is assessed [...] new data can be used to refine or reformulate existing ideas'. Ibid., p. 15.
6. See C. Chinkin, S. Wright and H. Charlesworth, 'Feminist Approaches to International Law: Reflection from Another Century', in D. Buss and A. Manji (eds), *International Law: Modern Feminist Approaches* (Oxford and Portland, Oregon: Hart Publishing, 2005), pp. 17–45; C.G. Bowman and E.M. Schneider, 'Feminist Legal Theory, Feminist Law-Making, and the

Legal Profession', *Fordham, Law Rev* 67 (1998), pp. 249–71. See also M. Chamallas, *Introduction to Feminist Legal Theory* (New York: Wolters Kluwer Law & Business/Aspen Publishers, 2013); S.E. Merry, *Human Rights and Gender Violence: Translating International Law into Local Justice* (Chicago: University of Chicago Press, 2006); Charlesworth, Chinkin and Wright, 'Feminist Approaches to International Law', *American Journal of International Law*, Vol. 85, 1991, pp. 613–45.

7. Zoe Pearson, 'Feminist Project(s): The Spaces of International Law', in S. Kouvo and Zoe Pearson (eds), *Feminist Perspectives on Contemporary International Law: Between Resistance and Compliance?* (Oxford, UK and Portland, Oregon: Hart Publishing, 2011).

8. UN World Conference on Human Rights, Vienna Declaration and Programme of Action, 25 June 1993, *UN Doc A/Conf. 157/23*, 1993, paras 1 & 18.

9. Report of the International Conference on Population and Development, Cairo, *UN Doc A/Conf. 171/13/Rev.1*, 1995.

10. Optional Protocol to the Convention on the Elimination of All Forms of Discrimination Against Women, GA Res 54/4 of 6 October 1999, entered into force 22 December 2000, *2131 UNTS 83*.

11. D. Buss and A. Manji, 'Introduction', in D. Buss and A. Manji (eds), *International Law: Modern Feminist Approaches* (Oxford and Portland, Oregon: Hart Publishing, 2005), p. 7.

12. Ibid.

13. In the 1990s, feminist scholars began to ask the 'woman question', which aims to find out whether the interests of women have been adequately dealt with in every legal analysis. Chinkin, Wright and Charlesworth, for instance, asked where the women in international law have been, and how might international law be made to work better for women. They criticised the public/private dichotomy based on gender, which has a normative, as well as descriptive, dimension. According to this, law and regulations are part of the public domain, which is dominated by men, while there is no place for law in the private sphere of life. Another feminist critique of human rights is the non-discrimination principle, according to which women should be treated in the same way as men. However, according to some feminist theories, the interests and needs of women are not the same as those of men. Therefore, the non-discriminative or equal treatment of men and women effectively brings about even more discrimination against the latter. See H. Charlesworth and C. Chinkin, *The Boundaries of International Law: A Feminist Analysis* (Manchester: Manchester University Press, 2000, p. 60. See also H. Charlesworth, 'Human Rights as Men's Rights' in J. Peters and A. Wolper (eds), *Women's Rights Human Rights: International Feminist Perspectives* (New York and London: Routledge, 1995), pp. 103–13.

14. K.T. Bartlett, 'Feminist Legal Methods', *Harvard Law Review* 103/4 (1990), pp. 829–88 at pp. 836–7.

15. Many ethnic and religious minorities live in Iran, but the official religion is Islam and the Twelver Ja'fari school (in usual al-Din and *feqh*), and – according to the constitution – this principle will remain eternally immutable. Other Islamic schools, including the Hanafi, Shafi'i, Maliki, Hanbali and Zaydi, are to be accorded full respect, and their followers are free to act in accordance with their own jurisprudence in performing their religious rites. These schools enjoy official status in matters pertaining to religious education, affairs of personal status (marriage, divorce, inheritance, and wills) and related litigation in courts of law. There are two laws covering matters of personal status and religious education of recognised non-Shia religious minorities. One was ratified on 1312/04/31 (22 July 1933) and the other was ratified by the Expediency Council on 1372/04/03 (24 June 1993). These laws make provisions for non-Shia and other recognised religious minorities to enjoy their own personal status regulations. According to Article 13 of the constitution, the only recognised religious minorities are Zoroastrians, Jews and Christians, who are at liberty to 'perform their own religious rites and ceremonies' and act according to their own religion in personal matters and religious teaching for as long as it falls within the boundaries of Iranian law. All other religious minorities who are not recognised by the constitution fall under Iran's legal system. For example, because the Baha'i faith is not recognised by the constitution, Iranian Baha'is are treated as Shia Muslim. See Advisory Opinion of the Legal Department of the Judiciary, *No. 7/6965- 1366/5/9, No. 7/2665- 1369/5/9, No. 7/802–1372/2/11, No. 7/3263- 1372/5/10* and *No. 7/7989- 1376/9/23*.

16. A considerable amount of Persian-language literature has been produced on the issue of women's rights in Iranian law. Some authors, such as Shirin Ebadi, Mostafa Mohaghegh Damad, Hasan Emami and Naser Katuziyan, have written about women's rights in Iran. For instance, Shirin Ebadi in her book, *Women's Rights under the Law of the Islamic Republic of Iran* evaluates laws and regulations pertaining to women in various facets of their lives – within the family and in society with attempts to elucidate and discuss different aspects of women's lives in relation to the law. The book, as explained in the introduction, targets a general readership, to bring awareness to women about their legal rights in Iran. See S. Ebadi, *Hoquq-e Zan dar Qavānin-e Jomhuri-ye Islami-ye Iran {Women's Rights under the Law of the Islamic Republic of Iran}* (Tehran: Ganj-e Dānesh, 1381 [2002]). See also N. Katuziyan, *Doreh-ye Hoqouq-e Madani: Khānevādeh, Jeldeh Aval, Nekāh va Talāq, {Civil Rights: Family, Marriage and Divorce}* (Tehran: Sherkat-e Sahāmi-ye Enteshār, 1387 [2009]); A. Emami, and H. Safai, *Mokhtasar-e Hoquq-e Khānevādeh {Concise Family Law}* (Tehran: Nashr-e Mizān, 1387 [2009]); M. Mohaqegh Damad, *Barrasi-ye Feghhi-ye Hoqugh-e Khānevādeh: Nekāh va Enhelāl-e Ān {A Study of Islamic Jurisprudence With Respect to Family Law: Marriage and Its Termination}* (Tehran: Shābok, 2008). Comparative studies of Iranian laws and the CEDAW have also been carried out by several

researchers and scholars. Mehrangiz Kar's account, *inter alia*, is more comprehensive as it compares different laws concerning women within the Iranian legal system with related articles in the CEDAW and provides solutions for reform whenever possible within the Islamic framework and political context of Iran. See M. Kar, *Raf'-e Tab'iz Az Zanān: Moqāyese-ye Konvānsion-e Raf'-e Tab'iz Az Zanān Bā Qavānin-e Dākheli-ye Iran {Elimination of Discrimination Against Women: A Comparison Between the Convention on the Elimination of All Forms of Discrimination Against Women and Iranian Law}* (Tehran: Nashr-e Qatreh, 1379 [2000]); see also M. Mohammadi, *Māde-ye Shānzdahom-e Konvānsion-e Zanān az Negāhe Feqh-e Shi'eh ({Article 16 of the Women's Convention from the Perspective of Islamic Jurisrudence})* (Qom: Boostān-e Ketāb, 2007); D. Mehrizadegan, M.A. Daeinejad and M. Taher, *Hoqugh-e Zanān:Naqd va Barasi-ye Konvānsion-e-Raf'-e Tab'iz alayhe Zanān {Women's Rights: A Review of the Convention on the Elimination of All Forms of Discrimination Against Women}* (Tehran: Shurā-ye Farhangi Ejtemāei Zanān, 2004); A. Hajari, M. Kaveh Marban, Zahra Ayatollahi, *Hoquq-e Jahāni Zanān:Konvānsion-e-Raf'-e Tab'iz alayhe Zanān {Universal Rights of Women: The Convention on the Elimination of All Forms of Discrimination Against Women}* (Tehran: Shurā-ye Farhangi Zanān, 1381 [2003]); M. Raeisi, *Konvānsion-e Zanān: Barrasi-ye Feqhi va Hoquqi-ye Elhāq ya Edame-ye Elhāqe Jomhuri-ye Islami-ye Iran be Konvānsion-e-Raf'-e Koliye-ye Ashkāle Tab'iz Alayhe Zanān {Women's Convention: Examination of Iran's Accession to the Convention on the Elimination of All Forms of Discrimination against Women from the Legal and Jurisprudential Perspectives}* (Qom: Nasime-Qods, 1381 [2002]).

17. All necessary measures have been taken to ensure that those interviewed for this research have been informed and fully understand its aims and implications. By selecting different groups of interviewees, I tend to utilise different perspectives on the phenomena of my research. The experiences of women activists illuminate my research questions in invaluable ways. Their daily experiences as they struggle for equality within their own households, as well as in society at large, have provided me with tangible examples of the impact of Shari'a in Iran, and also shed light on how this transcends the private sphere and becomes part of Iranian law. I could not interview the clerical figures discussed here, but I have studied their work and interviews provided in a variety of circumstances. The sample of clerics is divided into two subcategories. The fundamentalists are pro-government and follow the patriarchal interpretation of Shari'a, e.g., Ayatollah Ahmad Jannati and Ayatollah Mohammad Taghi Mesbah Yazdi. They do not believe in equality of rights between the sexes. The second group are reformists, such as Ayatollah Yousef Sanei, who object to the governmental interpretation of Shari'a, and has issued *fatwās* in favour of strengthening women's rights. In my view, it is crucial to have his view regarding the reinterpretation of Islamic law in order for it to be more compatible with the needs of modern life.

18. I interviewed Noushin Ahmadi Khorasani, Parvin Ardalan, Maryam Hossein Khaah, Khadijeh Moghadam, Mansooreh Shojaee, Asieh Amini and Sussan Tahmasebi.
19. I interviewed human rights lawyers, e.g., Shirin Ebadi, Nasrin Sutoudeh and Mahnaz Parakand.
20. Some of these MPs have left Iran. I interviewed Mrs Fatemeh Haghighat Joo and Mr Ali Akbar Moosavi.
21. Shirin Ebadi and Hadi Ghaemi, 'The Human Rights Case against Attacking Iran', *The New York Times*, 8 February 2005, p. 25.

Chapter 1 The Development of Universal Standards on Gender Equality: The Convention on the Elimination of All forms of Discrimination Against Women

1. For instance, Ayatollah Mazaheri, head of the Islamic seminary at Esfahan and a traditional religious jurist, is among those who believe that human rights are a Western concept. On the occasion of the possibility of Iran ratifying the CEDAW, he stated that the UN is trying to establish Western dominance and bring about the global hegemony of Western materialistic culture. Cited in P. Ardalan, 'Joining on the Condition to Discriminate', *Bad Jens: Iranian Feminist Newsletter* 5, 22 May 2002, www.badjens.com/fifthedition/joining.htm (accessed 15 January 2017).
2. E. Yahyaoui Krivenko, *Women, Islam and International Law: Within the Context of the Convention on the Elimination of All Forms of Discrimination Against Women* (Leiden and Boston: Martinus Nijhoff Publishers, 2009), p. 3.
3. It might be argued that in this case the term 'Muslim women' only represents the elite and women from the privileged social classes and excludes women from different social sects. This book argues that due to the lack of development in a number of Muslim states, many women are not well empowered, but this does not mean that they do not understand the concept of equality and do not support it. It might be acceptable that they may not be familiar with the legal instruments and international treaties like CEDAW, but the fact that they know the concept of equality of rights between men and women is enough to allow them to contextualise these international standards in their domestic context.
4. Article 2 of the CEDAW.
5. I. Jaising, 'The Convention on the Elimination of All Forms of Discrimination Against Women (CEDAW) and Realization of Rights: Reflection on Standard Settings and Culture', in M. Shivdas and S. Coleman (eds), *Without Prejudice: CEDAW and the Determination of Women's Rights in a Legal and Cultural Context* (London: Commonwealth Secretariat, 2010), p. 13.
6. L.J. Rupp, *Worlds of Women, the Making of an International Women's Movement* (Princeton, New Jersey: Princeton University Press, 1977), pp. 15–33.

NOTES TO PAGES 11–12   221

7. M. Afkhami, 'The Women's Organization of Iran: Evolutionary Politics and Revolutionary Change', in L. Beck and G. Nashat (eds), *Women in Iran: From 1800 to the Islamic Republic* (Urbana and Chicago: University of Illinois Press, 2004), pp. 107–35 at pp. 110–15.
8. The Charter of the United Nations, signed on 26 June 1945. Several provisions of the charter reiterate the goal of achieving gender equality. Article 1(3) provides for the cooperation of member states in solving international problems of an economic, social, cultural or humanitarian character, and in promoting and encouraging respect for human rights and for fundamental freedoms for all without distinction as to race, sex, language or religion. Article 55(c) calls for universal respect for, and observance of human rights and fundamental freedom for all without distinction as to race, sex, language or religion. Article 76(c) asserts an aim to encourage respect for human rights and for fundamental freedoms for all without distinction as to race, sex, language or religion, and to encourage recognition of the interdependence of the peoples of the world.
9. Ibid.
10. Article 68 of the UN Charter states that: 'The Economic and Social Council shall set up Commissions in economic and social fields and for the promotion of human rights, and such other commissions as may be required for the performance of its functions.'
11. Report of the CSW to ECOSOC on the first session of the commission, held at Lake Success, New York, from 10 to 24 February 1947. *UN. Doc.E/281/Rev.1*, 25 February 1947.
12. *193 U.N.T.S. 135*, entered into force 7 July 1954. The Convention on the Political Rights of Women is based on the Charter of the United Nations. Under this convention, State parties commit themselves to grant women, on equal terms with men and without discrimination, the right to vote, to stand for election and to hold public office.
13. *309 U.N.T.S. 65*, entered into force 11 August 1958. In accordance with the provisions of this convention married women have the right to retain their own nationality, and that the loss or acquisition of nationality of a woman shall not be influenced as a result of marriage, dissolution of marriage or change of nationality by the husband during marriage.
14. *521 U.N.T.S. 231*, entered into force 9 December 1964. This convention recognised the requirement of the consent of both parties to entering marriage. The CSW has also assisted a number of specialised UN agencies, such as the United Nations Educational, Social, and Cultural Organisation (UNESCO), and the International Labor Organisation (ILO). Its work with ILO led to the 1951 Convention on Equal Remuneration for Men and Women Workers for Work of Equal Value, which enshrined the principle of equal pay for work of equal value. Adopted on 29 June 1951 by the General Conference of the International Labour Organisation at its thirty-fourth session.

15. Both covenants were adopted by the General Assembly Resolution 2200 A (XXI) of 16 December 1966 and entered into force in 1976.
16. J. Morsink, *The Universal Declaration of Human Rights: Origins, Drafting, and Intent* (Philadelphia, Pennsylvania: University of Pennsylvania Press, 1999), pp. 117–18. See also R. Barlow, *Women's Human Rights and the Muslim Question: Iran's One Million Signature Campaign* (Melbourne, Australia: Melbourne University Press, 2012), p. 39.
17. Morsink, *The Universal*, p. 118.
18. Ibid. See also Barlow, *Women's*, p. 40.
19. Ibid.
20. S. E. Waltz, 'Universal Human Rights: The Contribution of Muslim States', *Human Rights Quarterly* 26 (2004), pp. 799–844 at p. 820. See also Barlow, *Women's*, p. 40.
21. Morsink, *The Universal*, p. 121. See also Barlow, *Women's*, p. 40.
22. Ibid., p. 123.
23. Ibid. For example, Van Istendael, the representative of various Christian groups, pointed out 'if the Declaration proclaimed the right to dissolve marriage, it would be unaccepted to hundreds of millions of Christians in countries that were Members of the United Nations'. Catherine Schaeffer, representative of the International Union of Catholic Women's Leagues, stated that 'her organisation comprised 36 million women divided among 120 associations in 60 countries', all of whose consciences would be offended by the 'principle of the dissolution of marriage'.
24. Sixth Summary Record of the Working Group of the Second Session of the United Nations Human Rights Commission, p. 3, cited in Morsink, *The Universal*, p. 122.
25. Regarding paragraph (1), Article 16 covering the eligibility for marriage, Jamil Baroody of Saudi Arabia argued that the phrase 'full age' did not incorporate the notion of physiological development and should be replaced by the expression 'legal matrimonial age.' Waltz, 'Universal Human Rights', pp. 820–1.
26. United Nations General Assembly Official Records, Third Committee, 3rd Session (7 September–7 December 1948), p. 370.
27. Ibid., p. 347.
28. This word was recommended by the Lebanese delegation and was added with a vote of three to zero, with five abstentions.
29. This phrase was proposed by the Soviet Union and passed by a comfortable two-to-one margin. Morsink, *The Universal*, p. 123.
30. Ibid., p. 125.
31. Report of the Commission on Human Rights to the second session of the Economic and Social Council, 21 May 1946. *UN.Doc. E/38/Rev.1*.
32. Waltz, 'Universal Human Rights', p. 822.
33. The delegate from Yemen noted that the article on equality before the law and equal protection of the law 'did not take into consideration the differences

between the laws of the various countries in particular with regards to marriage, divorce and inheritance.' In response to his statement the Iraqi delegate argued that 'the question of religion had been raised. If all nations lived in accordance with the spirit and the letter of their religion, there would be no need for a covenant on human rights. No covenant could, in any case, demand so much in respect of human rights as Islam did. The Commission on Human Rights should concentrate its attention on the similarities rather than the differences conflicting views on human rights and thereby draft a covenant to protect the common interest of humanity.' Afnan asserted that her delegation 'believed it imperative that the equality of women in regard to [economic, social and cultural rights] should be unequivocally stated. That was the purpose of her amendment.' United Nations General Assembly, Third Committee, 5th Session, 1950, pp. 122, 131 and 258.

In relation to Article 23 covering the right to marry and found a family, some delegations believed that the language used in the article was not strong enough. The representative of Libya, for example, argued that 'the text [m]ust be formulated in such a way as to guarantee the equality of the rights and responsibilities of the spouses, without prejudicing existing family relationship and in conformity with the Charter of the United nations.' She further pointed out that, 'behind the emancipation of women through the world, it was the equality of rights and responsibilities which furnished the incentive and not the privilege and prerogatives.' United Nations General Assembly, Third Committee, 16th Session, 1961, p. 162.

34. Waltz, 'Universal Human Rights', p. 823. Article 3 provides that: 'The States Parties to the present Covenant undertake to ensure the equal right of men and women to the enjoyment of all civil and political rights set forth in the present Covenant.'
35. *The United Nations and the Advancement of Women, 1945–1996* (New York: Department of Public Information, UN, 1995), p. 35.
36. A.S. Fraser, *The UN Decade for Women: Documents and Dialogue* (Boulder, Colorado: Westview Press, 1987), p. 26.
37. Report of the World Conference of the International Women's Year, E/Conf.66/34, http://daccessdds.un.org/doc/UNDOC/GEN/N76/353/95/PDF/N7635395.pdf?OpenElement (accessed 29 March 2017).
38. Afkhami, 'The Women's Organisation of Iran', p. 109.
39. Ibid.
40. Ibid., pp. 115–16.
41. Ibid., pp. 116–23.
42. Ibid., pp. 124–5.
43. *The United Nations and the Advancement of Women, 1945–1996*, p. 43.
44. J.S. Jaquette, 'Losing the Battle/Winning the War: International Politics, Women's Issues, and the 1980 Mid-Decade Conferences', in A. Winslow (ed.), *Women, Politics and the United Nations* (Westport, Connecticut: Greenwood Press, 1995), p. 45. See Also Barlow, *Women's*, p. 46.

45. Barlow, *Women's*, p. 46.
46. Ibid.
47. N. Tohidi, 'Modernity, Islamisation, and Women in Iran', in V. M. Moghadam (ed.), *Gender and National Identity* (London and New Jersey: Zed Books, 1994), p. 126. See also Barlow, *Women's*, p. 47.
48. Ibid. Modernity.
49. For full account of the 8 March event see M. Matin and N. Mohajer, *Khizesh-e Zanān-e Iran dar Esfand-e 1357: Tavalodi Digar {Iranian Women's Uprising, 8 March 1979: Renaissanc}*, Vol. I (Berkeley: Noqteh, 2013). See also, J. Afari and K.B. Anderson, *Foucault and the Iranian Revolution: Gender and the Seductions of Islamism* (Chicago and London: University of Chicago Press, 2005), pp. 111–20.
50. The United Nations and the Advancement of Women, 1945–1996, pp. 44 and 248.
51. ISIS International Bulletin 17 (1980), pp. 30–1. Cited in Fraser, *The UN Decade for Women*, p. 155.
52. *The United Nations and the Advancement of Women, 1945–1996*, pp. 46–7.
53. General Assembly resolution endorsing the Nairobi Forward-Looking Strategies for the Advancement of Women and calling on Governments to take measures toward their implementation. *A/RES/40/108*, 13 December 1985.
54. See Document 84, Report of the World Conference to Review and Appraise the Achievements of the United Nations Decade for Women: Equality, Development and Peace, held in Nairobi from 15 to 26 July 1985. *UN.Doc. A/CONF.116/28/Rev.1* (85.IV.10) 1989. *The United Nations and the Advancement of Women, 1945–1996*. p. 300.
55. See R.P. Dawson, 'When Women Gather: The NGO Forum of the Fourth World Conference on Women, Beijing 1995', *International Journal of Politics, Culture, and Society* 10/1 (Fall 1996), pp. 7–27 and C.H. Bunch and S. Fried, 'Beijing '95: Moving Women's Human Rights from Margin to Center', *Signs* 22/1 (Autumn 1996), pp. 200–204.
56. Report of the Fourth World Conference on Women, *A/CONF.177/20*, 17 October 1995.
57. N. Heyzer and I. Landsberg-Lewis, 'UNIFEM and Women's Climb to Equality: No Turning Back', in M. Afkhami and E. Friedl (eds), *Muslim Women and the Politics of Participation: Implementing the Beijing Platform* (Syracuse, New York: Syracuse University Press, 1997), pp. 153–61 at p. 159.
58. J. Sharifiyan, Rāhbord-e Jomhuri-ye Islami-ye Irān dar Zamineh-ye Hoquq-e Bashar dar Sazmān-e Melal-e Motahed {The Strategy of Islamic Republic of Iran with Respect to Human Rights in the United Nations} (Tehran: Markaz-e Chāp va Enteshārt-e Vezārat-e Omur-e Khārejei, 2001), p. 510.
59. Ibid.
60. For the full text of the speech, see 'Speech of H.E. Ms Shahla Habibi, Presidential Advisor on Women's Affairs for The Fourth World Conference on

Women Beijing September 1995', www.un.org/esa/gopher-data/conf/fwcw/conf/gov/950913181415.txt (accessed 30 January 2017).
61. The United Nations and the Advancement of Women 1945–1996, p. 68.
62. However, the Iranian representative registered the reservation of the Islamic Republic of Iran on the following issues: 'Although the family is the basic unit of society and as such plays a significant role in the advancement of women and promotion of human development, the Platform for Action falls short in recognizing its contribution and the importance of its stability and integrity. Concerning paragraphs 96 and 232 (f), our understanding is that the provisions of those paragraphs can only be interpreted in the context of health and the framework of marital relations between men and women. The Islamic Republic of Iran holds that the rights referred to in those paragraphs fall in the category of existing human rights and do not establish any new rights. The Islamic Republic of Iran upholds the principle that safe and responsible sexual relationships between men and women can only be legitimised within the framework of marriage. Moreover, the phrase "couples and individuals" should also be interpreted in that context. Concerning programmes aimed at sexual and reproductive health, education and services, the Islamic Republic of Iran believes that such education and services should be guided by ethical and moral values and respect the responsibilities, rights and duties of parents, taking into account the evolving capacities of adolescents. With respect to the issue of inheritance, the Islamic Republic of Iran interprets the references in the Platform for Action to this matter in accordance with the principles of the economic system of Islam. The concept of equality in our interpretation takes into account the fact that although women are equal in their human rights and dignity with men, their different roles and responsibilities underline the need for an equitable system of rights, where the particular priorities and requirements of the woman in her multiple roles are accounted for. The Islamic Republic of Iran affirms its commitment to the implementation of the Platform for Action with full respect for Islam and the ethical values of our society'. Fourth World Conference on Women, Beijing, China, 4–15 September 1995, A/CONF.177/20, 17 October 1995.
63. For detailed analysis of this issue see Barlow, *Women's*, pp. 55–8.
64. J. Rostam-Kolayi, 'The Politics of Women's Rights in the Contemporary Muslim World', *Journal of Women's History* 10/4 (1999), pp. 205–15, at 209.
65. Bralow, *Women's*, p. 55. See also Heyzer and Landsberg-Lewis, 'UNIFEM', p. 153.
66. M. Afkhami and E. Friedl, 'Introduction', in M. Afkhami and E. Friedl (eds), *Muslim Women and the Politics of Participation Implementing the Beijing Platform* (Syracuse: Syracuse University Press, 1997), pp. ix–xx.
67. M. Afkhami, 'Claiming Our Rights: A Manual for Women's Human Rights Education in Muslim Societies', in M. Afkhami and E., Friedl (eds), *Muslim Women and the Politics of Participation.* pp. 109–20 at p. 109.

68. Barlow, *Women's*, p. 57. 'The General Assembly, in resolution 52/100, decided to convene a special session to review progress in the implementation of the Nairobi Forward-looking Strategies for the Advancement of Women and the Beijing Declaration and Platform for Action. The special session was to take place five years after the Fourth World Conference on Women (FWCW) which was held in Beijing in 1995.' Five-year Review of the implementation of the Beijing Declaration and Platform for Action (Beijing +5) held in the General Assembly, 5 – 9 June 2000. Available from www.un.org/womenwatch/daw/followup/beijing+5.htm (accessed 8 April 2012. In June 2000, the UN General Assembly adopted a political declaration according to which member states agreed to 'assess regularly further implementation of the Beijing Platform for Action with a view to bringing together all parties involved in 2005 to assess progress and consider new initiatives, as appropriate, ten years after the adoption of the Beijing Platform for Action'. Resolution adopted by the General Assembly, A/RES/S–23/2, 16 November 2000. Ten-year Review and Appraisal of the implementation of the Beijing Declaration and Platform for Action and the outcome of the twenty-third special session of the General Assembly held during the forty-ninth session of the CSW, 28 February to 11 March 2005.
69. 'Iran's Reply to the Questionnaire on the Implementation of the Beijing Platform for Action', www.un.org/womenwatch/daw/followup/responses/Iran.pdf (accessed 29 March 2017).
70. Ibid., p. 4.
71. Ibid., p. 5.
72. Ibid., pp. 4, 7.
73. Barlow, *Women's*, p. 57.
74. The Answer of the Government of the Islamic Republic of Iran to the Questionnaire to Governments on Implementation of the Beijing Platform for Action (1995) and the Outcome of the Twenty-Third Special Session of the General Assembly (2000), www.un.org/womenwatch/daw/Review/responses/IRAN-English.pdf, pp. 33, 38–41 (accessed 1 May 2018).
75. Statement by Delegation of the Islamic Republic of Iran, Fifty-Second Session of the Commission on the Status of Women, Agenda Item 3: Financing for gender equality and empowerment of women, New York, 3 March 2008.
76. After the revolution in 1992, Bureau of Women's Affairs was established. The office was renamed to the Centre for Women's Participation Affairs under administration of Mohammad Khatami. In 2005, under Mahmud Ahmadinejad, the office was renamed to the Centre for Women and Family Affairs. In 2013, the officeholder was promoted to a vice presidency and the office became the Vice Presidency for Women and Family Affairs.
77. H.E. Mrs Maryam Mojtahedzadeh, Advisor to the President and Head of the Centre for Women and Family Affairs of the Islamic Republic of Iran before the 57th Session of the Commission on the Status of Women, New York, 5 March 2013.

78. The other three sections of the UN which merged with UN Women are: the International Research and Training Institute for the Advancement of Women (INSTRAW); the Office of the Special Adviser on Gender Issues and Advancement of Women (OSAGI); and the United Nations Development Fund for Women (UNIFEM). For more information on UN Women see its official website: www.unwomen.org/en/about-us/about-un-women (accessed 1 May 2018).
79. Statement by H.E. Mr Gholamali Khoshroo, Ambassador and Permanent Representative of the Islamic Republic of Iran to the United Nations before the Sixtieth Session of the Commission on the Status of Women, New York, 18 March 2016.
80. Ibid.
81. See W. Vandenhole, *Non-discrimination and Equality in the View of the UN Treaty Bodies* (London: Hart Publishing, 2005).
82. R. Kapur, 'Un-Veiling Equality: Disciplining the "Other" Woman Through Human Rights Discourse', in A.M. Emon, M.S. Eliss and B. Glahn (eds), *Islamic Law and International Human Rights Law: Searching for Common Grounds?* (Oxford: Oxford University Press, 2012), p. 267.
83. Ibid., pp. 267–9.
84. Ibid., p. 271.
85. L. Welchman, 'Musawah, CEDAW, and Muslim Family Laws in the 21st Century', in A.M. Emon, M.S. Eliss and B. Glahn (eds), *Islamic Law and International Human Rights Law: Searching for Common Grounds?* (Oxford: Oxford University Press, 2012), p. 310. See also General Recommendation No. 21 on the core obligations of the States Parties under Article 2 of the Convention on the Elimination of All Forms of Discrimination Against Women, CEDAW/C/2010/47/GC.2, 19 October 2010. Paragraph 5 states: '[a]n identical or neutral treatment of women and men might constitute discrimination against women if such treatment resulted in or had the effect of women being denied the exercise of a right because there was no recognition of the pre-existing gender-based disadvantage and inequality that women face'.
86. General Recommendation No. 28 on the core obligation of the States Parties under Article 2 of the Convention on the Elimination of All Forms of Discrimination Against Women, CEDAW/C/2010/47/GC.2, 19 October 2010, para 8.
87. R. Kapur, 'Un- Veiling Equality', pp. 270–1.
88. Ibid., p. 273.
89. A.E. Mayer, *Islam and Human Rights: Tradition and Politics*, 4th edition (Boulder, Colorado and Oxford: Westview Press, 2007), p. 104.
90. Iran ratified the ICESCR on 24 June 1975. It also ratified ICCPR on the same date without entering any reservations.
91. Human Rights Committee General Comment No. 28 on Equality of Rights between Men and Women (Article 3), 29/03/2000. *CCPR/C/21/Rev.1/Add.10*.

92. Human Rights Committee General Comment No. 18 on Non-discrimination, 21 November 1989, *CCPR/C/21/Rev.1. Add.1*, para. 12.
93. See the Convention on the Elimination of All Forms of Discrimination Against Women, Part 1, available from www.un.org/womenwatch/daw/cedaw/text/econvention.htm (accessed 28 December 2016).
94. In relation to human rights and the question of universality, the existing literature is dominated by two schools of thought. In the view of some academics, the concept of human rights is a strictly Western phenomenon. It is therefore of limited practical value within the context of non-Western societies. This relativist opinion is upheld by scholars such as Adamantia Polis, Peter Schwabb and Makau Mutua. For detailed arguments on the relativist approach, see A. Pollis and P. Schwabb, 'Human Rights: A Western Construct with Limited Applicability', in A. Pollis and P. Schwabb (eds), *Human Rights: Cultural and Ideological Pespectives* (New York: Praeger Publisher, 1979) pp. 1–18; and M. Mutua, 'The Complexity of Universalism in Human Rights', in A. Sajo (ed.), *Human Rights with Modesty: The Problem of Universalism* (Leiden: Martinus Nijhoff Publishers, 2004), pp. 51–64. Supporters of the concept of the universality of human rights, such as Eva Brems and Laith Kubba, posit that the concept of human rights is applicable across the world, despite being a European concept. To understand the view of those authors, see E. Brems, *Human Rights: Universality and Diversity* (The Hague: Martinus Nijhoff Publishers, 2001); and L. Kubba, 'Faith and Modernity: What is liberal Islam?' *Journal of Democracy* 14/2 (2003), pp. 45–49. Some scholars, such as Susan Waltz, have done extensive research to show that Muslim countries were present at the creation of the international standards of human rights, and in fact played a major role in establishing those norms. S.E. Waltz, 'Universal Human Rights: The Contribution of Muslim States', *Human Rights Quarterly* 26 (2004), pp. 799–844 and also S.E. Waltz, 'Universalizing Human Rights: The Role of Small States in the Construction of the Universal Declaration of Human Rights', *Human Rights Quarterly* 23 (2001), pp. 44–72.
95. Baderin in his book *International Human Rights and Islamic Law* argues that: 'Projecting human rights as a strictly Western concept subject to complete West-oriented interpretation was met by counter arguments advocating a culturally relative interpretation of international human rights norms'. The 'cultural relativists' approach generally 'endorses the idea that all values and principles are culture-bound and that there are no universal standards by which culture may be judged'. The advocates of cultural relativism, who are mostly non-Western, claim that 'human rights cannot be interpreted without regard to the cultural differences of people'. M.A. Baderin, *International Human Rights and Islamic Law* (Oxford: Oxford University Press, 2003), p. 27
96. R. Afshari, *Human Rights in Iran: The Abuse of Cultural Relativism* (Philadelphia, Pennsylvania: University of Pennsylvania Press, 2001), p. 4.
97. *Keyhān*, 25 July 1995. The translation of the text is cited in ibid at p. 4.

98. Mayer, *Islam*, p. 72. See also 'Islam a Champion of Human Rights, Official Says', *Compass Newswire*, 28 October 1997, available in Lexis Nexis Library, ALLWLD file.
99. *Āzād*, 6 February 2002. Quoted in P. Ardalan, 'Joining on the Condition to Discriminate', *Bad Jens: Iranian Feminist Newsletter* 5, 22 May 2002, www.badjens.com/fifthedition/joining.htm (accessed 18 January 2017).
100. M. Torabi, 'Interview with the Head of the Parliament's Committee for Women and Family Affairs, Fatemeh Alia', *Press TV*, 8 December 2007, http://edition.presstv.ir/detail/34194.html (accessed 28 January 2017).
101. Ibid.
102. Ibid. See also President Ahmadinejad's view of the West's 'instrumental' approach towards women; he has argued that 'Nothing is left of women's prestige in Europe and some other countries'. In his view, the Western countries 'take advantage of women there to advertise for their goods, and this shows how worthless they consider the value of women there.' While addressing Western societies, he reiterated: 'The atmosphere you have created for the women in your countries has deprived them of the opportunity for growth and perfection, while we believe in a way women and men are equals, but this equality is regarding their basic rights.' Ahmadinejad, 'Reform Needed in West's Instrumental Approach Towards Women', January 2010, www.women.gov.ir/en/pages/content.php?id=553 (accessed 30 January 2017). See also Shahla Habibi's speech at the Fourth World Conference on Women, where she stated: 'As reiterated by the Symposium on the Role of Women in Islamic Society, which was held in Tehran (17–19 April 1995), and sponsored by the Organization of the Islamic Conference, Islam views men and women as two partners complementing and not competing with each other. They are equal in creation, human dignity, human rights, and responsibility towards the welfare of the family as well as their society. Islam 1400 years ago has recognised and ensured through its principles, the economic, social and political rights of women. Women, in divine conception, are not created to be exploited as sex objects or become victims of profit oriented economic growth'. 'Speech of H.E. Ms Shahla Habibi, Presidential Advisor on Women's Affairs for The Fourth World Conference on Women, Beijing, September 1995'. Available at www.un.org/esa/gopher-data/conf/fwcw/conf/gov/950913181415.txt (accessed 30 January 2017).
103. Quoted in Ardalan, 'Joining on the Condition to Discriminate'.
104. Ibid.
105. See Baderin, *International*, pp. 58–66, 133–53.
106. Ibid., pp. 60, 65.
107. Quoted in ibid., p. 60. The full text of the Cairo Declaration on Human Rights in Islam is available from: http://hrlibrary.umn.edu/instree/cairodeclaration.html (accessed 1 May 2018).
108. Mayer, *Islam*, pp. 101–102.
109. Ibid., pp. 102–103.

110. Z. Mir-Hosseini, 'Islam and Gender Justice', in V.J. Cornell and O. Safi (eds), *Voices of Islam*, Vol. 5: Voices of Diversity and Change (Westport, Connecticut: Praeger, 2007), pp. 85–113.
111. Ibid., pp. 87–103.
112. F. Mernissi, *The Veil and the Male Elite*, Mary Jo Lakeland (trans) (New York: Basic Books, 1991), p. 195.
113. Ibid.
114. A. Pal, 'Shirin Ebadi's Interview', *The Progressive*, September 2004. http://progressive.org/magazine/helen-thomas-interview/ (accessed 5 February 2017).
115. Z. Mir-Hosseini, 'Women in Search of Common Ground: Between Islamic and International Human Rights Law', in A.M. Emon, M.S. Eliss and B. Glahn (eds), *Islamic Law and International Human Rights Law: Searching for Common Grounds?* (Oxford: Oxford University Press, 2012), p. 302.
116. One of the major tasks of the CSW was to draft the Convention on the Elimination of All Forms of Discrimination Against Women. The CSW aimed at preparing the draft to be presented at the Copenhagen conference in 1980, and with this task the commission adopted the draft, which was prepared by the special working group, and sent it to the UN General Assembly for approval. On December 1979, the draft was debated at the Third Committee of the General Assembly and a working group was established to carefully consider the text of the convention. On 18 December 1979, the General Assembly adopted the Convention on the Elimination of All Forms of Discrimination Against Women. The convention was presented during the opening ceremony of the Copenhagen conference.
117. In accordance with Article 27, paragraph 1 of the CEDAW.
118. For more information about States Parties to the Convention see the UN website: http://treaties.un.org/Pages/ViewDetails.aspx?src=TREATY&mtdsg_no=IV-8&chapter=4&lang=en (accessed 1 May 2018).
119. The protocol aims to strengthen the convention by providing a means to enable individuals or groups of people to bring complaints of violation of the provisions of the CEDAW. The protocol provides for an individual complaint procedure and provides for an inquiry procedure under which the Committee can initiate inquiries into situations of grave or systematic violations of women's rights. Articles 2, 8, 9 and 10 of the Optional Protocol to the CEDAW.
120. B. Andrew, 'The Convention on the Elimination of All Forms of Discrimination Against Women', in W. Benedek, E.M. Kisaakye and G. Oberleitner, *The Human Rights of Women: International Instruments and African Experiences* (London: Zed Books, 2002), p. 120.
121. Article 1 of the CEDAW.
122. Charlesworth, *The Boundaries*, p. 217.
123. Andrew, *The Convention*, p. 120.
124. Yahyaoui Krivenko, *Women, Islam*, p. 22.

NOTES TO PAGES 34-35   231

125. Article 2 (f)–(g) of the CEDAW. Provision of Article 2 (f) is related to the obligations in Article 5 (a).
126. See, for example, Concluding Observation (CO) Thailand, *A/61/38*, 34th Session (2006) paras 274–5.
127. See, for example, Concluding Observation (CO) Uganda, *A/57/38* (Supp) part II, Exceptional session (2002) paras 153–4; Concluding Observation (CO) Mozambique, *A/62/38*, 38th Session (2007) paras 167–8.
128. See, for example, Concluding Observation (CO) Gabon, *A/60/38*, 32nd Session (2005), para 231.
129. See M.A. Freeman, C. Chinkin and B. Rudolf (eds), *The UN Convention on the Elimination of All Forms of Against Discrimination Women* (Oxford: Oxford University Press, 2012), p. 90.
130. Concluding Observation (CO) Kyrgyzstan, *CEDAW/C/KGZ/CO/3* (2008) paras 11–12; Concluding Observation (CO) Kenya, *CEDAW/C/KEN/CO/6* (2007) paras 17–18.
131. See, for example, Concluding Observation (CO) Lebanon, *A/60/38*, 33rd Session (2005) paras 97–8; CO Mongolia, *CEDAW/C/MNG/CO/7* (2008) para 17; Concluding Observation (CO) Cameroon, *CEDAW/C/CMR/CO/3* (2009) paras 14–15; Concluding Observation (CO) Mozambique, *A/62/38*, 38th Session (2007) paras 165 and 168.
132. And also, Article 5 (a) of the CEDAW.
133. Freeman et al., *The UN Convention*, p. 91.
134. See General Recommendation 28, para 22 and General Recommendation 27, paras 16 and 36.
135. Freeman et al., *The UN Convention*, p. 91. See also CO Burkina Faso, *A/55/38*, 22.
136. Ibid., p. 92. See *UN Doc E/CN.6/SR.638* paras 29–39.
137. See UN Doc E/CN.6/SR.638 para 32.
138. Freeman et al., *The UN Convention*, p. 92.
139. See, for example, Concluding Observation (CO) Lebanon, *A/6038*, 33rd Session (2005) paras 103–104; Concluding Observation (CO) Iraq, *A/55/38*, 22nd Session (2000) paras 193–4; Concluding Observation (CO) Syrian Arab Republic, *A/6238*, 38th Session (2007) paras 129–30.
140. Concluding Observation (CO) Yemen, *CEDAW/C/YEM/CO/6* (2008) paras 18–19.
141. See, for example, Concluding Observation (CO) Lebanon, *CEDAW/C/LBN/CO/3* (2008) para 26 and Concluding Observation (CO) Syrian Arab Republic, *A/6238*, 38th Session (2007) paras 129–30.
142. See Chapter 5 for a detailed analysis of the opposition to article 2 which emerged during the Majles sessions dedicated to discussion of the CEDAW.
143. Iran is a signatory to the ICCPR and ICESCR. Article 3 of both covenants deal with gender equality.
144. Freeman et al., *The UN Convention*, p. 422.

145. See, for example, Concluding Observation (CO) Turkey, *CEDAW/C/TUR/CO/6*(2010) paras 40–1 and Concluding Observation (CO) Japan, *CEDAW/C/JPM/CO/6*(2009), paras 17–18.
146. For detailed analysis of this issue see chapter 2, pp. 104–21.
147. See Chapter 2, pp. 83–91.
148. The Committee on the Elimination of Discrimination Against Women, General Recommendation No. 21: Equality in Marriage and Family Relations, 13th Session, 1994, para 16.
149. See Freeman et al., *The UN Convention*, pp. 422–4.
150. General Recommendation No. 21, para 17.
151. Ibid., paras 11 and 13.
152. Ibid., para 12.
153. Ibid.
154. Ibid., paras 14–29.
155. See Chapter 3.
156. For a comprehensive examination of the regime of reservations to the CEDAW see B. Clark, 'The Vienna Convention Reservations Regime and the Convention on Discrimination Against Women', *The American Journal of International Law*, 85/2 (April 1991), pp. 281–321; R.J. Cook, 'Reservations to the Convention on the Elimination of All Forms of Discrimination against Women', *Virginia Journal of International Law* 30 (1989–1990), p. 643; A. Jenefsky, 'Permissibility of Egypt's Reservation to the Convention on the Elimination of All Forms of Discrimination Against Women', *Maryland Journal of International Law and Trade*, 15/2 (Fall 1991), pp. 199–233; Yahyaoui Krivenko, *Women, Islam*, pp. 115–208; M. Brandt and J.A. Kaplan, 'The Tension between Women's Rights and Religious Rights: Reservations to CEDAW by Egypt, Bangladesh and Tunisia', *Journal of Law and Religion*, 12/1 (1995–1996), pp. 105–42; J. Riddle, 'Making CEDAW Universal: A Critique of the CEDAW's Reservation Regime under Article 28 and the Effectiveness of the Reporting Process', *George Washington Law Review* 23 (2002), pp. 605–38; Reservations to the Convention on the Elimination of All Forms of Discrimination Against Women: Weakening the Protection of Women from Violence in the Middle East and North Africa Region (Amnesty International, 2004).
157. A. An-Na'im, 'The Rights of Women and International Law in the Muslim Context', *Whittier Law Review* 9 (1987), pp. 491–516 at p. 493.
158. A reservation is a 'unilateral statement, however phrased or named, made by a State, when signing, ratifying, accepting, approving, or acceding to a treaty, whereby it purports to exclude or to modify the legal effect of certain provisions of the treaty in their application to the State'. Vienna Convention on the Law of treaties, Article 2 (d).
159. For instance, Egypt entered a general reservation to Article 2, declaring 'The Arab Republic of Egypt is willing to comply with the content of this article, provided that such compliance does not run counter to the Islamic

Shari'a'. Therefore, although Egypt did not submit reservations to every provision of the convention that is in contradiction with the Shari'a, its reservation to Article 2 allows Egypt to not abide by provisions that are contradictory to the Shari'a. As Anna Jenefsky has noted: 'Such a broad reservation to the central provision of the Women's Convention appears to frustrate the Convention's primary purpose of eliminating discrimination against women at the domestic level. The argument that permitting Egypt to make its reservation to Article 2 may be the only way to elicit Egypt's adoption of the Convention carries little force because Article 2 is the most important provision of the Convention. Egypt's broad reservation to Article 2 is therefore incompatible with the object and purpose of the Women's Convention'. Jenefsky, *Permissibility of Egypt's Reservation*, p. 211. See also Brandt, *The Tension*, pp. 110–21.

160. For instance, Algeria, Bahrain, Egypt, Iraq, Jordan, Kuwait, Malaysia, Morocco, Oman, Syria and the UAE have entered reservations to Article 9. Some reservations entered regarding the article are not based on Shari'a. For example, Egypt's reservation, which is about providing equal rights to men and women where the nationality of their children is concerned, may be due more to the country's national policy than the Shari'a.

161. Algeria, Bahrain, Jordan, Niger, Oman, Syria, Tunisia and the UAE are amongst those countries that have entered reservations on Article 15.

162. For instance, Iraq's reservation to Article 16 reads as follows: 'Reservation to this article shall be without prejudice to the provisions of the Islamic Shari'a according women rights equivalent to the rights of their spouses so as to ensure a just balance between them'. Islamic law is the primary source of the Personal Statue Code in Iraq and, therefore, the reason for reservation to Article 16 was 'Iraq's concern to meet its international obligations under the Convention, on the one hand, and its commitment to its own cultural and legal heritage, as represented by Islamic law, on the other.' See Combined Second and Third Periodic Reports of Iraq, submitted on 19 October 1999, *CEDAW/C/IRQ/2–3*, p. 25. The issue of the dissolution of marriage is one of the most complicated issues and therefore a main cause for concern for the Iraqi Government. The claim that 'the Iraqi legislation regulating marriage, its legal effects and its dissolution guarantee the equal rights of the spouses in accordance with Islamic law' gives rise to the question regarding to which extent Islamic law is compatible with the concept of equality framed under the CEDAW. For instance, as it is clear from the reports, the grounds for and procedures of the dissolution of marriage are not the same for men and women. See Combined Second and Third Periodic Reports of Iraq, submitted on 19 October 1999, *CEDAW/C/IRQ/2–3*, pp. 26–29. Since the fall of Saddam Hussein's regime in Iraq in 2003 and due to subsequent political and social changes, the correct application of the existing laws has been severely affected. A new constitution was adopted in 2005 according to which Islam is the official religion and source of legislation. According to Article 41 of the constitution 'Iraqis are free in their commitments to their personal status

according to their religious, sects, beliefs, or choice, and this shall be regulated by law'. This article welcomes different interpretations, which in fact would be detrimental to the situation of women. See Krivenko, *Women, Islam*, p. 146, and Article 41 of the Constitution of Iraq. Cited in ibid.
163. One hundred and eighty-eight countries have ratified the CEDAW. This means that over 90 per cent of the members of the United Nations are party to the convention. Many States Parties to the convention have entered reservations to one or more of its articles to limit or qualify their obligations under the related provisions set out in the convention. Although reservations about a treaty are acceptable under international law, states are not free to enter any kind of reservation. Article 28 (2) of the CEDAW permits reservations that are not 'incompatible with the object and purpose' of the convention.
164. C. Chinkin, 'Thoughts on the UN Convention on the Elimination of All Forms of Discrimination Against Women (CEDAW)', in M. Shivdas and S. Coleman, *Without Prejudice: CEDAW and the Determination of Women's Rights in a Legal and Cultural Context* (London: Commonwealth Secretariat, 2010), p. 7.
165. Arguments surrounding Iran's ratification of the CEDAW will be discussed in full detail in the next chapter.
166. Yahyaoui Krivenko, *Women, Islam*, p. 169.
167. For the full text of the basic law, see the Saudi foreign ministry's official website: www.mofa.gov.sa/sites/mofaen/aboutKingDom/SaudiGovernment/Pages/BasicSystemOfGovernance35297.aspx (accessed 1 April 2017).
168. S. Mtango, 'A State of Oppression? Women's Rights in Saudi Arabia', *Asia-Pacific Journal on Human Rights and the Law* 5 (2004), pp. 49–67 at p. 49.
169. Ibid., p. 52.
170. E. Doumato, 'The Ambiguity of Shari'a and the Politics of "Rights" in Saudi Arabia', in M. Afkhami (ed.), *Faith and Freedom: Women's Human Rights in the Muslim World* (Syracuse: Syracuse University Press, 1995), p. 135 at p. 143.
171. Ibid., p. 146.
172. Ibid.
173. Mtango, 'A State of Oppression?', p. 53.
174. Yahyaoui Krivenko, *Women, Islam*, p. 167.
175. Combined Initial and Second Periodic Report of Saudi Arabia Submitted on 29 March 2007, *UN Doc. CEDAW/C/SAU/2*, pp. 10–11.
176. Ibid., p. 11.
177. Saudi Arabia Response to Questions Listed in Document Number *CEDAW/C/SAU/Q/2*, 18 December 2007, *UN Doc. CEDAW/C/SAU/Q/2/Add.1*, question 16 at pp. 14–15. Elections for office are not allowed in general except in two capacities: elections for 3/4 seats of the municipal councils, made permissible for women in 2015, and elections for the seats of the chambers of commerce made up mainly from business-affiliated women, open to women since 2005.
178. For further information see: https://www.nytimes.com/2018/06/22/opinion/saudi-arabia-salman-women-driving.html and https://agsiw.org/womens-labor-force-participation-across-gcc/

179. R. Newcomb, *Women of Fes: Ambiguities of Urban Life in Morocco* (Philadelphia, Pennsylvania: University of Pennsylvania Press, 2009), p. 192.
180. J. Hursh, 'Advancing Women's Rights Through Islamic Law: The Example of Morocco, *Berkeley Journal of Gender, Law and Justice* 27 (2012), pp. 252–305 at p. 256.
181. Ibid.
182. Ibid., p. 257.
183. L.H. Skalli, Through a Local Prism: Gender, Globalisation, and Identity in Moroccan Women's Magazines (Lanham, Maryland: Lexington Books, 2006), p. 177. Cited in ibid.
184. For the full text of Morocco's reservations and declarations, see the UN Women website: www.un.org/womenwatch/daw/cedaw/reservations-country.htm (accessed 2 April 2017).
185. The reservation to Article 16 goes further and states: 'The provisions of the Islamic Shari'a oblige the husband to provide a nuptial gift upon marriage and to support his family, while the wife is not required by law to support the family. Further, at dissolution of marriage, the husband is obliged to pay maintenance. In contrast, the wife enjoys complete freedom of disposition of her property during the marriage and upon its dissolution without supervision by the husband, the husband having no jurisdiction over his wife's property. For these reasons, the Shari'a confers the right of divorce on a woman only through the decision of a Shari'a judge'. Ibid.
186. Ibid.
187. F. Sadiqi and M. Ennaji, 'The Feminisation of Public Space: Women's Activism, the Family Law, and Social Change in Morocco', *Journal of Middle East Women's Studies* 12/2 (Spring 2006), pp. 86–114 at p. 105.
188. See K. Zoglin, 'Morocco's Family Code: Improving Equality for Women', *Human Rights Quarterly* 31 (2009), pp. 649–984 at p. 968. See also: Z. Mir-Hosseini, 'How the Door of Ijtihad Was Opened and Closed: A Comparative Analysis of Recent Family Law Reform in Iran and Morocco', Washington and Lee Law RevieD, Vol. 64 (2007), pp. 1499–151. And Z. Salime, Between Feminisim and Islam: Human Rights and Sharia Law in Morocco, University of Minnesota Press, 2011.
189. Ibid., p. 969.
190. Hursh, 'Advancing Women's Rights', p. 259. See also M. Ennaji, The New Muslim Personal Status Law in Morocco: Context, Proponents, Adversaries, and Arguments. www.fmyv.es/ci/in/family/1.pdf (accessed 2 April 2017).
191. Yahyaoui Krivenko, *Women, Islam*, pp. 162–3. According to Article 8 of the Moroccan Law of Personal Status which was applicable previously, the age of marriage for boys was eighteen and for girls was fifteen. Cited in Ibid.
192. Article 51 of the Family Code of Morroco (2004). Cited in ibid.
193. 'Morocco: Morocco Withdraws Reservations to CEDAW', *Women Living under Muslim Laws*, 18 December 2008, www.wluml.org/node/4941 (accessed 2 April 2017).

194. Ibid.
195. Weingartner categorises Moroccan women's problem in four types: '1) adequacy of formation of judges and functionaries to implement the reforms; 2) investment in education of the public at large regarding the reforms; 3) inherent injustice of polygamy in any case; and 4) remaining perception of ambiguities regarding divorce and child custody'. L.A. Weingartner, 'Family Law & Reform in Morocco – The Mudawana: Modernist Islam and Women's Rights in the Code of Personal Status', *University of Detroit Mercy Law Review* 82 (2005), pp. 687–713, p. 711. See also L.H. Skalli, 'Women and Poverty in Morocco: The Many Faces of Social Exclusion', *Feminist Review* 69, The Realm of the Possible: Middle Eastern Women in Political and Social Spaces (Winter 2001), pp. 73–89.
196. C.H. Bunch, 'Women's Human Rights: The Challenges of Global Feminism and Diversity', in M. Dekoven (ed.), *Feminist Locations: Global and Local, Theory and Practice* (New Brunswick, New Jersey and London: Rutgers University Press, 2001) pp. 129–46 at p. 131.
197. Ibid., p. 134.
198. Benazir Bhutto, Beijing, 4 September 1995. www.cfwd.org.uk/uploads/Benazir%20Bhutto.pdf (accessed 1 May 2018).
199. In the words of Rebecca Barlow, 'The contemporary Iranian women's movement can be seen as part of an ongoing tradition of Muslim women's meaningful engagement with, and contributions to, the international framework on women's rights and gender equality'. Barlow, *Women's*, p. 58.
200. Chinkin, 'Thoughts on the UN Convention', p. 7.

Chapter 2   The Political and Legal System of the Islamic Republic of Iran

1. For example, in case of polygamy Grand Ayatollah Sanei stated: 'If the first wife does not permit her husband to take another wife, the marriage will not be legitimate, even if a man can support both wives financially'. This statement is available from his official website at http://saanei.org/?view=02,01,09,15,0#02,00,00,00,0 (accessed 10 December 2017).
2. For a detailed analysis of the process of the law-making in Iran see: N. Katuziyan, Moqadameh-ye Elm-e Hoquq va Motāle'-e dar Nezām Hoquqi-ye Iran [Introduction to Jurisprudence and Study in the Legal System of Iran] (Tehran: Sherkat-e Sahāmi-ye Enteshār, 1373 [1994]), pp. 119–220.
3. Ibid., p. 119. Therefore, this definition only includes the laws enacted by the Majles and approved by the Guardian Council or adopted by the Expediency Council. Some writers consider a general definition of law, arguing that law is the total legal culture, comprising not only rules and institutions, but also the response of the society to law. P. Konz, 'Legal Development in Developing Countries', *Proceedings of the American Society of International Law* 63 (1969), pp. 91, 94–5, 97–100. Cited in A. Ansaripour, 'The Role of the Council of

NOTES TO PAGES 48–51   237

Guardians in the Islamicization of Iranian Law', in E. Cotran and M. Lau, *Yearbook of Islamic and Middle Eastern Law* 16: 2010–2011 (Leiden and Boston: Brill, 2012), pp. 127–46 at p. 128.

4. S. Ebadi, Hoquq-e Zan dar Qavānin-e Jomhuri-ye Islami-ye Iran [Women's Rights under the Law of the Islamic Republic of Iran] (Tehran: Ganj-e Dānesh, 1381 [2002]), pp. 20–1.
5. For a detailed account of the history of ancient Iran see H. Pirniya, *Irān-e Bāstān yā Tārikh-e Mofasal-e Irān-e Qadim {Ancient Iran or a Detailed History of Ancient Persia}*, Vol. 1 (Tehran: Majles, 1311 [1932]).
6. A. Perikhanian, *The Book of a Thousand Judgements: A Sasanian Law-Book*, Translated from Russian by Nina Garsoïan (Costa Mesa, California and New York: Mazda Publishers in association with Bibliotheca Persica, 1997).
7. For a detailed analysis of Iran's legal and political history see, among others, F. Adamiyat, *Andisheh-ye Taraqi va Hokumat-e Qānun: Asr-e Sepahsālār {Progressive Thought and Rule of Law: Sepehsalar Era}* (Tehran: Sherkat-e Sahāmi-ye Entesharāt-e Khārazmi, 1352 [1973]); E. Abrahamian, *A History of Modern Iran* (New York: Cambridge University Press, 2008); F. Adamiyat, *Fekr-e Demokrāsi-ye Ejtemāi dar Nehzat-e Mashrutiyat-e Iran {The Idea of Democracy in the Constitutional Movement}* (Tehran: Entesharāt-e Payām, 1355 [1976]); E. Abrahamian, *Iran Between Two Revolutions* (Princeton, New Jersey: Princeton University Press, 1983).
8. A. Abghari, Introduction to the Iranian Legal System and the Protection of Human Rights in Iran [Moqaddame-i Bar Nezām-e Hoquqi-ye Iranan Va Hemāyat az Hoquq-e Bashar dar Iran] (London: British Institute of International and Comparative Law, 2008), p. 31.
9. M. Mohammadi, *Judicial Reform and Reorganization in 20th Century Iran: State-Building, Modernization and Islamicization* (New York and London: Routledge, 2008), p. 46.
10. Abghari, Introduction, pp. 36–8.
11. Mohammadi, *Judicial Reform*, pp. 42, 44.
12. P. Paidar, *Women and the Political Process in Twentieth-Century Iran* (Cambridge: Cambridge University Press, 1995), p. 40. For a detailed analysis of State and society under the Qajars see E. Abrahamian, *A History*, pp. 8–62. See also W. Floor, 'Changes and Development in the Judicial System of Qajar Iran (1800–1925)', in E. Bosworth and C. Hillenbrand (eds), *Qajar Iran* (Edinburgh, 1983).
13. Paidar, *Women*, p. 40.
14. Adamiyat, *Andisheh-ye Taraqi*, pp. 196–207.
15. Ibid., p. 217.
16. Mohammadi, *Judicial Reform*, p. 47.
17. Abrahamian, *A History*, p. 35.
18. Ibid., p. 45.
19. The constitution was ratified in December 1906 and the supplementary laws were adopted in October 1907. The constitutional text of 1906 consisted of a short preamble and fifty-one articles. For the English text of the constitution, see

A.A. Marayati, *Middle Eastern Constitutions and Electoral Laws* (New York, Washington and London, 1965), pp. 4–31. 'These two documents, with minor amendments, survived as the fundamental laws of the land all the way to the 1979 revolution at least on paper'. Abrahamian, *A History*, p. 47.
20. For the historical background of the Constitutional Revolution see A. Kasravi, *Tarikh-e Mashruteh-ye Iran {The History of the Constitutional Revolution of Iran}* (Tehran: Moaseseh-ye Entesharat-e Amir Kabir, 1363 [1984]); H. Moaser, *Tarikh-e Esteqrar-e Mashrutiyat dar Iran: Mostakhrajeh az Asnad Mahramaneh Vezarat-e Omur-e Kharejeh Englestan {History of the Constitutional Movement in Iran: Based On Documents from the British Foreigh Office Archives}*, Vols. 1 & 2 (Tehran: Entesharat-e Ebn-e Sina, 1352 [1973]); N.I. Kermani (with the assistance of Ali Akbar Saeidi Sirjani), *Tarikh-e Bidari-ye Iranian {History of the Iranian Awakening}*, Vols. 1 & 2 (Tehran: Moaseseh Entesharat-e Agah, 1361 [1982]) and F. Adamiyat *Ideoloji-ye Nehzat-e Mashrutiyat-e Iran {On the Ideology of the Constitutional Movement in Iran}*, Vol. 1 (Tehran: Entesharat-e Payam, 2535 Shahanshahi [1974]).
21. Article 27 of the constitution guaranteed the separation of powers. For the full text of Article 27 of the Constitution of Iran (1906) see Abghari, *Introduction*, p. 39.
22. Ibid., p. 41.
23. Ettehadieh, M., 'The Origins and Development of the Women's Movement in Iran, 1906–41', in L. Beck and G. Nashat (eds), *Women in Iran: From 1800 to the Islamic Republic* (Urbana and Chicago: University of Illinois Press, 2004), pp. 86–95 at pp. 91–4.
24. Mohammadi, *Judicial Reform*, p. 68.
25. Ibid., pp. 68–9.
26. Abrahamian, *A History*, pp. 54–62.
27. Ibid., p. 65.
28. As a result, the judicial power of clerical courts became less significant even at the provincial level and in religious cities like Mashhad and Qom.
29. Mohammadi, *Judicial Reform*, pp. 83–6.
30. Abrahamian, *A History*, pp. 87–8.
31. These civil matters were disputes about the validity of marriage and divorce; hearing of disputes where resolution is not possible except by witnesses or oaths and cases dealing with the appointment of a trustee, guardian or executor of a will.
32. Mohammadi, *Judicial Reform*, pp. 96–7.
33. Watson, 1983, p. 1156. Cited in ibid., p. 95.
34. Afkhami M., 'The Women's Organisation of Iran: Evolutionary Politics and Revolutionary Change', in L. Beck, *Women in Iran*, p. 126. Written correspondence with Mahnaz Afkhami, former head of WOI, 21 May 2014.
35. Cited in Paidar, *Women*, p. 142.
36. Afkhami, *Women's*, p. 114.
37. Paidar, *Women*, p. 148; See also Abrahamian, *A History*, pp. 149–54.

38. SAVAK or *Sāzemān-e Ettelā'āt va Amniyat-e Keshvar {Organisation of Intelligence and National Security}* was established by Mohammad Reza Pahlavi to maintain domestic security. This organisation, which acted as a secret police and intelligence service, operated from 1957 to 1979. According to Paidar, SAVAK was created with 'the help of the CIA and the Israeli secret service MOSAD'. Paidar, *Women*, p. 135.
39. Ibid., pp. 172, 186.
40. Mohammadi, *Judicial Reform*, p. 109.
41. By the mid-1970s, more than 68 per cent of civil servants; 82 per cent of registered companies; 50 per cent of manufacturing production; 66 per cent of university students, 50 per cent of doctors; 42 per cent of hospital beds; 40 per cent of the cinema-going public; 70 per cent of travellers abroad; 72 per cent of printing presses; 80 per cent of newspaper readers belonged to Tehran, which only constituted 20 per cent of Iran's population. F. Kazemi, *Poverty and Revolution in Iran* (New York: New York University Press, 1980), p. 25.
42. FitzGerald, 'Giving the Shah Everything He Wants'. Cited in Abrahamian, *A History*, pp. 142–3.
43. For a detailed analysis of the 'social and political tensions' that led to the revolution, see Abrahamian, *A History*, pp. 123–54.
44. Ebadi, interview by the author, London, June 2017.
45. Mohammadi, *Judicial Reform*, p. 130.
46. Ibid., p. 131.
47. Interview of the Ayatollah Khomeini by Reuters on 26 October 1978. Cited in A. Schirazi, *The Constitution of Iran: Politics and the State in the Islamic Republic*, J. O'Kane (trans) (London: I.B.Tauris, 1997), p. 24.
48. Ibid.
49. For a detailed account of this issue see S. Randjbar-Daemi, 'Building the Islamic State: The Draft Constitution of 1979 Reconsidered', *Iranian Studies*, 46/4 (2013), pp. 641–63.
50. Schirazi, *Constitution*, p. 22.
51. Bazargan was appointed prime minister of the provisional government in a decree on 4 February 1979 issued by Ayatollah Khomeini.
52. M. Hashemi, Qānun-e Asāsi-ye Jomhuri-ye Islami-ye Iran [The Constitution of the Islamic Republic of Iran] (Tehran: Mizān Publication, 1386 [2008]), p. 54.
53. Ibid., p. 55.
54. Schirazi, *Constitution*, p. 31.
55. Ibid., p. 33.
56. Ibid.
57. Article 1 of the Constitution of Iran (1979). For the English text of the constitution before the amendment, see R.K. Ramazani, 'Document: Constitution of the Islamic Republic of Iran', *The Middle East Journal* 34 (1980), pp. 181–204. And for the English text after its amendment, see

A.P. Blaustein and G.H. Flanz (eds), *Constitution of the Countries of the World*, Vol. VIII (New York, 1994).
58. Article 12 of the Constitution of Iran (1979).
59. Article 4 of the Constitution of Iran (1979). See the following section of this chapter for an explanation of the Guardian Council.
60. Article 72 of the Constitution of Iran (1979).
61. Article 170 of the Constitution of Iran (1979).
62. Article 19 of the Constitution of Iran (1979).
63. Article 20 of the Constitution of Iran (1979).
64. Article 4 of the Constitution of Iran (1979).
65. Paidar, *Women*, p. 257.
66. Ibid., p. 258.
67. 'Women in the Constitution', Preamble of the Constitution of Iran (1979).
68. The goals mentioned in Article 21 are as follows:

   (1) create a favourable environment for the growth of a woman's personality and the restoration of her rights, both the material and intellectual;
   (2) the protection of mothers, particularly during pregnancy and child-rearing, and the protection of children without guardians;
   (3) establishing competent courts to protect and preserve the family;
   (4) the provision of special insurance for widows, aged women, and women without support;
   (5) the awarding of guardianship of children to worthy mothers to protect the interests of the children in the absence of a legal guardian.

69. Paidar, *Women*, p. 260.
70. Ibid., p. 262.
71. According to the preamble of the constitution: 'the basic characteristic of this revolution, which distinguishes it from other movements that have taken place in Iran during the past hundred years, is its ideological and Islamic nature. After experiencing the anti-despotic constitutional and the anti-colonialist nationalization of oil movements, the Muslim people of Iran learned from these costly experiences that the obvious and fundamental reason for these movements' failures was their lack of an ideological basis. Although the Islamic line of thought and the direction provided by militant religious leaders played an essential role in these recent movements, the struggles waged in the course of those movements quickly fell into stagnation due to their departure from genuine Islamic positions. Thus, it was that the awakened conscience of the nation, under the leadership of Imam Khomeini, came to perceive the necessity of pursuing a genuinely Islamic and ideological line in its struggles. This time, the militant *'olamā'* of the country, who had always been at the forefront of popular movements, together with committed writers and intellectuals, found new impetus by following his leadership'. The English translation of the constitution is available at: www.servat.unibe.ch/icl/ir00000_.html (accessed 10 February 2017).

NOTES TO PAGES 60-61

72. Article 1108 of the Civil Code of Iran. Cited in F. Badrian, *The Civil Code of Iran* (Tehran: Entesharat-e Daneshvar, 2001).
73. Article 1106 of the Civil Code of Iran.
74. According to the constitutional text amended in 1989 and currently valid, Article 110 defines this supervisory authority.
75. For detailed information about the functioning of the Majles and Guardian Council, see Hashemi, *Hoquq-e Asasi-ye*, pp. 85–264.
76. For detailed analyses of the Expediency Council, see ibid., pp. 539–603.
77. Article 73 of the Constitution of Iran (1979).
78. The Majles' commissions include:

    (6) Education and research;
    (7) Social;
    (8) Economy;
    (9) National security and foreign policy;
    (10) Energy
    (11) Planning and budget;
    (12) Health;
    (13) Industry and mining;
    (14) Development;
    (15) Culture;
    (16) Judicial and legal affairs;
    (17) Agriculture;
    (18) Petitions commission, which has the task of investigating complaints of the public against government organisations.

    Articles 29–45 of the Rules of Procedure of the Majles. The Persian version of this law is available from: http://rc.majlis.ir/fa/law/show/99673 (accessed 12 February 2017).

79. Article 94 of the Constitution of Iran (1979).
80. According to Mohammadi, '*Hokm-e hokumati* is neither an executive order/decree-law on the one hand nor a statute law. It is an afterthought to create a *feqhi* (jurisprudential) category, first to justify public law and later to put the *vali-ye faqih* (ruling jurist) above the law'. See Mohammadi, *Judicial Reform*, p. 116. The Supreme Leader's most controversial intervention was in mid-2000, when he ordered a bill proposing to reform Iran's repressive press laws removed from the docket.
81. Schirazi, *Constitution*, p. 230.
82. Ayatollah Hossein Rasti Kashani made this statement in an article in the *Resalat* newspaper, 7 Mordad 1368 [29 July 1989]. Cited in Schirazi, *Constitution*, p. 232, foonote 26.
83. Ibid.
84. Rafsanjani, 9/12/1987. Cited in Schirazi, *Constitution*, p. 232, footnote 27.

85. Information on this council is available at www.iranculture.org (accessed 2 May 2018).
86. For a detailed analysis of the role of the Guardian Council in the Islamicisation of Iranian law see Ansaripour, 'The Role'.
87. A *faqih* or *mojtahed* is a high-ranking religious scholar who has attained the right to engage in *ejtehād*, or independent reasoning in Islamic jurisprudence. According to Ansari, a *mojtahed* 'is a person who has gained the quality of *ejtehād*. In other words, he is a person who has the necessary knowledge and ability to look at the original sources of Islamic law and find a solution to a given legal problem. He must be well-versed in several disciplines including Arabic, especially Arabic grammar, logic, the jurisprudence (*usul-e feqh*) and Islamic law itself. In addition, he must know in detail the meaning of 500 verses which comprise the Qur'anic commandments and he must know the tradition (*hadith and rijal*)'. Ibid., p. 130.
88. Article 91 of the Constitution of Iran (1979).
89. Ibid. Article 92 of the Constitution of Iran (1979).
90. Ibid. Article 110 of the Constitution of Iran (1979).
91. Available at the official website of the Guardian Council under the section 'about the Guardian Council' available from: www.shora-gc.ir/Portal/Home/Default.aspx?CategoryID=8fac823a-5745-41b6-a9e2-b879c74deb7b (accessed 20 February 2017).
92. Articles 91, 94 and 96 of the Constitution of Iran (1979).
93. Articles 98 and 99 of the Constitution of Iran (1979).
94. See F. Hedayatniya Ganji, 'Nezārat-e Showrā-ye Negahbān Bar Qavānin va Moqararāt' [Guardian Council's Supervision of Laws and Regulations], *Ravāq-e Andisheh* 11, Mehr 1381 [October 2002], pp. 61–79.
95. See the Guardian Council's decision of 17.07.1361, No. 5736, in H. Mehrpur (ed.), *Majmu'h-ye Nazariyāt-e Shurā-ye Negahbān (The Collection of Gurdian Council's Decisions)*, Vol. 3 (Tehran, 1371 [1992]), pp. 208–209.
96. 'Q & A: Iran's election Crisis', *BBC News*, http://news.bbc.co.uk/1/hi/world/middle_east/3389017.stm (accessed 2 March 2017).
97. See, for example, 'Akharin Āmār-e Taid Salāhiyat Shodegān-e Majles-e Nohom' [The Latest Figures of the Approved Candidates for the Ninth Majles Election]. www.tabnak.ir/fa/news/225746/%D8%A2%D8%AE%D8%B1%DB%8C%D9%86-%D8%A2%D9%85%D8%A7%D8%B1-%D8%AA%D8%A7%DB%8C%DB%8C%D8%AF-%D8%B5%D9%84%D8%A7%D8%AD%DB%8C%D8%AA-%D8%B4%D8%AF%DA%AF%D8%A7%D9%86-%D9%85%D8%AC%D9%84%D8%B3-%D9%86%D9%87%D9%85, for a list of statistics related to the 2012 parliamentary elections, which point out how approximately 67 per cent of candidates had been approved (accessed 4 April 2018).
98. 'Chand Darsad az Namāyandegān Taeid Salāhiyat Shodand [The qualifications of how many of candidates were approved], *Afkār News*, 28 Bahman 1394 [17 February 2016]. www.afkarnews.ir/%D8%A8%D8%AE%D8%B4-%

D8%B3%DB%8C%D8%A7%D8%B3%DB%8C-3/489211-%DA%86%
D9%86%D8%AF-%D8%AF%D8%B1%D8%B5%D8%AF-%D8%A7%
D8%B2-%D8%AF%D8%A7%D9%88%D8%B7%D9%84%D8%A8%
D8%A7%D9%86-%D9%85%D8%AC%D9%84%D8%B3-%D8%AA%
D8%A3%DB%8C%DB%8C%D8%AF-%D8%B5%D9%84%D8%A7%
D8%AD%DB%8C%D8%AA-%D8%B4%D8%AF%D9%86%D8%AF%AF (accessed 20 March 2016).
99. Article 94 of the Constitution of Iran (1979).
100. Article 10 of the Internal Regulations of the Guardian Council.
101. Article 12 of the Internal Regulations of the Guardian Council.
102. 'Elhāq Be Konvānsion-e Por Dardesar bā Haq-e Tahafoz Ham Nashod' [The Accession to the Troubled Convention was not Successful Even with Reservations], *Tose'e*, 27 Mordad 1382 [18 August 2003]).
103. See Article 112 of the Constitution of Iran (1979). For detailed information about the creation of the council and its function see H. Mehrpur and M.H. Malayeri's interview with Hashemi Rafsanjani, 'Naqādi-ye Nazarvarzihā Darbāreh-ye Majma'-ye Tashkhis-e Maslahat-e Nezām' [Criticism of Views on the Expediency Discernment Council of the System], *Rāhbord*, No. 26, Zemestān 1382 [Winter 2003], pp. 8–48.
104. Mohammadi, *Judicial Reform*, p. 151.
105. See A. Bashiri, 'Majma'-ye Tashkhis-e Maslahat-e Nezām, Farātar az Qānun-e Asāsi va Majles?' [The Expediency Discernment Council of the System, Beyond the Constitution and Parliament?], *Gozāresh* 114, Mordād 1379 [July 2000], pp. 24–31.
106. Katuziyan, *Qānun-e Madani*, p. 635.
107. Katuziyan, *Moqadameh-ye*, p. 120. For a general understanding of the concept of law see H.L.A. Hart, *The Concept of Law*, 2nd edition (Oxford: Oxford University Press, 1994).
108. Articles 71 and 72 of the Constitution of Iran (1979).
109. Article 59 recognises mandatory referendum. According to this article: 'In extremely important economic, political, social, and cultural matters, the functions of the legislature may be exercised through direct recourse to popular vote through a referendum. Any request for such direct recourse to public opinion must be approved by two-thirds of the members of the Islamic Consultative Assembly'.
110. Ebadi, *Hoquq-e Zan*, p. 22.
111. Katuziyan, *Moqadameh-ye*, p. 128.
112. Ibid., pp. 189–90.
113. Ebadi, *Hoquq-e Zan*, pp. 27–8.
114. Ibid., p. 26.
115. Katuziyan, *Moqadameh-ye*, p. 200.
116. Ebadi, *Hoquq-e Zan*, pp. 28–9.
117. A. An-Na'im, *Toward an Islamic Reformation: Civil Liberties, Human Rights, and International Law* (New York: Syracuse University Press, 1990), p. 19.

118. Baderin, *International*, pp. 34–5.
119. An-Na'im, *Toward an Islamic Reformation*, p. 19.
120. Baderin, *International*, p. 35.
121. Ibid.
122. M. Shafi'i, *al-Risālah*, cited in ibid.
123. Qur'an 33:21. See also Qur'an 3:31 and Qur'an 4:59.
124. S. Ebadi and M. Zaimaran, Sonat va Tajadod dar System-e Hoquqi-ye Iran [Modernity and Tradition in the Iranian Legal System] (Tehran: Ganje-Danesh, 1375 [1996]), p. 136.
125. Baderin, *International*, pp. 36–7.
126. Ebadi, *Sonat va Tajadod*, pp. 136–7.
127. An-Na'im, *Toward an Islamic Reformation*, p. 23.
128. Qur'an 4:115
129. An-Na'im, *Toward an Islamic Reformation*, p. 23.
130. Ibid.
131. Ebadi, *Sonat va Tajadod*, p. 140.
132. Ibid.
133. An-Na'im, *Toward an Islamic Reformation*, p. 27. See also J. Copper, 'Allama al-Hilli on the Imamate and Ijtihad', in S.A. Arjomand (ed.), *Authority and Political Culture in Shi'ism* (New York, 1988), pp. 243–8; D.B. Macdonald, 'Ijtihad', in *The Encyclopaedia of Islam*, Vol. 3 (1971), pp. 1026–7.
134. A. Mashhour, 'Islamic Law and Gender Equality: Could There Be a Common Ground?: A Study of Divorce and Polygamy in Shari'a Law and Contemporary Legislation in Tunisia and Egypt', *Human Rights Quarterly* 27/2 (May 2005), pp. 562–96 at p. 567.
135. An-Na'im, *Toward an Islamic Reformation*, p. 27.
136. Ibid.
137. V.B. Halagh, translated by A. Kazemi Najafabadi, 'Ejtehād dar Miyān-e Ahl-e Sonat' [Ejtehād among Sunnis], *Majaleh-ye Andisheh-ye SādEqn* 10 (Spring 2003), pp. 32–51 at p. 32.
138. H. Nasr, H. Dabashi and V.R. Nasr, *Expectation of the Millennium: Shi'ism in History* (Albany, New York: State University of New York Press, 1989), p. 281.
139. Ibid., p. 280.
140. For definition of *mojtahed* see footnote 87 on page 94.
141. Nasr et al., Expectation of the Millennium, p. 280.
142. Ibid., p. 282.
143. Mashhour, 'Islamic Law and Gender Equality', p. 590.
144. Ibid.
145. A. Arshad, 'Ijtehad as a Tool for Islamic Legal Reform: Advancing Women's Rights in Morocco', *Kansas Journal of Law & Public Policy* 16 (200), p. 139.
146. Ibid.
147. Mashhour, 'Islamic Law and Gender Equality', p. 591.

148. Article 2 of the Constitution of Iran (1979).
149. Z. Mir-Hosseini, 'How the Door of *Ijtihad* was Opened and Closed: A Comparative Analysis of Recent Family Law Reforms in Iran and Morocco', *Washington & Lee Law Review*, 64/4 (Fall 2007), pp. 1499–1511 at p. 1501. Mir-Hosseini argues, 'Reason for this divergence must be sought in the configuration of domestic and international events between 1977 and 2004 that shaped the politics of gender and family law reform in each country'. Ibid., pp. 1509–15011.
150. Tabari and Yeganeh, *In the Shadow of Islam*, p. 51.
151. Mashhour, 'Islamic Law and Gender Equality', p. 594.
152. F. Roudi-Fahimi and M. Mederios Kent, 'Challenges and Opportunities – The Population of the Middle East and North Africa', *Population Bulletin* 62 (2): [24], June 2007. p. 9.
153. Hursh, 'Advancing Women's Rights', p. 296.
154. e.g., Articles 20, 21, 26 and 28 of the Constitution of Iran (1979).
155. e.g., Articles 24 and 26 of the Constitution of Iran (1979).
156. e.g., Articles 22, 25, 23 and 33 of the Constitution of Iran (1979).

Chapter 3   Deliberation over the adoption of CEDAW by Islamic Republic of Iran

1. For instance, in the words of Baderin 'equality of women is recognised in Islam on the principle of equal but not equivalent'. M.A. Baderin, *International Human Rights and Islamic Law* (Oxford: Oxford University Press, 2003), p. 60. Different views on equality were discussed in Chapter 1. It should be borne in mind that the definition of gender equality under the convention is, to some extent, in contradiction with the traditional understanding of gender equality within the Muslim world. In Islamic jurisprudence, gender equality, in its traditional sense, is understood and defined as 'complementarity' and a 'balance' of rights.
2. Ayatollah Khamenei's Word on Women's Dignity, available from the official website of the Supreme Leader, Ayatollah Ali Khamenei: http://farsi.khamenei.ir/newspart-index?tid=3249 (accessed 15 May 2017).
3. N. Ahmadi Khorasani, *The Spring of the Iranian Women's Movement* (Tehran, Shahrivar 1391 [August 2012]), p. 46. Due to the persistent censorship, publishers in Iran are not allowed to legally and openly publish this type of book.
4. For the full account of this case see Chapter 5, pp. 200–202.
5. For more details on this case see S. Ebadi, *Iran Awakening: A Memoir of Revolution and Hope* (New York: Random House, 2006), pp. 122–7.
6. In August 1997, Arian's case was reported to the SPRC. Her mother claimed that Arian's father and stepmother were abusing her. Ebadi accepted the case pro bono and the SPRC used all its power to make the case public.
7. Ebadi, *Iran Awakening*, p. 124.

8. Khorasani, *The Spring*, pp. 74–8.
9. Article 125 of the Constitution of Iran (1979).
10. Article 9 of the Civil Code of Iran.
11. These issues include: the nationality of a woman after her marriage, the nationality of children born to an Iranian mother, right to divorce, custody of children, marriage of children, the headship of the family, the marriage of a Muslim woman with a non-Muslim, free movements of women, equality before the law, sending students abroad, abolition of contradictory regulations to the convention and accepting the arbitration of the International Court of Justice. M. Raisi, 'Elhāq yā Adam-e Elhāq be Konvānsion-e Raf'-e Tab'iz az Zanān' [Accession or No Accession to the Convention on the Elimination of All Forms of Discrimination Against Women], *Nashriyeh-ye Feqh va Hoquq-e Khānevādeh* 29 (Bahār 1382 [Spring 2003]), pp. 44–82 at pp. 55–6.
12. 'Gozāresh-e Tahlili az Ravand-e Elhāq-e Irān be Konvānsion' [An Analytical Report on the Process of Iran's Accession to the Women's Convention], in *Konvānsion-e Mahv-e Koliye-ye Ashkāl-e Tab'iz Alayh-e Zanān: Majmue-ye Maqālāt va Goftoguhā* (Qom: Daftar-e Mutāleāt va Tahqiqāt-e Zanān, 2004), pp. 27–34.
13. The supporters consisted of women rights activists, the reformists, and some religious figures like Mousavi Bujnordi. The opponents included conservatives, the Supreme Leader and his supporters.
14. Ayatollah Tabrizi, Makarem Shirazi, Safi, Mazaheri and Nuri Hamedani were among those *foqahā* who disagreed with the CEDAW. Zarif, a representative from the foreign ministry, and Fatemeh Hashemi, secretary general of the International Union of Muslim Women NGOs, reported the opinions of the advocates of the CEDAW to the committee appointed by SCCR. The Supreme Council of Cultural Revolution and Research Centre of the Islamic Republic of Iran Broadcast (IRIB) reflected the opponents' opinion to this committee.
15. Konvānsion-e Mahv-e, p. 29.
16. Z. Mir-Hosseini, 'The Conservative–Reformist Conflict over Women's Rights in Iran', *International Journal of Politics, Culture, and Society* 16/1 (Fall 2002), pp. 37–53 at p. 38.
17. There was no organisation working on women's issues until 1987, when the Supreme Council of the Cultural Revolution proposed the initiation of a Social and Cultural Council to cover the issues pertaining to women. This council was established 9 June 1987 and its by-laws were published in *Ruznameh-ye Rasmi-ye Keshvar*, No. 12533 (10 Bahman 1366 [30 January 1988]). These by-laws were amended in 1997 and can be seen at *Ruznameh-ye Rami-ye Keshvar*, No. 15277 (22 Mordād 1379 [13 August 2000]). Among its initial members were Ateqe Rajaei (Sadighi), Goharolsharieh Dastqeyb, Marziyeh Dastgerdi, Mina Khajeh Nouri, Zahra Rahnavard, Zahra Shojaei, Shokohe Navabi Nejad, Marziyeh Mohamadiyan Fard, Ali Shariatmadari, Ahmad Ahmadi and Soraya Maknoon. Zahra Shojaei was elected vice president and held this position until 1991 when she became the president of the council. The council suggested thirteen plans to

improve women's status; only one was ratified by the Supreme Council of Cultural Revolution. To be more effective in implementing the plans in relation to the women's status, the Social and Cultural Council, during the presidency of Hashemi Rafsanjani suggested the vice president for executive affairs within the presidential office. President Rafsanjani disagreed with the position of the vice president and instead recommended the bureau for executive affairs within the presidential office. Ms Habibi became the person in charge in the bureau. Six years later, during the presidency of Mohammamd Khatami, the office was upgraded to the Center for Women's Participation. With the start of the ninth government, Mahmood Ahmadinejad proposed a broader idea on the social and religious necessities and the central role of women in the stabilisation of families. He therefore expanded the centre to the Centre for Women and Family Affairs and appointed Dr Nasrin Soltankhah as the head of the centre and advisor to the president in women and family affairs on 22 September 2005. Nasrin Soltankhah resigned in February 2006 following her decision to continue with her work at the Tehran city council. Following this, Dr Zohreh Tabibzadeh Nouri was appointed by the president as his advisor on women affairs. She commenced her role on 21 February as the head of the Centre for Women and Family Affairs'. On 8 October 2013 President Rowhani appointed Shahindokht Molaverdi as vice president for women and family affairs and subsequently the name of the centre was changed to Department for Women and Family Affairs. See the official website of the Department for Women and Family Affairs, http:// women.gov.ir/ (accessed 19 May 2017). See also, Z. Shojaei, 'Dar Bahs-e Konvānsion Ghoghā Sālāri kardand' [An Exaggerated Discussion About the Convention], *Yās-e Now*, 22 Esfand 1379 [21 March 2001].

18. The bill commission is a permanent commission of the government to draft bills to be approved by the council of ministers and send to the Majles for ratification. Hojat-ol-Islam Shooshtari (minster of justice), Mohajerani (minister of culture), Goodarz Eftekhar Jahromi (jurists), Danesh Yazdi, Hadi and Afsaneh Nadi Pur (all from the foreign affairs ministry), Mir-Mohamamdi and Meymanet Choobak (from the judiciary), Mirzaei (the state administrative and employment organisation) and Shojaei, Jahangir and Mulavardi (all from the Centre for Women's Participation) were the members of the subcommittee. Moreover, the ministries of education, judiciary, labour, social affairs, culture and higher education, health and medical education, foreign affairs, state administrative and employment organisations, legal and parliamentary affairs of the president's office and the planning and budget organisation presented their ideas to disagree with Iran's accession to the CEDAW in written documents to the subcommittee. Cited in *Konvānsion-e Mahv-e*, p. 31.
19. Konvānsion-e Mahv-e, p. 32.
20. According to its official website: 'The Islamic Culture and Relations Organisation (ICRO) is an independent legal entity affiliated with the Ministry of Culture and Islamic Guidance and carries out its activities under

the quidance of the Leader of the Islamic Republic of Iran, and the supervison of the Supreme Council of the ICRO, in accordance with the foreign policies of the Islamic Republic of Iran and the rules and regulations framed by its constitution'. See: http;//en.icro.ir/index.aspx?siteid=257&pageid=9292 (accessed 2 April 2017).
21. The legal and parliamentary affairs division of of the presidential office objected in particular to Article 2 of the CEDAW.
22. Amongst the positive consequences would be that of Islamic values and the national interest; the creation of an active role for the country in the international community; the laying of ground work for cultural, legal and political affairs to benefit from the capacities of the CEDAW to strengthen women's role and present appropriate representation of women in Islam and Iran; the prevention or reduction of negative consequences of disapproval of the CEDAW; and enjoyment the benefits of Iran's accession to the CEDAW. See the Report of the Bills Commission, *No. 16235*, p. 3.
23. Letter from the president of the Centre for Women's Participation, *No. 8346*, 25 Dey 1380 [15 January 2002].
24. Konvānsion-e Mahv-e, p. 39.
25. Ibid.
26. E. Kulaei, 'Bā Morur-e Zamān Negareshhā Taqir Mikonad' [Attitudes Will Change over Time], *Zanān-e Fardā*, Vol. 1, 1 Mehr 1381 [23 September 2002], p. 58.
27. 'Nāmeh-ye Jāme'h-ye Modaresin-e Hozeh-ye Elmiyeh-ye Qom Be Rais-e Majles-e Showrā-ye Islami Hojat-ol-Islam Valmoslemin Karroubi dar Mored-e Elhāq-e Iran Be Konvānsion' [Letter from the Society of Seminary Teachers of Qom to Majles Speaker Hojat-ol-Islam Karroubi Regarding Iran's Accession to the CEDAW Dated 18 March 2002], *Jomhuri-ye Islami*, 20 Mordād 1382 [11 August 2003], p. 4.
28. 'Movāfeqat-e Olamā Jalb Nashod' [The Olamā's Agreement Was Not Forthcoming], *Hambastegi*, 7 Ordibehesht 1382 [27 April 2003], p. 9.
29. *Maraje'* is the plural form of *marja* – also written *marja'-e taqlid* – a high-ranking Shi'ite ayatollah who has the highest authority on religious law. His decisions are to be obeyed by his followers and less-credential clerics.
30. 'Nazar-e Se Marja'-e Taqlid Darbāreh-ye Peyvastan-e Iran be Konvānsion-e Beynolmelali-ye Zanān' [The View of Three Religious Figures Regarding Iran's Accession to the Women's Convention], *Keyhān*, 25 Ordibehesht 1381 [15 May 2002]. See also Ayatollah Makarem Shirazi, 'Bandhā-ye Mota'adedi Az Konvānsion-e Raf'-e Tab'iz Sarihan Bar Khalāf-e Shar'-e Islam Ast' [Some Articles of the Convention Explictly Contradict Islam], *Hemāyat*, 12 Mordād 1382 [3 August 2003], and *Konvānsion-e Mahv-e*, pp. 41–2.
31. Konvānsion-e Mahv-e, p. 42.
32. 'Movāfeqat-e Olamā'.

33. 'Hoquq-e Madani-ye Zanān va Kudakān Bāznegari Mishavad' [The Civil Rights of Women and Children Will Be Revised], *Khorāsān*, 9 Ordibehesht 1382 [29 April 2003], p. 7.
34. 'Bā Morur-e Zamān'.
35. Z. Mir-Hosseini, 'Fatemeh Haqiqatjoo and the Sixth Majles: A Woman in Her Own Right', *Middle East Report* 233 (Winter 2004), www.merip.org/mer/mer233/mir-hosseini.html (accessed 2 May 2018).
36. Ibid.
37. In 2012 it was renamed to Woman and Family Reserah Centre.
38. Konvānsion-e Mahv-e, pp. 46–7.
39. Ayatollah Makarem Shirazi, 'Mabādā Ta'limāt-e Dini-ye Mā Rā Qarbihā Entekhāb Konand' [Lest Westerners Choose Our Religious Education], *Keyhān*, 10 Tir 1382 [1 July 2003], p. 6.
40. 'Mozākerāt-e jalase-ye Alani-ye Majles-e Shurā-ye Islami, Jalaseh-ye 342' [Official Record of the Majles, Session 342], *Ruznāme-ye Rasmi*, 1 Mordād 1382 [23 July 2003], p. 21.
41. These laws will be examined in Chapter 5.
42. The laws concerning family issues will be discussed in the next chapter.
43. 'Mozākerāt-e jalase-ye Alani-ye Majles-e Shurā-ye Islami, Jalaseh-ye 342' [Official Record of the Majles, Session 342], *Ruznāme-ye Rasmi*, 1 Mordād 1382 [23 July 2003], pp. 22–3.
44. Ibid., p. 30.
45. 'Rāhpeymāi Dar Eterāz be Konvānsion-e Raf'-e Tab'iz Alayhe Zanān Dar Qom Bargozār Shod' [A Demonstration Was Held in Qom in Objecting to the Convention on the Elimination of All Forms of Discrimination Against Women], *Khorāsān*, 12 Mordād 1382 [3 August 2003], p. 16.
46. Konvānsion-e Mahv-e, p. 49.
47. Ibid.
48. 'Dabir-e Shorā-ye Negahbān Konvānsion-e Raf'-e Tab'iz Alayhe Zanān Rā Khalāf-e Shar' va Moghāyer ba Qānun-e Asāsi E'lām Kard' [The Secretary-General of the Guardian Council Declares the Convention on the Elimination of all Forms of Discrimination Against Women Contradicts the Shari'a and the Constitution], *Khorāsān*, 29 Mordād 1382 [13 August 2003], p. 2.
49. 'Mozākerāt jalase-ye Alani-ye Majles-e Shurā-ye Islami, Jalase-ye 365' [Official Recored of the Majles, Session 365], *Ruznāme-ye Rasmi*, 23 Mehr 1382 [15 October 2003], p. 14.
50. Ibid.
51. Ibid., pp. 15–16, 19.
52. For a detailed overview of the views of the supporters and opponents of Iran's accession to the CEDAW see Z. Ebrahimi, 'Movāfeqan va Mokhālefān-e Elhāq' [The Supporters and Opponents of Accession], *Baztāb-e Andishe* 42 (Mehr 1382 [October 2003]), pp. 32–8; *Konvānsion-e Mahve Koliye-ye*, pp. 69–88; and M. Raei, 'Elhāq be Konvānsion az Manzar-e Movāfeqān va Mokhālefān' [Accession to the Convention From the Perspective of Supporters and

Opponents], *Bāztāb-e Andishe* 46 (Bahman 1382 [February 2004]), pp. 51–62.
53. See Z. Lantsel, 'Konvānsion-e Raf'-e Tab'iz va Payāmadhā-ye Ejtemāi-ye Ān' [The Convention on the Elimination of All Forms of Discrimination Against Women and Its Social Consequences], *Bānovān-e Shi'e* 3 Bahār 1383 [Spring 2005]), pp. 147–76; A. Hosseini, 'Chāleshhā-ye Konvānsion-e Raf'-e Tab'iz Alayhe Zanān' [The Challenges of the Convention on the Elimination of All Forms of Discrimination Against Women], *Ravāq Andisheh* 4 (Ābān va Āzar 1380 [October and November 2001]), pp. 95–108 and L. Zafaranchi, 'Naqdi Ejmāli bar Konvānsion-e Raf'-e Tab'iz Alayhe Zanān' [A Comprehensive Critique of the Convention on the Elimination of All Forms of Discrimination Against Women], *Ketāb-e Naqd* 27 & 28 (Bahar va Tabestan 1381 [Spring and Summer 2003]), pp. 267–76.
54. 'Dar Bahs-e Konvānsion'.
55. Ibid.
56. For a detailed analysis on the necessity of Iran joining the CEDAW see M. Jalali, M.A. Basiri and S. Bani Najariyan, 'Zarurat-e Elhāq-e Iran be Konvānsion-e 1979 Man'e Koliyeh-ye Ashkāl-e Tab'iz Alayhe Zanān' [The Necessity of Iran's Accession to the 1979 Convention on the Elimination of All Forms of Discrimination Against Women], *Nāmeh Mofid* 55, Shahrivar 1385 [September 2006], pp. 66–102.
57. As stated previously Ayatollah Fazel Lankarani, Ayatollah Makarem Shirazi, Ayatollah Tabrizi, Ayatollah Meshkini, Ayatollah Sāfi and Ayatollah Imami Kashani were among those who objected to the CEDAW. See 'Paziresh-e Konvānsion Zanān Ta'til-e Mosalamāt-e Shar' Ast' [The Acceptance of the Convention is the Closure of Islamic Principles], *Yālsārāt* 238, 24 Mordād 1382 [15 August 2003].
58. As discussed in the Introduction of the book, some scholars argue that Islam does not believe in the similarity of rights between men and women; rather, it acknowledges the difference between the two sexes. Biologically men and women are different and due to this fact, Islam provides dissimilar rights and responsibilities for men and women in the interests of life balance. For instance, men are asked to pay for family expenses and women to stay home and take care of children.
59. For detailed analysis of this argument see: A. Heydari, 'Lāyehe-ye Elhāq be Konvānsion Mahv-e Koliye-ye Ashkāle Tab'iz Az Zanān: Mokhālefathā' [The Bill of Accession to the CEDAW: Disagreemnets], *Nashriye-ye Payāme Zan* 140, Khordād 1394 [May 2015]; A. Fathi, 'Ta'ārozāt-e Konvānsion Mahve Tab'iz Alayhe Zanān Ba Islam va Hoquq-e Bashar' [The Convention's Contradiction of Islam and Human Rights], *Resālat* 6, 29 Mehr 1382 [21 October 2003]; F. Alasvand, *Konvānsion-e Raf'-e Koliye-ye Ashkāl-e Tab'iz Alayhe Zanān {Convention on the Elimination of All forms of Discrimination Against Women}* (Qom: Markaz-e Modiriyat Hozeh Elmiyeh, 1382 [2003]), p. 53; B. Mohammad Zadeh, 'Negāhi be Hoquq-e Zan dar Islam: Naqdi Bar

Konvānsion-e Raf'-e Koliye-ye Ashkāl-e Tab'iz Alayhe Zanān' [An Overview of Women's Rights in Iran: A Critique of the Convention on the Elimination of All Forms of Discrimination Against Women], *Ma'refat* 70, Mehr 1382 [October 2003], pp. 8–28.

60. Rezazadeh, 'Ta'āroz-e Konvānsion-e Mahve-e Koliye-ye Ashkāle Tab'iz Alayhe Zanān bā Hoquq-e Vāghei-ye Zanān' [The Contradictions of the Convention on the Elimination of All Forms of Discrimination Against Women with Women's Real Rights], *Jomhuri-ye Islami*, 7 Mordād 1378 [29 July 1999]. See also Fathi, 'Ta'ārozāt-e Konvānsion Mahve'; and 'Elhāq be Konvānsion-e Zanān Khodbākhtegi dar Barābar-e Farhang-e Gharb Ast' [Accession to the Women's Convention is Submission to Western Culture], *Resālat*, 19 Mordād 1382 [10 August 2003].

61. According to Article 7 (b), States Parties shall ensure to women on equal terms with men, the right to participate in the formulation of government policy and the implementation thereof and to hold public office and perform all public functions at all levels of government.

62. Article 9 of the CEDAW urges States Parties 'to grant women equal rights with men to acquire, change or retain their nationality. They shall ensure in particular that neither marriage to an alien nor change of nationality by the husband during marriage shall automatically change the nationality of the wife, render her stateless or force upon her the nationality of the husband'. According to Article 11 (a): 'States Parties should provide equal rights for women to work and ensure this right as an inalienable right of all human beings'. States Parties in accordance with Article 15 (4): 'shall accord to men and women the same rights with regard to the law relating to the movement of persons and the freedom to choose their residence and domicile'.

63. Article 16 of the CEDAW was discussed in depth in the previous chapter.

64. The difference of rights of men and women in inheritance will be discussed in Chapter 4.

65. Heydari, 'Lāyehey-e Elhāq'.

66. Qur'an 4:1.

67. Qur'an 49:13 states: 'O mankind! Lo! We have created you from male and female and have made you nations and tribes that ye may know one another. Lo! The noblest of you, in the sight of Allah, is the best in conduct. Lo! Allah is Knower, Aware.'

68. Heydari, 'Lāyehey-e Elhāq'.

69. Ibid.

70. Payāmadhā-ye Elhāq be Konvānsion-e Raf'-e Tab'iz az Zanān' [Consequences of Iran's Accession to the Convention], *Khorāsān*, 11 Ordibehesht 1385 [1 May 2006]. See also 'Bāzshenāsi-ye Āsibhā-ye Roykard-e Elhāq-e Iran be Konvānsion Gharbi-ye Mosum be Raf'-e Tab'iz az Zanān' [A Study of the Damages Incurred by the Views against Iran's Accession to the Western Convention Known as Elimination of Discrimination], *Keyhān* 25 & 26, 25 Mordād 1382 [16 August 2003].

71. Konvānsion-e Mahve, p. 74.
72. Article 14 of the CEDAW.
73. Fathi, 'Ta'ārozāt-e Konvānsion Mahv-e'.
74. Ibid.
75. Article 5 (a) of the CEDAW.
76. S. Sadr, 'Barābari-ye Mashrut-e Zan va Mard: Be Angizeh-yeTasvibe-e Elhāq be Konvānsion-e Raf'-e Hameh Goobneh Tab'iz Alayhe Zanān' [Conditional Equality of Men and Women: On the Occasion of the Ratification of the Convention on the Elimination of All Forms of Discrimination Against Women], *Zanān* 84, Bahman 1380 [January 2002], pp. 8–10.
77. Article 21 (3) of the UDHR.
78. According to Articles 2, 3 and 18 of the CEDAW.
79. Fathi, 'Ta'ārozāt-e Konvānsion-e Mahv-e'.
80. This principle derived from Qur'an 4:141 that states: 'Those who wait upon occasion in regard to you and, if a victory cometh unto you from Allah, say: Are we not with you? and if the disbelievers meet with a success say: Had we not the mastery of you, and did we not protect you from the believers? – Allah will judge between you at the Day of Resurrection, and Allah will not give the disbelievers any way (of success) against the believers'.
81. Heydari,'Lāyehe-ye Elhāq'.
82. Z. Ayatollahi, a member of the Women's Cultural and Social Council, listed the contradictory articles in the civil code. Z. Ayatollahi, 'Konvānsion-e Beynolmelali-ye Zanān bā Osul-e Islami Moghāyerat Dārad' [The International Convention on Women Contradcits Islam], *Keyhān* 26, 1381 [2003]. These statistics, which have emerged from a thorough comparison between the CEDAW principles and the *corpus* of Iranian laws, represent a marked increase with respect to the number of contraventions flagged in a more generic fashion by clerical figures such as Mesbah Yazdi. See also, Z. Ayatollahi, 'Haq-e Shart dar Konvānsion-e Raf'-e Tamāmi-ye Ashkāl-e Tab'iz Alayhe Zanān' [Rezervation to the Convention on the Elimination of All Forms of Discrimination Against Women], *Ketāb-e Zanān* 15, 1 Farvardin 1381 [21 March 2002]; and Z. Ayatollahi, 'Paziresh-e Konvānsion Mokhālef-e Masāleh-he Meli Ast' [Acceptance of the Convention is Against the National Interest], *Resālat*, 22 Farvardin 1381 [11 April 2002].
83. 'Raf'e Tab'iz Yā Hākemiyat-e Arzeshhāy-e Feministi: Negāhi be Mabāhes-e Matrooheh Darbāreh-ye Konvānsion-e Raf'e Har Gooneh Tab'iz az Zanān' [Elimination of Discrimination or Domination of the Feminist's Values: Examining Different Discussion About the Convention on the Elimination of All Forms of Discrimination Against Women], *Nashriyeh-ye Tarbiyat-e Siyasi* 13 (1), pp. 60–3.
84. Z. Tabibzadeh Nuri, 'Nemigozāram Iran be Konvānsion Bepeyvandad' (I will not Allow Iran to Join the Convention), *Aftāb* News, 9 Khordād 1385 [31 July 2006], www.aftabnews.ir/vdcdnz0o.yt05o6a22y.html (accessed 1 April 2017).

85. E. Kulaei, *Yāse Now*, 10 Esfand 1381 [1 March 2003].
86. Ibid.
87. N. Tariqi, 'Movāfeqān va Mokhālefān Che Migooyand, Tazāhorkonandegān Dar Qom: Zanān-e Mā Bidārand Az Konvānsion Bizārand' [What the Opponents and Supporters Say, Demonstrators in Qom: Our Women Are Awake and Hate the Convention], *Zanān* 101, Tir va Mordād 1382 [June–July 3003], pp. 14–19 at p. 17.
88. Ibid.
89. Article 12 (2) of the CEDAW.
90. 'Ta'ārozāt-e Konvānsion-e Mahve'.
91. Article 10 (c) of the CEDAW.
92. Konvānsion-e Mahv-e, p. 155.
93. Preamble of the CEDAW.
94. Ibid.
95. For a detailed analysis of the issue of Iran's ratifying the convention with reservation see, among others, 'Elhāq be Konvānsion-e Por Dardesar ba Haq-e Tahafoz ham Nashod' [The Accession to the Challenging Convention Was Not Accepted Even With Reservation], *Tose'e*, 27 Mordād 1382 [18 August 2003]; and M. Fazaeli, 'Konvāsion-e Raf'-e Tab'iz Alayhe Zanān va Shorut-e Koli-ye Vāred bar Ān' [The Convention on the Elimination of All Forms of Discrimination Against Women and Its General Reservations], *Hoquq-e Beynolmelal* 34, Bahār va Tabestān-e 1385 [Spring and Summer 2006], pp. 57–110.
96. Konvānsion-e Mahv-e, p. 152.
97. 'Konvānsion-e Tab'iz Alayhe Zanān dar Dastor-e Kāre Majles Qarār Girad' [The Convention Should Be Considered in the Majles' Agenda], *Yās-e Now*, 20 Tir 1380 [11 July 2001].
98. 'Yek Bam va Do Hava: Piramoon-e Elhāq-e Iran be Konvānsion-e Raf'-e Tab'iz az Zanān' [Double Standards: On Iran's Accession to the Convention on the Elimination of All Forms of Discrimination Against Women], *Yās-e Now*, 3 Shahrivar 1382 [25 August 2003].
99. M. Kar, 'Shart-e Dolat Besyār Koli va Mobham Ast' [The Reservation is Too General and Vague], *Zanān* 84, Bahman 1380 [February 2002], pp. 12–14.
100. Ibid.
101. S. Sadr, 'Barābari-ye Mashrut-e'.
102. Z. Mir-Hosseini, *The Conservative*, p. 50.
103. Mir-Hosseini, 'Fatemeh Haqiqatjoo'.

Chapter 4 Iranian Women's Struggle for Gender Equality: The Case of Iran's Civil Code

1. *The Civil Code of Iran*, Translated by M.A.R. Taleghany (Littleton, Colorado: Fred. B. Rothman, 1995), Preface.

2. Z. Mir-Hosseini, *Marriage on Trial: Islamic Family Law in Iran and Morocco* (London and New York: I.B.Tauris, 2000), p. 24.
3. In this book, use of the term 'international standards' in this context refers to the Convention on the Elimination of All Forms of Discrimination Against Women, which provides, in Article 16, equal rights in marriage and its dissolution.
4. Z. Mir-Hosseini, *Islam and Gender: The Religious Debate in Contemporary Iran* (London and New York, I.B.Tauris, 2000), p. 160.
5. Ibid.
6. Ibid.
7. This law was revised in 1937.
8. Qānun-e Hemāyat-e Khānevādeh.
9. Mir-Hosseini, *Marriage on Trial*, p. 24.
10. For instance, according to Ayatollah Khomeinei, 'the Family Law, which has as its purpose the destruction of the Muslim family unit, is contrary to the ordinances of Islam. Those who have imposed [this law] and those who have voted [for it] are criminals from the standpoint of both the Shari'a and the law. The divorce of women divorced by court order is invalid; they are still married women, and if they marry again, they become adulteresses. Likewise, anyone who knowingly marries a woman so divorced becomes an adulterer, deserving the penalty laid down by the Shari'a. The issue of such union will be illegitimate, unable to inherit, and subject to all other regulations concerning illegitimate offspring. All of the foregoing applies equally whether the court itself awards the divorce directly, orders the divorce to take place, or compels the husband to divorce his wife'. See R. Khomeini, *Islam and Revolution: Writings and Declaration of Imam Khomeini*, Translated and annotated by Hamed Algar (Berkeley: Mizan Press, 1981), p. 441. This is also cited in A. Schirazi, *The Constitution of Iran: Politics and the State in the Islamic Republic*, translated by J. O'Kane (London: I.B.Tauris, 1997), p. 216.
11. Schirazi, *Constitution*, p. 217.
12. Mir-Hosseini, *Marriage on Trial*, pp. 24–6.
13. The Civil Procedural Law was ratified on 9 April 2000, *Ruznāmeh-ye Rasmi-ye Keshvar*, No. 16070, 30 April 2000. See also Article 167 of the Constitution of Iran (1979).
14. See Introduction, p. 22.
15. In Persian, the adjective used to describe intimate relations outside marriage is *āzad* (free).
16. According to Article 233 of the Islamic Criminal Code of Iran (2013), *lāvāt* consists of sexual intercourse with a male. Based on Article 234, where the act of *lāvāt* is proven, the active person will be executed if he committed this crime forcefully and if he is wedded to a permanent wife with whom he has had intercourse and may have intercourse when he so desires. Otherwise, his punishment consists of 100 lashes. In either case, the punishment of the passive person is execution (whether he is wedded and has *ehsān* conditions or not).

NOTES TO PAGES 105–107   255

Article 238 of the code defines lesbianism as homosexuality of women through sexual activity. According to Article 239, the punishment for lesbianism is 100 lashes. The full text of this law is available in Persian from the official website of the Majles: http://rc.majlis.ir/fa/law/show/845048 (accessed 20 March 2017).

17. Article 1062 of the Civil Code of Iran. F. Badrian, *The Civil Code of Iran* (Tehran: Entesharāt-e Dāneshvar, 2001).
18. Article 1063 of the Civil Code of Iran.
19. Article 1067 of the Civil Code of Iran.
20. Article 1065 of the Civil Code of Iran.
21. Article 1070 of the Civil Code of Iran states that: 'Consent of the marrying parties is the condition upon which depends the enforcement of the marriage contract, and if a party showing at first reluctance authorises the making of the contract subsequently, the contract will be binding unless the reluctance is so acute that the reluctant person cannot be considered as having been in possession of any intention'.
22. Article 1062 of the Civil Code of Iran.
23. Article 1059 of the Civil Code of Iran states: 'Marriage of a female Muslim to a non-Muslim is not allowed'.
24. M.A. Baderin, *International Human Rights and Islamic Law* (Oxford: Oxford University Press, 2003), p. 144. For detailed discussion on marriage of a Muslim with a non-Muslim see, e.g., M. Jabaran, *Ezdevāj bā Qeyr-e Mosalmānān {Marriage with non-Muslims}* (Qom: Entesharāt-e Daftar-e Tablighāt-e Islami-ye Huzeh-ye Elmiye-ye Qom, 1382 [2003]).
25. Article 13 of the Constitution of Iran (1979).
26. According to Article 13 of of the Constitution of Iran (1979): 'Zoroastrian, Jewish, and Christian Iranians are the only recognised religious minorities, who, within the limits of the law, are free to perform their religious rites and ceremonies, and to act according to their own canon in matters of personal affairs and religious education.'
27. Article 167 of the Constitution of Iran (1979). See Nazariyeh-ye Edāreh-ye Hoquqi-ye Qoveh-ye Qzāiyeh Dar Mored-e Ezdevāj Mard-e Mosalmān Ba Zan-e Qeyr-e Mosalmān {Legal Department of the Judiciary's Opinion on Marriage of a Muslim Man with a Non-Muslim Woman}, *Opinion No. 7/3800*, 11 Mordād 1379 {1 August 2000}.
28. M. Mohaqeq Damad, Barrasi-ye Feghhi-ye Hoqugh-e Khānevādeh: Nekāh va Enhelāl-e Ān {A Study of Islamic Jurisprudence with Respect to Family Law: Marriage and Its Termination} (Tehran: Shābok, 2008), p. 151. According to Baderin, 'Qur'an 5:5 permits Muslim men to marry women of the people of the book.' Baderin, International, p. 144.
29. Mohaqeq Damad, *Barresi-ye*, p. 151.
30. Ibid.
31. Ibid., p. 155. See also H. Emami, *Hoquq-e Madani {Civil Rights}*, Vol. 4, 12th edition (Tehran: Ketāb Forushi-ye Eslāmiyeh, 1374 [1995]), p. 343.

32. Article 1060 of the Civil Code of Iran.
33. 'Bāzkhāni-ye Tab'izāt-e Qānuni-ye Ezdevāj-e Zanān-e Irāni bā Mardān-e Afqāni' [Readout of Legal Discrimination of Marriage of Iranian Women with Afghan Men], *Aftab Online*, 30 Tir 1386 [21 July 2007], www.aftabir.com/articles/view/social/law/c4c1185009901_spousal_p1.php/ (accessed 22 March 2017).
34. Ibid.
35. Y. Bazgir, *Qānun-e Madani dar Āine-ye Ārāy-e Divān-e Āliye Keshvar {The Civil Code as it Pertains to Supreme Court Verdicts}*, Vol. 1 (Tehran: Ferdosi, 1380 [2001]), p. 101. According to Article 17 of the 1931 marriage law, a foreign national will be punished with between one and three years of imprisonment if he marries an Iranian woman without the permission from the Iranian Government.
36. H. Hamidian, *Maqālāt-e Hoquq-e Khānevādeh {Articles on Family Law}* (Tehran: Hamun, 1387 [2008]), pp. 123–4.
37. H. Safai and A. Emami, *Mokhtasar-e Hoquq-e Khānevādeh {Concise Family Law}* (Tehran: Enteshārāt-e Mizān, 1387 [2009]), pp. 88–9.
38. Ibid.
39. Article 1061 of the Civil Code of Iran.
40. Ain Nāmeh-ye Ezdevāj-e Mardān-e Irāni bā Zanān-e Khāreji-ye Āvāreh (Dārande-ye Kārt-e Hoviyat-e Atbā'-e Khāreji [The By-law Regulating the Marriage of Iranian Men with Homeless Foreigner Women (Who Hold a Foreign National Identity Card)], Majmue'-ye Qavānin-e 1381 [2002], *Ruznāmeh-ye Rasmi-ye Keshvar*, Vol. 2, p. 1708.
41. Article 1051 of the Civil Code of Iran. See Mohaqeq Damad, *Barresi-ye*, pp. 161–2.
42. Article 987 of the Civil Code of Iran.
43. Article 976 (2) of the Civil Code of Iran.
44. 'Dāstān-e Ezdevāj-e Zan-e Irani bā Mard-e Afqān' [The Story of a Marriage Between an Iranian Woman and an Afghan Man], *BBC Persian*, www.bbc.co.uk/persian/iran/2011/05/110525_121_married_iranian_women_afghan_men.shtml (accessed 19 March 2017).
45. As Mohaqeq Damad argues, marriage of an Iranian woman to a non-Iranian Muslim man is allowed by Islam and is therefore valid. But its registration would be a government regulation that should be observed. Mohaqeq Damad, *Barresi-ye*, pp. 161–2.
46. L. Alikarami, Iran's political paranoia includes the children of foreign fathers, *Al Monitor*, Available: www.al-monitor.com/pulse/originals/2016/12/iranian-mothers-foreign-fathers-children-citizenship-law.html#ixzz4W2uRuLpd (accessed 12 June 2017).
47. R. Mosharaf, 'Barrasi-ye Payāmadhā-ye Ezdevāj-e Qeyr-e Qānuni-ye Zanān-e Irani ba Atbā'-e Bigāneh dar Khorāsān-e Razavi' [Analysing the Consequences of Illegal Marriage of Iranian Women with non-Iranian Men in Khorasan], *Khorāsān*, www.khorasan.ir/banovan/tabid/7403/Default.aspx (accessed 20 March 2017).

NOTES TO PAGES 110–112   257

48. Qanun-e Taein-e Taklif-e Tābeiyat-e Farzandān-e Hāsel az Ezdevāj-e Zanān-e Irāni bā Mardān-e Khāreji [The Bill of Amendment of the Single-clause Bill Determining the Citizenship for Children of Iranian Women Married to Foreign Men], 2 Mehr 1385 [24 September 2006].
49. Legal and Judicial Commission's Report to the Majles, K GH/1572, 26 August 2011.
50. 'Tarhe Tāb'iyat-e Irāni-ye Farzandān-e Zanān-e Irāni va Mardān–e Khāreji Moshkel-e Amniyati Dārad' [The Bill on Iranian Nationality for Children Those Born to Iranian Mothers has National Security Implications], Khabar Online, 6 Mehr 1390 [28 September 2011].
51. 'Vaziyat-e Tāb'iyat-e Farzandān-e Hāsel az Ezdevāj-e Zanān-e Irani bā Mardān-e Khāreji Moshakhas Shod' [The Situation of Nationality of Children Born to Iranian Mothers Is Determined], Hamshahri Online, www.hamshahrionline.ir/details/169311 (accessed 20 March 2017).
52. 'Sodur-e Shenāsnāmeh Brāye Farzandān-e Hāsel az Ezdevāj-e Zanān-e Irani bā Mardān-e Khāreji' [Issuing Birth Certificate for Children Born to Iranian Mothers and Foreign Men], www.salamatnews.com/news/223071/-%D8%B5%D8%AF%D9%88%D8%B1-%D8%B4%D9%86%D8%A7%D8%B3%D9%86%D8%A7%D9%85%D9%87-%D8%A8%D8%B1%D8%A7%DB%8C-%D9%81%D8%B1%D8%B2%D9%86%D8%AF%D8%A7%D9%86-%D8%AD%D8%A7%D8%B5%D9%84-%D8%A7%D8%B2-%D8%A7%D8%B2%D8%AF%D9%88%D8%A7%D8%AC-%D8%B2%D9%86%D8%A7%D9%86-%D8%A7%DB%8C%D8%B1%D8%A7%D9%86%DB%8C-%D8%A8%D8%A7-%D9%85%D8%B1%D8%AF%D8%A7%D9%86-%D8%AE%D8%A7%D8%B1%D8%AC%DB%8C 8C (accessed 20 March 2016).
53. Ray-e Manfi-ye Majles be Tarhe E'tāy-e Tāb'iyat be Farzandān-e Hāsel az Ezdevāj-e Zanān-e Irāni ba Mardān-e Khāreji [Majles Negative Vote to the Bill on Iranian Nationality for Children Borne to Iranian Mothers and Foregin Fathers], Hamshahri Online (5 Mehr 1394 [27 September 2015]), www.hamshahrionline.ir/details/308609/Iran/legislative (accessed 24 March 2017).
54. The civil code does not provide a definition of a virgin girl. As defined by some legal experts and jurists, a virgin is a girl who has never had sexual intercourse with a man. Therefore, her husband would be the first person who will end her chastity. See, e.g., Mohaqeq Damad, Barresi-ye, pp. 52–3; and Safaei and Emami, Mokhtasar-e, p. 79.
55. Article 1041 of the Civil Code of Iran, amended on 22 June 2002 by the Expediency Council. N. Katuziyan, Qānun-e Madani dar Nazm-e Hoquqi-ye Konuni {The Civil Code in the Current Legal Order}, 22nd edition (Tehran: Bonyād-e Hoghughi-ye Mizān, 1387 [2008]), p. 635.
56. Ibid.
57. N. Katuziyan, Khānevādeh: Nekāh va Talāq {Family: Marriage and Divorce}, Vol. 1 (Tehran: Sherkat-e Sahāmi-ye Enteshār, 1387 [2008]), p. 70.

The punishment according to article 3 of the marriage law of 1931 was six months to two years' imprisonment. Ibid., p. 79.
58. Ibid., pp. 76–9.
59. Article 210 of the Civil Code of Iran.
60. Article 211 of the Civil Code of Iran.
61. Article 213 of the Civil Code of Iran.
62. Katuziyan, Khānevādeh: Nekāh va Talāq, p. 77.
63. Article 1210 of the code states that: 'No one, when reaching the age of majority, can be treated as under disability in respect of insanity or immaturity unless his immaturity or insanity is proved'.
Note 1 – the age of majority for boys is fifteen lunar years and for girls nine lunar years. Badrian, *Civil Code of Iran*.
64. Article 1041 of the Civil Code of Iran, amended on 22 June 2002 by the Expediency Council. Katuziyan, *Qānun-e Madani*, p. 635.
65. The One Million Signatures Campaign will be discussed in more detail in Chapter 6.
66. S. Olyai Zand, 'Ezdevāj-e Nāmonāseb Bastari Zamine Saz Barāye Ruspigari' [Improper Marriage is a Cause of Prostitution], *Faslnāme-ye Refāh-e Ejtemāi* 6, Pāeiz 1381 [Autumn 2002].
67. Concluding Observations on the Combined Third and Fourth Periodic Reports of the Islamic Republic of Iran, CRC/C/IRN/CO/3-4. 13 March 2016. http://tbinternet.ohchr.org/_layouts/treatybodyexternal/Download.aspx?symbolno=CRC%2fC%2fIRN%2fCO%2f3-4&Lang=en (accessed 2 May 2018).
68. Katuziyan, Khānevādeh: Nekāh va Talāq, pp. 80–1.
69. Article 1043 of the Civil Code of Iran. Katuziyan, *Qānun-e Madani dar Nazm-e Hoquqi-ye Konuni*, p. 636.
70. Safaei and Emami, *Mokhtasar-e*, p. 77. Among these jurists are: Sheykh Tusi, Seyed Morteza, Ebne Jonayd, Ebne Edris, Shahid Aval, Fakhrol Mohagheghin, Shahid Sani, Saheb Javaher and Abu Hanifeh. N. Qorban Niya, *Bāzpajuhi-ye Hoquq-e Zan: Barrasi-ye Qavānin-e Marbut be Zanān dar Jomhuri-ye Islami-ye Iran {Re-Assesment of Women's Rights Under the Laws of the Islamic Republic of Iran}*, Vol. 2 (Tehran: Enteshārāt-e Ruz-e Now,1384 [2005]), pp. 11–12.
71. Katuziyan, Khānevādeh: Nekāh va Talāq, p. 83.
72. For more detail, see the official website of Ayatollah Makarem Shirazi: http://makarem.ir/websites/farsi/estefta/?mit=637&sid=1145#1145 (accessed 5 May 2012); and 'Ayā Barāye Dokhtar-e Bākereh dar Ezdevāj-e Dāem ya Movaqat Ezn-e Pedar Lāzem ast?' [Is Father's Consent Necessary for Either Permanent or Temporary Marriage of a Virgin Girl?], www.shia-news.com/fa/news/12791/ (accessed 25 March 2017).
73. Katuziyan, Khānevādeh: Nekāh va Talāq, p. 83.
74. Ibid.
75. Emami, *Hoquq-e Madani*, p. 286.
76. Ibid.

NOTES TO PAGES 115–120   259

77. Article 1044 of the Civil Code of Iran. Katuziyan, *Qānun-e Madani*, p. 638.
78. Katuziyan, *Khānevādeh: Nekāh va Talāq*, pp. 82–4 and Emami, *Hoquq-e Madani*, p. 285.
79. The Supreme Court, Verdict No.1, 18.04.1984, *Ruznāmeh-ye Rasmi-ye Keshvar*, No.11445, 14.06.1984. There were different decisions from different courts about similar cases where a marriage was conducted without the father's permission. To ensure the uniformity of judicial procedures, the Supreme Court issued this verdict.
80. Cited in Mir-Hosseini, *Islam and Gender*, p. 153.
81. This case was defended by the author when practicing law in Iran.
82. Human Rights Committee, General Comment 28, Equality of rights between men and women (Article 3, *U.N. Doc. CCPR/C121/Rev.1/Add.10* (2000), para. 24.
83. Ahmadi Khorasani, Jonbesh-e Yek Million Emzā: Revāyati az Darun [One Million Signatures Demanding Change to Discriminatory Laws: An Internal Narrative] (Tehran, 1386 [2007]), p. 29.
84. Ibid., pp. 35–9.
85. Inheritance will be discussed later in the present chapter.
86. The Guardian Council, *Decision No. 21056*, 25 August 1984.
87. Katuziyan, Khānevādeh: Nekāh va Talāq, p. 117.
88. Safai and Emami, *Mokhtasar-e*, p. 96.
89. 'Sabt-e Āmār-e Ejdevāj-e Mojadad va Movaqat dar Sabt-e Ahvāl' [Registration of Temporay and Second Marriages in the Registry of Personal Status Office], http://khabarfarsi.com/ext/1799020 (accessed 19 March 2017).
90. R. Ramezan Nargessi, 'Bāztāb-e Chand Hamsari dar Jāme'e' [The Reflection of Polygamy in Society], *Ketāb-e Zanān* 27, Bahār 1384 [Spring 2005], pp. 145–74 at p. 155.
91. Etemad Newspaper, 6 Tir 1382 [27 June 2003], cited in ibid at p. 155.
92. Ebadi, interview with the author, London, April 2012.
93. In their view, by allowing polygamy women can marry and have family. Moreover, biological differences between men and women enable men to have more than one wife. Safai and Emami, *Mokhtasar-e*, p. 95.
94. A. Hossein Abadi, 'Erāeh-ye Lāyeheh-ye Hemāyat az Khānevādeh Zarurati Nadāsht' [It Was Not Necessary to Introduce the New Family Protection Bill], *Majaleh-ye Vekālat* 37 & 38,12 Mehr 1387 [3 October 2008], pp. 6–8.
95. This information is available from the website of Iran's census centre: http://amar.sci.org.ir (accessed 25 March 2017).
96. On 2 April 2012 Ali Larijani, the head of the Majles, sent the ratified Family Protection Law to the Guardian Council for approval. Letter Number 136/12–2 April 2012. The GC approved the Bill on 27 February 2013.
97. 'Natāyej-e Tarh-e Hamsarkoshi dar 15 Ostān-e Keshvar' [The Result of Research on Intra-Marital Homicide in 15 Provinces of the Country], *Ruznāmeh-ye Iran*, 18 Bahman 1381 [7 February 2003]. See also 'The Effect of

Laws on Women's Lives', *Change for Equality*, www.sign4change.info/english/spip.php?article41 (accessed 25 March 2017).
98. It is not necessary for the temporary marriage to be registered. The permission of the first wife is only necessary in the case of permanent marriage.
99. Maryam Hosseinkhah, interview with the author, London, September 2012.
100. Qur'an 4:3, which states: 'Marry women of your choice, two, three, or four; but if you fear that you shall not be able to deal justly [with them] then only one, or [a captive] that your right hands possess. That is nearer to prevent you from doing injustice.'
101. See Badrin, *International*, pp. 41–2.
102. See e.g. Tanzil-ur- Rahman, *A Code of Muslim Personal Law*, 1978, Vol. 1, pp. 92–101; and Al-Zuhayli, W. *Al-Fiqh Al-Islami wa-Adillatuh* (Arabic), Vol. 9, pp. 6669–70. Cited in Baderin, *International*, p. 140.
103. They refer to the concluding part of the verses 4:3, which provides that '(monogamy) is best to prevent you from doing injustice.' Baderin, *International*, p. 140.
104. Ibid.
105. Ayatollah Yousef Sanei, 'A Second Marriage without the First Wife's Permission is Harām and Null and Void', availabe at: http://saanei.org/?view=01,02,48,218,0#01,01,05,9,0 (accessed 27 March 2017).
106. Ibid.
107. See N.A. Shah, Women, *the Koran and International Human Rights Law: The Experience of Pakistan* (Leiden: Martinus Nijihoff Publishers, 2006), p. 49.
108. See Y. Ali, *The Meaning of the Holy Qur'an* (Maryland: Amana Corporation, 1989).
109. Badrin, *International*, pp. 142–3.
110. Mir-Hosseini, 'Women in Search of Common Ground', p. 300. See also Z. Mir-Hosseini, 'The Construction of Gender in Islamic Legal Thought and Strategies for Reform', *Hawwa Journal of Women in the Middle East and the Islamic World* 1/1 (2003), pp. 1–28 at p. 23.
111. Article 1120 of the Civil Code of Iran.
112. Katuziyan, Khānevādeh: Nekāh va Talāq, p. 255.
113. Article 1132 of the Civil Code of Iran.
114. Article 1140 of the Civil Code of Iran.
115. According to Article 1075 of the Civil Code of Iran marriage is deemed temporary when it is for a limited period of time.
116. Katuziyan, Khānevādeh: Nekāh va Talāq, p. 256.
117. Article 438 of the Civil Code of Iran states that: 'Trickery denotes conduct which causes the other party to the transaction to be misled'.
118. Article 1128 of the Civil Code of Iran.
119. Article 1121 of the Civil Code of Iran.
120. Article 1125 of the Civil Code of Iran.
121. Article 1124 of the Civil Code of Iran states that: 'The defects of the wife entitle the man to a right of cancellation of marriage if they existed at the time of marriage'.

122. Article 1126 of the Civil Code of Iran.
123. Article 1122 of the Civil Code of Iran.
124. Article 1125 of the Civil Code of Iran.
125. Katuziyan, Khānevādeh: Nekāh va Talāq, p. 257.
126. Article 1126 of the Civil Code of Iran. This article states that: 'Any one of the married couple who was cognisant of the existence of the defects mentioned in the other party before the marriage was celebrated, has no right after that date to cancel the marriage'. Badrian, *The Civil Code of Iran.*
127. Article 1124 of the Civil Code of Iran.
128. Article 1131 of the Civil Code of Iran.
129. See, for example, Mir-Hosseini, *Marriage on Trial*, pp. 36–8. Safaei and Emami, *Mokhtasar-e*, pp. 201–203, and Katuziyan, *Khānevādeh: Nekāh va Talāq*, pp. 273–82.
130. For the English translation of Article 8 see Mir-Hosseini, *Marriage on Trial*, p. 57.
131. As previously said, Imam Khomeini was among those religious figures who strongly opposed the Family Protection Law.
132. Mir-Hosseini, *Marriage on Trial*, p. 55.
133. Schirazi, *Constitution*, p. 217.
134. R. Khomeini, *Ruznāmeh-ye Enqelāb-e Islāmi*, No. 107, Mehr 1358 [October 1979]. English translation is cited in Shirazi, *Constitution*, p. 217.
135. Schirazi, *Constitution*, p. 217.
136. Mir-Hosseini, *Marriage on Trial*, p. 57.
137. Ibid. The provisions are almost the same as those mentioned in article 8 of the Family Protection Law of 1975.
138. Article 1129 of the Civil Code of Iran states that: 'If the husband refuses to pay the cost of maintenance of his wife, and if it is impossible to enforce a judgment of the court and to induce him to pay the expenses, the wife can refer to the judge applying for and the judge will compel the husband to divorce her.' Badrian, *The Civil Code of Iran.*
139. According to Article 1130 of the Civil Code of Iran, a wife can refer to an Islamic judge and request a divorce in the following circumstances: 'When it is proved to the Court that the continuation of the marriage causes difficult and undesirable conditions, the judge can for the sake of avoiding harm and difficulty compel the husband to, divorce his wife. If this cannot be done, then the divorce will be made on the permission of the Islamic judge.' Badrian, *The Civil Code of Iran.*
140. Mir-Hosseini discussed the ruling on 'denial of harm' with the clerics in Qom in her book *Islam and Gender*, pp. 123–8.
141. The case was defended by the author in a civil court in Tehran.
142. Note on Article 1130 of the Civil Code of Iran.
143. Article 1023 of the Civil Code of Iran.
144. During *eddeh*, except in the case of the death of the husband, the husband can return to the marriage whenever he desires. Therefore, during this period

divorce is not completed and the wife is still under the control of her husband. The period of *eddeh* for a divorce or for the dissolution of a marriage consists of three consecutive monthly periods of a woman unless the woman concerned though of child-bearing age has no monthly period, in which case the period of *eddeh* will be three months. The period of *eddeh* for divorce or dissolution of marriage or waiver of the remaining period or its expiry in the case of temporary marriage for a non-pregnant woman is the expiry of two monthly periods unless contrary to the nature of her age, she no longer has such periods, in which case the waiting period will be forty-five days. The period of *eddeh* for divorce or dissolution of marriage act or waiver or expiry of the period of marriage in the case of a woman who is pregnant will be until she given birth to a child. There is no *eddeh* in the case of a wife who has not had any matrimonial intercourse with her husband, or in the case of a wife beyond the age of conception who is not affected by any *eddeh* for divorce or for dissolution of marriage. These two kinds of divorce are irrevocable, and the husband cannot return to the marriage after the divorce. In both cases, if the husband dies the *eddeh* for death must be observed.

145. The period of *eddeh* in the case of death (of the husband) in both permanent and temporary marriages is four months and ten days, unless the wife is pregnant when the *eddeh* comes to an end with the birth of the child provided that the interval between the death of the husband and the birth of the child is longer than four month and ten days: if not, the period of *eddeh* will be the same four months and ten days.

146. Article 1030 of the Civil Code of Iran.

147. According to Articles 225 and 226 of the Criminal Code of Iran (2013) adultery is punishable by stoning in the following cases: '(1) Adultery by a married man who is wedded to a permanent wife with whom he has had intercourse and may have intercourse when he so desires; (2) Adultery of a married woman with an adult man provided the woman is permanently married and has had intercourse with her husband and is able to do so again'. Although the punishment is same for both men and women, one should bear in mind that polygamy and temporary marriage are allowed for men in Iran. Therefore, they can easily escape the punishment by relying on these legal provisions that support them.

148. Article 1119 of the Civil Code of Iran. For Katuziyan's discussion on the stipulation conditions to the marriage contract, see Katuziyan, *Khānevādeh: Nekāh va Talāq*, pp. 227–47.

149. See Khomeini, R., *Sahifeh-ye Imam*, Vol. 10 (Tehran: Moasseseh-ye Tanzim va Nashr-e Asār-e Hazrat Imam Khomeini, 1378 [1999]).

150. Ebadi, interview with the author, London, September 2016.

151. Mir-Hosseini, *Islam and Gender*, pp. 160–4.

152. Ibid., p. 162.

153. Article 1119 of the Civil Code of Iran.

154. Schirazi, *Constitution*, p. 217.

155. Safaei and Emami, *Mokhtasar-e*, p. 219.
156. M. Esmaeili, Shorut-e Zemn-e Aqd dar Nekāh [Stipulated Conditions in the Marriage Contract] (Tehran: Nashr-e Harir, 1389 [2010]), p. 22.
157. Katuziyan, Khānevādeh: Nekāh va Talāq, pp. 240–4.
158. Article 1144 of the Civil Code of Iran.
159. Article 1148 of the Civil Code of Iran.
160. *Khul'* will be discussed further below.
161. According to Article 1147 of the Civil Code of Iran: 'A *mobāarāt* divorce occurs when the dislike is mutual in which case the compensation must not be more than the marriage portion.'
162. Article 1145 of the Civil Code of Iran.
163. Article 1146 of the Civil Code of Iran.
164. Qur'an 2:229.
165. Article 1146 of the Civil Code of Iran.
166. The Legal Department of the Judiciary Opinion, *No. 7/193*, 14 April 2007.
167. Article 1149 of the Civil Code of Iran.
168. Katuziyan, Khānevādeh: Nekāh va Talāq, p. 388.
169. J. Basedow and N. Yassari, *Iranian Family and Succession Laws and their Application in German Courts* (Tubingen: Mohr Siebeck, 2004), p. 87.
170. Katuziyan, Khānevādeh: Nekāh va Talāq, p. 413.
171. Mohaqeq Damad, *Barresi-ye*, p. 438.
172. Ebadi, interview with the author, London, June 2017.
173. For detailed analysis on temporary marriage see S. Haeri, *Law of Desire: Temporary Marriage in Shi'i Iran* (Syracuse, New York: Syracuse University Press, 1989).
174. Mir-Hosseini, *Marriage on Trial*, p. 164. See also Mohaqeq Damad, *Barresi-ye*, p. 209.
175. J. Afary, *Sexual Politics in Modern Iran* (Cambridge, Cambridge University Press, 2011), p. 60.
176. M.A. Daykandi, 'Ezdevāj-e Movaqat dar Quran-e Karim' [Temporary Marriage in the Qur'an], *Nashriyeh-ye Safir* 1, Esfand 1385 [March 2007], pp. 157–202 at p. 162.
177. M. Motahhari, *Nezām-e Hoquq-e Zan dar Islam* [The Structure of Women's Rights in Islam] (Tehran: Sadrā, 1358 [1979]), pp. 66–7.
178. H. Mousavi, 'Ezdevāj-e Movaqat: Hekmathā va Zarurathā' [Temporary Marriage: Wisdoms and Necessities], *Mobaleqān* 85, Azar 1385 [December 2006], pp. 38–52 at p. 46.
179. M. Pur Tehrani, 'Ezdevāj-e Movaqat: Be Har Do Ruye Sekeh Bengarim [Temporary Marriage: Consider Both Sides of the Coin], *Gozāresh* 100, Ordibehesht 1378 [May 1999], pp. 22–4 at p. 23.
180. Ibid.
181. For his detailed analysis on this issue see Motahhari, *Nezām-e*, pp. 47–61.
182. N. Makarem Shirazi, 'Ezdevāj-e Movaqat Yek Zarurat-e Ejtenāb Nāpazir-e Ejtemāi Ast [Temporary Marriage is an Unavoidable Social Need]', 23/07/1389

[15 Pctober 2010], https://makarem.ir/main.aspx?lid=0&typeinfo=1& catid=25445&pageindex=0&mid=252812 (accessed 20 April 2018).
183. Two articles deal with duration and the rest with *mahr*.
184. 'A marriage is temporary', states Article 1075 of the Civil Code of Iran, 'when the duration is specified.' It can be for a very short period, such as twenty-four hours, or very long, such as ninety-nine years.
185. Mohaqeq Damad, *Barresi-ye*, p. 213.
186. 'In Islamic jurisprudence this type of marriage is referred to as 'marriage of pleasure': *mut'a* in Arabic denotes pleasure.' Mir-Hosseini, *Marriage on Trial*, p. 164.
187. Ibid., p. 165.
188. Article 1133 of the Civil Code of Iran.
189. Article 940 of the Civil Code of Iran.
190. 'Mokhālefat-e Majles bā Elzāmi Shodan-e Sabt-e Ezdevāj-e Movaqat' [Majles Rejection of the Mandatory Registration of Temporary Marriage], *Fars News Agency*, 15 Esfand 1390 [5 March 2012], www.farsnews.com/newstext.php?nn=13901215000667 (accessed 27 March 2017).
191. 'Discrimination in Iran's Temporary Marriage Law Goes Unchecked', *Guardian*, 6 March 2012, www.guardian.co.uk/world/iran-blog/2012/mar/06/iran-temporary-marriage-law-sigheh (accessed 24 March 2017).
192. Ibid.
193. Article 1139 of the Civil Code of Iran.
194. Article 1097 of the Civil Code of Iran.
195. Mir-Hosseini, *Marriage on Trial*, p. 165.
196. Article 1152 of the Civil Code of Iran.
197. Article 1153 of the Civil Code of Iran.
198. Mir-Hosseini, *Marriage on Trial*, p. 166.
199. Qur'an 4:12 states that: 'You get half of what your wives leave behind, if they had no children. If they had children, you get one-fourth of what they leave. All this, after fulfilling any will they had left, and after paying off all debts. They get one-fourth of what you leave behind, if you had no children. If you had children, they get one-eighth of what you bequeath. All this, after fulfilling any will you had left, and after paying off all debts. If the deceased man or woman was a loner, and leaves two siblings, male or female, each of them gets one-sixth of the inheritance. If there are more siblings, then they equally share one-third of the inheritance. All this, after fulfilling any will, and after paying off all debts, so that no one is hurt'.
200. Articles 899 and 900 of the Civil Code of Iran.
201. In this regard Qur'an 4:11 provides that: 'God directs your children's [inheritance]: to the male, a portion equal to that of two females'.
202. Article 901 of the Civil Code of Iran.
203. Baderin, *International*, p. 147.
204. Qur'an 4:7.

205. To support his idea, he quotes Badawi where he justifies the double-share rule. See Baderin, *International*, p. 147.
206. Mir-Hosseini asked Ayatollah Azari-Qomi, one of the most influential clerics of the first decade of the Islamic Republic, why women do not have equal rights with men in inheritance? He responded: 'At a time when patriarchy ruled in different human societies and women was but a slave, the result of women's work belonged totally to men. Islam gave women economic independence and the Holy Qur'an explicitly declares woman to possesses her own wealth; Islam has instituted the right of mothers to demand wages from their husbands for breast-feeding and caring for their children; according to Islamic instructions, a man has no right to order his wife to do housework, and a woman can demand wages for cooking and sewing and even for work she does for herself; also a woman has the right to demand that her husband pay her dower, however large; provision of complete personal maintenance for a wife is incumbent on her husband, even if she is rich. Unlike a man, who is bound to provide for his wife and children and his own parents if they are poor', [women have no duty]. Mir-Hosseini, *Gender and Islam*, p. 61.
207. Baderin, *International*, p. 148.
208. Article 946 of the Civil Code of Iran.
209. Iran: Ayatollah Support Women's Right to Inheritance and Abortion, www.payvand.com/news/08/feb/1170.html and 'Iran Enforces New Women's Inheritance Law', www.presstv.ir/Detail.aspx?id=88367&sectionid=351020101 (accessed 25 March 2017).
210. Ibid.
211. Mir-Hosseini, *Gender and Islam*, p. 131.

Chapter 5 Iranian Women Demanding Equal Rights: The Case of Iran's Criminal Code

1. P. Paidar, *Women and the Political Process in Twentieth-Century Iran* (Cambridge: Cambridge University Press, 1995), p. 113.
2. Article 179 of the Criminal Code of 1926. The Persian version of this code is available from the Majlis's website, http://rc.majlis.ir/fa/law/show/91023 (accessed 26 March 2017). This will be discussed further in the present chapter.
3. In 1936, Reza Shah issued a decree that barred women from appearing on the streets with *hejāb*. He also ordered the police to remove women's *chādor* or scarf should they come out veiled.
4. Articles 1–195 were ratified on 25 August 1982 and Articles 196–218 were ratified on 17 October 1982.
5. Z. Saidzadeh, 'Jāye Khāliye-h Hoquq-e Jensi dar Lāyehe-ye Mojāzāt-e Islami' [The Absence of Gender Related Rights in the Criminal Code], *Meydaan*, www.meydaan.org/ShowArticle.aspx?arid=692 (accessed 25 March 2017).

6. According to Article 1 of the Civil Code of Iran: 'The Islamic Consultative Assembly's enactments and the results of the referendum, having gone through legal procedures will be notified to the President of the Republic. The President shall within five days sign them and notify them to executors, and issue instruction to have them published, and the Official Gazette shall be required to publish them within 72 hours after notification thereof'.
7. The Supreme Leader can intervene through *hokm-e hokumati*, which was discussed in Chapter 1. For a detailed account of the process of the approval of the criminal code of 2013 see 'Sarnevesht-e Lāyeheh-ye Qānun-e Mojāzāt-e Islami dar Hālehi az Ebhām' [The Vague Situation of the Islamic Criminal Code], http://lawyerman.persianblog.ir/post/155 (accessed 26 March 2017).
8. Article 14 of the Islamic Criminal Code of Iran (2013).
9. Article 16 of the Islamic Criminal Code of Iran (2013). It is therefore equivalent to the Western notion of 'talion law'.
10. Article 17 of the Islamic Criminal Code of Iran (2013).
11. Article 15 of the Islamic Criminal Code of Iran (2013).
12. Articles 18 and 19 of the Islamic Criminal Code of Iran (2013).
13. Article 49 of the Islamic Criminal Code of Iran (2013).
14. S. Ebadi, *The Rights of the Child: A Study on Legal Aspects of Children's Rights in Iran* (Tehran: UNICEF, 1994), p. 23.
15. Ibid.
16. Article 1210 (1) of the Civil Code of Iran, amended on 5 November 1991.
17. Article 49 of the Islamic Criminal Code of Iran (1991).
18. Articles 147, 88 and 89 of the Islamic Criminal Code of Iran (2013). For detailed analysis of the age of criminal responsibility under the new criminal code see M.H. Nayyeri, 'Criminal Responsibility of Children in the Islamic Republic of Iran's New Penal Code', www.iranhrdc.org/english/publications/legal-commentary/1000000054-criminal-responsibility-of-children-in-the-islamic-republic-of-irans-new-penal-code.html#.T-g4gytYs0M (accessed 26 March 2017).
19. Article 91 of the Islamic Criminal Code of Iran (2013).
20. Article 1 of the Convention on the Rights of the Child.
21. For a detailed analysis of women's testimony in Islam see F. Sanei, *Shahādat-e Zan dar Islam {Women's Testimony in Islam}* (Qom: Meysam-e Tamār, 1386 [2007]).
22. According to Article 181 of the Islamic Criminal Code of Iran (2013) an *ādel* (just) person is one who in the opinion of the judge or a person who testifies to his righteousness is not a sinner. The testimony of one who has a reputation for debauchery and commits a mortal sin or venial sins is not accepted until changes in his behaviour have become evident and his competence and righteousness have been established.
23. Article 237 of the Islamic Criminal Code of Iran (1991). The English translation of the articles can be found at http://mehr.org/Islamic_Penal_Code_of_Iran.pdf (accessed 26 March 2017).

24. Article 117 of the Islamic Criminal Code of Iran (2013).
25. Article 128 of the Islamic Criminal Code of Iran (2013).
26. *Qazf*, according to Article 139 of the Islamic Criminal Code of Iran (1991) is the act of falsely accusing another person of a wrongdoing, which according to Article 153 of the code can only be substantiated by two male witnesses.
27. According to Article 135 of the Islamic Criminal Code of Iran (1991), *qavvādi* is the act of 'collecting and connecting two or more people for the purpose of *zenā* and *lavāt*'. Only two (just) men can serve as witness (Article 137).
28. Felonious theft, according to Article 201 of the Islamic Criminal Code of Iran (1991) is punishable by amputation of four fingers of the right hand at their base. A second offense will cost the thief a left foot, amputated above the toes, with half the instep remaining. The third offence brings a life-sentence. The fourth is conducive to a death sentence. Article 199 only allows the testimony of two just men.
29. *Mohārebeh* has been translated into English variously as 'waging war against God', 'war against God and the state' and 'enmity towards God'.
30. According to Article 183 of the Islamic Criminal Code of Iran (1991), anyone who endangers public security or creates fear and terror by taking up arms is considered *mohāreb* (seditious) and *mofsed* (corrupt). Article 189 calls for two (just) men to establish the crime.
31. Article 170 of the Islamic Criminal Code of Iran (1991).
32. Article 459 of the Islamic Criminal Code of Iran (1991).
33. Ebadi, *Hoquq-e Zan*, pp. 81–2.
34. Article 199 of the Islamic Criminal Code of Iran (2013).
35. Ibid.
36. 'According to Article 155 of this law, the requirements for a witness are: adulthood, sanity, legitimate birth, justness, non-personal interest, non-animosity with either side of the dispute and not being a tramp or beggar'. Abghari, *Introduction*, pp. 123–4.
37. Cited in Afshar, *Islam and Feminisms*, p. 105.
38. Baderin, *International*, p. 101.
39. See N.A. Shah, 'Women's Human Rights in the Koran: An Interpretive Approach', *Human Rights Quarterly* 28 (2006), pp. 869–903 at p. 899.
40. Ibid., p. 903.
41. S. El-Bahnassawi, *Women Between Islam and World Legislation* (Safat: Dār-ul-Qalam, 1985), p. 132. Cited in Baderin, *International*, p. 102.
42. Baderin, *International*, p. 101.
43. Qur'an 65:1–2.
44. Qur'an 5:106 states: 'Oh you who believe! When death approaches any of you, [take] witnesses among yourselves when making bequests- two just persons of your own'.
45. The Qur'an (4:15) in this regard provides that: 'And those of your women who commit lewdness [illegal sexual intercourse], take the evidence of four witnesses from amongst you against them'.

46. Baderin, *International*, p. 102.
47. *Report Iran: Honour Killing*, Landinfo, 22 May 2009, p. 6. For detailed analysis of honour killings in Iran see S. Zarabadi, 'Bā Ejāzeh-ye Khodam Nāmusam Rā Mikosham' [I Kill My Honour with My Own Permission], *Zanān* 109, Khordād 1383 [May 2004], pp. 29–33 and S. Sadr, 'Nāmus-e Zanān Vābasteh be Yek Mard' [Women's Honour Depending on a Single Man], *Zanān* 93, Abān 1381 [October 2002], pp. 10–13.
48. A. Gill, 'Honour Killings and the Quest for Justice in Black and Minority Ethnic Communities in the UK and Moving Toward a 'Multiculturalism Without Culture': Constructing a Victim-Friendly Human Rights Approach to Forced Marriage in the UK. United Nations Division for the Advancement of Women, United Nations Economic Commission for Africa, Expert Group Meeting on Good Practices in Legislation to Address Harmful Practices Against Women, United Nations Conference Centre, Addis Ababa, Ethiopia, 25 to 28 May 2009. EGM/GPLHP/2009/EP.03, 12 June 2009, p. 3. Honour killing is also defined as follows: 'murders by families on family members who are believed to have brought 'shame' on the family name. The apparent 'shame' could be caused by a victim refusing to enter into an arranged marriage or for having a relationship that the family considers to be inappropriate. Some victims are driven to suicide from the pressure of their families'.
49. *Report Iran*, p. 7.
50. Integration of the Human Rights of Women and a Gender Perspective: Violence Against Women, Report of the Special Rapporteur on violence against women, its causes and consequences, Yakin Ertürk, Mission to the Islamic Republic of Iran (29 January to 6 February 2005), *E/CN.4/2006/61/Add.3*, 27 January 2006, p. 11.
51. *Report Iran*, p. 8.
52. Ibid.
53. Integration of the Human Rights, p. 11.
54. A. Qarai Moghadam, 'Qatlhā-ye Nāmusi yā 'nahve-h kardan' dar Miyān-e Qabāyel-e Arab-e Khuzestan' [Honour Killings among Khuzestan's Arab Tribes], *Majaleh-ye Dādgostari* 32, Pāeiz 1379 [Autumn 2000], pp. 75–92, p. 81.
55. Ibid., pp. 81 and 83–5.
56. Article 381 of the Islamic Criminal Code of Iran (2013).
57. 'A Man Hanged His Own Sister Because She Wanted to Marry a Man She Loved', https://iranhr.net/en/articles/194/ (accessed 28 March 2017).
58. Article 301 of the Islamic Criminal Code of Iran (2013).
59. 'A Suspicious Father Strangles his 14-year-old Daughter'. *Quds* newspaper, www.qudsdaily.com/archive/1387/html/8/1387–08–12/page8.html#1 (accessed 22 October 2010). For the case of Zahra, a nine-year-old girl who was killed by her father, see N. Rostami, 'Khon-e Man Cheqadr Miarzad' [How Much is My Blood Worth], *Zanān*, Khordād 1383 [May 2004], pp. 23–5. For a detailed report on the issue of killing girls by their fathers

NOTES TO PAGES 149–150   269

see R. Karimi Majd, 'Yek Jenāyat-e Kāmelan Ma'muli' [An Ordinary Crime], *Zanān* 93, Abān 1381 [October 2002], pp. 2–9.

60. Ebadi, interview wth the author, London, May 2012.
61. Article 630 of the Islamic Criminal Code of Iran (1996) states that: 'When a man catches his wife in the act of *zenā* with an unknown man and if he has knowledge of his wife's consent, he can kill both perpetrators. If his wife did not give her consent, the husband can only kill the man. In cases of assault and battery, the judgment is the same as in the case of murder'.
62. 'The Effect of Laws on Women's Lives'. 28 August 2006, *Change for Equality*, http://we-change.org/site/english/spip.php?article41 (accessed 27 March 2017).
63. Article 83(b) of the Islamic Criminal Code of Iran (1991) defined a married woman as someone who 'has a permanent husband who has had intercourse with her while she was cognisant and aware, and who has had the opportunity to have intercourse with her husband'. Article 86 also provided for the following stipulation, 'Fornication between a man or woman who each have a permanent spouse but who have no access to them due to travel, imprisonment, or such like, with legitimate proof, is not punishable by *rajm* (stoning).'
64. According Article 167 of the Constitution of Iran (1979): 'the judge is bound to endeavour to judge each case on the basis of the codified law. In case of the absence of any such law, he has to deliver his judgement on the basis of authoritative Islamic sources and authentic *fatāwā*. He, on the pretext of the silence of or deficiency of law in the matter, or its brevity or contradictory nature, cannot refrain from admitting and examining cases and delivering his judgement'.
65. The punishment of *zenā* was changed to execution in the 2013 code. See Article 224.
66. M.J. Habibzadeh and H. Babai, 'Qatl dar Farāsh' [Honour Killings], *Modares* 4, Zemestān 1378 [Winter 1999], pp. 89–90. See also H. Mehrpur, 'Seyri dar Mabāni-ye Feqhi va Hoquqi-ye Mādeh-ye 630 Qānun-e Mojāzāt-e Islami' [Analysis of Legal and Jurisprudential Basis of Article 630 of the Islamic Criminal Code], *Majaleh-ye Nāmeh-ye Mofid* 8, 1375 [1996], pp. 167–88.
67. Article 179 of the Criminal Code of Iran (1926). The Persian-language version of this code is available from the Majles website: http://rc.majlis.ir/fa/law/show/91023 (accessed 27 March 2017).
68. Article 324 of the Penal Code of France (1810). Available at: www.napoleon-series.org/research/government/france/penalcode/c_penalcode3b.html (accessed 27 March 2016). This provision is omitted from the 1992 French penal code. Habibzadeh and Babai, 'Qatl dar Farāsh', p. 82. For more details on comparisons between Article 179 of the 1926 Iranian code and Article 324 of the 1810 French code, see A.A. Samadi, 'Mādeh-ye 179 Qānun-e Mojāzāt-e Iran va Moqāyeseh-ye ān bā Shaq-e 2 az Mādeh-ye 324 Qānun-e Mojāzāt-e Farānseh' [Comparative Analysis of Article 170 of Iran's Criminal

Code with Article 324(2) of the French Penal Code], *Majaleh-ye Kānun-e Vokalā* 78 (1961).
69. Habibzadeh and Babai, 'Qatl dar Farāsh', pp. 88–9.
70. Under the Islamic Criminal Code of Iran (2013) *diyeh* is defined as 'monetary compensation that Shar'ia has specified for the loss or damage caused in crime against a life or bodily harm, which is paid to the victim or his next of kin.' See Articles 17, 448 and 450.
71. Articles 448 and 450 Islamic Criminal Code of Iran (2013).
72. According to the code: 'blood money shall be paid in the case of a non-intentional act, as a result of pure mistake that results in death, loss of limb or infliction of bodily injury, such as, for example, the accidental shooting of a person while hunting, resulting in death or bodily injury; a non-intentional act as a result of pure mistake that results in death, loss of limb or infliction of bodily injury, where the person intends to do an act that is not on its own criminal, such as while punishing a person, or administering medical treatment that accidently results in the death or injury of a patient and intentional offences to which *qesās* is not applicable'. See Articles 448 and 450 of the Islamic Criminal Code of Iran (2013).
73. Article 347 of the Islamic Criminal Code of Iran (2013).
74. Article 550 of the Islamic Criminal Code of Iran (2013).
75. For an analysis of *qesās* under Islamic law see Z.S. Kermanshahi, 'Jāygāh-e Zan dar Feqh-e Keyfari-ye Islami' [Women's Status under Islamic Criminal Feqh], *Zanān* 13, Shahrivar 1372 [August 1993], pp. 56–9.
76. Article 382 of the Islamic Criminal Code of Iran (2013).
77. Ibid.
78. Article 448 of the Islamic Criminal Code of Iran (2013).
79. A. Mohammadi Jurkuye, '*Diyeh va Qesās va Taklif-e Hokumat va Haq-e Zanān*' [*Diyeh* and *Qesās*: Women's Rights and the Government's Obligation], *Majale-ye Bāztāb-e Andisheh* 52, 1383 [2004], pp. 46–56 at p. 49. For an analysis of the views of some *foqahā* on the issue of *diyeh*, see A. Bagheri and N. Mokhtari Afrakati, 'Bāzpajuhi-ye Motun-e Qurani va Ravāi dar Bāb-e Diyeh-ye Zan va Mard' [Re-examination of the Qur'an's Text in Relation to Men and Women's Blood Money], *Majaleh-ye Hoquq-e Dāneshkadeh-ye Hoquq va Olum-e Siyāsi-ye Dāneshgāh-he Tehran* 74, Zemestān 1385 [Winter 2006], pp. 47–68.
80. Zan-e Ruz, 28 May 1994. Cited in H. Afshar, *Islam and Feminisms*, p. 110.
81. 'Barge Ākhar dar Parvande-ye Qatl-e Leila Fathi' [Last Chapter in Leila Fathi's Case], http://khabarfarsi.com/ext/2548735 (accessed 28 March 2017).
82. Zan-e Ruz, 28 May 1994. Cited in H. Afshar, *Islam and the Feminisms*, p. 111.
83. S. Ebadi, *Iran Awakening: A Memoir of Revolution and Hope* (New York: Random House, 2006), p. 117.
84. Ibid.
85. This issue was discussed in the final meeting that Mir-Hosseini had with the *Payam-e Zan* clerics. Cited in Mir-Hosseini, *Islam and Gender*, pp. 184–5.

86. Ibid.
87. Article 716 (6) of the Islamic Criminal Code of Iran (2013).
88. Ibid.
89. Article 388 of the Islamic Criminal Code of Iran (2013).
90. 'Amendment of the Law of Compulsory Insurance for the Civil Liability of the Owners of Motor Vehicles Against Third Parties', ratified on 6 July 2008. Article 2 (2) provides for equal compensation for men and women in car accidents. The Persian version of the law is available on the Majlis website: http://rc.majlis.ir/fa/law/show/134253 (accessed 27 March 2016).
91. 'Iran Women to Get Equal 'Blood Money' in Car Crashes', *Reuters*, 27 May 2008, www.reuters.com/article/us-iran-women-bloodmoney-idUSDAH 7353562008052 (accessed 27 March 2017).
92. Qur'an 4:92.
93. Y. Sanei, Feqh va Zendegi 3: Barabari-ye Diyeh [Feqh and Life Vol. 3: Equality of Blood Money] (Qom: Meysam Tamar, 1386 [2007]), pp. 60–8.
94. For example, he refers to Qur'an 10:44 'Indeed, Allah does not wrong the people at all, but it is the people who are wronging themselves'; Qur'an 40:31 'Allah wants no injustice for his servants'; Qur'an 6:115 'And the word of your Lord has been fulfilled in truth and in justice' and Qur'an 4:1 'O mankind, fear your Lord, who created you from one soul and created from it its mate and dispersed from both of them many men and women. And fear Allah, through whom you ask one another, and the wombs. Indeed, Allah is ever, over you, an observer'.
95. Qur'an 5:45. Grand Ayatollah Yusef Sanei's perspective on *diyeh* is available from his official website: www.saanei.org/index.php?view=01,01,04,318,40 (accessed 3 April 2018).
96. Ibid.
97. Qur'an 49:13.
98. *Jāme'eh-ye Sālem*, September 1995, Cited in Mir-Hosseini, *Islam and Gender*, p. 186.
99. Ibid., pp. 186–8.
100. Ibid.
101. Ibid.
102. See J.H. Beckstrom, 'Transplantation of Legal System: An Early Report on the Reception of Western Laws in Ethiopia', *American Journal of Comparative Law* 21/3 (Summer 1973), pp. 557–83 at pp. 557–8.

Chapter 6 The One Million Signatures Campaign: Domestic Discourse on Gender Equality

1. 'Campaign Khod Dalil-e Zendegi Ast' [The Campaign Itself is a Reason for Life], *The Feminist School*, www.feministschool.com/campaign/spip.php?article18 (accesssed 3 April 2017).

2. 'Pāsokh be Porsesh hā-ye Motadāvel dar Mored-e Campain-e Yek Milion Emzā' [Answers to the Most Popular Questions about the One Million Signatures Campaign], *The Feminist School*, www.feministschool.com/campaign/spip.php?article1 (accessed 3 April 2017).
3. N. Ahmadi Khorasani, translated by D. Simin, 'The Two Storytellers of the Women's Prison and the Imaginary Literature of the One Million Signatures Campaign', 28 April 2007, *Change for Equality*, http://we-change.org/site/english/spip.php?article74 (accessed 3 April 2017).
4. According to Tahmasebi, 'the past few years have witnessed the re-emergence of the Iranian women's movement as a strong voice for justice, which has attracted both national and international attention. Perhaps the reason explaining the current strength of the women's movement can be partly attributed to the fact that it is focused on the broad demand of equality within the legal system and under the law'. See S. Tahmasebi, 'Empowering Iranian Women through the One Million Signatures Campaign', 1 September 2007, *Change for Equality*, http://we-change.org/site/english/spip.php?article139 (accessed 3 April 2017).
5. E'telāf-e Ābādgarān-e Īrān-e Eslāmī, usually shortened to Ābādgarān, was an alliance of some right-wing Iranian political parties and organisations.
6. 'Natije-ye Pāyāni-ye Dahomin Entekhābāt-e Riyāsat-e Jomhuri' [The Final Result of the Tenth Presidential Elections], *Tabnāk*, 23 Khordād 1388 [13 June 2009], www.tabnak.ir/fa/news/51716/%D9%86%D8%AA%DB%8C% D8%AC%D9%87-%D9%BE%D8%A7%DB%8C%D8%A7%D9%86% DB%8C-%D8%AF%D9%87%D9%85%DB%8C%D9%86-%D8%A7% D9%86%D8%AA%D8%AE%D8%A7%D8%A8%D8%A7%D8%AA-% D8%B1%DB%8C%D8%A7%D8%B3%D8%AA-%D8%AC%D9%85% D9%87%D9%88%D8%B1%DB%8C (accessed 22 April 2017).
7. P. Ardalan, translated by Sholeh Shahrokhi, 'Women's Movement into the Streets', 29 May 2007, *Change for Equality*, http://change4equality.com/english/spip.php?article95 (accessed 22 April 2017).
8. Hamandishi-ye Zanān or the 'Intellectual Partnership of Women' was formed in the aftermath the awarding of the Nobel Peace Prize to Shirin Ebadi.
9. This movement was established after 8 March 2005 to press the larger and more global demands of women based on the Universal Declaration of Human Rights.
10. Ardalan, Women's Movement.
11. Ebadi. interview with the author, London, July 2012. The author herself was among the defence lawyers in this case.
12. Ardalan, *Women's Movement*. For a detailed analysis of this issue see 'Rāhbordhā-ye Jonbesh-e Zanān Roy-e Yek Miz: Neshasti Bā Fa'ālān Gorohhā-ye Mokhtalef-e Jonbesh-e Zanān' [Women's Strategies on the Table: A Meeting with Women's Rights Activists from Different Groups], *Zanān* 145 (Khordād 1386 [May 2007]), pp. 2–11; and 'Khāb-e Āshofteh-ye Khiyābān: Revāyathā-ye Khārej az Tārikh' [A Disterest Street Dream: Tails outside of History],

NOTES TO PAGES 162–167   273

Change for Equality, www.we-change.org/IMG/pdf/khabe-ashofte.pdf (accessed 4 April 2017).
13. N. Keshavarz, translated by MS, 'Interview with Jelveh Javaheri: From a Reading Group to the Campaign for One Million Signatures', 30 December 2007, *Change for Equality*, http://topicsandroses.free.fr/spip.php?article275 (accessed 4 April 2017).
14. Ardalan, *Women's Movement*.
15. Keshavarz, 'Interview with Jelveh Javaheri'.
16. Ahmadi Khorasani, *Jonbesh-e yek Miliyon Emzā*, p. 8.
17. Ahmadi Khorasani, *The Two Storytellers*. The author was among the participants.
18. 'About One Million Signatures Demanding Changes to Discriminatory Laws', 28 August 2006, *Change for Equality*, http://we-change.org/site/english/spip.php?article18 (accessed 4 April 2017).
19. 'Launching of the One Million Signatures Campaign Demanding Changes to Discriminatory Laws', 27 August 2006, *Change for Equality*, http://we-change.org/site/english/spip.php?article20 (accessed 4 April 2017).
20. Barlow, *Women's*, pp. 101–102.
21. Ibid., p. 101.
22. 'About One Million Signatures'. Discriminatory laws against women were discussed in more detail in Chapters 2 and 3. The campaign expressly pointed to some discriminatory laws including: marriage, divorce, number of partners, age of criminal responsibility, blood money, inheritance, laws that support honour killing, bearing witness, *hejāb* or compulsory prescribed dress for women, social security laws, stoning to death and some other laws. For more details see the campaign's website: http://we-change.org/site/english/spip.php?article18.
23. 'About One Million Signatures'.
24. P. Ardalan, translated by Ali G. Scotten, 'A Matter of Life: Report on the Preliminary Three-Month Activities of the One Million Signatures Campaign', 10 March 2007, *Change for Equality*, http://we-change.org/site/english/spip.php?article46 (accessed 4 April 2017).
25. According to Jelveh Javaheri 'The Campaign's method of collecting signatures through face-to-face canvassing is very important. The only other groups to do something similar were environmental groups who went door-to-door at a more limited scope. I have never seen this method used before where advocacy is done among people through face-to-face discussion. Several times, people have commented on how interesting our method is. The Campaign has been able to establish and use this method to good effect'. Keshavarz, 'Interview with Jelveh'.
26. Ardalan, 'A Matter of Life'.
27. Ibid. The author ran some of the campaign's legal training.
28. According to Jelveh Javaheri 'Another positive impact is that the Campaign has been able to integrate the discourse of equality into people's religious

discourse. Many people have written about the relationship of the two discourses in a positive manner and there has been lots of discussions. I think the Campaign is the first social action that has been able to articulate the issue of women's rights and Islam so broadly among people'. Keshavarz, 'Interview with Jelveh'.
29. Barlow, *Women's*, p. 109.
30. 'Officials' here does not necessarily mean people with official positions in the government, but rather people associated with the State who may or may not be in office or hold an official position.
31. K. Mozaffari, translated by P. Saeedi, 'The Campaign and Future Political Challenges', 15 March 2008, *Change for Equality*, http://we-change.org/site/english/spip.php?article237 (accessed 5 April 2017).
32. K. Mozaffari, 'The Minimums to Design an Interaction with the Political Parties', http://articlesjelvehkaveh.blogfa.com/post-11.aspx (accessed 5 April 2017).
33. B. Hedayat, 'Promotion of Equal Rights Discourse Among Political Groups', 29 July 2007, *Change for Equality*, http://we-change.org/site/english/spip.php?article124 (accessed 5 April 2017).
34. Ibid.
35. S. Tahmasebi, interview with the author, London, 25 May 2013.
36. Tahmasebi, 'Empowering Iranian Women'.
37. N. Tohidi, 'Iran's Women's Rights Movement and the One Million Signatures Campaign', November 2006, www.payvand.com/news/06/dec/1174.html (accessed 30 March 2017).
38. Ibid.
39. Tahmasebi, interview with the author, London, 25 May 2013.
40. Ibid.
41. For a full account of inheritance see chapter 4, pp. 181–3.
42. Tahmasebi, interview with the author, London, 25 May 2013.
43. Keshavarz, Interview with Jelveh.
44. K. Moghadam, translated by Leila Sheernejad, 'An Alarming Experience', 18 March 2007, *Change for Equality*, http://we-change.org/site/english/spip.php?article47 (accessed 4 April 2017).
45. For full account on *diyeh* see chapter 5, pp. 199–205.
46. Tasmim Barāy-e Barābari-ye Diyeh-ye Zan va Mard (Decission on Equal Diyeh for Men and Women) (1 Khordād 1386 [22 May 2007]), http://iraninsurance.ir/en/display-news/-/asset_publisher/vdWtKGtk9KxK/content/%D8%AA%D8%B5%D9%85%D9%8A%D9%85-%D8%A8%D8%B1%D8%A7%D9%8A-%D8%A8%D8%B1%D8%A7%D8%A8%D8%B1%D9%8A-%D8%AF%D9%8A%D9%87-%D8%B2%D9%86-%D9%88%D9%85%D8%B1%D8%AF-%D8%A7%D8%B9%D8%AA%D9%85%D8%A7%D8%AF/pop_up?_101_INSTANCE_vdWtKGtk9KxK_viewMode=print (accessed 20 April 2018).
47. Ibid.

NOTES TO PAGES 172–173   275

48. Rafsanjani went further to emphasise that the reform of certain laws in the civil code, which have created problems for women, is essential. He stated, 'Currently, lack of compatibility of some laws which are not in line with the current needs of society can be felt'. Ibid. See also Barlow, *Women*, p. 111.
49. *Etemād*, 2 Khordād 1387 [22 May 2008].
50. 'Nāmeh-ye Sargoshādeh-ye Barkhi Tashakolhā-ye Zanān Be Majles Darbāreh-ye Barābari-ye Diyeh-ye Zan va Mard' [An Open Letter of Some Women's Organisations to the Majles about Equal Diyeh for Men and Women], *Zanestān*, 12 Tir 1386 [3 July 2007], http://zanestan.es/news/07,07,03,06,08,15/ (accessed 31 March 2017).
51. Ibid. This letter pointed to Article 21 of the constitution and asked the government to ensure the rights of women in all respects.
52. Note 2 to Article 4 of the Law on Compulsory Insurance of Civil Liability for the Owners of Motor Vehicles Against Third Parties. The bill first was ratified by the economic committee of the Majles on 27 April 2008 and subsequently was sent to the Majles to undergo legal procedures. The Majles ratified it on its session on 2 May 2008. It was sent to the Guardian Council to be approved on 22 May 2008. The Guardian Council asked the Majles to amend some of its articles. Finally, the Guardian Council approved it on 6 August 2008. The bill was sent to the executive on 11 August 2008.
53. 'Iran Women Get Equal Blood Money in Car Crashes', *Reuters*, 27 May 2008, www.reuters.com/article/us-iran-women-bloodmoney/iran-women-to-get-equal-blood-money-in-car-crashes-idUSDAH73535620080527 (accessed 31 March 2017).
54. President Ahmadinejad sent the bill to the Majles speaker, Gholam-Ali Haddad Adel, to undergo the proper legal procedures. Ahmadinejad's explanation of the need for such a law was as follows: 'With respect to the special role and status of the family in the legal and educational classifications of Islam and noting the illegalisation of a portion of the law related to family rights, and the existence and absence of a legal procedure in this matter and due to dispersion and an absence of clarity on the abrogating body and abolishing of the laws cause repeated issues such as confusion for the Prosecution offices in processing family claims and in light of certain short comings and defects in laws governing the family and their lack of concurrence with the realities of the day and in order to act upon the content of Article 21 of the Constitution of the Islamic Republic of Iran and in order to achieve removal of judgment and to reduce the existing problems in regulations of Family Law and remove ambiguity, expostulation and absence of law in the current family related law and to uphold section (2) of Article (158) of the Constitution, the act below is submitted to undergo proper legal procedures.' *Islamic Republic of Iran, Islamic Consultative Assembly*, Legal and Judicial Commission's Report, 28 July 2008, *No. 25/K.GH*.
55. Lāyehe-ye Jadid-e Mojāzāt-e Islāmi Zarf-e See Mah-e Āyandeh be Majles Ersāl Mishavd [The New Islamic Penal Code will be Sent to Parliament within

three months], www.farsnews.com/newstext.php?nn=8605240449 (accessed 4 April 2018).
56. Ibid.
57. The first version of Article 22 stated that: 'Registering permanent marriage, annulment and its voiding, divorce, revocation and announcement of marriage, annulment and divorce is mandatory.

Note- registering temporary marriage is subject to procedural code ratified by the minister of justice. Legal and Judicial Committee's Report, 28 July 2008, *No. 25/K.GH*.
58. The first draft of Article 23 stated: 'Taking a second temporary wife is subject to permission from court after approval of the man's financial ability and his guarantee for executing justice between his wives'.

'Note – In case of multiple marriage, if the *mahriyeh* is prompt and the first wife requests it, permission to register the second marriage is dependent upon payment of *mahriyeh* to the first wife'. Legal and Judicial Commission's Report, 28 July 2008, *No. 25/K.GH*.
59. Article 25 of the bill stated that: 'The Ministry of Economics and Finances is duty bound to tax excessively and uncommonly high *mahriyeh* at the time of registering them in accordance to the situation of the couple and economic situation of the country and in compliance with the increase of the amount of *mahriyeh* based on inflation. Acceptable amount of *mahriyeh* and the taxing of it accordingly will be with attention to the economic situation of the country and based on a circular suggested by the Ministry of Economic and Finances and approved by the cabinet'.
60. 'Taqdir-e Shorā-ye Zanān az Jāme Negari-ye Lāyehe ye Hemāyat az Khānevādeh' [Women's Council Appriciation of the Family Protection Bill], *Mehr News Agency* (3 Shahrivar 1386 [25 August 2007]), available from: www.mehrnews.com/news/540659 (accessed 19 May 2017).
61. Rafat Bayan: Namāyandegān Zan Majles bā Lāyeheh-ye Hemāyat az Khānevādeh-ye Dolat Mokhālef Hastand [Rafat Bayat: Women MPs disagree with the Government's Family Protection Bill], *Iran Zanan Network*, 27 Shahrivar 1386 [18 September 2007], www.iranzanan.com/news/cat_21/000470.php (accessed 19 May 2017).
62. 'Lāyehe-ye Hemāyat az Khānevādeh va Janjālhā-ye Māde-ye 23' [Family Protection Bill and Article 23 Controversies], *Harmshahri Online*, 14 August 2007, www.hamshahrionline.ir/details/28924/Society/-institution (accessed 19 May 2017).
63. Ibid.
64. 'Khātami: Dādan-e Haq-e Yektarafe-ye Ezdevāj Mojadad be Mardān Jafā be Zanān Ast [Khatami: Polygamy is a Great Violation of the Rights of Women], *Asri Iran*, 6 Shahrivar 1386 [28 August 2007], www.asriran.com/fa/news/24396/ (accessed 19 May 2017).
65. 'Fatwa-ye Jadid-e Ayatollah Sanei: Ezdevāj-e Mojadad Bedoon-e Ejāze-ye Hamsar-e Aval Harām Ast' [Ayatollah Sanei's New Fatwa: Husband's Second

Marriage Without the Consent of the First Wife is Illegal], *Etemād* 1471, 7 Shahriver 1386 [29 August 2007], p. 1.

66. 'Amniyate Khānevādeha bā Tasvib-e Lāyehe-ye Hemāyat az Kānevāde be ham Khāhad Rikht' [Households' Security Will Be Poured Together with the Adoption of the Family Protection Bill], *Etemad* 1501, 4 Mehr 1386 [26 September 2007], www.magiran.com/npview.asp?ID=1490104 (accessed 20 May 2017).

67. 'Mokhālefat-e Jame-ye Zeynab bā Lāyehe-ye Hemāyat az Khānevādeh' [Zeynab Society Disagrees with the Family Protection Bill], *Donyā-ye Eghtesād*, 16 Mordād 1387 [6 August 2008], http://donya-e-eqtesad.com/news/465347 (accessed 19 May 2017).

68. 'Neshast-e Lāyehe-ye Hemāyat az Khānevādeh' [Gathering about the Family Protection Bill], *Iranian Students' News Agency*, 13 Shahrivar 1386 [4 September 2007], www.isna.ir/news/8606-07054/ (accessed 19 May 2017).

69. G. Esfandiari, 'Controversial Family Bill Returns to Iranian's Parliament's Agenda', *Radio Free Europe*, 24 August 2010, www.rferl.org/content/Controversial_Family_Bill_Returns_To_Iranian_Parliaments_Agenda/2136632.html (accessed 31 March 2017).

70. Ibid. Sociologist Shala Ezazi described the bill as an attempt by the authorities to have greater control over Iranian women. She believed that in practice it would be rejected by both women and men. She further pointed out that the bill couldn't be applied in practice; the conditions are such that even threats as laid out in it would not force women to sit at home and accept a series of inopportune demands.

71. Qānun-e Hemāyat az Khānevādeh 46 Sāl be Aghab Bordeh Shode', [The Family Protection Bill Went Back to Fourty Years Ago], www.pyknet.net/1386/07shahrivar/10/PAGE/40EBADI.htm (accessed 21 May 2017).

72. The European Parliament's delegation for relations with Iran travelled to Tehran from 7–10 December, for the 2nd EP/Iran interparliamentary meeting. The 11-member delegation was led by its chair, Angelika Beer (Greens/EFA, DE). Their statement is available from: www.europarl.europa.eu/meetdocs/2004_2009/documents/dv/afet_171207_iranpress/afet_171207_iranpressen.pdf (accessed 21 May 2017).

73. 'Moj-e Eterāz be Lāyehe-ye Khānevādeh dar Rāh Ast' [Wave of Objection to Family Protection Bill Is on Its Way], www.akhbar-rooz.com/news.jsp?essayId=16446 (accessed 21 May 2017).

74. 'Shast va Panj Namāyandeh-ye Majles-e Haftom va Hashtom Do Zan Dārand [65 Male MPs of the Seventh and Eighth Majles Have A Second Wife', http://iranianuk.com/20080212101200018/%DB%B6%DB%B5 (accessed 21 May 2017).

75. The name of the MPs practising polygamy was published on this weblog: 'Shalvārhā-ye Nāzok-e Ehsās dar Khāneh-ye Mellat [Sensitive Thin Trousers in the House of the Nation], https://chandzane.wordpress.com/ (accessed 21 May 2017).

76. 'Zahra Rahnavard Khāstār-e Khoru-je Bandhāyi az Lāyehe-ye Hemāyat az Khānevāde az Dastur-e Kār-e Majles Shod' [Zahra Rahnavard Called for the Withdrawal of Some Parts of the Family Protection Bill from the Parliamentary Agenda], www.radiofarda.com/a/2172815.html (accessed 1 April 2018). She further pointed that that Qu'ranic references to polygamy have been misinterpreted in the bill.
77. For the full account of the meeting see 'Women's United Front Against the "Family Protection Bill" Wins Dividends', translated by: Karineh Kanantz, 2 September 2008, *The Feminist School*, www.feministschool.com/english/spip.php?page=print&id_article=141 (accessed 31 March 2017).
78. 'Iran's Women Say No to Polygamy: Women Achieve Temporary Victory over Iran Family Protection Bill', 23 September 2008, www.alternet.org/reproductivejustice/100941/iran_women_say_no_to_polygamy (accessed 31 March 2017).
79. She further explained, 'Today, we had a duty, and our duty was to voice the concerns of the women in our country to the representatives. Our visit to the Parliament and our objection was because we don't want future generations to wonder why we did not protest such a bill. So, visiting the Parliament and meeting with the MPs was important and necessary.' 'Women's United Front'.
80. 'Controversial Articles of Iran's Family Protection Bill to be Reviewed', *Radio Zamaneh*, 17 December 2010, www.zamaaneh.com/enzam/2010/08/controversial-articles-of.html (accessed 4 April 2017).
81. The second amendment was made on 23 June 2010 and the third on 26 October 2010.
82. Article 22 was amended as follows: 'The judicial system of the Islamic Republic of Iran supports permanent marriage in order to strengthen and make pivotal the familial relations. Temporary marriage, however, is subject to the Shari'a laws and regulations stated in the civil code and its registration is necessary in the cases below:

1. Pregnancy of the wife;
2. Agreement of the two sides;
3. Conditions of the marriage.

Note – Registering the matters subject to this article and article 21 of this law in official registration offices for marriage and divorce is itself subject to a procedural code that will be issued within a year by the minister of Justice and approved by the head of the Judiciary. Until the issuance of that law, the regulations subject of Article 1 of the Law of Marriage, ratified on May 19, 1937 are still valid and enforced'. Articles 23 and 25 were removed from the bill. Islamic Republic of Iran, Islamic Consultative Assembly, Legal and Judicial Commission's Report, 27 July 2011, No 2/ 1219/K.GH.
83. Tahmasebi, 'Empowering Iranian Women'.

84. There is a vast literature on the issue of Islam and feminism and Islamic feminists who believe that Islam itself does not discriminate against women. Rather, patriarchal norms and traditions which were inserted into Islamic law deprive women from enjoying equal rights. See, among others, Najmabadi, 'Feminism in the Islamic Republic'; V.M. Moghadam, 'Islamic Feminism and Its Discontents: Toward a Resolution of the Debate', *Chicago Journals* 27/4 (Summer 2002), pp. 1135–71 and A. Kian, 'Feminism-e Dolati va Jonbesh-e Mostaqel-e Zanān' [Governmental Feminism and Independent Women's Movement], interview with M.H. Saburi, *Zanān* 124 (Shahrivar 1384 [August 2005]), pp. 44–9. For more sources see footnotes 76 and 87 at pp. 36, 39.
85. See, among others: F. Farhi, 'Religious Intellectuals, the "Women Question", and the Struggle for the Creation of a Democratic Public Sphere in Iran', *International Journal of Politics, Culture, and Society* 15/2 (Winter 2001), pp. 315–39; A. Alavi Tabar, 'Masaleh-ye Zanān dar Iran [Women's Problem in Iran], *Zanān* 65 (1378 [1999]); A. Abdi, 'Roshanfekri-ye Dini va Masāel-e Foritar az Masale-ye Zanān' [Religious Intellectualism and More Urgent Problems Than the Women's Problem], *Zanān* 58 (Āzar 1378 [December 1999]), p. 38; J. Tavakolian, 'Roshanfekri va Masaleh-ye Zanān' [Religious Intellectualism and the Women Issue], *Zanān* 82 (Āzar 1380 [December 2002]), pp. 44–9; E. Baghi, 'Masaleh-ye Zanān Kodām Ast' [What is the Women Issue], *Zanān* 57 (Abān 1378 [November 1999]), pp. 23–4; A. Sorush, 'Zabt va Bast-e Hoquq-e Zanān' [Contraction and Expansion of Women's Rights], *Zanān* 59 (Dey 1378 [January 2000]), pp. 32–7; V.M. Moghadam, 'Rhetorics and Rights of Identity in Islamist Movements', *Journal of World History* 4/2 (Fall, 1993), pp. 243–64; N. Ahmadi Khorasani, 'Feminizm-e Islami dar Negāhi be Ruznāmeh-ye Zan va Majaleh-ye Zanān' [Islamic Feminism through the Prisms of Zan and Zanān], *Andisheh-ye Jāmeh*, 1377 [1998], pp. 68–70; H. Moghissi, *Feminism and Islamic Fundamentalism: The Limits of Postmodern Analysis* (London and New York: Zed Books, 1999); V.M. Moghadam, 'Islamic Feminism', pp. 1135–71.
86. See among their works H. Afshar, *Islam and Feminisms: An Iranian Case-Study* (Houndsmills, Baskingstoke, UK: Macmillan, 1998); Z. Mir-Hosseini, 'Stretching the Limits: a Feminist Reading of the Shari'a in Post-Khomeini Iran', in Mai Yamani (ed.), *Islam and Feminism: Legal and Literary Perspectives* (London: Ithaca Press, 1996), pp. 285–319; A. Najmabadi, 'Feminism in the Islamic Republic: Years of Hardship, Years of Growth' in Y.Y. Haddad and J.L. Esposito (eds), *Islam, Gender and Social Change* (Oxford: Oxford University Press, 1998).
87. H. Afshar, 'Islam and Feminism: An Analysis of Political Strategies', in M. Yamani (ed.), *Feminism and Islam, Legal and Literary Perspectives* (Berkshire, UK: Garnet Publishing, 1996), pp. 197–216 at p. 197.
88. Moghadam, 'Islamic Feminism', p. 1145.
89. Ibid., p. 1144.

90. Ibid.
91. Z. Anwar, 'Malaysia: Advocacy for Women's Rights Within the Islamic Framework', *Sisters in Islam* (2003), www.wluml.org/node/1186 (accessed 5 February 2016).
92. Ibid.
93. Moghissi, Feminism and Islamic Fundamentalism, p. 141.
94. Moghadam, 'Islamic Feminism', p. 1149.
95. H. Shahidian, *Women in Iran: Emerging Voices in the Women's Movement* (Westport, Connecticut and London, Greenwood Press, 2002), p. 107.
96. Mir-Hosseini, 'The Quest for Gender Equality: Between Islamic Law and Feminism', *Critical Inquiry* Vol. 32, No. 4 (Summer 2006), pp. 629–45. At 644.
97. This approach is also taken by Rebecca Barlow in her book, *Women's Human Rights and the Muslim Question: Iran's One Million Signature Campaign* (Melbourne: Melbourne University Pres, 2012), p. 11.
98. For discussion on clerical support for the campaign's goals, see Barlow, *Women's*, p. 112.
99. Elnaz Ansari interview with Ayatollah Mousavi Tabrizi, translated by Sussan Tahmasebi, 'Ayatollah Mousavi Tabrizi: The Charge of Actions Against National Security Is Political', 11 November 2007, *Change for Equality* http://we-change.org/site/english/spip.php?article169 (accessed 31 March 2017).
100. Barlow, *Women's*, p. 112. He issued this *fatwā* to the question that was posed to him as follows: 'given the fact that pregnancy out of wedlock is extremely difficult for an unwed mother and will in all likelihood bring shame to her and her family, would she under these circumstances be allowed to obtain an abortion?' To answer this question, the Grand Ayatollah replied as follows: 'given these circumstances, [an abortion] is permissible'. 'Grand Ayatollah Mazaheri Issues Fatwā Allowing Abortion of Unwed Mothers', 23 January 2008, *Change for Equality*, http://we-change.org/english/spip.php?article207 (accessed 1 April 2017).
101. The *fatwā* by Ayatollah Sanei was issued in response to the following interpellation: 'if a man passes away and his only heir is his wife, how much of his assets should be given to his wife?' He has responded that when a man with no heirs besides his wife, passes away, his wife becomes the sole heir of his assets. 'Ayatollah Sanei Issues Fatwā in Support of Women's Inheritance', 16 February 2008, *Change for Equality*, http://we-change.org/site/english/spip.php?article217 (accessed 3 April 2017).
102. Barlow, *Women's*, p. 112.
103. Ayatollah Fazel Maybodi, interviewed by Elnaz Ansari, translated by Sussan Tahmasebi, 'Ayatollah Fazel Maybodi: The Demands of the Campaign Can Be Met Through Dynamic Jurisprudence', 6 June 2007, *Change for Equality*. http://we-change.org/site/english/spip.php?article97 (accessed 3 April 2017).
104. Ibid.

105. Ardalan, 'Joining on the Condition to Discriminate'.
106. Ibid.
107. Ebadi, interview with the author, London, 10 July 2012.
108. Ibid.
109. Ebadi, *Iran Awakening*, pp. 191–2.
110. A. Yaghoub-Ali, translated by Sussan Tahmasebi, 'Interesting Reactions to the Campaign', 20 July 2007, *Change for Equality*, http://we-change.org/site/english/spip.php?article114, 20 July 2007 (accessed 20 March 2017).
111. Tahmasebi, interview with the author, London, 25 May 2013.
112. Mehdi Karroubi was the first presidential candidate to outline his view on the status of women. He issued several statements in which 'he emphasised the need to review laws that discriminate against women, the need to ensure the presence of women in governmental and state decision making positions, including as ministers, as members of the Guardian Council, the Expediency Council and the Council of Experts. Karubi has emphasised the need to implement articles in the Constitution that support women's rights and to try to sign on to the Convention on the Elimination of All Forms of Discrimination Against Women (CEDAW). He has also emphasised the need for women's access to education, the reversal of limiting educational policies pertaining to women adopted during the Presidency of Ahmadinejad and the important role of housewives'. D. Iran Ardalan, NPR Interview with Sussan Tahmasebi, *Iranian Women Demand Change*, 5 June 2009, www.npr.org/blogs/sundaysoapbox/2009/06/women_rights_factors_in_irans.html (accessed 12 March 2017).
113. Mirhossein Mousavi, who has been identified as the main challenger to President Ahmadinejad, also issued a statement outlining his thinking and programs for women. 'This statement is very comprehensive and rather detailed in terms of policy initiatives he intends to adopt as president and calls for the re-examination of laws that discriminate against women, the joining of the CEDAW with exceptions to ensure that it is in line with Islamic and cultural values, and working to empower women in the social, economic, professional and education spheres, through the adoption of policies addressing these issues as well as inclusion of women in decision-making roles as ministers and high level managers. In this statement he also commits to reversing some of the policies that Mr Ahmadinejad had adopted with respect to placing quotas on the university entrance of female students.' Ibid.
114. N. Tohidi, 'Women and the Presidential Elections: Iran's New Political Culture', 9 March 2009, www.juancole.com/2009/09/tohidi-women-and-presidential-elections.html (accessed 12 March 2017).
115. *Iranian Women Demand Change*. It is interesting to note that Ahmadinejad himself was silent on women's issues. However, his advisor on women's issues and the head of the Centre for Women and Families attacked the policies of reformists who had tried to join the CEDAW during the previous administration. She also attacked the members of the One Million Signatures

Campaign and also Shirin Ebadi. It is important to highlight that President Ahmadinejad's administration took several major steps on the issues pertaining to women which were not tolerable by human rights activists. These include changing the name of the Centre for Women's Participation to the Centre for Women and Families, which has worked ever since to promote the role of women as mothers and wives. The adoption of the social safety program, which targets women on the streets for their Islamic dress, the adoption of quotas limiting the entrance of women into university and proposals designed to ensure that women attend university in their local communities, unless they have the permission of their fathers or husbands to do otherwise – a concession after the proposal received great criticism. Additionally, Ahmadinejad included two contested and highly criticized provisions in the family protection bill put forth to the parliament by the judiciary. The two provisions sought to ease restrictions on polygamy and impose a tax on *mahriyeh*. Both measures have since been taken out of the bill after an outcry by women's rights activists and their march on parliament. *Iranian Women Demand Change.*
116. Keshavarz, 'Interview with Jelveh Javaheri'.
117. Ibid.
118. For more information about the experience of the members of the campaign see: P. Naeemi, 'Interesting Reactions to the Campaign, I Returned Empty-Handed, Yet My Heart Is Filled with Confidence That My Decision from Five Years Earlier Was the Right One', 7 February 2007, Change for Equality, http://we-change.org/site/english/spip.php?article330 (accessed on 4 April 2018); and A. Roshani, translated by SZ, 'In Memory of Amir: In Prison, but Freer than Most of Us', 7 August 2007, *Change for Equality*, http://we-change.org/site/english/spip.php?article129 (accessed 4 April 2018).
119. P. Ardalan, 'Who is Accused of Being a "Threat to Civil Security?"', translated by ST, *Rooz Online*, 25 May 2007. Available at: www.roozonline.com/english/news3/newsitem/article/who-is-accused-of-being-a-threat-to-civil-security.html (accessed 27 March 2017).
120. Keshavarz, 'Interview with Jelveh Javaheri'.
121. For more information about individual cases see: M. Hosseinkhah, 'Detentions and Summons Against Campaigners for Gender Equality', translated by H. Milan, 24 February 2008, *Change for Equality*, http://we-change.org/site/english/spip.php?article225 (accessed 4 April 2017).
122. She was arrested on 2 March 2010 after security officers stormed her home and searched and seized property. The court order to search her property had been issued six days prior and in relation to her alleged participation in protests following the disputed results of the presidential elections. She was released after spending 170 days in detention on 18 August 2010 on a bail order in the amount of 500 million Iranian tomans (roughly US$500,000). On 15 May 2011, she was asked to introduce herself to the Evin prison to serve her three-year mandatory prison term. She is now in prison. Prior to this arrest,

Mahbubeh had been arrested on five occasions. She had been acquitted in relation to charges brought against her in all five cases. 'Increased Concern on the Implementation of 3 Year Prison Sentence for Mahbubeh Karami', 15 May 2011, *Change for Equality*, http://we-change.org/site/english/spip.php?article889 (accessed 31 March 2017).
123. Article 169 of the Constitution of Iran (1979) and Article 2 of the Islamic Criminal Code of Iran (2013).
124. S. Ebadi, interview with the author, London, May 2013.
125. The Revolutionary Court was established during the 1979 Revolution to deal with 'revolutionary cases.' In fact, this court was established for a specific period in the early years after the revolution, but it still exists. Currently, based on Article 303 of the Criminal Procedure Code Revolutionary Courts investigate the following offences:

1. Crimes against national and foreign security of the IRI, enmity with god (*mohārebeh*), *corruption on earth (efsaāde fel arz)*, armed rebellion, conspiracy against the regime, armed action, terrorism and sabotage, profiteering and forestalling the market of public commodities;
2. Insulting the Founder of the Islamic Republic of Iran and the Supreme Leader;
3. Narcotics crimes and arms smuggling;
4. Espionage with foreign entities;
5. Other crimes when pursuant to particular legislation.

The fact is that the majority of so-called political cases are heard in the revolutionary courts, which are controlled by extra-judicial elements and the security forces. These courts operate outside of the constitution, and do not allow for robust defence of the accused.
126. In the revolutionary court cases, lawyers are not allowed to enter the courtroom without permission from the judges even though the law of criminal procedure provides that lawyers should have access to their clients and to the official case notes. However, judges have the discretion to bar defendants' access to lawyers in 'sensitive cases' under a note to Article 128 of the Code of Criminal Procedures of Iran. In practice, defendants are routinely barred from access to a lawyer during the investigative stage of their detention, which can be extended indefinitely.
Article 3 of the Law on Respect for Legitimate Freedoms and Safeguarding Citizens' Rights, enacted in 2004, requires courts and prosecutors' offices to respect the right of the accused and defendants to a legal defence and to provide them with the opportunity to be represented by a lawyer and to use the services of experts. This appears to remove the limitations provided under the note to Article 128 of the Code of Criminal Procedures of Iran, but in practice, prosecutors and courts have ignored this new legislation and have continued to invoke this note to deny defendants their right to a lawyer.

127. According to Article 165 of the Constitution of Iran (1979), trials are to be held openly and members of the public may attend without any restriction unless the court determines that an open trial would be detrimental to public morality or discipline, or if, in private disputes, both the parties request that the public be excluded. Article 168 of the Constitution of Iran (1979) provides that: 'Political and press offenses are to be tried openly and in the presence of a jury. The manner of the selection of the jury, its powers, and the definition of political offenses, are to be determined by law in accordance with Islamic criteria.'
128. The working group is an independent and impartial body of the UN currently composed of human rights experts from Chile, Norway, Pakistan, Senegal and Ukraine. *Opinion No. 21/2011 (ISLAMIC REPUBLIC OF IRAN)*.
129. Mozaffari, 'The Campaign and Future Political Challenges'.
130. For instance, Tahmasebi stated that: 'The Campaign is not an opposition group or opposed to the government. It seeks to work within the existing system to create change and to express the demands of a major segment of the Iranian population to the government. The Campaign's petition is directly addressing the Iranian public and the Iranian legislature (Parliament). Some within the government or within political groups have supported and signed the Campaign's petition, especially reformists, including many former parliamentarians, some current reformist parliamentarians, people from ruling-religious families, etc. Some Campaign members have even reached out to parliamentarians and other political figures to introduce the Campaign and speak about its demands. Since the start of the Campaign, there has also been much discussion among decision-makers and religious leaders about the need to reform laws on women. Activists hope that through this effort, the urgency of the matter will be conveyed to the Parliament, forcing them to act with expedience and greater resolve, than they would if left up to their own accord. Since the start of the Campaign, the discourse on women's rights has become common place, among grassroots groups and citizens as well as those in the highest levels of public office and this is a major achievement and source of pride, demonstrating the success of the Campaign and its peaceful and civic strategies.' S. Tahmasebi, 'Answer to Your Most Frequently Asked Questions About the Campaign', 24 February 2008, *Change for Equality*, http://we-change.org/english/spip.php?article226 (accessed 28 March 2017).
131. Keshavarz, 'Interview with Jelveh Javaheri'.
132. Tahmasebi, 'Answer to Questions'.
133. According to Jelveh Javaheri, since the presidential election of June 2009, 'the pressure on the Campaign has been such that even if a meeting was organised over the phone, police and security forces would appear at the location of the meeting and interrogate the owner'. However, she explains how the Campaign was successful to advance its work during the past two years. By splitting to smaller groups, keeping a low profile and without media publicity, the Campaign has continued its works. This model, i.e., making the groups

smaller and networking amongst them, according to Jelveh had a significant impact on the continuation of the campaign. J. Javaheri, 'We Struggle for Progressive Change', *Change for Equality*, 5 June 2010, http://we-change.org/site/english/spip.php?article712 (accessed 31 March 2017).
134. S. Tahmasebi, interview with the author, London, 25 May 2013.
135. S. Tahmasebi, 'Four Years of Engaging Face-to-Face on Women's Rights', 29 August 2010, *Change for Equality*, http://we-change.org/site/english/spip.php?article757 (accessed 31 March 2017).
136. 'Iran: Allow Women's March for Equality', Human Rights Watch Statement on Iran, 8 March 2011, *Change for Equality*, http://we-change.org/site/english/spip.php?article858 (accessed 31 March 2017).
137. 'Violence against women in Iran', www.cedaw-iran.org/impact-of-cedaw-violence-against-women (accessed 4 April 2017).
138. Karami, interview with the author, London, 25 June 2012.
139. Tahmasebi, 'Answer to Questions'.
140. Ebadi, interview with the author, London, August 2013.
141. 'Pāsokh be Porsesh hā-ye Motadāvel'.
142. N. Ahmadi Khorasani, 'The Women's Movement in the Run-up to the Presidential Elections in Iran', 10 June 2009, *The Feminist School*, www.feministschool.com/english/spip.php?article305 (accessed 14 March 2017).
143. *Majale-ye Zanān*, January and February 1996. The group include 'Network of Islamic Republic of Iran's Women's Non-Governmental Organisations' and 'Solidarity Council of Women's Sport', or 'Shorā-ye Hambastegi-ye Varzesh-e Bānovān'.
144. *Hafte Nameh-ye Sobh*, 16 April 1996.
145. *Salam*, May 1996.
146. *Zanān*, January and December 1998.
147. *Zanān*, April 1999.
148. N. Ahmadi Khorasani, *The Spring of the Iranian Women's Movement* (Tehran, August 2012), pp. 325–7.
149. N. Ahmadi Khorasani, *The Spring*, pp. 335–6.
150. The coalition reminded the candidates that the proposal to ratify the CEDAW was submitted to the sixth parliament during the first cabinet of Mohammad Khatami and was ratified by parliament but rejected by the Council of Guardians. This proposal was later presented to the Expediency Council, of which the president was a member. Therefore, the coalition urged the presidential candidates to place this proposal at the top of their priorities with respect to the principles of equality and non-discrimination of citizens. In relation to the elimination of the discriminatory articles of the constitution, the coalition announced that it is aware that the president has no power to change laws but was also aware that the government is able to utilise its capabilities and encourage the parliament to include the principle of equality in the constitution if it is committed to the principle of equality and views it as its duty to implement.

151. Tohidi, 'Women and the Presidential *Elections*'. The coalition of women's movement aims are as follows: 'To divert the dominant state-machismo discourse towards a more conciliatory tone in order to address the needs of the civil society, especially women's delayed demands; to attract the attention of the authorities and to their responsibilities to the public, especially the most deprived and marginalised sectors; to address the presidential candidates such that if they require the votes of women, students, teachers and other social groups, they must include their needs and demands in their programmes; to show that even under harshest social and political conditions it is possible to be an effective and responsible citizen and press for a better and just society. To achieve these goals, we women must prove that we have the ability and the courage to seek all peaceful and civil avenues. Our past experiences demonstrated that whenever a window of opportunity has opened for women, the misogynists interfered, and the women faced further discrimination, limitations and inhumane violence'. See: 'The Coalition of the Iranian Women's Movement for Voicing their Demands in the Election', *The Feminist School*, www.feministschool.com/english/spip.php?article281 (accessed 16 March 2017).
152. For the names and statements of these activists see: 'Hamgarāyān-e Jonbesh-e Zanān Che Miguyand' [What Does the Coalition for Women Say?], 21 Tir 1388 [12 July 2009], *The Feminist School*, www.feministschool.com/spip.php?article2599 (accessed 15 February 2017).
153. 'Kārgāhhā-ye Āmuzeshi-ye Konvānsion-e Raf'-e Tab'iz az Zanān dar Shiraz Kelid Khord' [CEDAW Workshops Started in Shiraz], 31 Ordibehesht 1388 [21 May 2009], *The Feminist School*, www.feministschool.com/spip.php?article2556 (accessed 20 March 2017).
154. Article 177 of the Constitution of Iran (1979) provides for contitutional revision through referendum or a revision council, the selection process for which is specified within the article.
155. 'Pāyan-e Hamgarāei: Āqazi Digar Barāye Tarh-e Motālebāt Zanān' [End of The Coalition: Another Beginning for Women's Demands], 8 June 2009, *The Feminist School*, www.feministschool.com/spip.php?article2635 (accessed 12 January 2016).
156. Tohidi, 'Women and the Presidential Elections'.
157. For the full account of the meeting see: 'Dovomin Neshast-e Hamandishi: Talāsh barāy-e Hambastegi va Sāzmāndehi-ye Bishtar' [The Second Meeting of the Hamandishi-ye Zanān: Trying to Become More Organised and United], 12 Tir 1392 [3 July 2013], *The Feminist School*, www.feministschool.com/spip.php?article7328 (accessed 4 April 2018).
158. N. Tohidi, Iran: A Small Window of Hope, Open Democracy, 1 July 2013, http://www.opendemocracy.net/5050/nayereh-tohidi/iran-small-window-of-hope (Accessed 7 January 2017).
159. http://www.rohani92.com/portal/ondex.php/2013-06-05-06-25-27/women/2013-06-12-08-31-00/309-2013-06-11-12-36-51 (Accessed 7 February 2017).

160. See pages 187–189 of this chapter for a description of Mousavi and Karroubi's attitudes with respect to CEDAW during the presidential campaign of 2009.
161. 'Anger as Iran Bars Women from US Volleyball Game', *BBC news*, 20 June 2015, available from: www.bbc.co.uk/news/world-middle-east-33205360 (accessed 3 April 2017).
162. Ibid.
163. 'Iranian Vice-President Attacks Hardliners Over Vollaybale Ban for Female Fans', *Guardian*, 20 June 2015. Available from: www.theguardian.com/world/2015/jun/20/iran-vice-president-attacks-hardliners-over-volleyball-ban-for-female-fans (accessed 3 April 2017).
164. Ibid.
165. 'Iran Vice President Shahindokht Molaverdi Scolds Hardliners After Women Banned from Volleyball Match', *Australian Broadcasting Network*, 20 June 2015. Available from: www.abc.net.au/news/2015-06-20/iran-vp-scolds-hardliners-over-volleyball-ban/6561202 (accessed 3 April 2017).
166. N. Ahmadi Khorasani, 'Ten Days that Shook Iran', 30 July 2009, www.feministschool.com/english/spip.php?page=print&id_article=322 (accessed 27 March 2017).

BIBLIOGRAPHY

Persian Sources

1. Primary Sources in Persian

Publications of official bodies

Ain Nāmeh-ye Ezdevāj-e Mardān-e Irāni bā Zanān-e Khāreji-ye Āvāreh (Dārande-ye Kārt-e Hoviyat-e Atbā'-e Khāreji [By-Law Regulating the Marriage of Iranian Men with Homeless Foreigner Women (Who Hold a Foreign National Identity Card)], *Majmue'-ye Qavānin-e 1381*[The Law Collection of 2002], Ruznāmeh-ye Rasmi-ye Keshvar, Vol. 2, p. 1708.

Jomhuri-ye Islami-ye Iran, Majles Shurā-ye Islami, Gozāresh-e Comisiun-e Qazāei va Hoquqi-ye Majle [Islamic Republic of Iran, Islamic Consultative Assembly, Legal and Judicial Commission Report], 13 Tir 1387 [28 July 2008], No. 25/K.GH.

Jomhuri-ye Islami-ye Iran, Majles Shurā-ye Islami, Gozāresh-e Comisiun-e Qazāei va Hoquqi-ye Majle [Islamic Republic of Iran, Islamic Consultative Assembly, Legal and Judicial Commission Report], 5 Mordad 1390 [27 July 2011], No. 2/1219/K.GH.

Khomeini, R., *Sahifeh-ye Imam* [The Official Compilation of the Sayings and Declarations of Ayatollah Khomeini], Vol. 10 (Tehran: Moassesseh-ye Tanzim va Nashr-e Āsār-e Hazrat-e Imam Khomeini, 1378 [1999]).

———. *Sahifeh-ye Imam* [The Official Compilation of the Sayings and Declarations of Ayatollah Khomeini], Vol. 13, Tehran, Moassesseh-ye Tanzim va Nashr-e Āsār-e Hazrat-e Imam Khomeini, 1378 [1999].

———. *Sahifeh-ye Imam* [The Official Compilation of the Sayings and Declarations of Ayatollah Khomeini], Vol. 14, Tehran: Moassesseh-ye Tanzim va Nashr-e Āsār-e Hazrat-e Imam Khomeini, 1378 [1999].

———. *Sahifeh-ye Imam* [The Official Compilation of the Sayings and Declarations of Ayatollah Khomeini], Vol. 18, Tehran: Moassesseh-ye Tanzim va Nashr-e Āsār-e Hazrat-e Imam Khomeini, 1378 [1999].

———. *Sahifeh-ye Imam* [The Official Compilation of the Sayings and Declarations of Ayatollah Khomeini], Vol. 19, Tehran: Moassesseh-ye Tanzim va Nashr-e Āsār-e Hazrat-e Imam Khomeini, 1378 [1999].

BIBLIOGRAPHY 289

———. *Sahifeh-ye Imam* [The Official Compilation of the Sayings and Declarations of Ayatollah Khomeini], Vol. 20, Tehran: Moassesseh-ye Tanzim va Nashr-e Āsār-e Hazrat-e Imam Khomeini, 1378 [1999].

Gozāresh-e Comisiun-e Qazāei va Hoquqi-ye Majles [Legal and Judicial Commission's Repor to the Majles], *KGH/1527*, 4 Shahrivar 1390 [26 August 2011].

Nameh-ye Raeis-e Markaz-e Mosharekat-e Zanān [Letter from the President of the Centre for Women's Participation], *No. 8346*, 25 Dey 1380 [15 January 2002].

Majmu'e-ye Qavānin-e 1389 [The Law Collection of 2010], Tehran: Ruznāmeh-ye Rasmi-ye Keshvar [Official Gazette], Bahār-e 1390 [Spring 2011].

Majmu'e-ye Qavānin-e 1388 [The Law Collection of 2009], Tehran: Ruznāmeh-ye Rasmi-ye Keshvar [Official Gazette], 1388 [2009].

Majmu'e-ye Qavānin-e 1387 [The Law Collection of 2008], Tehran: Ruznāmeh-ye Rasmi-ye Keshvar [Official Gazette], 1387 [2008].

Majmu'e-ye Qavānin-e 1386 [The Law Collection of 2007], Tehran: Ruznāmeh-ye Rasmi-ye Keshvar [Official Gazette], 1387 [2007].

Majmu'e-ye Qavānin-e 1385 [The Law Collection of 2006], Tehran: Ruznāmeh-ye Rasmi-ye Keshvar [Official Gazette], 1385 [2006].

Majmu'e-ye Qavānin-e 1382 [The Law Collection of 2003], Tehran: Ruznāmeh-ye Rasmi-ye Keshvar [Official Gazette], 1382 [2003].

Majmu'e-ye Qavānin-e 1381 [The Law Collection of 2002], Tehran: Ruznāmeh-ye Rasmi-ye Keshvar [Official Gazette], 1381 [2002].

Majmu'e-ye Qavānin-e 1380 [The Law Collection of 2001], Tehran: Ruznāmeh-ye Rasmi-ye Keshvar [Official Gazette], 1380 [2001].

Majmu'e-ye Qavānin-e va Moqararāt-e Yeksad Sāleh, Asr-e Mashrutiyat 1285–1299 [One Hundred Year Law Collection, Constitutional Era 1906–1920], Vol. 1, Tehran: Ruznāmeh-ye Rasmi-ye Keshvar [Official Gazette].

Majmu'e-ye Qavānin-e va Moqararāt-e Yeksad Sāleh, 1300–1320, Bakhshe Aval 1300–1312 [One Hundred Year Law Collection, 1921–1941], Vol. 2, 1921–1933, Tehran: Ruznāmeh-ye Rasmi-ye Keshvar [Official Gazette].

Majmu'e-ye Qavānin-e va Moqararāt-e Yeksad Sāleh, 1300–1320, Bakhshe Dovom 1313–1320 [One Hundred Year Law Collection, 1921–1941], Vol. 3, 1934–1941, Tehran: Ruznāmeh-ye Rasmi-ye Keshvar [Official Gazette].

Majmu'e-ye Qavānin-e va Moqararāt-e Yeksad Sāleh, 1321–1330 [One Hundred Year Law Collection, 1942–1951], Vol. 4, Tehran: Ruznāmeh-ye Rasmi-ye Keshvar [Official Gazette].

Majmu'e-ye Qavānin-e va Moqararāt-e Yeksad Sāleh, 1331–1335 [One Hundred Year Law Collection, 1952–1956], Vol. 5, Tehran: Ruznāmeh-ye Rasmi-ye Keshvar [Official Gazette].

Majmu'e-ye Qavānin-e va Moqararāt-e Yeksad Sāleh, 1336–1340 [One Hundred Year Law Collection, 1957–1961], Vol. 6, Tehran: Ruznāmeh-ye Rasmi-ye Keshvar [Official Gazette].

Majmu'e-ye Qavānin-e va Moqararāt-e Yeksad Sāleh, 1341–1344 [One Hundred Year Law Collection, 1962–1965], Vol. 7, Tehran: Ruznāmeh-ye Rasmi-ye Keshvar [Official Gazette].

Majmu'e-ye Qavānin-e va Moqararāt-e Yeksad Sāleh, 1345–1347 [One Hundred Year Law Collection, 1966–1968], Vol. 8, Tehran: Ruznāmeh-ye Rasmi-ye Keshvar [Official Gazette].

Majmu'e-ye Qavānin-e va Moqararāt-e Yeksad Sāleh, 1348–1350 [One Hundred Year Law Collection, 1969–1971], Vol. 9, Tehran: Ruznāmeh-ye Rasmi-ye Keshvar [Official Gazette].

Majmu'e-ye Qavānin-e va Moqararāt-e Yeksad Sāleh, 1351–1353 [One Hundred Year Law Collection, 1972–1974], Vol. 10, Tehran: Ruznāmeh-ye Rasmi-ye Keshvar [Official Gazette].

Majmu'e-ye Qavānin va Moqararāt-e Hoqughi, Daftar-e Aval, [A Collection of Civil Laws], Vol. 1, Tehran: Ruznāmeh-ye Rasmi-ye Keshvar [Official Gazette], 1381 [2002]).

Majmu'e-ye Qavānin va Moqararāt-e Hoqughi, Daftar-e Dovom [A Collection of Civil Laws], Vol. 2, Tehran: Ruznāmeh-ye Rasmi-ye Keshvar [Official Gazette], 1383 [2004].

Majmu'e-ye Nazarhā-ye Mashverati-ye Edāreh-ye Hoquqi-ye Qoveh-ye Qazāiyeh dar Masāel-e Madani, 1362–1387 [A Collection of Advisory Opinions of the Legal Department of the Judiciary in Civil Matters, 1983–2008], Tehran: Ruznāmeh-ye Rasmi-ye Keshvar [Official Gazette].

Mehrpur, H. (ed.), Majmu'h-ye Nazariyāt-e Shurā-ye Negahbān [Collection of the Gurdian Council's Opinion], Vol. 3, Tehran: 1371 [1992].

'Mozākerāt-e jalase-ye Alani-ye Majles-e Shurā-ye Islami, Jalaseh-ye 342 [Official Record of the Majles, Session 342]', *Ruznāme-ye Rasmi*, 1 Mordād 1382 [23 July 2003], p. 21.

'Mozākerāt-e jalase-ye Alani-ye Majles-e Shurā-ye Islami, Jalaseh-ye 342 [Official Record of the Majles, Session 342]', *Ruznāme-ye Rasmi*, 1 Mordād 1382 [23 July 2003], pp. 22–3.

'Mozākerāt-e jalase-ye Alani-ye Majles-e Shurā-ye Islami, Jalaseh-ye 342 [Official Record of the Majles, Session 365], *Ruznāme-ye Rasmi*, 23 Mehr 1382 [15 October 2003], p. 365.

Nazariyeh-ye Edāreh-ye Hoquqi-ye Qoveh-ye Qzāiyeh Dar Mored-e Ezdevāj Mard-e Mosalmān Ba Zan-e Qeyr-e Mosalmān [Legal Department of the Judiciary's Opinion on Marriage of a Muslim Man with a Non-Muslim Woman], *Opinion No. 7/3800*, 11 Mordād 1379 [1 August 2000].

Nazariyeh-ye Edāreh-ye Hoquqi-ye Qoveh-ye Qzāiyeh [Advisory Opinion of the Legal Department of Judiciary], *Opinion No. 7/6965* – 9 Mordād 1366 [31 July 1987].

Nazariyeh-ye Edāreh-ye Hoquqi-ye Qoveh-ye Qzāiyeh [Advisory Opinion of the Legal Department of Judiciary], *Opinion No. 7/2665* – 9 Mordād 1369 [31 July 1990].

Nazariyeh-ye Edāreh-ye Hoquqi-ye Qoveh-ye Qzāiyeh [Advisory Opinion of the Legal Department of Judiciary], *Opinion No. 7/802* – 11 Ordibehesht 1372 [1 May 1993].

Nazariyeh-ye Edāreh-ye Hoquqi-ye Qoveh-ye Qzāiyeh [Advisory Opinion of the Legal Department of Judiciary], *Opinion No. 7/3263* – 10 Mordād 1372 [1 August 1993].

Nazariyeh-ye Edāreh-ye Hoquqi-ye Qoveh-ye Qzāiyeh [Advisory Opinion of the Legal Department of Judiciary], *Opinion No. 7/7989* – 23 Āzar 1376 [14 December 1997].

Qānun-e Hemāyat-e Khānevādeh [The Family Protection Law], Tehran: Ruznāmeh-ye Rasmi-ye Keshvar [Official Gazette], Bahār-e 1392 [Spring 2013].

BIBLIOGRAPHY

Qānun-e Mojāzāt-e Islami [Islamic Criminal Code], Tehran: Ruznāmeh-ye Rasmi-ye Keshvar [Official Gazette], Bahār-e 1392 [Spring 2013].

Qānun-e Mojāzāt-e Omumi [Criminal Code], 1304 [1926].

Qanun-e Taein-e Taklif-e Tābeiyat-e Farzandān-e Hāsel az Ezdevāj-e Zanān-e Irāni bā Mardān-e Khāreji [The Bill of Amendment of the Single-clause Bill Determining the Citizenship for Children of Iranian Women Married to Foreign Men], 2 Mehr 1385 [24 September 2006].

Rules of Procedure of the Majles. Available from: http://rc.majlis.ir/fa/law/show/99673 (accessed 12 February 2017).

Ruznāmeh-ye Rasmi-ye Keshvar [Official Gazette, contains the full Majles records], Tehran: Edāreh-ye Kol-e Umur-e Farhangi va Ravābet-e Umumi-ye Majles-e Showrā-ye Islami, 1979–2009.

Electronic Sources from Official Bodies

Internet archive of Ayatollah Khamene'i, http://farsi.khamenei.ir/archive/.
Website of the Assembly of Experts, http://www.majlesekhobregan.ir/.
Website of the Departement for Women and Family Affairs, http://women.gov.ir/.
Website of the Guardian Council, www.shora-gc.ir/.
Iranian judiciary, www.dadiran.ir/.
Majles Library, www.ical.ir/.
Majles Research Centre, www.majlis.ir.
Repository of Laws and Bills approved by the Majles and other official bodies, http://tarh.majlis.ir/.
The Islamic Culture and Relations Organisation (ICRO), http://en.icro.ir.

Other Electronic Sources Containing Primary Material

www.amontazeri.com.
www.feministschool.com.
www.hoqooq.net.
www.irna.com.
www.isna.ir.
Website of Ayatollah Makarem Shirazi, http://makarem.ir/websites/farsi/estefta/?mit=637&sid=1145#1145.
www.saanei.org.
www.we-change.org.

2. Secondary Sources in Persian

Books

Abazari-ye Fumani, M., Enhelāle Nekāhe Dāem az Nazar-e Qānun-e Madani-ye Iran: Negāhi bar Avāmel-e Ejtemāi-ye Talāq dar Iran [Disolution of Marriage under Iran's Civil Code: Reviewing Divorce From a Social Prespective] (Tehran: Nashr-e Khayām, 1377 [1998]).

Adamiyat, F., Andisheh-ye Taraqi va Hokumat-e Qānun: Asr-e Sepahsālār [Progressive Thought and Rule of Law: Sepehsalar Era] (Tehran: Sherkat-e Sahāmi-ye Enteshārāt-e Khārazmi, 1352 [1973]).

———. Fekr-e Demokrāsi-ye Ejtemāi dar Nehzat-e Mashrutiyat-e Iran [The Idea of Democracy in the Constitutional Movement] (Tehran: Enteshārāt-e Payām, 1355 [1976]).

———. Ideoloji-ye Nehzat-e Mashrutiyat-e Iran [On the Ideology of the Constitutional Movement in Iran] Vol. 1 (Tehran: Enteshārāt-e Payām, 2535 Shāhanshahi [1974]).

Ahmadi Khorasani, N., Bahār-e Jonbesh-e Zanān: Revāyati Az Ashkhā va Labkhandhā [The Spring of the Iranian Women's Movement] (Tehran: Nevisandeh, Shahrivar 1391 [September 2012]).

———. Hejāb va Roshanfekrān [Hejāb and the Intellectuals] (Tehran: Nevisandeh, 1390 [2012]).

———. Jonbesh-e Yek Million Emzā: Revāyati az Darun [One Million Signatures Demanding Change to Discriminatory Laws: An Internal Narrative] (Tehran, 1386 [2007]).

Alameh Haeri, A., Ezdevāj-e Movaqat dar Hoquq-e Iran [Temporary Marriage under Iranian Law] (Tehran: Enteshārāt-e Khāghāni, 1380 [2001]).

Alasvand, F., Naqd-e Konvānsion-e Raf'-e Koliye-ye Ashkāl-e Tab'iz Alayh-e Zanān [A Critique of the Convention on the Elimination of All Forms of Discrimination Against Women] (Qom: Markaz-e Motāleāt va Pajoheshha-ye Farhangi-ye Hozeh-ye Elmiyeh, 1382 [2003]).

———. Zanān va Hoquq-e Barābar: Naqd va Barresi-ye Konvānsion-e Raf'-e Tab'iz Alayhe Zanān va Sanad-e Pekan [Women and Equal Rights: A Critique and an Examination of the Convention on the Elimination of All Forms of Discrimination Against Women and the Beijing Declaration] (Tehran: Shurā-ye Farhangi- Ejtemāei-ye Zanān, Ravābet-e Omumi, 1382 [2003]).

———. Konvānsion-e Raf'-e Koliye-ye Ashkāl-e Tab'iz Alayhe Zanān [Convention on the Elimination of All forms of Discrimination Against Women] (Qom: Markaz-e Modiriyat Hozeh Elmiyeh, 1382 [2003]).

Arjomand Danesh, J., Barrasi-ye Qāedeh-ye Osr va Haraj: Kārborde Ān dar Tlāq va Barrasi-ye Masādiq-e Jadid-e Mādeh-ye 1130 Qānun-e Madani [Examination of the Hardship Principle: Its Function in Divorce and Evaluation of New Examples of Article 1130 of the Civil Code] (Tehran: Enteshārāt-e Behnāmi, 1388 [2009]).

Artidar, T., Qavānin va Moqararāt-e Vijeh-ye Zanān dar Jomhuri-ye Islami Iran [Laws and Regulations Pertaining to Women in the Islamic Republic of Iran] (Tehran: Barge Zeytoon, 1378 [1999]).

Bahrami Khoshkar, M., Qavāed-e Ers dar Feqh-e Emāmiye va Qānun-e Madani [Inheritance under Feqh and the Civil Code] (Tehran: Nashr-e Kalame-ye Allāh, 1390 [2011]).

Bazgir, Y., Qānun-e Madani dar Āine-ye Ārāy-e Divān-e Āliye Keshvar [The Civil Code as it Pertains to Supreme Court Verdicts], Vol. 1 (Tehran: Ferdosi, 1380 [2001]).

———. Qānun-e Madani dar Āeineh-ye Ārāy-e Divāne Āli- ye Keshvar: Hoquq-e Khānevadeh [Civil Code Relating to Supreme Court Verdicts], Vol. 2 (Tehran: Ferdosi, 1380 [2001]).

Davani, A., *Zan Dar Quran* [Woman in the Qur'an] (Qom: Daftar-e Enteshārāt-e Islami, 1378 [1999]).

Bibliography 293

Ebadi, S. and M. Zaimaran, Sonat va Tajadod dar System-e Hoquqi-ye Iran [Modernity and Tradition in the Iranian Legal System] (Tehran: Ganje-Danesh, 1375 [1996]).
Ebadi, S., Tārikhcheh va Asnāde Hoquq-e Bashar Dar Iran [History and Documentation of Human Rights in Iran] (Tehran: Enteshārāt-e Roshangarān, 1373 [1994]).
———. Hoquq-e Zan dar Qavānin-e Jomhuri-ye Islami-ye Iran [Women's Rights under the Law of the Islamic Republic of Iran] (Tehran: Ganj-e Dānesh, 1381 [2002]).
Emami, H., *Hoquq-e Madani (Civil Rights)*, Vol. 4, 12th edition (Tehran: Ketāb Forushi-ye Eslāmiyeh, 1374 [1995]).
Esmaeili, M., Shorut-e Zemn-e Aqd dar Nekāh [Stipulated Conditions in the Marriage Contract] (Tehran: Nashr-e Harir, 1389 [2010]).
Fazaeli, M., Shorut-e Qeyr-e Mo'tabar va Āsār-e Ān dar Konvāsion-e Raf'-e Koliyeh-ye Ashkāl-e Tab'iz Alayh-e Zanān [Invalid Reservation and its Effects on the Convention on the Elimination of All Forms of Discrimination Against Women] (Qom: Daftar-e Motāleāt va Tahghighāt-e Zanān, Zemestān, 1382 [2004]).
Ganji, A., Talaqi-ye Fāshisti az Din va Hokumat [Fascism's Understanding of Religion and State] (Tehran: Tarh-e Now, 1379 [2000]).
Hafeziyan, M.H., Zanan va enqelāb: Dāstān-e Nagofteh [Women and the Revolution: An Untold Story] (Tehran: Andisheh-ye Bartar, 1380 [2001]).
Hajari, A., M. Kaveh Marban, Zahra Ayatollahi, Hoquq-e Jahāni Zanān: Konvānsion-e-Raf'-e Tab'iz alayhe Zanān [Universal Rights of Women: The Convention on the Elimination of All Forms of Discrimination Against Women] (Tehran: Shurā-ye Farhangi Zanān, 1381 [2003]).
Hakimpoor, M., Hoquq-e Zan dar Keshākesh-e Sonat va Tajadod: Ta'amoli dar Mabādi-ye Hermonetik-e Hoquq-e Zan [Women's Rights in the Conflict between Modernity and Tradition: A Reflection on the Hermeneutic Principles of Women's Rights] (Tehran: Naqmeh Nonandish, 1382 [2003]).
Hamidiyan, H., Maqālāt-e Hoquq-e Khānevādeh [Articles on Family Law] (Tehran: Hamun, 1387 [2008]).
Hasani, A., Faskh-e Nekāh dar Hoquq-e Iran va Nahve-ye Eqāmeh-ye Da'āvi-ye Marbuteh [Cancellation of Marriage under Iran's Law and Means of Litigation] (Tehran: Entesharāt-e Fekrsāzān, 1383 [2004]).
Hashemi, M., Qānun-e Asāsi-ye Jomhuri-ye Islami-ye Iran [The Constitution of the Islamic Republic of Iran] (Tehran: Mizān Publication, 1386 [2008]).
Jabaran. M., *Ezdevāj bā Qeyr-e Mosalmānān* [Marriage with non-Muslims] (Qom: Enteshārāt-e Daftar-e Tablighāt-e Islami-ye Huzeh-ye Elmiye-ye Qom, 1382 [2003]).
Jahangiri, M., Barresi-ye Tamāyozhā-ye Feqhi-ye Zan va Mard [A Study on the Differences Between Men and Women from Feqh's Perspective] (Qom: Bustān-e Qom, 1385 [2006]).
Jori, M.E., Ers: Bā Negāh-e Tatbiqi Hoquq, Mazāheb-e Panjgāneh Islam, Masihi, Kalimi va Zartoshti [A Comparative Analysis of Inheritance in Christianity, Islam, Judaism and Zoroastrianism] (Tehran: Nashr-e Daftar Elm, 1389 [2011]).
Kar, M., Raf'-e Tab'iz az Zanān: Moqāyese-ye Konvānsion Raf'-e Tab'iz Az Zanān Bā Qavānin-e Dākheli-ye Iran [Elimination of Discrimination Against Women:

A Comparison Between the Convention on the Elimination of All Forms of Discrimination Against Women and Iranian Law] (Tehran: Nashr-e Qatreh, 1379 [2000]).

———. Pajoheshi Darbāre-ye Khoshunat Alayh-e Zanān dar Iran [A Study on Violence against Women in Iran] (Tehran: Entesharāt-e Roshangarān, 1380 [2002]).

Kasravi, A., Tarikh-e Mashruteh-ye Iran [The History of the Constitutional Revolution of Iran] (Tehran: Moaseseh-ye Entesharāt-e Amir Kabir, 1363 [1984]).

Katuziyan, N., Zendegi-ye Man [My Life] (Tehran: Sherkat-e Sahāmi-ye Enteshār, 1385 [2007]).

———. Moqadameh-ye Elm-e Hoquq va Motāle'-e dar Nezām Hoquqi-ye Iran [Introduction to Jurisprudence and Study in the Legal System of Iran] (Tehran: Sherkat-e Sahāmi-ye Enteshār, 1373 [1994]).

———. Gāmi be Suye Edālat [Step Toward Justice], Vol. 1 (Tehran: Entesharāt-e Mizān, 1386 [2008]).

———. Gāmi be Suye Edālat [Step Toward Justice], Vol. 2 (Tehran: Entesharāt-e Mizān, 1386 [2008]).

———. Gāmi be Suye Edālat [Step Toward Justice], Vol. 3 (Tehran: Entesharāt-e Mizān, 1386 [2008]).

———. Doreh-ye Moqadamāti- ye Hoquq-e Madani: Ers [Civil Rights: Inheritance] (Tehran: Entesharāt-e Mizān, 1385 [2007]).

———. Doreh-ye Hoqouq-e Madani: Khānevādeh, Nekāh va Talāq [Civil Rights: Family, Marriage and Divorce] (Tehran: Sherkat-e Sahāmi-ye Enteshār, 1387 [2009]).

———. Qānun-e Madani dar Nazm-e Hoquqi-ye Konuni [The Civil Code in the Current Legal Order], 22nd edition (Tehran: Bonyād-e Hoghughi-ye Mizān, 1387 [2008]).

———. Khānevādeh: Nekāh va Talāq [Family: Marriage and Divorce], Vol. 1 (Tehran: Sherkat-e Sahāmi-ye Enteshār, 1387 [2008]).

Kazem Zadeh, A., Tafāvot-e Hoquqi-ye Zan va Mard: Dar Nezām-e Hoqouqi-ye Iran Mabāni va Masādiq [Examples of Legal Differences Between Men and Women in the Iranian Legal System] (Tehran: Entesharāt-e Mizān, 1382 [2003]).

Kermāni, N.I. (with the assistance of Ali Akbar Saeidi Sirjani), Tārikh-e Bidāri-ye Irāniān [History of the Iranian Awakening] Vols 1 & 2 (Tehran: Moaseseh Entesharāt-e Āgāh, 1361 [1982]).

Keshvari, I., Qāede-ye Osr va Haraj: Motāle'-ye Tatbiqi-ye Kārbord-e Qavāed-e Feqh dar Hoquq [Hardship Principle: A Comparative Analysis of Feqh Principles in Law] (Tehran: Entesharāt-e Jāvdāneh, 1388 [2010]).

Khalili, H., Talāq: Hoquqi- Ejtemāi [Divorce: A Social Right] (Qom: Ebtekār-e Dānesh, 1389 [2011]).

Konvānsion-e Mahv-e Koliye-ye Ashkāl-e Tab'iz Alayh-e Zanān: Majmue-ye Maqālāt va Goftoguhā [The Convention on the Elimination of All Forms of Discrimination Against Women: A Collection of Articles] (Qom: Daftar-e Mutāleāt va Tahqiqāt-e Zanān, 1383 [2004]).

Mahmudi, A., Nazariyeh-ye Jadid darbāreh-ye barābari-ye Zan va Mard dar Qesās [A New Theory of Equality Between Man and Woman in Qesās] (Tehran: Entesharāt-e besat, 1365 [1986]).

BIBLIOGRAPHY

Matin, M. and N. Mohajer, Khizesh-e Zanān-e Iran dar Esfand-e 1357: Tavalodi Digar [Iranian Women's Uprising, 8 March 1979: Renaissance], Vol. I (Berkeley: Noqteh, 2013).

———. Khizesh-e Zanān dar Esfand-e 1357: Hambastegi-ye Jahāni [Iranian Women's Uprising, 8 March 1979: International Solidarity], Vol. II (Berkeley: Noghteh, 2013).

Mehra, N., Zan va Hoquq- Keyfari: Majmu'e-ye Maqālāt, Natāyej-e Kār-e Goruhā va Asnād-e Nakhostin Hamāyesh-e Beynolmelali-ye Zan va Hoquq-e Keyfari: Gozashteh, Hāl, Āyandeh [Women and Criminal Law: Collection of Essays, Workshops, Guidelines of the First International Seminar on Women and Criminal Law: Past, Present and Future] (Qom: Salsabil, 1384 [2005]).

Mehrizi, M., Shakhsiyat va Hoquq-e Zan Dar Islam [Woman's Personality and Rights in Islam] (Tehran: Sherkat-e Entesbārāt-e Elmi va Farhangi, 1382 [2003]).

Mehrizadegan, D., M.A. Daeinejad and M. Taher, Hoqugh-e Zanān:Naqd va Barasi-ye Konvānsion-e-Raf'-e Tab'iz alayhe Zanān [Women's Rights: A Review of the Convention on the Elimination of All Forms of Discrimination Against Women] (Tehran: Shurā-ye Farhangi Ejtemāei Zanān, 1383 [2004]).

Mehrpoor, H., Barresi-ye Mirās-e Zojeh dar Hoquq-e Islam va Iran: Tahlil-e Feqhi va Hoquqi-ye Ers-e Zan az Dārāi-ye Shohar [Analysis of Woman's Inheritance under Iranian Law and Islam: Legal and Feqh Interpretation of Woman's Inheritance of Man's Assets] (Tehran: Etelāāt, 1375 [1997]).

Mirkhani, E., Ruykardi Novin dar Ravābet-e Khānevādeh [New Perspectives on Family Relationships] (Tehran: Safir-e Sobh, 1378 [2000]).

Mir-Shamsi, F., Hoquq va Takālif-e Zan dar Ezdevāj: Az Didgāh-e Feqh-e Emāmiyeh [Women's Rights and Obligations in Marriage under the Imami Feqh Perspective] (Tehran: 1380 [2001]).

Moaser, H., Tarikh-e Esteqrār-e Mashrutiyat dar Iran: Mostakhrajeh az Asnād Mahramāneh Vezārat-e Omur-e Khārejeh Englestān [History of the Constitutional Movement in Iran: based on Documents from the British Foreign Office Archives], Vols 1 & 2 (Tehran: Entesbārāt-e Ebn-e Sinā, 1352 [1973]).

Mohaqeq Damad, M., Barresi-ye Feghhi-ye Hoqugh-e Khānevādeh: Nekāh va Enhelāl-e Ān [A Study of Islamic Jurisprudence with Respect to Family Law: Marriage and Its Termination] (Tehran: Shābok, 2008).

Mohammadi, M., Māde-ye Shānzdahom-e Konvānsion-e Zanān az Negāhe Feqh-e Shi'eh [Article 16 of the Women's Convention from the Perspective of Islamic Jurisrudence] (Qom: Boostān-e Ketāb, 1386 [2007]).

Molavardi, S., Moqābeleh ba Khoshunat Alayheh Zanān dar Keshvarhāye Islami [Combatting Violence Against Women in Islamic Countries] (Tehran: Entesbārāt-e Hoquqdān, Dānesh Negār, 1384 [2005]).

Moradifar, B., Tahavolāt-e Hoquq-e Khānevādeh Ba'd az Enqelāb-e Islami [The Evolution of Family Rights After the Islamic Revolution] (Tehran: Entesbārāt-e Behnāmi, 1388 [2009]).

Motahhari, M., Nezām-e Hoquq-e Zan dar Islam [The Structure of Women's Rights in Islam] (Tehran: Sadrā, 1358 [1979]).

Mousavi Bojnurdi, M., Andishebhā-ye Hoquqi-ye1: Hoquq-e Khānevādeh [Legal Thoughts 1: Family Law] (Tehran: Majm'-e Elimi va Farhangi-ye Majd, 1385 [2006]).

———. Elm-e Osul [The Science of Principles] (Tehran: Majd, 1385 [2006]).
Nuri, R., Khānevādeh: Hoquq-e Khānevādeh dar Hoquq-e Madani [Family Law in the Civil Code] (Tehran: Pazhang, 1378 [2000]).
Pirniya, H., Irān-e Bāstān yā Tārikh-e Mofasal-e Irān-e Qadim [Ancient Iran or a Detailed History of Ancient Persia], Vol. 1 (Tehran: Majles, 1311 [1932]).
Qorban Niya, N., Bāzpajuhi-ye Hoquq-e Zan: Barrasi-ye Qavānin-e Marbut be Zanān dar Jomhuri-ye Islami-ye Iran [Re-Assesment of Women's Rights Under the Laws of the Islamic Republic of Iran], Vol. 2 (Tehran: Enteshārāt-e Ruz-e Now, 1384 [2005]).
Raeisi, M., Konvānsion-e Zanān: Barrasi-ye Feqhi va Hoquqi-ye Elhāq ya Edame-ye Elhāqe Jomhuri-ye Islami-ye Iran be Konvānsion-e-Raf'-e Koliye-ye Ashkāle Tab'iz Alayhe Zanān [Women's Convention: Examination of Iran's Accession to the Convention on the Elimination of All Forms of Discrimination Against Women from the Legal and Jurisprudential Perspectives] (Qom: Nasime-Qods, 1381 [2002]).
Rafiei, A., Talāq va Āsār-e Ān dar Hoquq-e Zojeh [Divorce and its Effect on Woman's Rights] (Tehran: Enteshārāt-e Majd, 1379 [2000]).
Rajabiyan, Z., Z. Ayatollahi, and M. Godazgar, Sen-e Ezdevāj-e Dokhtarān: Mādeh-ye 1041 va Tabsare-ye Madeh-ye 1210 Qānun-e Madani [Marriage Age for Girls: Article 1041 and Note to Article 1210 of the Civil Code] (Tehran: Safir-e Sobh, 1379 [2000]).
Rudijani, M.M., Vekālat dar Talāq [Power of Attorney for Divorce] (Tehran: Nashr-e Ketāb-e Āvā, 1388 [2009]).
Safaei, H. and A. Emami, Mokhtasar-e Hoqouq-e Khānevādeh [Concise Family Law] (Tehran: Enteshārāt-e Mizān, 1387 [2009]).
Sanei, F., Shahādat-e Zan dar Islam [Women's Testimony in Islam] (Qom: Meysam-e Tamār, 1386 [2007]).
Sanei, Y., Feqh va Zendegi 3: Barabari-ye Diyeh [Feqh and Life Vol. 3: Equality of Blood Money] (Qom: Meysam Tamar, 1386 [2007]).
Shafie Sarvestani, E., Jaryān Shenāsi-ye Defāe az Hoquq-e Zanān dar Iran [A Study of the Process of Defending Women's Rights in Iran] (Qom: Ketāb-e Tāhā, 1385 [2006]).
Sharifi, H., Ezdevāj-e Movaqat va Chāleshhā [Temporary Marriage and its Challenges] (Qom: Bustān-e Ketāb, 1385 [2006]).
Sharifiyan, J., Rāhbord-e Jomhuri-ye Islami-ye Irān dar Zamineh-ye Hoquq-e Bashar dar Sazmān-e Melal-e Motahed [The Strategy of the Islamic Republic of Iran with Respect to Human Rights in the United Nations] (Tehran: Markaz-e Chāp va Enteshārt-e Vezārat-e Omur-e Khārejeh, 1380 [2001]).
Toghrangar, H., Hoquq-e Siyāsi Ejtemāi-ye Zanān Qabl va Ba'd Az Piruzi-ye Enqelāb-e Islāmi-ye Iran [Women's Political and Social Rights Before and After the Revolution] (Tehran: Markaz-e Asnād-e Enqelāb-e Islami, 1388 [2009]).
Zibaei-Nejad, M.R. and M.T. Sobhani, Darāmadi Bar Nezām-e Shakhsiyat-e Zan dar Islam: Barresi-ye Moqāyesehi-ye Didgah-e Islam va Qarb [Women's Personality in Islam: A Comparative Analysis of Islam and the West] (Qom: Darolnoor, 1380 [2001]).

Journal Articles and Online Resources

Abdi, A., 'Roshanfekri-ye Dini va Masāel-e Foritar az Masale-ye Zanān' [Religious Intellectualism and More Urgent Problems than the Women's Problem], *Zanān* 58, Āzar 1378 [December 1999], p. 38.

Ahmadi Khorasani. N., 'Feminizm-e Islami dar Negāhi be Ruznāmeh-ye Zan va Majaleh-ye Zanān' [Islamic Feminism through the Prisms of Zan Newspaper and Zanān Magazine], *Andisheh-ye Jāmeh*, 1377 [1998]), pp. 68–70.

Alasvand, F., 'Zanān va Hoquq-e Barābar' [Women and Equal Rights], *Ketāb-e Naqd* 26 & 27, Bahār va Tābestān 1382 [Spring and Summer 2003].

'Akharin Āmār-e Ta'id Salāhiyat Shodegān-e Majles-e Nohom' [The Latest Figures of the Approved Candidates for the Ninth Majles Election], *Tābnāk*, 21 Bahman 1390 [10 February 2012]. www.tabnak.ir/fa/news/225746/%D8%A2%D8% AE%D8%B1%DB%8C%D9%86-%D8%A2%D9%85%D8%A7%D8%B1- %D8%AA%D8%A7%DB%8C%DB%8C%D8%AF-%D8%B5%D9%84% D8%A7%D8%AD%DB%8C%D8%AA-%D8%B4%D8%AF%DA%AF% D8%A7%D9%86-%D9%85%D8%AC%D9%84%D8%B3-%D9%86% D9%87%D9%85 (accessed 4 April 2018).

Alavi Tabar, A., 'Masaleh-ye Zanān dar Iran' [Problems for Women in Iran], *Zanān* 65 (1378 [1999]).

'Amniyat-e Khānevādeha bā Tasvib-e Lāyehe-ye Hemāyat az Kānevāde be ham Khāhad Rikht' [Households' Security Will Be Poured Together with the Adoption of the Family Protection Bill], *Etemad* 1501, 4 Mehr 1386 [26 September 2007], www.magiran.com/npview.asp?ID=1490104 (accessed 20 May 2017).

Anvari, H.A., 'Konvānsion-e Zanān va Chāleshhā-ye Dini' [Women's Convention and Religious Challenges], *Jāme'e-ye Fārda* 3, Zemestān 1385 [Winter 2007].

———. 'Haq-e Shart dar Konvānsion-e Raf'-e Tamāmi-ye Ashkāl-e Tab'iz Alayhe Zanān' [Reservation to the Convention on the Elimination of All Forms of Discrimination Against Women], *Ketāb-e Zanān* 15, 1 Farvardin 1381 [21 March 2002].

———. 'Paziresh-e Konvānsion Mokhālef-e Masāleh-e Meli Ast' [Acceptance of the Convention is against National Interest], *Resālat*, 22 Farvardin 1381 [11 April 2002].

Arfa'niya, B., 'Konvānsion-e Mahv-e Koliyeh-ye Ashkāl-e Tab'iz Alayhe Zanān' [Convention on the Elimination of All Forms of Discrimination Against Women], *Kānun-e Vokalā* 188 & 189, Bahār va Tabestān 1384 [Spring and Summer 2005], pp. 170–95.

Atai Ashtiyani, Z., 'Konvānsion va Sahm-e Zanān Dar Tasmim Sāzhāye Beynolmelali' [The Women's Convention and Women's Share in the International Decision-Making Process], *Ketāb-e Naqd* 29, Zemestān 1382 [Winter 2003], pp. 91–106.

'Ayā Barāye Dokhtar-e Bākereh dar Ezdevāj-e Dāem ya Movaqat Ezn-e Pedar Lāzem ast?' [Is Father's Consent Necessary for Either Permanent or Temporary Marriage of a Virgin Girl?], *Shia News*. www.shia-news.com/fa/news/12791/ (accessed 25 March 2017).

Ayatollah Makarem Shirazi, 'Bandhā-ye Mota'adedi Az Konvānsion-e Raf'-e Tab'iz Sarihan Bar Khalāf-e Shar'-e Islam Ast' [Some Articles of the Convention Explictly Contradict Islam], *Hemāyat*, 12 Mordād 1382 [3 August 2003]).

---. 'Mabādā Ta'limāt-e Dini-ye Mā Rā Qarbihā Entekhāb Konand' [Lest Westerners Choose Our Religious Education], *Keyhān*, 10 Tir 1382 [1 July 2003].

---. 'Ezdevāj-e Movaqat Yek Zarurat-e Ejtenāb Nāpazir-e Ejtemāi Ast' [Temporary Marriage is an Unavoidable Social Need] (23/07/1389 [15 October 2010]). https://makarem.ir/main.aspx?lid=0&typeinfo=1&catid=25445 &pageindex=0&mid=252812 (accessed 20 April 2018).

Ayatollah Yousef Sanei, 'A Second Marriage without the First Wife's Permission is Harām and Null and Void', available at http://saanei.org/?view=01,02,48,218,0#01,01,05,9,0 (accessed 27 March 2017).

'Ayatollah Sanei Issues Fatwā in Support of Women's Inheritance', 16 February 2008, *Change for Equality*, http://we-change.org/site/english/spip.php?article217 (accessed 3 April 2017).

Ayatollahi, Z., 'Konvānsion-e Beynolmelali-ye Zanān Bā Osul-e Islami Moqāyerat Dārad' [The International Convention on Women is in Contradiction with Islam], *Keyhān* 26 (1381 [2003]).

---. 'Paziresh-e Konvānsion Mokhālef-e Masāleh-he Meli Ast' [Acceptance of the Convention is Against the National Interest], *Resālat*, 22 Farvardin 1381 [11 April 2002].

Bagheri, A. and N. Mokhtari Afrakati, 'Bāzpajuhi-ye Motun-e Qurani va Ravāi dar Bāb-e Diyeh-ye Zan va Mard' [Re-Examination of the Qur'an in Relation to Men and Women's Blood Money], *Majaleh-ye Hoquq-e Dāneshkadeh-ye Hoquq va Olum-e Siyāsi-ye Dāneshgāh-he Tehran* 74, Zemestān 1385 [Winter 2006], pp. 47–68.

Baghi, E., 'Masaleh-ye Zanān Kodām Ast' [What is the Women's Issue?], *Zanān* 57 (Abān 1378 [November 2000]), pp. 23–4.

Bāqerzadeh, M., 'Negāhi be Hoquq-e Zan dar Islam: Naqdi Bar Konvānsion-e Raf'-e Koliye-ye Ashkāl-e Tab'iz Alayhe Zanān' [An Overview of Women's Rights in Iran: A Critique of the Convention on the Elimination of All Forms of Discrimination Against Women], *Ma'refat* 70 (Mehr 1382 [October 2003]), pp. 8–28.

'Barge Ākhar dar Parvande-ye Qatl-e Leila Fathi' [Last Chapter in Leila Fathi's Case], http://khabarfarsi.com/ext/2548735 (accessed 28 March 2017).

'Barresi-ye Elhāq Iran Be Konvānsion-e Mahv-e Koliyeh-ye Ashkāl-e Tab'iz Alayhe Zanān' [Analysis of Iran's Accession to the Convention on the Elimination of All Forms of Discrimination Against Women], *Jomhuri-ye Islami*, 13 Esfand 1380 [4 March 2002].

'Barresi-ye Konvānsion-e Raf'-e Koliyeh-ye Ashkāl-e Tab'iz Alayhe Zanān' [Examination of the Convention on the Elimination of All Forms of Discrimination Against Women], *Qezāvat* 17 (Mehr 1382 [October 2003]), pp. 37–43.

Bashiri, A., 'Majma'-ye Tashkhis-e Maslahat-e Nezām, Farātar az Qānun-e Asāsi va Majles?' [The Expediency Discernment Council of the System, Beyond the Constitution and Parliament?], *Gozāresh* 114 (Mordād 1379 [July 2000]), pp. 24–31.

'Bastarhā-ye Fekri-ye Defā'az Konvānsion-e Man'-e Tab'iz' [Intellectual Context of the Defense the Convention on the Elimination of All Forms of Discrimination Against Women], *Resālat*, 10 Mehr 1382 [2 October 2003].

'Bāzshenāsi-ye Āsibha-ye Rooykar-de Elhāq Iran Beh Konvānsion-e Qarbi-ye Mosum Be Raf'e-e Tab'iz az Zanān' [A Study of the Damages Incurred by the Views against Iran's Accession to the Western Convention Known as Elimination of Discrimination], *Keyhān* 25 & 26 (25 Mordād 1382 [16 August 2003]).

Bayan, R., 'Namāyandegān Zan Majles bā Lāyeheh-ye Hemāyat az Khānevādeh-ye Dolat Mokhālef Hastand' [Rafat Bayat: Women MPs disagree with the Government's Family Protection Bill], *Iran Zanan Network*, 27 Shahrivar 1386 [18 September 2007], www.iranzanan.com/news/cat_21/000470.php (accessed 19 May 2017).

'Campaign Khod Dalil-e Zendegi Ast' [The Campaign Itself is a Reason for Life], *The Feminist School*, www.feministschool.com/campaign/spip.php?article18 (accesssed 3 April 2017).

'Chāleshhā va Zarurathā: Lāyeh-ye Elhāq-e Iran Be Konvānsion-e Mahv-e Koliyeh-ye Ashkāl-e Tab'iz Alayhe Zanān' [Challenges and Needs: The Bill of Iran's Accession to the CEDAW], *Mardom Sālāri*, 30 Bahman 1380 [19 February 2002], pp. 285–9.

'Chand Darsad az Namāyandegān Taeid Salāhiyat Shodand [The qualifications of how many of candidates were approved], *Afkār News*, 28 Bahman 1394 [17 February 2016]. www.afkarnews.ir/%D8%A8%D8%AE%D8%B4-%D8% B3%DB%8C%D8%A7%D8%B3%DB%8C-3/489211-%DA%86%D9% 86%D8%AF-%D8%AF%D8%B1%D8%B5%D8%AF-%D8%A7%D8%B2- %D8%AF%D8%A7%D9%88%D8%B7%D9%84%D8%A8%D8%A7% D9%86-%D9%85%D8%AC%D9%84%D8%B3-%D8%AA%D8%A3%DB %8C%DB%8C%D8%AF-%D8%B5%D9%84%D8%A7%D8%AD%DB% 8C%D8%AA-%D8%B4%D8%AF%D9%86%D8%AF (accessed 20 March 2016).

'Dabir-e Shorā-ye Negahbān Konvānsion-e Raf'-e Tab'iz Alayhe Zanān Rā Khalāf-e Shar' va Moghāyer ba Qānun-e Asāsi E'lām Kard' [The Secretary-General of the Guardian Council Declares the Convention on the Elimination of all Forms of Discrimination Against Women Contradicts the Shari'a and the Constitution], *Khorāsān*, 29 Mordād 1382 [13 August 2003].

'Dāstān-e Ezdevāj-e Zan-e Irani bā Mard-e Afqān' [The Story of a Marriage Between an Iranian Woman and an Afghan Man], *BBC Persian*, www.bbc.co.uk/persian/iran/2011/05/110525_121_married_iranian_women_afghan_men.shtml (accessed 19 March 2017).

'Davā-ye Siyāsi Barāye Yek Chālesh-e Ejtemāei: Lāyeheh-ye Peyvastan Be Konvānsion-e Man'-e Tab'iz Az Zanān' [A Political Dispute for a Social Challenge: The Bill of Iran's Accession to the Convention on the Elimination of all Forms of Discrimination Against women], *Tose'e*, 15 Mordād 1381 [6 August 2002].

Daykandi, M.A., 'Ezdevāj-e Movaqat dar Quran-e Karim' [Temporary Marriage in the Qur'an], *Nashriyeh-ye Safir* 1 (March 2007), pp. 157–202.

'Dolat Shobahāte Lāyehe-ye Raf'-e Tab'iz az Zanān Rā Bartaraf Konad' [The Government Should Remove Lingering Doubts Over the Convention on the Elimination of All Forms of Discrimination Against Women], *Entekhāb* (1382 [2003]).

'Dovomin Neshast-e Hamandishi: Talāsh barāy-e Hambastegi va Sāzmāndehi-ye Bishtar' [The Second Meeting of the Hamandishi-ye Zanān: Trying to Become

More Organised and United], 12 Tir 1392 [3 July 2013], *The Feminist School*. www.feministschool.com/spip.php?article7328 (accessed 4 April 2018).

Ebrahimi, Z., 'Movāfeqān va Mokhālefān-e Elhāq' [The Supporters and Opponents of Accession], *Baztāb-e Andishe* 42 (Mehr 1382 [October 2003]), pp. 32–8.

———. 'Lāyeheh-ye Elhāq-e Iran Be Konvānsion-e Raf'-e Tab'iz Az Zanān az Dastur Khārej Shod' [The Bill of Iran's Accession to the Convention on the Elimination of All Forms of Discrimination Against Women Was Removed from the Majles' Proceeding], *Zanān*, Vol. 85.

'Elhāq Be Konvānsion-e Por Dardesar bā Haq-e Tahafoz Ham Nashod [The Accession to the Troubled Convention was not Successful Even with Reservations]', *Tose'e*, 27 Mordad 1382 [18 August 2003]).

'Elhaq Be Konvānsion-e Raf'-e Koliyeh-ye Ashkāl-e Tab'iz Alayhe Zanān va Pāsokh be Barkhi Ebhāmāt va Shobahāt' [Accession to the Convention on the Elimination of All Forms of Discrimination Against Women and Answer to Some Doubts], *Mardom Sālāri*, 18 Dey 1380 [8 January 2002].

'Elhāq Be Konvānsion-e Zanān, Khodbākhtegi Dar Barābar-e Farhang-e qarb Ast' [Accession to Women's Convention is Submission to Western Culture], *Resālat*, 19 Mordād 1382 [10 August 2003].

'Ezat-e Islami Be Mā Ejāzeh-ye Elhāq Be Konvānsion Ra Nemidahad' [Our Islamic Honour Does Not Allow Us to Join the Convention], *Zan-e Ruz*, Vol. 1915.

Fathi, A., 'Ta'ārozāt-e Konvānsion Mahve Tab'iz Alayhe Zanān Ba Islam va Hoquq-e Bashar' [The Convention's Contradiction of Islam and Human Rights], *Resālat* 6 (29 Mehr 1382 [21 October 2003]).

———. 'Negāhi Digar Be Ta'ārozāt-e Konvānsion-e Mosum Be Mahv-e Tab'iz Alayh-e Zanān ba Islam va Hoquq-e Bashar' [Other Views on the Contradiction of the Convention on the Elimination of All Forms of Discrimination Against Women with Islam and Human Rights], *Bāztāb-e Andishe* 44 (Āzar 1382 [December 2003]), pp. 40–50.

'Fatwa-ye Jadid-e Ayatollah Sanei: Ezdevāj-e Mojadad Bedoon-e Ejāze-ye Hamsar-e Aval Harām Ast' [Ayatollah Sanei's New Fatwa: Husband's Second Marriage Without the Consent of the First Wife is Illegal], *Etemād* 1471, 7 Shahriur 1386 [29 August 2007], p. 1.

Fazaeli, M., 'Konvāsion-e Raf'-e Tab'iz Alayhe Zanān va Shorut-e Koli-ye Vāred bar Ān' [The Convention on the Elimination of All Forms of Discrimination Against Women and Its General Reservations], *Hoquq-e Beynolmelal* 34 (Bahār va Tabestān-e 1385 [Spring and Summer 2006]), pp. 57–110.

Fazelian, P., 'Negāhi Digar Be Convānsion-e Raf'-e Har Guneh Tab'iz Alayhe Zanān' [Other Views on the Contradiction of the Convention on the Elimination of All Forms of Discrimination Against Women with Islam and Human Rights], *Farhang* 48 (Zemestān 1382 [Winter 2004]), pp. 209–20.

———. 'Zanān Rā Be Kodām Su Mibarand?' [Which Direction Women Are Taken To?], *Ketāb-e Naqd* 26 & 27, Bahār va Tābestān 1382 [Spring and Summer 2003], pp. 286–96.

———. 'Zan Dar Sotuh-e Meli va Beynolmelali' [Women's Rights at Domestic and International Levels], *Mabāhes-e Bānovān-e Shi'eh* 8 (Tābestān 1385 [Summer 2004]), pp. 105–38.

Gheyrat, F., 'Hemāyat va Nefrat az Konvānsion-e Zanān' [Support for and Aversion to the Women's Convention], *Sharq*, 21 Ābān 1381 [12 November 2002].

BIBLIOGRAPHY

'Gozāresh-e Tahlili az Ravand-e Elhāq-e Irān be Konvānsion' [An Analytical Report on the Process of Iran's Accession to the Women's Convention], in *Konvānsion-e Mahv-e Koliye-ye Ashkāl-e Tab'iz Alayh-e Zanān: Majmue-ye Maqālāt va Goftoguhā* (Qom: Daftar-e Mutāleāt va Tahqiqāt-e Zanān, 2004), pp. 27–34.

Habibzadeh, M.J. and H. Babai, 'Qatl dar Farāsh' [Honour Killings], *Modares* 4, Zemestān 1378 [Winter 1999], pp. 89–90.

Halagh, V.B., translated by A. Kazemi Najafabadi, 'Ejtehād dar Miyān-e Ahl-e Sonat' [Ejtehād among Sunnis], *Majaleh-ye Andisheh-ye SādEqn* 10 (Spring 2003]), pp. 32–51.

'Hamgarāyān-e Jonbesh-e Zanān Che Miguyand' [What Does the Coalition for Women Say?], 21 Tir 1388 [12 July 2009], *The Feminist School.* www.feministschool.com/spip.php?article2599 (accessed 15 February 2017).

'Harfi az Barresi-ye Tarh-e Ezdevāj-e Movaqat Nist' [Nothing Has Been Said on the Design of Temporary Marriage], *Sedāye Adālat*, 1382 [2003].

Hāshemi, H., 'Konvānsion-e Raf'-e Tab'iz Alayhe Zanān' [Convention on the Elimination of All Forms of Discrimination Against Women], *Ravāq Andishe* 22 (Mehr 1382 [October 2003]), pp. 3–8.

———. 'Gavāhi-ye Zanān' [Women's Testimony], *Ketāb-e Naqd* 12 (Paiz 1378 [Fall 1999]), pp. 176–205.

Hāshemi Golpāyegāni, H., 'Konvānsion-e Raf'-e Har Guneh Tab'iz Alayhe Zanān: Āri yā Na?' [The Convention on the Elimination of All Forms of Discrimination Against Women: Yes or No?], *Siyāsat-e Ruz*, 27 Dey 1390 [16 February 2012].

Hedayatniya Ganji, F., 'Nezārat-e Showrā-ye Negahbān Bar Qavānin va Moqararāt' [Guardian Council's Supervision of Laws and Regulations], *Ravāq-e Andisheh* 11, Mehr 1381 [11 October 2002], pp. 61–79.

Heydari, A., 'Lāyehe-ye Elhāq be Konvānsion Mahv-e Koliye-ye Ashkāle Tab'iz Az Zanān: Mokhālefathā' [The Bill of Accession to the CEDAW: Disagreements], *Nashriye-ye Payāme Zan* 140, Khordād 1394 [May 2015].

'Hoquq-e Madani-ye Zanān va Koodakān Bāznegari Mishavad' [Civil Rights of Women and Children will be Revised], *Khorāsān*, 9, Ordibehesht 1382 [29 April 2003].

'Hoquq-e Zanān va Rah-e Doshvār-e Peyvastan Be Konvānsion' [Women's Rights and Difficult Path of Accession to the Convention], *Zanān*, Vol. 102.

Hossein Abadi, A., "Erāeh-ye Lāyeheh-ye Hemāyat az Khānevādeh Zarurati Nadāsht' [It Was Not Necessary to Introduce the New Family Protection Bill], *Majaleh-ye Vekālat* 37 & 38, Mehr 1387 ([October 2008]).

Hosseini, A., 'Chāleshhā-ye Konvānsion-e Raf'-e Tab'iz Alayhe Zanān' [The Challenges of the Convention on the Elimination of all Forms of Discrimination Against Women], *Ravāq Andisheh* 4 (Ābān va Āzar 1380 [October and November 2001]).

———. 'Negāhi Be Mabāni Konvānsion-e Raf'-e Har Guneh Tab'iz Alayhe Zanān' [An Overview of the Convention on the Elimination of All Forms of Discrimination Against Women], *Ravāq Andisheh* 1 (Khordād va Tir 1380 [June–July 2001]).

Jalali, M., M.A. Basiri and S. Bani Najarian, 'Zarurat-e Elhāq-e Iran be Konvānsion-e 1979 Man'e Koliyeh-ye Ashkāl-e Tab'iz Alayhe Zanān' [The Necessity of Iran's Accession to the 1979 Convention on the Elimination of all Forms of Discrimination Against Women], *Nāmeh Mofid* 55 (Shahrivar 1385 [September 2006]), pp. 66–102.

'Jame va Tafriqi Dar Peyvastan Beh Konvānsion' [Pros and Cons of Adhering to the Convention], *Zan-e Ruz*, Vol. 1845.

Kamali, A., 'Rahyāft-e Moshārekat-e Zanān Dar Tose'e: Pish Sharthā va Mavāne' [Women's Participation in Development: Pre-conditions & Obstacles], *A Quarterly Journal of the Centre for Women's Studies* 1 (Fall 2001, pp. 3–20).

Kameli, E., 'Konvānsion-e Raf'-e Tab'iz az Zanān ra Behtar Beshnāsim' [A Better Understanding of the Convention on the Elimination of All Forms of Discrimination Against Women], *Farhang-e Kosar* 42 (Shahrivar 1379 [September 2000]), pp. 30–4.

Kar, M., 'Shart-e Dolat Besyār Koli va Mobham Ast' [The Reservation is Too General And Vague], *Zanān* 84 (Bahman 1380 [February 2002]), pp. 12–14.

'Kārgāhhā-ye Āmuzeshi-ye Konvānsion-e Raf'-e Tab'iz az Zanān dar Shiraz Kelid Khord' [CEDAW Workshops Started in Shiraz], 21 May 2009, *The Feminist School*. www.feministschool.com/spip.php?article2556 (accessed 20 March 2017).

'Karimi Majd, R., 'Konvānsion-e Raf'-e Tab'iz, Entezār-e Ākharin Rāhe Hal' [Convention on the Elimination of All Forms of Discrimination Against Women: The Last Solution], *Goftegu* 38 (Āzar 1382 [December 2003]).

———. 'Yek Jenāyat-e Kāmelan Ma'muli' [An Ordinary Crime], *Zanān* 93 (Abān 1381 [October 2002]), pp. 2–9.

Kermanshahi, Z.S., 'Jāygāh-e Zan dar Feqh-e Keyfari-ye Islami' [Women's Status under Islamic Criminal Feqh], *Zanān* 13 (Shahrivar 1372 [August 1993]), pp. 56–9.

'Khāb-e Āshofteh-ye Khiyābān: Revāyathā-ye Khārej az Tārikh' [A Disterest Street Dream: Tails outside of History], *Change for Equality*. www.we-change.org/IMG/pdf/khabe-ashofte.pdf (accessed 4 April 2017).

'Khātami: Dādan-e Haq-e Yektarafe-ye Ezdevāj Mojadad be Mardān Jafā be Zanān Ast [Khatami: Polygamy is a Great Violation of the Rights of Women], *Asri Iran* (6 Shahrivar 1386 [28 August 2007]), http://www.asriran.com/fa/news/24396/ (accessed 19 May 2017).

Kian, A., 'Feminism-e Dolati va Jonbesh-e Mostaqel-e Zanān' [Governmental Feminism and Independent Women's Movement, interview with M.H. Saburi], *Zanān* 124 (Shahrivar 1384 [August 2005]), pp. 44–9.

'Konvānsion-e Emhā-ye Hameh Ashkāl-e Tab'iz Alayhe Zanān' [Convention on the Elimination of All Forms of Discrimination Against Women], *Hemāyat*, 14 Ordibehesht 1391 [3 May 2012].

'Konvānsion Feministi Ast Ta'āroz-e Ān Bā Islam qeyr-e Qābel-e Enkār Ast' [The Convention is Feminist and is Against Islam], *Resālat* 8 (Āzar 1382 [29 November 2003]).

'Konvānsion-e Mahv-e Koliyeh-ye Ashkāl-e Tab'iz Alayhe Zanān Az Manzar-e Faqihān' [Convention on the Elimination of All Forms of Discrimination Against Women from Foqhhā's Perspective], *Mobaleqān* 10 (Āzar 1379 [December 2000]), pp. 78–88.

'Konvānsion-e Raf '-e Tab'iz Az Zanān va Hasāsiyathā' [The Convention on the Elimination of All Forms of Discrimination Against Women and Its Sensitivities], *Zan-e Ruz*, Vol. 1906.

'Konvānsion-e Tab'iz Alayhe Zanān dar Dastor-e Kāre Majles Qarār Girad' [The Convention Should Be Considered in the Majles' Agenda], *Yās-e Now*, 20 Tir 1380 [11 July 2001].

Kulaei, E., 'Bā Morur-e Zamān Negareshhā Taqir Mikonad' [Attitudes Will Change over Time], *Zanān-e Fardā* 1 (1 Mehr 1381 [23 September 2002]).
———. *Yāse Now*, 10 Esfand 1381 [1 March 2003].
———. 'Zanān: Zanān-e Irani Pas az Eslāhāt' [Women: Iranian Women after Reforms Era], *Āin* 9 (Āzar 1386 [December 2007]), pp. 46–50.
———. 'Zanān: Majles Sheshom va Hoquq-e Zanān' [The Sixth Majles and Women's Rights], *Āin* 5 (Dey 1385 [January 2007]).
———. 'Zanān Dar Arseh-ye Omumi, Motāle'eh-ye Muredi-ye Jomhuri-ye Islami Iran' [Women in Public Spaces: A Case Study of Iran], *Majaleh-ye Hoquq* 61 (Pāiz 1382 [Fall 2003]), pp. 217–38.
Lantsel, Z., "Konvānsion-e Raf'-e Tab'iz va Payāmadhā-e Ejtemāi-ye Ān' [The Convention on the Elimination of all Forms of Discrimination Against Women and Its Social Consequences], *Bānovān-e Shi'e* 3 (Bahār 1383 [Spring 2005]), pp. 147–76.
Lāyehe-ye Jadid-e Mojāzāt-e Islāmi Zarf-e See Mah-e Āyandeh be Majles Ersāl Mishavd' [The New Islamic Penal Code will be Sent to Parliament within three months]. www.farsnews.com/newstext.php?nn=8605240449 (accessed 4 April 2018).
Lorestani, F., 'Jonbesh-e Ejtemāi-ye Zanān-e Iran' [Iranian Women's Social Movement], *A Quarterly Journal of the Centre for Women's Studies* 6 (Summer 2003), pp. 23–42.
'Majles Āmādeh-ye Eslāh-e Koliyeh-e Qavānin-e Marbut be Zanān Ast' [Majles is Ready to Amend All Laws Related to Women], *Yās-e Now*, 10 Esfand 1381 [1 March 2003].
'Majles-e Showrā-ye Islami va Elhāq Be Konvānsion' [Majles and Accession to the Convention], *Yād* 75, Bahār 1384 [2005], pp. 293–310.
'Masāel-e Beynolmelali dar Peyvastan Be Konvānsion-e Man'-e Tab'iz Alayh-e Zanān Tasiri Nadārad' [International Policies Have no Effect on the Ratification of the Convention], *Yās-e Now*, 24 Farvardin 1382 [13 April 2003].
Mashini, F., 'Motālebāt-e Zanān' [Women's Demands], *Baztāb-e Andisheh* 49 (Ordibehesht 1383 [May 2004]), pp. 43–7.
Mehrpur, M., and M.H. Malayeri., Interview with Hashemi Rafsanjani, 'Naqādi-ye Nazarvarziha Darbāreh-ye Majma'-ye Tashkhis-e Maslahat-e Nezām' [Criticism of Views on the Expediency Discernment Council of the System], *Rāhbord* 26 (Zemestān 1382 [Winter 2003]), pp. 8–48.
———. 'Seyri dar Mabāni-ye Feqhi va Hoquqi-ye Mādeh-ye 630 Qānun-e Mojāzāt-e Islami' [Analysis of Legal and Jurisprudential Basis of article 630 of the Islamic Criminal Code], *Majaleh-ye Nāmeh-ye Mofid* 8, 1375 [1996], pp. 167–88.
Mir-Khalili, A., 'Zan Dar Hoquq-e Khānevādeh' [Women under Family Law], *Ketāb-e Naqd* 12 (Pāiz 1378 [Fall 1999]), pp. 102–43.
Moein Al Eslam, M.,'Cheshm Andāzi Bar Barkhi az Vāqeiyathā-ye Penhān-e Konvānsion-e Raf'-e Tab'iz Alayhe Zanān' [Perspectives on the Realities of the Convention on the Elimination of All Forms of Discrimination Against Women], *Payām-e Zan*, Vol. 140.
Mohammadi Jurkuye, A., 'Diyeh va Qesās va Taklif-e Hokumat va Haq-e Zanān' [Diyeh and Qesās: Women's Rights and the Government's Obligation], *Majale-ye Bāztāb-e Andisheh* 52, 1383 [2004], pp. 46–56.

'Moj-e Eterāz be Lāyehe-ye Khānevādeh dar Rāh Ast' [Wave of Objection to Family Protection Bill is on its Way], http://www.akhbar-rooz.com/news.jsp?essayId=16446 (accessed 21 May 2017).

Mohammad Zadeh, B., 'Negāhi be Hoquq-e Zan dar Islam: Naqdi Bar Konvānsion-e Raf'-e Koliyeh-ye Ashkāl Tab'iz Alayhe Zanān' [An Overview of Women's Rights in Iran: A Critique of the Convention of the Elimination of All Forms of Discrimination Against Women], *Mo'refat* 70 (Mehr 1382 [October 2003]).

'Mokhālefat-e Jame-ye Zeynab bā Lāyehe-ye Hemāyat az Khānevādeh' [Zeynab Society Disagrees with the Family Protection Bill], *Donyā-ye Eghtesād*, 16 Mordād 1387 [6 August 2008]. http://donya-e-eqtesad.com/news/465347 (accessed 19 May 2017).

'Mokhālefat-e Majles bā Elzāmi Shodan-e Sabt-e Ezdevāj-e Movaqat' [Majles Rejection of the Mandatory Registration of Temporary Marriage], *Fars News Agency*, 15 Esfand 1390 [5 March 2012]. www.farsnews.com/newstext.php?nn=13901215000667 (accessed 27 March 2017).

Molai, S., 'Ejlās-e Zanān-e 2000 Gāmi Barā-ye Edālat, Solh va Tose'e' [2000 Women's Forum: A Step Towards Development, Justice and Peace], *Bāztāb-e Andishe* 3 (Khordād 1379 [June 2000]).

'Monāzerehi Keh Nabood' [A Discussion That Did Not Take Place], *Zanān* 97, p. 78.

'Mosāhebe-ye Matbuāti-ye Rowhāni' [Transcript of Rowhani's Press Conference], http://isna.ir/fa/news/92051508991 [2 April 2018].

Mosavari Manesh, A., 'Barkhi Nahādhā-ye Zanān ba Konvānsion-e Raff'-e Tab'iz Mokhālefand' [Some Women's Institutions Disagree with the Convention], *Mardom Sālāri*, 20 Mehr 1381 [12 October 2002].

Mosharaf, R., 'Barrasi-ye Payāmadhā-ye Ezdevāj-e Qeyr-e Qānuni-ye Zanān-e Irani ba Atbā'-e Bigāneh dar Khorāsān-e Razavi' [Analysing the Consequences of Illegal Marriage of Iranian Women with non-Iranian Men in Khorasan], *Khorāsān*. www.khorasan.ir/banovan/tabid/7403/Default.aspx (accessed 20 March 2017).

Moti', N., 'Goruhhā-ye Zanān Dar Harkat-e Tavānā Sāzi' [Women Groups on the Move to Empowerment], *A Quarterly Journal of Centre for Women's Studies* 6 (Summer 2003), pp. 7–22.

Mousavi, H., 'Ezdevāj-e Movaqat: Hekmathā va Zaruratha' [Temporary Marriage: Wisdoms and Necessities], *Mobaleqān* 85, Āzar 1385 [December 2006], pp. 38–52.

'Movāfeqat-e *olamā* Jalb Nashod' [The Olamā's Agreement Was Not Forthcoming], *Hambastegi* (7 Ordibehesht 1382 [27 April 2003]).

Namamiyan, P. and S. Tayebi, 'Barresi va Tahlil-e Mofād-e Konvānsion-e 1979 Majma'-e Omumi-ye Sāzmān-e Melal-e Motahed' [Analysis of the 1979 Convention Ratified by the UN General Assembly], *Edālat Ārā* 4 & 5 (Tābestān va Pāiz 1385 [Summer and Fall 2006]).

'Nāmeh-ye Āshofteh' [A Perturbed Letter], *Yās-e Now*, 30 Mordād 1382 [21 August 2003].

'Nāmeh-ye Jāme'h-ye Modaresin-e Hozeh-ye Elmiyeh-ye Qom Be Rais-e Majles-e Showrā-ye Islami Hojat-ol-Islam Valmoslemin Karroubi dar Mored-e Elhāq-e Iran Be Konvānsion' [Letter from the Society of Seminary Teachers of Qom to Majles Speaker Hojat-ol-Islam Karroubi Regarding Iran's Accession to the

CEDAW Dated 18 March 2002], *Jomhuri-ye Islami* (20 Mordād 1382 [11 August 2003]).

'Nāmeh-ye Sargoshādeh-ye Barkhi Tashakolhā-ye Zanān Be Majles Darbāreh-ye Barābari-ye Diyeh-ye Zan va Mard' [An Open Letter of Some Women's Organisations to the Majles about Equal Diyeh for Men and Women], *Zanestān*, 12 Tir 1386 [3 July 2007], http://zanestan.es/news/07,07,03,06,08,15/ (accessed 31 March 2017).

'Natāyej-e Tarh-e Hamsarkoshi dar 15 Ostān-e Keshvar' [The Result of Research on Intra-Marital Homicide in 15 Provinces of the Country], *Ruznāmeh-ye Iran*, 18 Bahman 1381 [7 February 2003].

Nāteqi, L., 'Peyvastan-e Iran Be Konvānsion-e Raf'-e Tab'iz Alayhe Zanān' [Iran's Accession to the Convention on the Elimination of All Forms of Discrimination Against Women], *Āftāb-e Yazd*, 6 Bahman 1380 [26 January 2002].

'Natije-ye Pāyāni-ye Dahomin Entekhābāt-e Riyāsat-e Jomhuri' [The Final Result of the Tenth Presidential Elections], *Tabnāk*, 23 Khordād 1388 [13 June 2009]. www.tabnak.ir/fa/news/51716/%D9%86%D8%AA%DB%8C%D8%AC% D9%87-%D9%BE%D8%A7%DB%8C%D8%A7%D9%86%DB%8C-% D8%AF%D9%87%D9%85%DB%8C%D9%86-%D8%A7%D9%86%D8% AA%D8%AE%D8%A7%D8%A8%D8%A7%D8%AA-%D8%B1%DB%8C %D8%A7%D8%B3%D8%AA-%D8%AC%D9%85%D9%87%D9%88% D8%B1%DB%8C (accessed 22 April 2017).

'Nazar-e Se Marja'-e Taqlid Darbāreh-ye Peyvastan-e Iran be Konvānsion-e Beynolmelali-ye Zanān' [The View of Three Religious Figures Regarding Iran's Accession to the Women's Convention], *Keyhān* (25 Ordibehesht 1381 [15 May 2002]).

Ne'mati, L., 'Konvānsion-e Zanān va Ebhāmāt-e Ān' [Women's Convention and its Ambiguities], *Resālat*, 26 Āzar 1390 [16 January 2012].

'Neshast-e Lāyehe-ye Hemāyat az Khānevādeh' [Gathering about the Family Protection Bill], *Iranian Students' News Agency*, 13 Shahrivar 1386 [4 September 2007]. www.isna.ir/news/8606-07054/ (accessed 19 May 2017)

'Niyāz Be Elhaq Be Konvānsion-e Raf'-e Tab'iz Az Zanān Nadārim' [There Is No Need to Accede to the Convention on the Elimination of All Forms of Discrimination Against Women], *Fekr-e Rooz*, Vol. 3.

Olyai Zand, S., 'Ezdevāj-e Nāmonāseb Bastari Zamine Saz Barāye Ruspigari' [Improper Marriage is a Cause of Prostitution], *Faslnāme-ye Refāh-e Ejtemāi*, Vol. 6 (Paeiz 1381 [Autumn 2002]).

'Pāsokh be Porsesh hā-ye Motadāvel dar Mored-e Campain-e Yek Milion Emzā [Answers to the Most Popular Questions' About the One Million Signatures Campaign], *The Feminist School*, http://www.feministschool.com/campaign/spip. php?article1 (accessed 3 April 2017.

'Payāmadhā-ye Elhāq be Konvānsion-e Raf'-e Tab'iz az Zanān' [Consequences of Iran's Accession to the Convention], *Khorāsān*, 11 Ordibehesht 1385 [1 May 2006].

'Payāmadhā-ye Peyvastan Be in Konvānsion Jobrān Nāpazir Ast: Barresi-ye Konvānsion-e Mahv-e Koliyeh-ye Ashkāl-e Tab'iz Alayh-e Zanān' [It Is Not Possible to Remedy the Consequences of Accession to the Convention: An Analysis of the Convention on the Elimination of All Forms of Discrimination Against Women], *Keyhān*, 19 Tir 1382 [10 July 2003].

'Pāyan-e Hamgarāei: Āqazi Digar Barāye Tarh-e Motālebāt Zanān' [End of The Coalition: Another Beginning for Women's Demands], 8 June 2009, *The Feminist School.* www.feministschool.com/spip.php?article2635 (accessed 12 January 2016).

'Paziresh-e Konvānsion Zanān Ta'til-e Mosalamāt-e Shar' Ast' [The Acceptance of the Convention is the Closure of Islamic Principles], *Yālsārāt* 238 (24 Mordād 1382 [15 August 2003]).

Pur Tehrani, M. 'Ezdevāj-e Movaqat: Be Har Do Ruye Sekeh Bengarim' [Temporary Marriage: Consider Both Sides of the Coin], *Gozāresh* 100 (Ordibehesht 1378 [May 1999]), pp. 22–4.

Qadir, M., 'Konvānsion-e Raf'-e Tab'iz az Zanān az Didgāh-e Hoquq-e Binolmelal' [The Convention on the Elimination of All Forms of Discrimination Against Womem from an International Law Perspective], *Keyhān*, 26 Esfand 1380 [17 March 2002].

'Qānun-e Hemāyat az Khānevādeh 46 Sāl be Aghab Bordeh Shode' [The Family Protection Bill Went Back to Fourty Years Ago], *Pyknet.* www.pyknet.net/1386/07shahrivar/10/PAGE/40EBADI.htm (accessed 21 May 2017).

Qarai Moghadam, A., 'Qatlhā-ye Nāmusi yā 'nahve-h kardan' dar Miyān-e Qabāyel-e Arab-e Khuzestan' [Honour Killings among Khuzestan's Arab Tribes], *Majaleh-ye Dādgostari* 32 (Pāeiz 1379 [Autumn 2000]).

'Raf '-e Tab'iz Yā Hākemiyat-e Arzeshhā-ye Femenisti? Negāhi Be Mabāhes-e Matruheh Darbāreh-ye Konvānsion-e Raf'-e Har Guneh Tab'iz Alayh-e Zanān' [Elimination of Discrimination or Domination of the Feminist's Values: Examining Different Discussion about the Convention on the Elimination of all Forms of Discrimination Against Women], *Nashriyeh-ye Tarbiyat-e Siyasi* 13 (1), pp. 60–3.

'Rāhbordhā-ye Jonbesh-e Zanān Roy-e Yek Miz: Neshasti Bā Fa'ālān Gorohhā-ye Mokhtalef-e Jonbesh-e Zanān' [Women's Strategies on the Table: A Meeting with Women's Rights Activists from Different Groups], *Zanān* 145 (Khordād 1386 [May 2007]), pp. 2–11.

'Rāhpeymāi dar E'terāz be Konvānsion Raf'-e Tab'iz Alayhe Zanān dar Qom Bargozār Shod' [A Demonstration Was Held in Qom in Objection to the Convention on the Elimination of All Forms of Discrimination Against Women], *Khorāsān*, 12 Mordād 1382 [3 August 2003].

Raei, M., 'Elhāq be Konvānsion az Manzar-e Movāfeqān va Mokhālefān' [Accession to the Convention From the Perspective of Supporters and Opponents], *Bāztāb-e Andishe* 46 (Bahman 1382 [February 2004]), pp. 51–62.

———. 'Zanān: Asnād-e Hoquq-e Bashar va Mavāzin-e Feqhi' [Women: Human Rights Documents and Feqh Principles], *Ravāq Andisheh* 36 (Āzar 1383 [December 2004]).

Raisi, M., 'Elhāq yā Adam-e Elhāq be Konvānsion-e Raf'-e Tab'iz az Zanān' [Accession or No Accession to the Convention on the Elimination of all Forms of Discrimination Against Women], *Nashriyeh-ye Feqh va Hoquq-e Khānevādeh* 29 (Bahār 1382 [Spring 2003]), pp. 44–82.

Ramezan Nargessi, R., 'Bāztāb-e Chand Hamsari dar Jāme'e' [The Reflection of Polygamy in Society], *Ketāb-e Zanān* 27 (Bahār 1384 [Spring 2005]), pp. 145–74.

Ray-e Manfi-ye Majles be Tarhe E'tāy-e Tāb'iyat be Farzandān-e Hāsel az Ezdevāj-e Zanān-e Irāni ba Mardān-e Khāreji' [Majles Negative Vote to the Bill on Iranian

Nationality for Children Borne to Iranian Mothers and Foregin Fathers],
Hamshahri Online (5 Mehr 1394 [27 September 2015]). www.hamshahrionline.
ir/details/308609/Iran/legislative (accessed 24 March 2017).
Rezazadeh., 'Ta'āroz-e Konvānsion-e Mahve-e Koliye-ye Ashkāle Tab'iz Alayhe Zanān bā Hoquq-e Vāghei-ye Zanān' [The Contradictions of the Convention on the Elimination of All Forms of Discrimination Against Women with Women's Real Rights], *Jomhuri-ye Islami* (7 Mordād 1378 [29 July 1999]).
Rostami, N., 'Khon-e Man Cheqadr Miarzad' [How Much Is My Blood Worth], *Zanān*, Khordād 1383 [May 2004], pp. 23–5.
'Ruh-e Hākem Bar Konvānsion Mardsālār Ast' [Patriarchy Is the Prevailing Spirit of the Convention], *Zan-e Ruz*, Vol. 1969.
Saberi, M., 'Naqd-e Konvānsion-e Koliyeh-ye Ashkāl-e Raf'-e Tab'iz az Zanān' [A Critique of the Convention on the Elimination of All Forms of Discrimination Against Women], *Tahurā* 13 (Tābestān 1391 [Summer 2012]), pp. 145–68.
'Sabt-e Āmār-e Ejdevāj-e Mojadad va Movaqat dar Sabt-e Ahvāl' [Registration of Temporay and Second Marriages in the Registry of Personal Status Office]'. Available from: http://khabarfarsi.com/ext/1799020 (accessed 19 March 2017).
Sadr, S., 'Barābari-ye Mashrut-e Zan va Mard: Be Angizeh-yeTasvibe-e Elhāq be Konvānsion-e Raf'-e Hameh Goobneh Tab'iz Alayhe Zanān [Conditional Equality of Men and Women: On the Occasion of the Ratification of the Convention on the Elimination of All Forms of Discrimination Against Women]', *Zanān* 84 [Bahman 1380 [January 2002]).
———. 'Darbāreh-ye Yek Nāmeh [About a Letter]', *Yās-e Now*, 20 Tir 1382 [11 July 2003].
———. 'Nāmus-e Zanān Vābasteh be Yek Mard [Women's Honour Depending on a Single Man]', *Zanān* 93 (Ābān 1381 [October 2002]), pp. 10–13.
Saidzadeh, Z., 'Jāye Khāliye-h Hoquq-e Jensi dar Lāyehe-ye Mojāzāt-e Islami [The Absence of Gender Related Rights in the Criminal Code]'. Available at www. meydaan.org/ShowArticle.aspx?arid=692 (accessed 25 March 2017).
Samadi, A.A., 'Mādeh-ye 179 Qānun-e Mojāzāt-e Iran va Moqāyeseh-ye ān bā Shaq-e 2 az Mādeh-ye 324 Qānun-e Mojāzāt-e Farānseh [Comparative Analysis of Article 170 of Iran's Criminal Code with Article 324(2) of the French Penal Code]', *Majaleh-ye Kānun-e Vokalā* 78, 1340 [1961], pp. 59–69.
'Shast va Panj Namāyandeh-ye Majles-e Haftom va Hashtom Do Zan Dārand' [65 Male MPs of the Seventh and Eighth Majles Have A Second Wife]. Available at http://iranianuk.com/20080212101200018/%DB%B6%DB%B5 (accessed 21 May 2017).
'Sarnevesht-e Lāyeheh-ye Qānun-e Mojāzāt-e Islami dar Hālehi az Ebhām [The Vague Situation of the Islamic Criminal Code]'. http://lawyerman.persianblog. ir/post/155 (accessed 26 March 2017).
Savizi, M., 'Konvānsion-e Raf'-e Koliyeh-ye Ashkāl-e Zolm Alayhe Zanān: Yek Zarurat' [The Convention on the Elimination of All Forms of Discrimination Against Women: A Necessity], *Motāle'āt-e Rābordi-e Zanān* 31, Bahār 1385 [Spring 2006], pp. 7–25.
Seyedi, Azad.,'Haq-e Shart Bar Konvānsion-e Emhā-ye Koliyeh-ye Ashkāl-e Tab'iz Alayhe Zanān' [Reservation to the Convention on the Elimination of All Forms of Discrimination Against Women], *Pajohesh Hoquq va Siyāsat* 15 & 16 (Paiz va Zemestān 1384 [Fall and Winter 2005]), pp. 283–316.

Shadlu, S., 'Jonbesh-e Ejtemāi-ye Zanān Dar Jahān-e Sevom' [Women's Social Movement in the Third World], *Hoquq Zanān* 17 (Ordibehesht va Khordād 1379 [May and June 2000]), pp. 6–11.

———. 'Jonbesh-e Ejtemāi-ye Zanān' [Women's Social Movement], *Hoquq Zanān* 15 (Ordibehesht va Khordād 1379 [May and June 2000]), pp. 13–18.

'Shalvārhā-ye Nāzok-e Ehsās dar Khāneh-ye Mellat' [Sensitive Thin Trousers in the House of the Nation]. Available at https://chandzane.wordpress.com/ (accessed 21 May 2017).

Shirafkan, A., 'Bāzkhāni-ye Tab'izāt-e Qānuni-ye Ezdevāj-e Zanān-e Irāni bā Mardān-e Afqāni' [Readout of Legal Discrimination of Marriage of Iranian Women with Afghan Men]. Available at www.aftabir.com/articles/view/social/law/c4c1185009901_spousal_p1.php/ (accessed 22 March 2017).

Shirazi, M., 'Bandhā-ye Mota'adedi az Konvānsion-e Raf'-e Tab'iz Sarihan bar Khalāf-e Shar'-e Islam Ast' [Some articles of the Convention are in Explicit Contradiction with Islam], *Hemāyat*, 12 Mordād 1382 [3 August 2003].

———. 'Mabādā Ta'limāt-e Dini-ye Mārā Gharbihā Entekhāb Konand' [Lest Westerns Choose Our Religious Education], *Keyhān*, 10 Tir 1382 [1 July 2003].

Shojaei, Z., 'Dar Bahs-e Konvānsion Ghoghā Sālāri kardand' [An Exaggerated Discussion About the Convention], *Yās-e Now* (22 Esfand 1379 [21 March 2001]).

Sobhani Tabrizi, J., 'Goftogui ba Hazrat-e Āyatollah Sobhāni Pirāmun-e Konvānsion-e Tab'iz Alayhe Zanān' [A Discussion with Ayatollah Sobhani Regarding the Convention on the Elimination of All Forms of Discrimination Against Women], *Darshāi az Maktab-e Islam* 9 (Āzar 1382 [December 2003]), pp. 28–36.

'Sodur-e Shenāsnāmeh Brāye Farzandān-e Hāsel az Ezdevāj-e Zanān-e Irani bā Mardān-e Khāreji' [Issuing Birth Certificate for Children Born to Iranian Mothers and Foreign Men]. Available at www.salamatnews.com/news/223071/-%D8%B5%D8%AF%D9%88%D8%B1-%D8%B4%D9%86%D8%A7%D8%B3%D9%86%D8%A7%D9%85%D9%87-%D8%A8%D8%B1%D8%A7%DB%8C-%D9%81%D8%B1%D8%B2%D9%86%D8%AF%D8%A7%D9%86-%D8%AD%D8%A7%D8%B5%D9%84-%D8%A7%D8%B2-%D8%A7%D8%B2%D8%AF%D9%88%D8%A7%D8%AC-%D8%B2%D9%86%D8%A7%D9%86-%D8%A7%DB%8C%D8%B1%D8%A7%D9%86%DB%8C-%D8%A8%D8%A7-%D9%85%D8%B1%D8%AF%D8%A7%D9%86-%D8%AE%D8%A7%D8%B1%D8%AC%DB%8C (accessed 31 March 2017).

Sorush, A., 'Zabt va Bast-e Hoquq-e Zanān' [Contraction and Expansion of Women's Rights], *Zanān* 59 (Dey 1378 [January 2001]), pp. 32–7.

Tabibzadeh Nuri, 'Nemigozāram Iran be Konvānsion Bepeyvandad' [I Will Not Allow Iran to Join the Convention], *Aftāb News*, 9 Khordād 1385 [31 July 2006]. Available at www.aftabnews.ir/vdcdnz0o.yt05o6a22y.html (accessed 1 April 2017).

Taheri, M., 'Ehqāq-e Hoquq-e Zan, Konvānsion yā Islam' [Establishing Women's Rights: Convention or Islam], *Ketāb-e Naqd* 26 & 27, Bahār va Tābestān 1382 [Spring and Summer 2003], pp. 277–88.

'Talāsh-e Zanān-e Majles Barāy-e Jolugiri az Tasvib-e Konvānsion' [The Efforts of Female MPs in Discouraging the Ratification of the Convention], *Zanān*, Vol. 113.

'Taqdir-e Shorā-ye Zanān az Jāme Negari-ye Lāyehe ye Hemāyat az Khānevādeh' [Women's Council Appriciation of the Family Protection Bill], *Mehr News Agency*, 3 Shahrivar 1386 [25 August 2007]. Available from: www.mehrnews. com/news/540659 (accessed 19 May 2017).

'Tashāboh Yā Tasāvi-ye Zanān va Mardān: Konvānsion Be Kodām Su Miravad?' [Equality or Similarity of Men and Women: What Is the Convention's Preferance?], *Resālat*, 29 Ābān 1382 [20 November 2003].

Tasmim Barāy-e Barābari-ye Diyeh-ye Zan va Mard [Decission on Equal Diyeh for Men and Women], 1 Khordād 1386 [22 May 2007]. Available at http://iranins urance.ir/en/display-news/-/asset_publisher/vdWtKGtk9KxK/content/%D8% AA%D8%B5%D9%85%D9%8A%D9%85-%D8%A8%D8%B1%D8%A7% D9%8A-%D8%A8%D8%B1%D8%A7%D8%A8%D8%B1%D9%8A-% D8%AF%D9%8A%D9%87-%D8%B2%D9%86-%D9%88%D9%85%D8% B1%D8%AF-%D8%A7%D8%B9%D8%AA%D9%85%D8%A7%D8%AF/ pop_up?_101_INSTANCE_vdWtKGtk9KxK_viewMode=print (accessed 20 April 2018).

Tariqi, N., 'Movāfeqān va Mokhālefān Che Migooyand, Tazāhorkonandegān dar Qom: Zanān-e Mā Bidārand az Convānsion Bizārand [What the Opponents and Supporters Say, Demonstrator in Qom: Our Women Are Awake and Hate the Convention]', *Zanān* 101, Tir va Mordād 1382 [June–July 2003], pp. 14–19.

'Tarhe Tāb'iyat-e Irāni-ye Farzandān-e Zanān-e Irāni va Mardān–e Khāreji Moshkel- e Amniyati Dārad' [The Bill on Iranian Nationality for Children Those Born From Iranian Mothers has National Security Implications], *Khabar Online*, 28 September 2011.

Tavakolian, J., 'Roshanfekri va Masaleh-ye Zanān' [Religious Intellectualism and the Women's Issues], *Zanān* 82 (Āzar 1380 [December 2002]).

Tohidi, A.R., 'Zanan va Sazeman Melal' [Women and the United Nations], in *The Convention on the Elimination of All Forms of Discrimination Against Women: Articles and Discussions* (Qom: Sadaf, 1381 [2003]), pp. 9–87.

'Tozih-e Chand Khabar' [Explaination of Some News], *Zanān*, Vol. 99.

'Vaziyat-e Tāb'iyat-e Farzandān-e Hāsel az Ezdevāj-e Zanān-e Irani bā Mardān-e Khāreji Moshakhas Shod' [The Situation of Nationality of Children Born to Iranian Mothers Is Determined]. Available at www.hamshahrionline.ir/details/ 16931 (accessed 20 March 2017).

'Zahra Rahnavard Khāstār-e Khoru-je Bandhāyi az Lāyehe-ye Hemāyat az Khānevāde az Dastur-e Kār-e Majles Shod' [Zahra Rahnavard Called for the Withdrawal of Some Parts of the Family Protection Bill from the Parliamentary Agenda]. Available at www.radiofarda.com/a/2172815.html (accessed 1 April 2018).

Zarabadi, S., 'Bā Ejāzeh-ye Khodam Nāmusam Rā Mikosham' [I Kill My Honour with My Own Permission], *Zanān* 109 (Khordād 1383 [May 2004]), pp. 29–33.

Zafaranchi, L., 'Naqdi Ejmāli bar Konvānsion-e Raf'-e Tab'iz Alayhe Zanān' [A Comprehensive Critique of the Convention on the Elimination of all Forms of Discrimination Against Women], *Ketāb-e Naqd* 27 & 28 (Spring and Summer 2003), pp. 267–76.

'Zanān, Sāzmān-e Melal va Neshast-e Pekan+5': Barresi-ye Tārikhcheh-ye Eqdāmāt-e Sazmān-e Melal Dar Masāel-e Zanān va Payāmadha-ye Konvānsion-e Pekan' [Women, United Nations and the Beijing Summite: An Evalution of United

Nations History on Women's Issues and the Results of the Beijing Convention], *Keyhān*,13 June 2000.

'Yek Bām va Do Havā: Pirāmoon-e Elhāq-e Iran be Konvānsion-e Raf'-e Tab'iz az Zanān' [Double Standards: On Iran's Accession to the Convention on the Elimination of All Forms of Discrimination Against Women], *Yās-e Now*, 3 Shahrivar 1382 [25 August 2003].

Interviews

Ahmadi Khorasani, N., written corespondence.
Ebadi, S., interviews with the author, May, April, June and July 2012 and June, July and August 2013, London.
Hosseinkhah, M., interview with the author, September 2012, London.
Karami, L., interview with the author, June 2012, London.
Moqaddam, K., interview with the author, May 2013, London.
Mousavi Khoini, A.A., written correspondence.
Tahmassebi, S., interview with the author, May 2013, London.

English Sources

1. Primary Sources in English

Treaties

Arab Charter on Human Rights 2004 (originally adopted 15 September 1994; revised version adopted 22 May 2004; entered into force 15 March 2008).
Charter of the United Nations (signed on 26 June 1945, entered into force 24 October 1945) 59 Stat. 1031, *T.S. 993, 3 Bevans 1153*.
Convention Concerning the Employment of Women Before and After Childbirth (ILO Convention No 3) (adopted 28 November 1919, entered into force 13 June 1921) *38 UNTS 53*.
Convention for the Protection of Human Rights and Fundamental Freedoms (European Convention on Human Rights) (Rome, 4 November 1950; *TS71 (1953)*).
Convention on Consent to Marriage, Minimum Age for Marriage and Registration of Marriage (adopted 7 November 1962, entered into force 9 December 1946) *521 UNTS 231*.
Convention on the Elimination of All Forms of Discrimination Against Women (CEDAW) (adopted 18 December 1979, entered into force 3 September 1981) *1249 UNTS 13*.
Convention on the Nationality of Married Women (adopted 29 January 1957, entered into force 11 August 1958) *309 UNTS 65*.
Convention on the Political Rights of Women (adopted 20 December 1952, entered into force 7 July 1954) *193 UNTS 135*.
Convention on the Rights of the Child (adopted 20 November 1989; entered into force 2 September 1990) *1577 UNTS 3*.
ILO Convention Concerning Night Work (ILO Convention No 171) (adopted 26 June 1990, entered into force 4 January 1995) 1855, *UNTS 305*.

International Convention on the Elimination of All Forms of Racial Discrimination (CERD) (adopted 21 December 1965, entered into force 4 January 1969) 660 UNTS 195.

International Covenant on Civil and Political Rights (ICCPR) (adopted by General Assembly Resolution 2200A (XXI) of 16 December 1966, entered into force 23 March 1967) 999 UNTS171.

International Covenant on Economic, Social and Cultural Rights (ICESCR) (adopted by General Assembly Resolution 2200A (XXI) of 16 December 1966, entered into force 3 January 1976) 993 UNTS 3.

Optional Protocol to the Convention on the Elimination of All Forms of Discrimination Against Women, GA Res 54/4 of 6 October 1999, entered into force 22 December 2000, 2131 UNTS 83.

Optional Protocol to the International Covenant on Civil and Political Rights (adopted 16 December 1966, entered into force 23 March 1976) 999 UNTS 171.

Rome Statute of the International Criminal Court (adopted 17 July 1998, entered into force 1 July 2002) 2187 UNTS90.

Universal Declaration of Human Rights adopted by UN General Assembly Resolution 217 A (III) of 10 December 1948 (UDHR).

Vienna Convention on the Law of Treaties (adopted 23 May 1969, entered into force 27 January 1980), 1155 UNTS 331.

Other International Instruments

Article 324 of the Penal Code of France (1810). Available at www.napoleon-series.org/research/government/france/penalcode/c_penalcode3b.html (accessed 27 March 2016).

Beijing Declaration and Platform for Action (15 September 1995). Reproduced in *International Legal Materials* 35, 404 (1996).

Cairo Declaration on Human Rights in Islam. Available from: http://hrlibrary.umn.edu/instree/cairodeclaration.html (accessed 1 May 2018).

CEDAW General Recommendation No. 1, 5th Session (1986) on Reporting Guidelines.

CEDAW General Recommendation No. 2, 6th Session (1987) on Reporting Guidlines.

CEDAW General Recommendation No. 4, 6th Session (1987) on Reservations.

CEDAW General Recommendation No. 11, 8th Session (1989) on Technical Advisory Service for Reporting.

CEDAW General Recommendation No. 12, 8th Session (1989) on Violence against Women.

CEDAW General Recommendation No. 19, 11th Session (1992) on Violence against Women.

CEDAW General Recommendation No. 20, 11th Session (1992) on Reservations to the Convention.

CEDAW General Recommendation No. 21, 13th Session (1994) on Equality in Marriage and Family Relations.

CEDAW General Recommendation No. 27, 47th Session (2010) on Older Women and Protection of their Human Rights, UN Doc CEDAW/C/GC/27.

CEDAW General Recommendation No. 28, 47th Session (2010) The Core Obligation of States Parties under Article 2 of the Convention on the

Elimination of All Forms of Discrimination Against Women, *UN CEDAW/C/ GC/28*.
Committee on Elimination of Discrimination Against Women, 22nd Session, Concluding Observation (CO) Iraq, *CEDAW/C/IRQ/2-3* (14 June 2000).
Committee on Elimination of Discrimination Against Women, 32nd Session, Concluding Observation (CO) Gabon, 32nd Session, *CEDAW/C/2005/I/CRP.3/ Add.3/Rev.1* (28 January 2005).
Committee on Elimination of Discrimination Against Women, 33rd Session, Concluding Observation (CO) Lebanon, *CEDAW/C/LBN/CO/2* (22 July 2005).
Committee on Elimination of Discrimination Against Women, 34th Session, Concluding Observation (CO) Tahailand, *CEDAW/C/THA/CO/5* (3 February 2006).
Committee on Elimination of Discrimination Against Women, 38th Session, Concluding Observation (CO) Mozambique, *CEDAW/C/MOZ/CO/2* (11 June 2007).
Committee on Elimination of Discrimination Against Women, 38th Session, Concluding Observation (CO) Syrian Arab Republic, *CEDAW/C/SYR/CO/1* (11 June 2007).
Committee on Elimination of Discrimination Against Women, 41st Session, Concluding Observation (CO) Yemen, *CEDAW/C/YEM/CO/6* (9 July 2008).
Committee on Elimination of Discrimination Against Women, 42nd Session, Concluding Observation (CO) Kyrgyzstan, *CEDAW/C/KGZ/CO/3* (14 November 2008).
Committee on Elimination of Discrimination Against Women, 42nd Session, Concluding Observation (CO) Mongolia, *CEDAW/C/MNG/CO/7* (7 November 2008).
Committee on Elimination of Discrimination Against Women, 43rd Session, Concluding Observation (CO) Cameroon, *CEDAW/C/CMR/CO/3* (6 February 2009).
Committee on Elimination of Discrimination Against Women, 44th Session, Concluding Observation (CO) Japan, *CEDAW/C/JPN/CO/6* (7 August 2009).
Committee on Elimination of Discrimination Against Women, 46th Session, Concluding Observation (CO) Turkey, *CEDAW/C/TUR/CO/6* (30 July 2010).
Committee on Elimination of Discrimination Against Women, Exceptional Session, Concluding Observation (CO) Uganda, *CEDAW/C/SR.575 and 576* (9 August 2002).
Committee on Elimination of Discrimination Against Women, 48th Session, Concluding Observation (CO) Kenya, *CEDAW/C/MNG/CO/7* (2 February 2011).
Compilation of Guidelines on the Form and Content of Reports to be Submitted by States Parties to the International Human Rights Treaties, *HIR/GEN/2/Rev.1/ Add.2* (5 May 2003).
Compilation of Guidelines on the Form and Content of Reports to be Submitted by States Partties to the International Human Rights Treaties, *HRI/GEN/2/Rev.1/ Add.6* (3 June 2009).
Concluding Comments of the Committee, Consideration of the Combined Third and Fourth Periodic Report by Morocco, Advanced United Version 1 February 2008, *UN Doc. CEDAW/C/MAR/CO/4*.

BIBLIOGRAPHY

Concluding Comments of the Committee, Consideration of the Initial Report Submitted by Syria, UN Doc. CEDAW/C/SYR/CO/1.

Concluding Observations on the Combined Third and Fourth Periodic Reports of the Islamic Republic of Iran, 13 March 2016, CRC/C/IRN/CO/3–4.

Consideration of the Initial Report Submitted by Iraq, 12th Session, Summary Record of the 212th Meeting, 20 January 1993, UN. Doc. CEDAW/C/SR.212.

Consideration of the Initial Report Submitted by Iraq, 13th Session, Summary Record of the 212th Meeting, 20 January 1993, UN. Doc. CEDAW/C/SR.213.

Consideration of the Initial Report Submitted by Morocco, 16th Session, Summary Record of the 312th Meeting, 14 January 1997, UN Doc. CEDAW/C/SR. 312.

Consideration of the Initial Report Submitted by Morocco, 16th Session, Summary Record of the 313th Meeting, 14 January 1997, UN Doc. CEDAW/C/SR. 313.

Consideration of the Initial Report Submitted by Morocco, 16th Session, Summary Record of the 320th Meeting, 20 January 1997, UN Doc. CEDAW/C/SR. 320.

Combined Initial and Second Periodic Report of Saudi Arabia Submitted on 29 March 2007, UN Doc. CEDAW/C/SAU/2.

Combined Second and Third Periodic Report of Iraq Submitted on 19 October 1999, NU Doc. CEDAW/C/IRAQ/2–3.

Combined Third and Fourth Periodic Report of Morocco Submitted on 18 September 2006, UN Doc. CEDAW/C/Mor4.

Commission on the Status of Women. Report on the Twenty-Fifth Session, 14 January–1 February 1974, UN Doc. E/CN.6/589.

Commission on the Status of Women, Twenty-Sixth Session, Summary Records of the 632nd Meeting held on 14 September 1976, UN Doc. E/CN.6/SR.632.

Commission on the Status of Women, Twenty-Sixth Session, Summary Records of the 650th Meeting held on 27 September 1976, UN Doc. E/CN.6/SR.650.

Commission on the Status of Women. Report on the Twenty-sixth and Resumed Twenty-Sixth Session, 13 September–1 October and 6–17 December 1976, UN Doc. E/5909 or E/CN.6/608.

Compilation of General Comments and General Recommendations Adopted by Human Rights Treaty Bodies. 8 May 2006, UN Doc. HRI/GEN/1/Rev.8.

Five-year Review of the implementation of the Beijing Declaration and Platform for Action (Beijing +5). Available at www.un.org/womenwatch/daw/followup/beijing+5.htm (accessed 8 April 2012).

Fourth World Conference on Women, Beijing, China, 4–15 September 1995, A/CONF.177/20, 17 October 1995.

Gill, A., Honour Killings and the Quest for Justice in Black and Minority Ethnic Communities in the UK and Moving Toward a 'Multiculturalism Without Culture': Constructing a Victim-Friendly Human Rights Approach to Forced Marriage in the UK. United Nations Division for the Advancement of Women, United Nations Economic Commission for Africa, Expert Group Meeting on Good Practices in Legislation to Address Harmful Practices Against Women, United Nations Conference Centre, Addis Ababa, Ethiopia, 25 to 28 May 2009. EGM/GPLHP/2009/EP.03, 12 June 2009.

General Assembly Resolution Adopting the Declaration on the Elimination of All Forms of Discrimination Against Women, 7 November 1967, A/RES/2263 (XXII) (DEDAW).

General Assembly Resolution Adopting the Recommendation on Consent to Marriage, Minimum Age for Marriage and Registration of Marriages *A/RES/2018* (XX), 1 November 1965, Principle II.

General Assembly Declaration on the Elimination of All Forms of Violence Against Women, 20 December 1993, *GA Res. 48/104* (DEVAW).

General Assembly Declaration Endorsing the Nairobi Forward-Looking Strategies for the Advancement of Women and Calling on Governments to Take Measures toward their Implementation. *A/RES/40/108*, 13 December 1985.

General Assembly Resolution, *A/RES/S-23/2*, 16 November 2000.

H.E. Mrs Maryam Mojtahedzadeh, Advisor to the President and Head of the Centre for Women and Family Affairs of the Islamic Republic of Iran before the 57th Session of the Commission on the Status of Women, New York, 5 March 2013.

Human Rights Committee General Comment No. 18 on Non-Discrimination, 21 November 1989, *CCPR/C/21/Rev.1.Add.1.*

Human Rights Committee General Comment No. 19 on Protection of the Family, the Right to Marriage and Equality of the Spouses (Article 23) 27/07/90 (39th Session 1990) *HRI/GEN/1/Rev.7.*

Human Rights Committee General Comment No. 28 on Equality of Rights between Men and Women (Article 3) (29/03/2000) *CCPR/C/21/Rev.1Add.10*, CCPR Comment 28.

Human Rights Committee, General Comment 31, Nature of the General Legal Obligation on States Parties to the Covenant, *U.N. Doc. CCPR/C/21/Rev.1/Add.13* (2004).

ICJ Advisory Opinion, Reservations to the Convention on the Prevention and Punishment of the Crime of Genocide, Pleadings, Oral arguments, Documents, 28 May 1951, pp. 15–69.

Initial Report of Iraq Submitted on 16 August 1990, *UN Doc. CEDAW/C/5/Add.66/Rev.1.*

Initial Report of Morocco Submitted on 29 February 2000, *UN Doc. CEDAW/C/MOR/2.*

Initial Report of Syria Submitted on 29 August 2005, *UN Doc. CEDAW/C/SYR/1.*

Integration of the Human Rights of Women and a Gender Perspective: Violence Against Women, *Report of the Special Rapporteur on violence against women, its causes and consequences*, Yakin Ertürk, Mission to the Islamic Republic of Iran (29 January to 6 February 2005), *E/CN.4/2006/61/Add.3*, 27 January 2006.

Morocco's reservations and declarations, *UN Women website*. www.un.org/womenwatch/daw/cedaw/reservations-country.htm (accessed 2 April 2017).

Report of the Committee on the Elimination of Discrimination Against Women, 3rd Session, General Assembly Official Records, 39th Session, Supplement No 45, 1984, *UN Doc. A/39/45.*

Report of the Committee on the Elimination of Discrimination Against Women, 5th Session, General Assembly Official Records, 41st Session, Supplement No 45, 1986, *UN Doc. A/41/45.*

Report of the Committee on the Elimination of Discrimination Against Women, 6th Session, General Assembly Official Records, 42nd Session, Supplement No 38, 1987, *UN Doc. A/42/38.*

Report of the Committee on the Elimination of Discrimination Against Women, 8th Session, General Assembly Official Records, 44th Session, Supplement No 38, 1990, *UN Doc. A/44/38.*

Report of the Committee on the Elimination of Discrimination Against Women, 9th Session, General Assembly Official Records, 45th Session, Supplement No 38, 1990, *UN Doc. A/45/38.*

Report of the Committee on the Elimination of Discrimination Against Women, 10th Session, General Assembly Official Records, 46th Session, Supplement No 38, 1993, *UN Doc. A/46/38.*

Report of the Committee on the Elimination of Discrimination Against Women, 11th Session, General Assembly Official Records, 47th Session, Supplement No 38, 1993, *UN Doc. A/47/38.*

Report of the Committee on the Elimination of Discrimination Against Women, 13th Session, General Assembly Official Records, 49th Session, Supplement No 38, 1994, *UN Doc. A/49/38.*

Report of the Committee on the Elimination of Discrimination Against Women, 14th Session, General Assembly Official Records, 50th Session, Supplement No 38, 1996, *UN Doc. A/50/38.*

Report of the Committee on the Elimination of Discrimination Against Women, 15th Session, General Assembly Official Records, 51st Session, Supplement No 38, 1996, *UN Doc. A/51/38.*

Report of the Committee on the Elimination of Discrimination Against Women, 16th and 17th Session, General Assembly Official Records, 52nd Session, Supplement No 38, 1997, *UN Doc. A/52/38/Rev.1.*

Report of the Committee on the Elimination of Discrimination Against Women, 18th and 19th Session, General Assembly Official Records, 53rd Session, Supplement No 38, 1998, *UN Doc. A/53/38/Rev.1.*

Report of the Committee on the Elimination of Discrimination Against Women, 20th and 21st Session, General Assembly Official Records, 54th Session, Supplement No 38, 1999, *UN Doc. A/54/38/Rev.1.*

Report of the Commission on Human Rights to the second session of the Economic and Social Council, 21 May 1946. *UN.Doc. E/38/Rev.1.*

Report of the CSW to ECOSOC on the first session of the Commission, held at Lake Success, New York, from 10 to 24 February 1947. *UN. Doc.E/281/Rev.1*, 25 February 1947.

Report of the International Conference on Population and Development, Cairo, *UN Doc A/Conf.171/13/Rev.1*, 1995.

Report of the Special Rapporteur on the situation of human rights in the Islamic Republic of Iran, Human Rights Council, twenty-second session, Agenda item 4, *A/HRC/22/56*, 28 February 2013.

Report of the World Conference to Review and Appraise the Achievements of the United Nations Decade for Women: Equality, Development and Peace, held in Nairobi from 15 to 26 July 1985. *UN.Doc.A/CONF.116/28/Rev.1* (85.IV.10), 1989.

Report of the World Conference of the International Women's Year, Mexico City, 19 June–2 July 1975, *UN Doc. E/CONF.66/34*, United Nations Publications Sales Number E.76.IV.1.

Response to the List of Issues and Questions for Consideration of the Combined Third and Fourth Report of Morocco, 15 November 2007, *UN Doc. CEDAW/C/MAR/Q/4/Add.1.*

Response to the List of Issues and Questions for Consideration of the Combined Initial and Second Periodic Report of Saudi Arabia, 18 December 2007, CEDAW/C/SAU/Q/2, *UN Doc. CEDAW/C/SAU/Q/2/Add.1*

Response to the List of Issues and Questions for Consideration of the Initial Periodic Report of Syria, 2 March 2007, *UN Doc. CEDAW/C/SYR/Q/1/Add.1*

Resolution adopted by the General Assembly, *A/RES/S-23/2*, 16 November 2000.

Statement by Delegation of the Islamic Republic of Iran, Fifty-Second Session of the Commission on the Status of Women, Agenda Item 3: Financing for gender equality and empowerment of women, New York, 3 March 2008.

The Answer of the Government of the Islamic Republic of Iran to the Questionnaire to Governments on Implementation of the Beijing Platform for Action (1995) and the Outcome of the Twenty-Third Special Session of the General Assembly (2000). Available at www.un.org/womenwatch/daw/Review/responses/IRAN-English.pdf (accessed 1 May 2018).

UN World Conference on Human Rights, Vienna Declaration and Programme of Action, 25 June 1993, *UN Doc A/Conf. 157/23*, 1993, paras 1 & 18.

UN Doc. CEDAW/C/1994/WG.I/Rev.1, 31 January 1994.

UN Doc. CEDAW/C/1994/WG.I/WP.1/Rev. 1, 31 January 1994.

United Nations General Assembly Official Records, Third Committee, 3rd Session (30 September–7 December 1948).

United Nations General Assembly Official Records, Third Committee, 5th Session, 1950.

United Nations General Assembly Official Records, Third Committee, 16th Session, 1961.

UN General Assembly, Thirty-Second Session, UN Decade for Women: Equality, Development and Peace. Draft Convention on the Elimination of Discrimination Against Women. Report of the Secretary-General, 21 September 1977, *UN Doc. A/32/218*.

UN General Assembly, Thirty-Second Session, UN Decade for Women: Equality, Development and Peace. Draft Convention on the Elimination of Discrimination Against Women. Report of the Secretary-General. Addendum, 12 October 1977, *UN Doc. A/32/218/Add.1*.

United Nations World Conference on Human Rights: Vienna Declaration and Programme of Action, 25 June 1993, *UN Doc, A/Conf. 157/23*.

Nasrin Sotoudeh v. Islamic Republic of Iran, Working Group on Arbitrary Detention, Opinion No. 21/2011, *U.N. Doc. A/HRC/WGAD/2011/21*.

Statement of the European Parliament's delegation for relations with Iran. Available at www.europarl.europa.eu/meetdocs/2004_2009/documents/dv/afet_171207_iranpress/afet_171207_iranpressen.pdf (accessed 21 May 2017).

Legislation

The Constitution of the Islamic Republic of Iran (1979, revised 1989). Available at: www.servat.unibe.ch/icl/ir00000_.html (accessed 10 February 2017).

The Civil Code of Iran, translated by M.A.R. Taleghany (Littleton, Colorado: Fred. B. Rothman, 1995).

The Civil Code of Iran, edited and translated by F. Badrian (Tehran: Daneshvar, 2001).

The Basic Law of Governance of the Kingdom of Saudi Arabia (1992). Available at www.mofa.gov.sa/sites/mofaen/aboutKingDom/SaudiGovernment/Pages/BasicSystemOfGovernance35297.aspx (accessed 1 April 2017).

2. Secondary Sources in English
Books and articles

Abghari, A., *Introduction to the Iranian Legal System and the Protection of Human Rights in Iran {Moqaddame-i Bar Nezām-e Hoquqi-ye Iranan Va Hemāyat az Hoquq-e Bashar dar Iran}* (London: British Institute of International and Comparative Law, 2008).

Abou El Fadl, Kh., *Speaking in God's Name: Islamic Law, Authority and Women* (Oxford: Oneworld, 2001).

'About One Million Signatures Demanding Changes to Discriminatory Laws', 28 August 2006. *Change for Equality*. Available at http://we-change.org/site/english/spip.php?article18 (accessed 4 April 2017).

Abrahamian, E., *Iran Between Two Revolutions* (Princeton, New Jersey: Princeton University Press, 1983).

———. *A History of Modern Iran* (New York: Cambridge University Press, 2008).

Afary, J., 'Seeking a Feminist Politics for the Middle East after September 11', *Frontiers* 25/1 (2004), pp. 1128–37.

———. *Sexual Politics in Modern Iran* (Cambridge: Cambridge University Press, 2011).

——— and K.B. Anderson, *Foucault and the Iranian Revolution: Gender and the Seductions of Islamism* (Chicago and London: University of Chicago Press, 2005).

Afkhami, M. (ed.) *Faith and Freedom: Women's Rights, Human Rights in the Muslim World* (London: I.B.Tauris, 1995).

———. 'The Women's Organization of Iran: Evolutionary Politics and Revolutionary Change', in L. Beck and G. Nashat (eds), *Women in Iran: From 1800 to the Islamic Republic* (Urbana and Chicago: University of Illinois Press, 2004), pp. 107–35.

———. 'Claiming Our Rights: A Manual for Women's Human Rights Education in Muslim Societies', in M. Afkhami and E., Friedl (eds), *Muslim Women and the Politics of Participation: Implementing the Beijing Platform* (Syracuse, New York: Syracuse University Press, 1997), pp. 109–20.

Afkhami, M., and Friedl, E., 'Introduction', in M. Afkhami and E. Friedl (eds), *Muslim Women and the Politics of Participation: Implementing the Beijing Platform* (Syracuse, New York: Syracuse University Press, 1997), pp. ix–xx.

Afshar, H., *Islam and Feminisms: An Iranian Case-Study* (Houndsmills, Baskingstoke: Macmillan, 1998).

———. 'Islam and Feminism: An Analysis of Political Strategies', in M. Yamani (ed.), *Feminism and Islam, Legal and Literary Perspectives* (Berkshire, UK: Garnet Publishing, 1996), pp. 197–216.

Afshari, R., *Human Rights in Iran: The Abuse of Cultural Relativism* (Philadelphia, Pennsylvania: University of Pennsylvania Press, 2001).

Ahmadi Khorasani, N., translated by D. Simin, 'The Two Storytellers of the Women's Prison and the Imaginary Literature of the One Million Signatures Campaign', *Change for Equality*, 28 April 2007. Available at http://we-change.org/site/english/spip.php?article74 (accessed 3 April 2017).

———. 'The Women's Movement in the Run-up to the Presidential Elections in Iran', 10 June 2009, *The Feminist School*. Available at www.feministschool.com/english/spip.php?article305 (accessed 14 March 2017).

———. 'Ten Days that Shook Iran', 30 July 2009, *The Feminist School*. Available at www.feministschool.com/english/spip.php?page=print&id_article=322 (accessed 27 March 2017).

Ahmadinejad, M., 'Reform Needed in West's Instrumental Approach Towards Women', January 2010. Available at www.women.gov.ir/en/pages/content.php?id=553 (accessed 30 January 2017).

Ahmed, L., 'Early Islam and the Position of Women: The Problem of Interpretation', in Nikki R. Keddie and Beth Baron, *Women in Middle Eastern History* (New Haven: Yale University Press, 1991).

———. *Women and Gender in Islam: Historical Roots of a Modern Debate* (New Haven: Yale University Press, 1992).

Al-Hibri, A., 'Islam, Law and Custom: Redefining Muslim Women's Rights', *American University Journal of International Law and Policy* 12 (1997), pp. 1–44.

Alikarami, L., 'Iran's political paranoia includes the children of foreign fathers', *Al Monitor*. Available at www.al-monitor.com/pulse/originals/2016/12/iranian-mothers-foreign-fathers-children-citizenship-law.html#ixzz4W2uRuLpd (accessed 12 June 2017).

Ali, S.S., *Gender and Human Rights in Islam and International Law: Equal before Allah, Unequal before Man?* (The Hague: Kluwer, 2000).

Ali, Y., *The Meaning of the Holy Qur'an* (Maryland: Amana Corporation, 1989).

'A Man Hanged His Own Sister Because She Wanted to Marry a Man She Loved'. Available at https://iranhr.net/en/articles/194/ (accessed 28 March 2017).

Amirahmadi, H. and M. Parvin (eds), *Post-Revolutionary Iran* (Boulder, Colorado and London: Westview Press, 1988).

Anderson, J.N., *Law Reforms in the Muslim World* (London: Athlone, 1967).

Andrew, B., 'The Convention on the Elimination of All Forms of Discrimination Against Women', in W. Benedek, E.M. Kisaakye and G. Oberleitner, *The Human Rights of Women: International Instruments and African Experiences* (London: Zed Books, 2002).

'Anger as Iran Bars Women from US Volleyball Game', *BBC news*, 20 June 2015. Available at www.bbc.co.uk/news/world-middle-east-33205360 (accessed 3 April 2017).

An-Na'im, A., 'The Rights of Women and International Law in the Muslim Context', *Whittier Law Review* 9 (1987), pp. 491–516.

———. *Toward an Islamic Reformation: Civil Liberties, Human Rights, and International Law* (New York: Syracuse University Press, 1990).

———. *Human Rights in Cross-Cultural Perspectives A Quest for Consensus* (Philadelphia, Pennsylvania: University of Pennsylvania Press, 1992).

———. 'State Responsibility Under International Human Rights Law to Change Religious and Customary Laws', in R.J. Cook (ed.), *Human Rights of Women: National and International Perspectives* (Pennsylvania: University of Pennsylvania Press, 1994), pp. 167–88.

———. 'Islam and Human Rights: Beyond the Universality Debate', *ASIL Proceedings* (2000), pp. 95–101.

———. (ed.), *Islamic Family Law in a Changing World: A Global Resource Book* (London and New York: Zed Books, 2002).

———. 'Toward a Cross-Cultural Approach to Defining International Standards of Human Rights: The meaning of Cruel, Inhuman, or Degrading Treatment or

Punishment', in A. An-Nai'm (ed.), *Human Rights in Cross-Cultural Perspectives: A Quest for Consensus* (Philadelphia, Pennsylvania: University of Pennsylvania Press, 1992), pp. 19–43.

———. 'Universality of Human Rights: An Islamic Perspective', in N. Ando (ed.), *Japan and International Law: Past, Present and Future* (The Hague: Kluwer Law International, 1999), pp. 311–23.

Ansari, S. and V. Martin (eds), *Women, Religion and Culture in Iran* (London and New York: Routledge, 2002).

Ansari E., Interview with Ayatollah Mousavi Tabrizi, translated by Sussan Tahmasebi, 'Ayatollah Mousavi Tabrizi: The Charge of Actions Against National Security Is Political', 11 November 2007, *Change for Equality*. Available at http://we-change.org/site/english/spip.php?article169 (accessed 31 March 2017).

Ansaripour, A. 'The Role of the Council of Guardians in the Islamicization of Iranian Law', in E. Cotran and M. Lau, *Yearbook of Islamic and Middle Eastern Law* 16: 2010–2011 (Leiden and Boston: Brill, 2012), pp. 127–46.

Anwar, Z., 'Malaysia: Advocacy for Women's Rights Within the Islamic Framework', *Sisters in Islam* (2003). Available at www.wluml.org/node/1186 (accessed 5 February 2016).

Ardalan, P., 'Joining on the Condition to Discriminate', *Bad Jens: Iranian Feminist Newsletter* 5, 22 May 2002. Available at www.badjens.com/fifthedition/joining.htm (accessed 18 January 2017).

———. translated by ST, 'Who is Accused of Being a "Threat to Civil Security?", *Rooz Online*, 25 May 2007. Available at www.roozonline.com/english/news3/newsitem/article/who-is-accused-of-being-a-threat-to-civil-security.html (accessed 27 March 2017).

———. translated by Ali G. Scotten, 'A Matter of Life: Report on the Preliminary Three-Month Activities of the One Million Signatures Campaign', 10 March 2007, *Change for Equality*. Available at http://we-change.org/site/english/spip.php?article46 (accessed 4 April 2017).

———. 'Women's Movement into the Streets', *Change for Equality*. 29 May 2007. Available at http://we-change.org/site/english/spip.php?article95 (accessed 22 April 2017).

———. 'Text of Speech Delivered at the Olaf Palme Foundation', 2008, *Change for Equality*. Available at http://www.we-change.org/english/spip.php?article231 (accessed 20 april 2017).

Arjomandi, S.A. (ed.), *Authority and Political Culture in Shi'ism* (Albany, New York: State University of New York Press, 1988).

Arnardottir, O.M., *Equality and Non-Discrimination under the European Convention on Human Rights* (The Hague, London and New York: Martinus Nijhoff Publishers, 2003).

Arshad, 'Ijtehad as a Tool for Islamic Legal Reform: Advancing Women's Rights in Morocco', *Kansas Journal of Law & Public Policy* 16 (2006–2007), p. 129.

Asgarizadeh, R., translated by SZ, 'Me and the Campaign on Vozara Street: A Laugh at a Chaotic Situation', *Change for Equality*. Available at www.we-change.org/English/spip.php?article136.

Askin, K. and D. Koenig (eds), *Women and International Human Rights Law* (Ardsley, New York: Transnational Publishers, 1999).

'A Suspicious Father Strangles his 14-year-old Daughter'. *Quds* newspaper. Available at www.qudsdaily.com/archive/1387/html/8/1387-08-12/page8.html#1 (accessed 22 October 2010).

Ayatollah Fazel Maybodi, interviewed by Elnaz Ansari, translated by Sussan Tahmasebi, 'The Demands of the Campaign Can be Met through Dynamic Jurisprudence', 6 June 2007, *Change for the Equality*. Available at http://we-change.org/site/english/spip.php?article97 (accessed 3 April 2017).

'Ayatollah Sanei Issues Fatwā in Support of Women's Inheritance', 16 February 2008, *Change for Equality*. Available at www.we-change.org/english/spip.php?article217 (accessed 3 April 2017).

Azari, F., *Women of Iran: The Conflict with Fundamentalist Islam* (London: Ithaca Press, 1983).

Baderin, M.A., *International Human Rights and Islamic Law* (Oxford: Oxford University Press, 2003).

———. 'Islam and the Realization of Human Rights in Muslim World: A Reflection on Two Essential Approaches and Two Divergent Perspectives', *Muslim World Journal of Human Rights* 4/1 (2007).

Banda, F., *Women, Law and Human Rights: An African Perspective* (Oxford and Portland, Oregon: Hart, 2005).

Barlow, R., *Women's Human Rights and the Muslim Question: Iran's One Million Signatures Campaign* (Melbourne, Australia: Melbourne University Press, 2012).

Bartlett, K.T., 'Feminist Legal Methods', *Harvard Law Review* 103/4 (1990), pp. 829–88.

Basedow, J. and N. Yassari., *Iranian Family and Succession Laws and their Application in German Courts* (Tubingen: Mohr Siebeck, 2004).

Bates, E., Avoiding Legal Obligations Created by Human Rights Treaties, *The International and Comparative Law Quarterly* 57/4 (October 2008), pp. 751–88.

Beckstrom, J.H.,'Transplantation of Legal System: An Early Report on the Reception of Western Laws in Ethiopia', *American Journal of Comparative Law* 21/3 (Summer 1973), pp. 557–83.

Beck, L. and G. Nashat (eds), *Women in Iran: From 1800 to the Islamic Republic* (Urbana and Chicago: University of Illinois Press, 2004).

Benedek, W., E. Kisaakye and G. Oberleitner (eds), *The Human Rights of Women: International Instruments and African Experiences* (London: Zed Books, 2002).

Benazir Bhutto, Beijing, 4 September 1995. Available at www.cfwd.org.uk/uploads/Benazir%20Bhutto.pdf (accessed 1 May 2018).

Blaustein, A.P. and G.H. Flanz (eds), *Constitution of the Countries of the World*, Vol. VIII (New York, 1994).

Bodman, H.L. and N. Tohidi (eds), *Women in Muslim Societies: Diversity Within Unity* (London: Lynne Rienner, 1998).

Bowman, C.G and E.M. Schneider, 'Feminist Legal Theory, Feminist Law-Making, and the Legal Profession', *Fordham Law Rev* 67 (1998), pp. 249–71.

Bradley, C.A. and J.L. Goldsmith, 'Treaties, Human Rights, and Conditional Consent', *University of Pennsylvania Law Review* 149/2 (December 2000), pp. 399–468.

Brandt, M. and J.A. Kaplan, 'The Tension between Women's Rights and Religious Rights: Reservations to CEDAW by Egypt, Bangladesh and Tunisia', *Journal of Law and Religion*, 12/1 (1995–1996), pp. 105–42.

Brems, E., *Human Rights: Universality and Diversity* (The Hague: Martinus Nijhoff Publishers, 2001).
Bunch, C.H., 'Women's Human Rights: The Challenges of Global Feminism and Diversity', in M. Dekoven (ed.), *Feminist Locations: Global and Local, Theory and Practice* (New Brunswick, New Jersey and London: Rutgers University Press, 2001), pp. 129–46.
───── and S. Fried, 'Beijing '95: Moving Women's Human Rights from Margin to Center', *Signs* 22/1 (Autumn 1996), pp. 200–204.
Buskens, L., 'Recent Debates on Family Law Reform in Morocco: Islamic Law as Politics in an Emerging Public Sphere', *Islamic Law and Society* 10/1 (2003), pp. 69–131.
Buss, D. and A. Manji (eds), *International Law: Modern Feminist Approaches* (Oxford and Portland, Oregon: Hart Publishing, 2005).
Byrnes, A., 'The Convention on the Elimination of All Forms of Discrimination Against Women', in W. Benedek, E. Kisaakye and G. Oberleitner (eds), *The Human Rights of Women: International Instruments and African Experiences* (London: Zed Books, 2002).
───── and J. Connors, *The Bill of Rights for Women: The Impact of the CEDAW Convention* (Oxford: Oxford University Press, 2008).
Campbell, T., K.D. Ewing and A. Tomkins, *Sceptical Essays on Human Rights* (Oxford: Oxford University Press, 2001).
Chamallas, M., *Introduction to Feminist Legal Theory* (New York: Wolters Kluwer Law and Business/Aspen Publishers, 2013).
Charlesworth, H., 'Human Rights as Men's Rights' in J. Peters and A. Wolper (eds), *Women's Rights Human Rights: International Feminist Perspective* (New York and London: Routledge, 1995), pp. 103–13.
───── and C.M. Chinkin, *The Boundaries of International Law: A Feminist Analysis* (Manchester: Manchester University Press, 2000).
─────, C. Chinkin, S. Wright and H. Charlesworth, 'Feminist Approaches to International Law: Reflection from Another Century', in D. Buss and A. Manji (eds), *International Law: Modern Feminist Approaches* (Oxford and Portland, Oregon: Hart Publishing, 2005), pp. 17–45.
─────, C. Chinkin, S. Wright and H. Charlesworth, 'Feminist Approaches to International Law', *American Journal of International Law*, Vol. 85, 199, pp. 613–45.
Chinkin, C., 'Thoughts on the UN Convention on the Elimination of All Forms of Discrimination Against Women (CEDAW)', in M. Shivdas and S. Coleman, *Without Prejudice: CEDAW and the Determination of Women's Rights in a Legal and Cultural Context* (London: Commonwealth Secretariat, 2010).
Clark, B., 'The Vienna Convention Reservations Regime and the Convention on Discrimination Against Women', *The American Journal of International Law*, 85/2 (April 1991), pp. 281–321.
Controversial articles of Iran's Family Protection Bill to be Reviewed, *Radio Zamaneh*, 17 December 2010. Available at www.zamaaneh.com/enzam/2010/08/controversial-articles-of.html (accessed 4 April 2017).
Cook, R.J., 'Reservations to the Convention on the Elimination of All Forms of Discrimination Against Women', *Virginia Journal of International Law* 30 (1989–1990), p. 643.

―――― (ed.), *Human Rights of Women: National and International Perspectives* (Philadelphia, Pennsylvania: University of Pennsylvania Press, 1994).
Copper, J., 'Allama al-Hilli on the Imamate and Ijtihad', in S.A. Arjomand (ed.), *Authority and Political Culture in Shi'ism* (New York, 1988).
Coulson, N. and D. Hinchcliffe, 'Women and Law Reforms in contemporary Islam', in Lois Beck and Nikki Keddie (eds), *Women in the Muslim World* (Cambridge, Massachusetts: Harvard University Press, 1978).
Dawson, R.P., 'When Women Gather: The NGO Forum of the Fourth World Conference on Women, Beijing 1995', *International Journal of Politics, Culture, and Society* 10/1 (Fall 1996).
'Demand of the Campaign Reviewed by Parliament: Reform of Diyeh on the Agenda of Iran's Parliament', 6 June 2007, *Change for Equality*. Available at www.we-change.org/english/spip.php?article98 (20 July 2017).
'Discrimination in Iran's Temporary Marriage Law Goes Unchecked', *Guardian*, 6 March 2012. www.guardian.co.uk/world/iran-blog/2012/mar/06/iran-temporary-marriage-law-sigheh (accessed 24 March 2017).
Doumato, E., 'The Ambiguity of Shari'a and the Politics of "Rights" in Saudi Arabia', in M. Afkhami (ed.), *Faith and Freedom: Women's Human Rights in the Muslim World* (Syracuse, New York: Syracuse University Press, 1995).
Ebadi, S., *The Rights of the Child: A Study on Legal Aspects of Children's Rights in Iran* (Tehran: UNICEF, 1994).
――――. *Iran Awakening: A Memoir of Hope* (New York: Random House, 2006).
―――― and H. Ghaemi, 'The Human Rights Case against Attacking Iran', *The New York Times*, 8 February 2005.
El Azhary Sonbol, A., *Women, the Family, and Divorce Laws in Islamic History* (Syracuse, New York: Syracuse University Press, 1996).
Emon, A.M., M.S. Ellis and B. Glahn, *Islamic Law and International Human Rights Law: Searching for Common Ground?* (Oxford: Oxford University Press, 2012).
Engineer, A.A., *The Rights of Women in Islam* (London: Hurst, 1992).
Engle, K., 'International Human Rights and Feminisms: When Discourses Keep Meeting', in D. Buss and A. Manji (eds), *International Law: Modern Feminist Approaches* (Oxford and Portland, Oregon: Hart Publishing, 2005).
Ennaji, M., 'The New Muslim Personal Status Law in Morocco: Context, Proponents, Adversaries, and Arguments'. Available at www.fmyv.es/ci/in/family/1.pdf (accessed 2 April 2017).
Esfandiari, G., 'Controversial Family Bill Returns to Iranian's Parliament's Agenda', *Radio Free Europe*, 24 August 2010. Available at www.rferl.org/content/Controversial_Family_Bill_Returns_To_Iranian_Parliaments_Agenda/2136632.html (accessed 31 March 2017).
Ettehadieh, M., 'The Origins and Development of the Women's Movement in Iran, 1906–41', in L. Beck and G. Nashat (eds), *Women in Iran: From 1800 to the Islamic Republic* (Urbana and Chicago: University of Illinois Press, 2004), pp. 86–95.
Evans, M.D., *International Law* (New York: Oxford University Press, 2003).
Evans, T., *US Hegemony and the Project of Universal Human Rights* (New York: St. Martin's Press, 1996).
Flanz, G.H., *Constitution of the Countries of the World*, Vol. VIII (New York, 1994).

Farhi, F., 'Religious Intellectuals, the "Women Question", and the Struggle for the Creation of a Democratic Public Sphere in Iran', *International Journal of Politics, Culture, and Society* 15/2 (Winter 2001), pp. 315–39.

Floor, W., 'Changes and Development in the Judicial System of Qajar Iran (1800–1925)', in E. Bosworth and C. Hillenbrand (eds), *Qajar Iran* (Edinburgh, 1983).

Foley, R., 'Muslim's Women Challenges to Islamic Law: The Case of Malaysia', *International Feminism Journal of Politics* 6/1 (2004), pp. 53–84.

Fraser, A.S., *The UN Decade for Women: Documents and Dialogue* (Boulder, Colorado: Westview Press, 1987).

Freeman, M.A., C. Chinkin and B. Rudolf (eds), *The UN Convention on the Elimination of All Forms of Against Discrimination Women* (Oxford: Oxford University Press, 2012).

Galtung, J., *Human Rights in Another Key* (Oxford: Polity Press, 1994).

Gamble, J.K., Jr., 'Reservations to Multilateral Treaties: A Macroscopic View of State Practice', *The American Journal of International Law* 74/2 (April 1980), pp. 372–94.

Goodman, R., 'Human Rights Treaties, Invalid Reservations, and State Consent', *The American Journal of International Law* 96/3 (July 2002), pp. 531–60.

'Grand Ayatollah Mazaheri Issues Fatwā Allowing Abortion of Unwed Mothers', 23 January 2008, *Change for Equality*. Available at http://we-change.org/english/spip.php?article207 (accessed 1 April 2017).

Habibi, S., 'Speech of H.E. Ms Shahla Habibi, Presidential Advisor on Women's Affairs for the Fourth Conference on Women, Beijing, September 1995'. Available at www.un.org/esa/gopher-data/conf/fwcw/conf/gov/9509131181415.txt (accessed 30 January 2017).

Haeri, S., *Law of Desire: Temporary Marriage in Shi'i Iran* (Syracuse, New York: Syracuse University Press, 1989).

Hamadan, S., 'Women Appointed to Saudi Council for First time', *The New York Times*, www.nytimes.com/2013/01/17/world/middleeast/women-appointed-to-saudi-council-for first time.html/ (accessed 1 April 2017).

Hallaq, W., 'Was the Gate of Ijtihad Closed?', in W. Hallaq (ed.), *Law and Legal Theory in Classical and Medieval Islam* (Aldershot: Variorum, 1995).

Hart, H.L.A., *The Concept of Law*, 2nd edition (Oxford: Oxford University Press, 1994).

Hathaway, O.A., 'Do Human Rights Treaties Make a Difference?', *The Yale Law Journal* 111/8 (January 2002), pp. 1935–2042.

Hedayat, B., 'Promotion of Equal Rights Discourse Among Political Groups', 29 July 2007, *Change for Equality*. Available at http://we-change.org/site/english/spip.php?article124 (accessed 5 April 2017).

Heyzer, N. and I. Landsbergs-Lewis, 'UNIFEM and Women's Climb to Equality: No Turning Back', in M. Afkhami and E. Friedl (eds), *Muslim Women and the Politics of Participation: Implementing the Beijing Platform* (Syracuse, New York: Syracuse University Press, 1997), pp. 153–61.

Hosseinkhah, M., 'Detentions and Summons Against Campaigners for Gender Equality', translated by H. Milan, 24 February 2008, *Change for Equality*. Available at http://we-change.org/site/english/spip.php?article225 (accessed 4 April 2017).

Hursh, J., 'Advancing Women's Rights Through Islamic Law: The Example of Morocco', *Berkeley Journal of Gender, Law and Justice* 27 (2012), pp. 252–305.

'Increased Concern on the Implementation of 3 Year Prison Sentence for Mahbubeh Karami', 15 May 2011, *Change for Equality*. Available at http://we-change.org/site/english/spip.php?article889 (accessed 31 March 2017).

'Iran: Allow Women's March for Equality', Human Rights Watch Statement on Iran, 8 March 2011, *Change for Equality*. Available at http://we-change.org/site/english/spip.php?article858 (accessed 31 March 2017).

Irfani, S., *Revolutionary Islam in Iran: Popular Liberation or Religious Dictatorship?* (London: Zed Books, 1983).

Iran Ardalan, D., 'NPR Interview with Sussan Tahmasebi, Iranian Women Demand Change', 5 June 2009. www.npr.org/blogs/sundaysoapbox/2009/06/women_rights_factors_in_irans.html (accessed 12 March 2017).

'Iran Enforces New Women's Inheritance Law'. Available at www.presstv.ir/Detail.aspx?id=88367&sectionid=351020101 (accessed 25 March 2017).

'Iran's Reply to the Questionnaire on the Implementation of the Beijing Platform for Action'. Available at www.un.org/womenwatch/daw/followup/responses/Iran.pdf (accessed 29 March 2017).

'Iran Women Get Equal Blood Money in Car Crashes', *Reuters*, 27 May 2008. Available at www.reuters.com/article/us-iran-women-bloodmoney/iran-women-to-get-equal-blood-money-in-car-crashes-idUSDAH73535620080527 (accessed 31 March 2017).

'Iran's Women Say No to Polygamy: Women Achieve Temporary Victory over Iran Family Protection Bill', 23 September 2008. Available at www.alternet.org/reproductivejustice/100941/iran_women_say_no_to_polygamy (accessed 31 March 2017).

'Iran: Ayatollah Support Women's Right to Inheritance and Abortion'. Available at www.payvand.com/news/08/feb/1170.html (accessed 25 March 2017).

'Iranian Vice-President Attacks Hardliners Over Vollaybale Ban for Female Fans', *Guardian*, 20 June 2015. Available at www.theguardian.com/world/2015/jun/20/iran-vice-president-attacks-hardliners-over-volleyball-ban-for-female-fans (accessed 3 April 2017).

'Iran Vice President Shahindokht Molaverdi Scolds Hardliners After Women Banned from Volleyball Match', *Australian Broadcasting Network*, 20 June 2015. Available at www.abc.net.au/news/2015-06-20/iran-vp-scolds-hardliners-over-volleyball-ban/6561202 (accessed 3 April 2017).

'Islam a Champion of Human Rights, Official Says', *Compass Newswire*, 28 October 1997, available in Lexis Nexis Library, ALLWLD file.

Jaising, I., 'The Convention on the Elimination of All Forms of Discrimination Against Women (CEDAW) and Realization of Rights: Reflection on Standard Settings and Culture', in M. Shivdas and S. Coleman (eds), *Without Prejudice: CEDAW and the Determination of Women's Rights in a Legal and Cultural Context* (London: Commonwealth Secretariat, 2010).

Jaquette, J.S., 'Losing the Battle/Winning the War: International Politics, Women's Issues, and the 1980 Mid-Decade Conferences', in A. Winslow (ed.), *Women, Politics and the United Nations* (Westport, Connecticut: Greenwood Press, 1995).

Javaheri, J., 'We Struggle for Progressive Change', *Change for Equality*, 5 June 2010. Available at http://we-change.org/site/english/spip.php?article712 (accessed 31 March 2017).

Jawad, H., *The Rights of Women in Islam: An Authentic Approach* (London, Macmillan, 1998).

Jenefsky, A., 'Permissibility of Egypt's Reservation to the Convention on the Elimination of All Forms of Discrimination Against Women', *Maryland Journal of International Law and Trade*, 15/2 (Fall 1991), pp. 199–233.
Kamali, M.H., *Principles of Islamic Jurisprudence* (Cambridge, UK: Islamic Texts Society, 1991).
Kanantz, Karineh (trans), 'Women's United Front Against the "Family Protection Bill" Wins Dividends', 2 September 2008, *The Feminist School*, www.feministschool.com/english/spip.php?page=print&id_article=141 (accessed 31 March 2017).
Kandiyoti, D. (ed.), *Women, Islam and the State* (Houndmills, Basingstoke, UK: Macmillan, 1991).
Kapur, R., 'Un-Veiling Equality: Disciplining the "Other" Woman Through Human Rights Discourse', in A.M. Emon, M.S. Eliss and B. Glahn (eds), *Islamic Law and International Human Rights Law: Searching for Common Grounds?* (Oxford: Oxford University Press, 2012).
Kazemi, F., *Poverty and Revolution in Iran* (New York: New York University Press, 1980).
Keddie, N.R., *Iran and the Muslim World: Resistance and Revolution* (New York: New York University Press, 1995).
Keshavarz, N., translated by MS, 'Interview with Jelveh Javaheri: From a Reading Group to the Campaign for One Million Signatures', 30 December 2007, *Change for Equality*. Available at http://topicsandroses.free.fr/spip.php?article275 (accessed 4 April 2017).
Khomeini, R., *Islam and Revolution: Writings and Declaration of Imam Khomeini*, translated and annotated by Hamed Algar (Berkeley: Mizan Press, 1981).
Kubba, L., 'Faith and Modernity: What is Liberal Islam?' *Journal of Democracy* 14/2 (2003), pp. 45–9.
'Launching of the One Million Signatures Campaign Demanding Changes to Discriminatory Laws', 27 August 2006, *Change for Equality*. Available at http://we-change.org/site/english/spip.php?article20 (accessed 27 May 2017).
'Lāyehe-ye Hemāyat az Khānevādeh va Janjālhā-ye Māde-ye 23' [Family Protection Bill and Article 23 Controversies], *Harmshahri Online*, 14 August 2007. Available at www.hamshahrionline.ir/details/28924/Society/-institution (accessed 19 May 2017).
Lijnzaad, L., *Reservations to UN Human Rights Treaties: Ratify and Ruin?* (Dordrecht: Martinus Nijhoff, 1995).
Macdonald, D.B., 'Ijtihad', in *The Encyclopaedia of Islam*, Vol. 3 (1971), pp. 1026–7.
Marayati, A.A., *Middle Eastern Constitutions and Electoral Laws* (New York, Washington and London, 1965).
Martin, V. (ed.), *Women, Religion and Culture in Iran* (Surrey, UK: Curzon Press, 2002).
Mashhour, A., 'Islamic Law and Gender Equality: Could There Be a Common Ground?: A Study of Divorce and Polygamy in Shari'a Law and Contemporary Legislation in Tunisia and Egypt', *Human Rights Quarterly* 27/2 (May 2005), pp. 562–96.
Masud, M.K., B. Messick and D.S. Powers (eds), *Islamic Legal Interpretation: Muftis and their Fatwas* (Cambridge, Massachusetts and London: Harvard University Press, 1996).

Mayer, A.E., *Islam and Human Rights: Tradition and Politics*, 4th edition (Boulder, Colorado and Oxford: Westview Press, 2007).

Mernissi, F., *The Veil and the Male Elite*, translated by Mary Jo Lakeland (New York: Basic Books, 1991).

―――. *Islam and Democracy: Fear of the Modern World* (New York: Addison Wesley Publishing Company, 1993).

―――. *Women and Islam: An Historical and Theological Enquiry* (New Delhi: Women Unlimited, 2004).

―――. 'The Internationalisation of Religious Position on Human Rights: How Religious Particularisms Are Uniting in a Campaign against Women's International Human Rights', in Ch. L. Eisqruber and A. Sajo (eds), *Global Justice and the Bluwark of Localism* (Leiden: Martinus Nijhoff Publishers, 2005), pp. 223–55.

Merry, S.E., *Human Rights and Gender Violence: Translating International Law into Local Justice* (Chicago: University of Chicago Press, 2006).

Meyer, M.K. and E. Prugl (eds), *Gender Politics in Global Governance* (New York and Oxford: Rowman & Littlefield Publishers, 1999).

Mir-Hosseini, Z., *Marriage on Trial: Islamic Family Law in Iran and Morocco* (London and New York: I.B.Tauris, 2000).

―――. 'The Conservative–Reformist Conflict over Women's Rights in Iran', *International Journal of Politics, Culture, and Society* 16/1 (Fall 2002), pp. 37–53.

―――. 'Debating Women: Gender and the Public Sphere in Post-Revolutionary Iran', in A. Sajoo (ed.), *Civil Society in Comparative Muslim Contexts* (London: I.B.Tauris and the Institute of Islamic Studies, 2002), pp. 95–122.

―――. 'How the Door of *Ijtihad* was Opened and Closed: A Comparative Analysis of Recent Family Law Reforms in Iran and Morocco', *Washington & Lee Law Review*, 64/4 (Fall 2007), pp. 1499–1511.

―――. 'Muslim Women's Quest for Equality: Between Islamic Law and Feminism', *Critical Inquiry* Vol. 32, No. 4 (Summer 2006), pp. 629–45.

―――. 'Islam and Gender Justice', in V.J. Cornell and O. Safi (eds), *Voices of Islam*, Vol. 5: Voices of Diversity and Change (Westport, Connecticut: Praeger, 2007), pp. 85–113.

Mir-Hosseini, Z., 'The Construction of Gender in Islamic Legal Thought and Strategies for Reform', *Hawwa Journal of Women in the Middle East and the Islamic World* 1/1 (2003), pp. 1–28 at p. 23.

―――. 'Classical Fiqh, Modern Ethics and Gender Justice', in K. Vogt, Lena Larsen and Christian Moe (eds), *Changeable and Unchangeable: New Directions in Islamic Thought and Practice* (London, I.B.Tauris, 2009), pp. 77–88.

――― and R. Tapper, 'Islamism: Ism or Wasm?' in Martin, R. and Barzegar, A. (eds), *Islamism: Contested Perspectives on Political Islam* (Stanford: Stanford University Press, 2010), pp. 81–6.

―――. 'Criminalising Sexuality: Zina Laws as Violence Against Women', The Global Campaign To Stop Killing And Stoning Women', Women Reclaiming And Redefining Culture Programme, Women Living Under Muslim Laws. Available at www.stop-stoning.org/node/882. 2010 (accessed 20 May 2017).

―――. 'Towards Gender Equality: Muslim Family Laws and the Shari'a', in Anwar, Z. (ed.), *Wanted: Equality and Justice in the Muslim Family* (Kuala Lumpur: Musawah; An Initiative of Sisters of Islam, 2009).

———. 'Broken Taboo in Post-Election Iran', *Middle East Report Online*, 17 December 2009. Available at www.merip.org/mero/mero121709 (accessed 15 July 2017).

———. 'Islamic Law and Feminism: The Story of a Relationship', in *Yearbook of Islamic & Middle Eastern Law* 9 (2004), pp. 32–42.

———. 'Divorce', *Encyclopedia of Islam and the Muslim World*, Vol. I (Macmillan Reference USA, 2004), pp. 182–3.

———. 'Marriage', *Encyclopedia of Islam and the Muslim World*, Vol. II (Macmillan Reference USA, 2004), p. 424.

———. 'Stretching the Limits: a Feminist Reading of the Shari'a in Post-Khomeini Iran', in Mai Yamani (ed.), *Islam and Feminism: Legal and Literary Perspectives* (London: Ithaca Press, 1996), pp. 285–319.

———. 'Mahr' (dowery), *Encyclopedia of Islam and the Muslim World*, Vol. II (Macmillan Reference USA, 2004), pp. 430–3.

———. 'Nikah' (marriage contract), *Encyclopedia of Islam and the Muslim World*, Vol. II (Macmillan Reference USA, 2004), p. 510.

———. 'Polygamy', *Encyclopedia of Islam and the Muslim World*, Vol. II (Macmillan Reference USA, 2004), pp. 552–3.

———. 'Fatemeh Haqiqatjoo and the Sixth Majles: A Woman in Her Own Right', *Middle East Report Online, Report* 233 (Winter 2004). Available at www.merip.org/mer/mer233/mir-hosseini.html (accessed 2 May 2018).

———.'Feminism in the Islamic Republic', *Encyclopedia Iranica* 9 (1999), pp. 498–503.

———. 'When a Woman's Hurt Becomes an Injury: "Hardship" as Grounds for Divorce in Iran', *Hawwa Journal of Women in the Middle East and the Islamic World* 5/1 (2007), pp. 111–26.

———. 'The Quest for Gender Equality: Between Islamic Law and Feminism', *Critical Inquiry* Vol. 32, No.4 (Summer 2006), pp. 629–45.

———, *Islam and Gender: The Religious Debate in Contemporary Iran* (London and New York, I.B.Tauris, 2000).

———. 'Women in Search of Common Ground: Between Islamic and International Human Rights Law', in A.M. Emon, M.S. Eliss and B. Glahn (eds), *Islamic Law and International Human Rights Law: Searching for Common Grounds?* (Oxford: Oxford University Press, 2012).

Moghadam, V.M., 'Feminism and Islamic Fundamentalism: A Secularist Interpretation', *Journal of Women's History* 13/1 (2001), pp. 42–6.

———. 'Islamic Feminism and Its Discontents: Toward a Resolution of the Debate', *Chicago Journals* 27/4 (Summer 2002), pp. 1135–71.

———. 'Rhetorics and Rights of Identity in Islamist Movements', *Journal of World History* 4/2 (Fall 1993), pp. 243–64.

———. *Globalizing Women: Transnational Feminist Network* (Baltimore, Maryland and London: The John Hopkins University Press, 2005).

Moghadam, K., translated by Leila Sheernejad, 'An Alarming Experience', 18 March 2007, *Change for Equality*. Available at http://we-change.org/site/english/spip.php?article47 (accessed 4 April 2017).

Moghissi, H., *Feminism and Islamic Fundamentalism: The Limits of Postmodern Analysis* (London and New York: Zed Books, 1999).

Mohammadi, M., *Judicial Reform and Reorganization in 20th Century Iran: State-Building, Modernization and Islamicization* (New York and London: Routledge, 2008).

'Morocco: Morocco Withdraws Reservations to CEDAW', *Women Living under Muslim Laws*, 18 December 2008, www.wluml.org/node/4941 (accessed 2 April 2017).

Morsink, J., *The Universal Declaration of Human Rights: Origins, Drafting, and Intent* (Philadelphia, Pennsylvania: University of Pennsylvania Press, 1999).

Mtango, S., 'A State of Oppression? Women's Rights in Saudi Arabia', *Asia-Pacific Journal on Human Rights and the Law* 5 (2004), pp. 49–67.

Mozaffari, K., translated by P. Saeedi, 'The Campaign and Future Political Challenges', 15 March 2008, *Change for Equality*. Available at http://we-change.org/site/english/spip.php?article237 (accessed 5 April 2017).

———. 'The Minimums to Design an Interaction with the Political Parties'. Available at http://articlesjelvehkaveh.blogfa.com/post-11.aspx (accessed 5 April 2017).

Mutua, M., 'The Complexity of Universalism in Human Rights', in A. Sajo (ed.), *Human Rights with Modesty: The Problem of Universalism* (Leiden: Martinus Nijhoff Publishers, 2004), pp. 51–64.

Naeemi, P., 'Interesting Reactions to the Campaign, I Returned Empty-Handed, Yet My Heart Is Filled with Confidence That My Decision from Five Years Earlier Was the Right One', 7 February 2007, *Change for Equality*, http://wechange.org/site/english/spip.php?article17 (accessed 4 April 2018).

Najmabadi, A., 'Feminism in the Islamic Republic: Years of Hardship, Years of Growth' in Y.Y. Haddad and J.L. Esposito (eds), *Islam, Gender and Social Change* (Oxford: Oxford University Press, 1998).

Naples, N.A. and M. Desai (eds), *Women's Activism and Globalization: Linking Local Struggles and Transnational Politics* (New York and London: Routledge, 2007).

Nashat, G., 'Introduction', in L. Beck and G. Nashat (eds), *Women in Iran: From 1800 to the Islamic Republic* (Urbana and Chicago: University of Illinois Press, 2004).

Nasr, H., H. Dabashi and V.R. Nasr, *Expectation of the Millennium: Shi'ism in History* (Albany, New York: State University of New York Press, 1989).

Nayyeri, M.H., 'Criminal Responsibility of Children in the Islamic Republic of Iran's New Penal Code'. Available at www.iranhrdc.org/english/publications/legal-commentary/1000000054-criminal-responsibility-of-children-in-the-islamic-republic-of-irans-new-penal-code.html#.T-g4gytYs0M (accessed 26 March 2017).

Newcomb, R., *Women of Fes: Ambiguities of Urban Life in Morocco* (Philadelphia, Pennsylvania: University of Pennsylvania Press, 2009).

Norman, R., *Free and Equal: A Philosophical Examination of Political Values* (Oxford: Oxford University Press, 1987).

Nouraie-Simone, F. (ed.), *On Shifting Ground: Muslim Women in the Global Era* (New York: The Feminist Press at the University of New York, 2005).

Novak, M., 'The Prohibition of Gender-based Discrimination in the International Convention on Civil and Political Rights', Benedekin, W., Kisaakye, E.M. and Oberletiner, G. (eds), *Human Rights of Women International Instruments and African Experiences* (London: Zed Books, 2002).

Osanloo, A., *The Politics of Women's Rights in Iran* (Princeton, New Jersey and Oxford: Princeton University Press, 2009).

Otte, D., 'Holding Half the Sky, But for Whose Benefit? A Critical Analysis of the Fourth World Conference on Women', *Australian Feminist Law Journal* 6 (1996), pp. 7–30.

Paidar, P., 'Feminism and Islam in Iran', in Kandiyoti, D. (ed.), *Gendering the Middle East: Emerging Perspectives* (London, I.B.Tauris, 1996), pp. 51–67.

———. *Women and the Political Process in Twentieth-Century Iran* (Cambridge: Cambridge University Press, 1995).

Pal, A., Shirin Ebadi's Interview, *The Progressive*, September 2004. http://progressive.org/magazine/helen-thomas-interview/ (accessed 5 February 2017).

Pearl D. and Menski, W., *Muslim Family Law*, 3rd edition (London, Sweet & Maxwell, 1998).

Perikhanian, A., *The Book of a Thousand Judgements: A Sasanian Law-Book*, translated from Russian by Nina Garsoïan (Costa Mesa, California and New York: Mazda Publishers in association with Bibliotheca Persica, 1997).

Peters, J. and A., Wolper (eds), *Women's Rights, Human Rights: International Feminist Perspectives* (New York, London: Routledge, 1995).

Piper, C.L., 'Reservations to Multilateral Treaties: The Goal of Universality', *Iowa Law Review* 71 (1985–1986), pp. 295–322.

Pollis, A. and P. Schwabb, 'Human Rights: A Western Construct with Limited Applicability', in A. Pollis and P. Schwabb (eds), *Human Rights: Cultural and Ideological Pespectives* (New York: Praeger Publisher, 1979), pp. 1–18.

———. 'Toward a New Universalism: Reconstruction and Dialogue', *Netherlands Quarterly of Human Rights* 16 (1998), pp. 3–23.

Povey, T and E. Rostami-Povey (eds), *Women, Power and Politics in 21st Century Iran* (Surrey and Burlington: Ashgate Publishing Limited, 2012).

'Q & A: Iran's election Crisis', *BBC News*. Available at http://news.bbc.co.uk/1/hi/world/middle_east/3389017.stm (accessed 2 March 2017).

Radin, M., 'The Pragmatist and the Feminist', *Southern California Law Review* 63 (1990), pp. 1699–1726.

Ragin, Charles, *Constructing Social Research: The Unity and Diversity of Method* (Thousand Oaks, California and London: Pine Forge Press, 1994).

Rahman, T., *A Code of Muslim Personal Law*, 1978, Vol. 1, pp. 92–101.

Ramazani, R.K., 'Document: Constitution of the Islamic Republic of Iran', *The Middle East Journal* 34 (1980), pp. 181–204.

Randjbar-Daemi, S., 'Building the Islamic State: The Draft Constitution of 1979 Reconsidered', *Iranian Studies*, 46/4 (2013), pp. 641–63.

Rehman, J., *International Human Rights Law*, 2nd edition (Essex, UK: Pearson Education Limited, 2010).

Report Iran: Honour Killing, Landinfo, 22 May 2009.

Reservations to the Convention on the Elimination of All Forms of Discrimination Against Women: Weakening the Protection of Women from Violence in the Middle East and North Africa Region (Amnesty International, 2004).

Ritchie, J., J. Lewis and G. Elam, 'Designing and Selecting Samples' in J. Ritchie and J. Lewis (eds), *Qualitative Research Practice: A Guide for Social Students and Researchers* (London: Sage, 2004).

Riddle, J., 'Making CEDAW Universal: A Critique of CEDAW's Reservation Regime under Article 28 and the Effectiveness of the Reporting Process', *George Washington Law Review* 23 (2002), pp. 605–38.

Roshani, A., translated by SZ, 'In Memory of Amir: In Prison, but Freer than Most of Us', 7 August 2007, *Change for Equality*. Available at www.we-change.org/english/spip.php?article129 (accessed 4 April 2018).

Ross, S.D., *Women's Human Rights: The International and Comparative Law Casebook* (Philadelphia, Pennsylvania: University of Pennsylvania Press, 2008).
Rostam-Kolayi, J., 'The Politics of Women's Rights in the Contemporary Muslim World', *Journal of Women's History* 10/4 (1999), pp. 205–15.
Roudi-Fahimi, F. and Mederios Kent, M., 'Challenges and Opportunities – The Population of the Middle East and North Africa', *Population Bulletin* 62 (2): [24], June 2007.
Ruda, J.M., 'Reservations to Treaties', *RCADI*, Vol. 146, 1975.
Rupp, L.J., *Worlds of Women, the Making of an International Women's Movement* (Princeton, New Jersey: Princeton University Press, 1977).
Sabbah, F., *Woman in the Muslim Unconscious* (New York: Pergamon, 1984).
Schirazi, A., *The Constitution of Iran: Politics and the State in the Islamic Republic*, translated by J. O'Kane (London: I.B.Tauris, 1997).
Sadiqi, F. and M. Ennaji, 'The Feminisation of Public Space: Women's Activism, the Family Law, and Social Change in Morocco', *Journal of Middle East Women's Studies* 12/2 (Spring 2006), pp. 86–114.
Shahidian, H., *Women in Iran: Gender Politics in the Islamic Republic* (Westport, Connecticut and London: Greenwood Press, 2002).
———. *Women in Iran: Emerging Voices in the Women's Movement* (Westport, Connecticut and London: Greenwood Press, 2002).
Siddiqi, M.M., *Women in Islam* (Lahore: Institute of Islamic Culture, 1952).
Shah, N.A., 'Women's Human Rights in the Koran: An Interpretive Approach', *Human Rights Quarterly* 28 (2006), pp. 869–903.
———. *Women, the Koran and International Human Rights Law: The Experience of Pakistan* (Leiden: Martinus Nijihoff Publishers, 2006).
Shivdas, M. and S. Coleman (eds), *Without Prejudice: CEDAW and the Determination of Women's Rights in a Legal and Cultural Context* (London: Commonwealth Secretariat, 2010).
Skalli, L.H., 'Women and Poverty in Morocco: The Many Faces of Social Exclusion', *Feminist Review* 69: The Realm of the Possible: Middle Eastern Women in Political and Social Spaces (Winter 2001), pp. 73–89.
———. *Through a Local Prism: Gender, Globalisation, and Identity in Moroccan Women's Magazines* (Lanham, Maryland: Lexington Books, 2006).
Slaughter, A.M. and W. Burke-White, 'The Future of International Law is Domestic (or, the European Way of Law)', *Harvard International Law Journal* 47 (2006), pp. 327–52.
Stowasser, B., 'Women's Issues in Modern Islamic Thought', in E.T. Judith (ed.), *Arab Women: Old Boundaries, New Frontiers* (Bloomington, Indiana: Indiana University Press, 1993).
Tabari, A. and N. Yeganeh, *In the Shadow of Islam: The Women's Movement in Iran* (London: Zed Press, 1982).
Tahmasebi, S., 'Empowering Iranian Women through the One Million Signatures Campaign', 1 September 2007, *Change for Equality*. Available at http://we-change.org/site/english/spip.php?article139 (accessed 3 April 2017).
———. 'Answer to Your Most Frequently Asked Questions About the Campaign', 24 February 2008, *Change for Equality*. Available at http://we-change.org/english/spip.php?article226 (accessed 28 March 2017).

———. 'Four Years of Engaging Face-to-Face on Women's Rights', 29 August 2010, *Change for Equality*. Available at http://we-change.org/site/english/spip.php?article757 (accessed 31 March 2017).

'The Effect of Laws on Women's Lives'. 28 August 2006, *Change for Equality*. Available at http://we-change.org/site/english/spip.php?article41 (accessed 27 March 2017).

'The Coalition of the Iranian Women's Movement for Voicing their Demands in the Election', *The Feminist School*. Available at www.feministschool.com/english/spip.php?article281 (accessed 16 March 2017).

The United Nations and the Advancement of Women, 1945–1996 (New York: Department of Public Information, UN, 1995).

Tohidi, N., 'Women and the Presidential Elections: Iran's New Political Culture', 9 March 2009. www.juancole.com/2009/09/tohidi-women-and-presidential-elections.html (accessed 12 March 2017).

———. 'Modernity, Islamisation, and Women in Iran', in V.M. Moghadam (ed.), *Gender and National Identity* (London and New Jersey: Zed Books, 1994).

———. 'Iran's Women's Rights Movement and the One Million Signatures Campaign', November 2006, www.payvand.com/news/06/dec/1174.html (accessed 30 March 2017).

———. 'Iran: A Small Window of Hope', *Open Democracy*, 1 July 2013, www.opendemocracy.net/5050/nayereh-tohidi/iran-small-window-of-hope (accessed 10 June 2017).

Torabi, M., Interview with Fatemeh Alai, Women's Rights in Islam and Iran, *Press TV*, 2007. Available at http://edition.presstv.ir/detail/34194.html (accessed 28 January 2017).

US Department of State, Background Note: Iran. Available at www.state.gov/r/pa/ei/bgn/5314.htm (accessed 10 May 2017).

'Violence against women in Iran'. Available at www.cedaw-iran.org/impact-of-ccdaw violence-against-women (accessed 4 April 2017).

Vandenhole, W., *Non-Discrimination and Equality in the View of the UN Treaty Bodies* (London: Hart Publishing, 2005).

Wallace, R.M.M., *International Human Rights: Text and Materials*, 2nd edition (London: Sweet & Maxwell, 2001).

Waltz, S.E., 'Reclaiming and Rebuilding the History of the Universal Declaration of Human Rights', *Third World Quarterly* 23/3 (2002), pp. 437–48.

———. 'Universal Human Rights: The Contribution of Muslim States', *Human Rights Quarterly* 26 (2004), pp. 799–844.

———. 'Universalizing Human Rights: The Role of Small States in the Construction of the Universal Declaration of Human Rights', *Human Rights Quarterly* 23 (2001), pp. 44–72.

Weiner, M. and Banuazizi, A. (eds), *The Politics of Social Transformation in Afghanistan, Iran, and Pakistan* (Syracuse, New York: Syracuse University Press, 1994).

Weingartner, L.A., 'Family Law & Reform in Morocco- The Mudawana: Modernist Islam and Women's Rights in the Code of Personal Status', *University of Detroit Mercy Law Review* 82 (2004–2005), pp. 687–713.

Welchman, L. (ed.), *Women's Rights and Islamic Family Law: Perspectives on Reform* (London and New York: Zed Books, 2004).

———. *Women and Muslim Family Laws in Arabs States: A Comparative Overview of Textual Development and Advocacy* (Amsterdam: Amsterdam University Press, 2007).

———. 'Musawah, CEDAW, and Muslim Family Laws in the 21st Century', in A.M. Emon, M.S. Eliss and B. Glahn (eds), *Islamic Law and International Human Rights Law: Searching for Common Grounds?* (Oxford: Oxford University Press, 2012).

West, L.A., 'The United Nations Women's Conferences and Feminist Politics', in M.K Meyer, and Prugl, E. (eds), *Gender Politics in Global Governance* (Maryland: Rowman & Littlefield, 1999).

Yaghoub-Ali, A., translated by Sussan Tahmasebi, 'Interesting Reactions to the Campaign', 20 July 2007, *Change for Equality*. Available at http://we-change.org/site/english/spip.php?article114 (accessed 20 March 2017).

Yahyaoui Krivenko, E., *Women, Islam and International Law: Within the context of the Convention of the Elimination of All Forms of Discrimination Against Women* (Leiden and Boston: Martinus Nijhoff Publishers, 2009).

Yamani, M. (ed.), *Feminism and Islam, Legal and Literary Perspectives* (Berkshire, UK: Garnet Publishing, 1996).

Yazbeck Haddad, Y. and Esposito, J.L., *Islam, Gender and Social Changes* (Oxford: Oxford University Press, 1998).

Zerfoss, S., 'The Convention on the Elimination of all Forms of Discrimination Against Women: Radical, Reasonable or Reactionary?', *Michigan Journal of International Law* 12 (1991), pp. 903–42.

Zoe Pearson, 'Feminist Project(s): The Spaces of International Law', in S. Kouvo and Zoe Pearson (eds), *Feminist Perspectives on Contemporary International Law: Between Resistance and Compliance?* (Oxford, UK and Portland, Oregon: Hart Publishing, 2011).

Zoglin, K., 'Morocco's Family Code: Improving Equality for Women', *Human Rights Quarterly* 31 (2009), pp. 949–84.

INDEX

adultery (zenā), 140, 145–47, 149–50, 262, 269
Ahmadi Khorasani, Noushin, 210
Ahmadi Pour, Zahra, 208
Ahmadinejad administration (2005–13)
  impact on Iranian women's rights, 22–23, 173, 183, 193, 201, 204–5, 214, 247, 282
Ahmadinejad, Mahmoud
  views on the status of women, 275
Alasvand, Fariba, 88, 90
Algeria, 233
Alinejad, Masih, 207
Amini, Asieh, 193
Aminzadeh, Elham, 172, 208
An-Na'im, Abdullahi Ahmed, 71
Anwar, Zainah, 181–82
apostasy, 191
Ardalan, Parvin, 161–62, 165–66, 193
Association for the Support of Women's Human Rights, 175
Association of Women Researchers in Islamic Science, 175
Ayatollahi, Zahra, 85, 90, 179

Baderin, Mashood, 29, 121, 137, 147
Baha'i faith, 107, 196, 218

Bahrain, 233
Bani-Etemad, Rakhshan, 177
Baniyaghoob, Jila, 203
Bayat, Rafat, 173
Bazargan, Mehdi, 57, 239
Beer, Angelika, 177, 277
Behbahani, Simin, 177–78
Behroozi, Maryam, 172, 174, 197, 202
Beijing Conference on Women (1995), 18–22, 80
blood money (compensation).
  See diyeh (blood money)
Bojnurdi, Ayatollah Mousavi, 28–29, 152, 153, 184–85, 246

Cairo Declaration on Human Rights in Islam, 29
CEDAW, 9–46, 230
  accession of Muslim states to, 38–45
  and shari'a law, 28–29
  as an issue in the 2009 elections in Iran, 203–4
  ratification debate in Iran, 4, 35, 82–100, 203–4, 212–15, 248, 250, 285
  shari'a-based objections to, 10, 38–45, 82, 90–91, 99–100
  state reservations to, 38–45, 232–33

Centre for the Defenders of Human
  Rights (Iranian women's rights
  group), 177
Centre for Women and Family Affairs of
  Iran, 23, 179, 226, 247
Centre for Women's Participation
  (CPW), 22, 83, 84–85, 282
Committee on the Rights of the
  Child (CRC), 114
Constitution of Iran (1979)
  popular ratification of, 56
  preamble on the character of the
    1979 revolution, 240
  provisions on women's rights in,
    142–44, 240
  recognised religious minorities in,
    255
Constitutional Revolution (1906),
  1, 6, 11, 49, 51, 237–38
Convention on the Elimination of All
  Forms of Discrimination Against
  Women (CEDAW). See CEDAW
Convention on the Political Rights of
  Women (1952), 11, 221
Criminal Code of Iran (1926), 150

Damad, Mohaqeq, 107, 218
Davoodi Mohajer, Fariba, 200
discretionary punishments (ta'zirāt),
  142
divorce (talāq), 125–32
diyeh (blood money), 79, 141, 151–56,
  171–73, 187, 209, 270
Dolatabadi, Shiva, 176

Ebadi, Shirin, 2, 8, 32, 78–79, 81–82,
  145, 153–54, 156, 163–64, 167,
  175–78, 185–86, 191, 193, 195,
  200, 203–4, 218
Ebtekar, Masoumeh, 208
eddeh, 22, 128–32, 128–32, 135,
  261–62
Egypt, 13, 14, 35, 232
ejtehād, 3, 32, 44, 68, 70–74, 184–86

Elham, Gholam-Hossein, 172, 179
Emami, Asdollah, 108
equality (concept)
  general perspectives on, 24–26
  Islamic perspectives on, 26–32, 75
Ertürk, Yakin, 148
eslāhāt (reform era, 1997–2005), 186,
  198, 213
European Parliament, 177, 277
Expediency Council (EC), 64–65
  Iranian CEDAW accession stalled in,
    65, 91
Ezazi, Shahla, 176, 277

Family Protection Law (2013),
  134–35, 259, 261
Family Protection Law (pre-1979), 1,
  54, 104–5, 112, 118–19, 125
Farhangkhah, Fatemeh, 203
Fatima (daughter of the Prophet
  Mohammad), 75
feminist legal theory, 4–7, 217
feraksiun-e zanān (women's caucus in
  the Majles), 87, 172, 174,
  200–201

Gheyrat, Farideh, 174–75, 176
Golpaygani, Ayatollah Lotfollah Safi,
  86, 115
Gorgani, Ayatollah Mohammad Ali
  Alavi, 206
Guardian Council (GC), 58, 61, 62–65
  rejection of Iran's accession to
    CEDAW (2003), 63, 87

Habibi, Shahla, 19–20, 247
Haft-e Tir protest (2006), 161–63, 201
Hamandishi-ye-Zanān [Intellectual
  Partnership of Women], 202–3,
  203, 272
Hamedani, Nuri, 246
Hamgerāi-ye Zanān (Convergence of
  Women), 196, 205
Haqiqatjoo, Fatemeh, 87, 200

INDEX 335

Hashemi, Faezeh, 197, 200
Hashemi, Fatemeh, 246
Hedayat Khah, Sattar, 134
Hedayat, Bahareh, 168
hejāb (mandatory veiling), 17, 53, 93, 140, 169, 207, 265, 273
hokm-e hokumati, 241, 266
homosexuality (lavāt), 140, 145, 146, 254–55
honour killing
  no shari'a-based justification for, 151
honour-related crimes, 148–51
Hosseinkhah, Maryam, 193
hudud (fixed punishments), 141, 143–44
hukumat-e Islami. See Islamic state (concept)
human rights
  debate over universality of, 26, 28, 220, 223, 228

India, 35
inheritance, 136–38, 171–73, 187, 209
International Covenant on Civil and Political Rights (ICCPR), 14, 25–26, 29, 164–65, 192, 227, 231
International Covenant on Economic, Social, and Cultural Rights (ICESCR), 14, 164–65, 227, 231
Iranian Revolution (1979), 1–2, 55–58, 61–62
Iranian Women Journalists Association, 175
Iran–Iraq War, 2, 3, 8, 89
Iraq, 13, 14, 16, 233
Islamic criminal code of Iran (2013), 140–42, 146, 151, 157
Islamic feminism, 72, 180–83, 279
Islamic Iran Participation Front, 177
Islamic Republic of Iran Women's NGO Network, 80, 201

Islamic Republic Women's Association, 199
Islamic state (concept), 56–60
Islamic criminal code of Iran (2013), 150

Jalaeipuor, Fatemeh, 199
Jamshidi, Alireza, 154, 173
Jannati, Ayatollah Ali, 27, 90, 219
Javaheri, Jelveh, 188–89, 190, 192
Jense Dovom [The Second Sex] (magazine), 76–77
Jolodarzadeh, Soheila, 174, 197, 200

Kadivar, Jamileh, 85, 87, 197, 199, 204
Kar, Mehrangiz, 78, 100, 200
Kārgozārān-e Sāzandegi (women's group), 77
Karroubi, Mehdi, 86, 188, 281
Kashani, Ayatollah Imami, 61, 250
Katuziyan, Naser, 108
Kazemi, Zahra, 88
Khalife, Nadya, 194
Khamenei, Ayatollah Ali, 26–27, 170
  views on human rights, 26
  views on the status of women, 75, 115, 146
Khaneh Ahzab [House of Parties], 175, 177
Khatami administration (1997–2005)
  impact on Iranian women's rights, 7, 21, 81–83, 83, 183, 198, 202
Khatami, Mohammad, 63, 174
  views on CEDAW, 91, 99–100
Khomeini, Ayatollah Ruhollah
  views on marriage and divorce, 125–26, 129, 254
  views on women's rights, 20, 53–54, 216
  writings on feqh (Islamic jurisprudence), 141
  writings on hukumat-e Islami, 56
Khorasani, Nushin Ahmadi, 77, 160–61

Khoshroo, Gholamali, 24
khul' divorce, 131–32
Kulaei, Elaheh, 85, 87–89, 203–4
Kuwait, 233
Kuye Daneshgah incident (1999), 199–200

Lahiji, Shahla, 200
Lankarani, Ayatollah Fazel, 27–28, 86, 89, *250*
Larijani, Ali, 138, 178–79, *259*
lavāt (homosexuality). *See* homosexuality (lavāt)
law (definition), 48, *236*
Lebanon, 14
legal system of Iran
   categories of punishments under, 141–42
   gender disparity in age of criminal responsibility, 142–44, 157
   historical development, 48–56, 103–5, 140–41
   post-1979 Islamicisation of, 55–56, 141, 211
   sources of law, 65–70
   unequal status of women's testimony, 145–47

Mahmoodzadeh, Maryam, 174
mahriyeh (dowry), 67, 133–34, 135, *276*
Majles (Iranian parliament), 60–64, *241*
Majles-e Showra-ye Islami [Islamic Consultative Assembly]. *See* Majles (Iranian parliament)
Majma'-ye Tashkhis-e Maslahat-e Nezām [Expediency Council for the Discernment of the Interest of Islamic Order]. *See* Expediency Council (EC)
Malaysia, 69, *233*
Manesh, Akram Mosavari, 86, 87, 97
marital rape, 35, 60, 114

marriage in Iran
   annulment, 123–25
   divorce (talāq), 125–32
   forms of dissolution, 122
   legal definition as civil contract, 105
   minimum legal age, 64–65, 111–17
   nationality status and, 109–11, *246*
   of Iranian woman to a foreign man, 110, *246*
   prohibition against same-sex, 105
   requirement of parties' mutual consent, 106, *255*
Mashini, Farideh, 177, 203–4
Mazaheri, Ayatollah Hossein, 28, 184, 220, *246*
Mernissi, Fatima, 31, 43
Meshkini, Ayatollah Ali, 85, *250*
Meybodi, Ayatollah Fazel, 184
Meydan-e Zanan (Iranian women's group), 176
Mir-Hosseini, Ziba, 30–31, 130, 134–35, 181, 183, 186
Moghissi, Haideh, 182
Mohammad VI, King of Morroco, 44–45
mohārebeh (sedition), 145, *267*, *283*
mojtahed
   definition of, *242*
Mojtahedzadeh, Maryam, 23
Molaverdi, Shahindokht, 92, 174–75, 177, 205–8, *247*
Moqadam, Khadijeh, 193
Moravati, Mehrangiz, 202
Morocco, *233*
   status of women in, 38–45
Mortazi Langarudi, Minoo, 200
Mostafavi, Zahra, 199
Mousavi, Mir Hossein, 178, 188, *281*
Mozafari, Kaveh, 167–68

Najmabadi, Afsaneh, 181
Niger, *233*
Noandishan-e Dini movement, 78
Nouri, Zohreh Tabibzadeh, *247*

INDEX   337

Oman, 233
One Million Signatures Campaign, 4, 114, 159–210, 214
Organisation of the Islamic Conference (OIC), 84, 88
osr va harag [difficult and undesirable conditions] (basis for divorce), 127–28

Pahlavi, Mohammad Reza Shah, 2, 42, 53–55, 140
Pahlavi, Princess Ashraf, 16
Pahlavi, Reza Shah, 52, 53, 140, 265
Pakistan, 13, 14, 16
patriarchal practices
   as impediment to gender equality in Iran, 21, 194–96
people of the book (ahl-e ketab), 107
polygamy, 103–4, 117–22, 173–75, 178, 184, 259
Pur Nejati, Ahmad, 88, 91

Qanun-e Eslah-e Moqararat-e Marbut be Talaq [Law on Divorce Regulations] (1982), 126
Qanun-e Ezdevaj [Law on Marriage] (1931), 104
Qur'an
   provisions on divorce in, 147
   provisions on marriage in, 109, 131, 132
   provisions on women's inheritance in, 264–65

Rafsanjani administration (1997–2005)
   impact on Iranian women's rights, 78, 80, 82
Rafsanjani, Faezeh Hashemi, 77
Rafsanjani, Hashemi, 61
   views on the status of women, 275
   views on Western feminism, 94
Rahnavard, Zahra, 178, 188
Rakei, Fatemeh, 87–88, 175, 177

Ramezanzadeh, Fatemeh, 200
Reformist Muslim Women Association, 175
religious minorities, 7, 105, 107, 182, 196, 218, 255
retribution as punishment (qesās), 141, 143–44, 149, 152
revocable divorce (talāq-e Raj'i), 132
Rezaei, Mohsen, 188
Rowhani administration (2013–)
   impact on Iranian women's rights, 92, 205, 207–8, 214

Sadeq, Ja'far (Sixth Shi'ia Imam), 132–33
Sadr, Shadi, 96, 100, 203
Safai, Hossein, 108
Safi, Ayatollah, 115, 246
Salahshouri, Parvaneh, 207
Salman bin Abdul-Aziz Al Saud, King of Saudi Arabia, 41–42
Sanei, Ayatollah Yousef, 47, 104, 115–16, 120, 130, 138, 174, 184, 209, 219
   views on diyeh (blood money), 155–56, 271
   views on polygamy, 236
   views on women's inheritance, 280
Saudi Arabia, 13, 14, 30, 38–42
SAVAK, 54, 239
Senegal, 35
Shaditalab, Jaleh, 200
Shari'a
   and gender equality, 30
   and religious minorities, 182
   as a source of law in Iran, 7, 47–50, 68–70, 104–5
   as a tool to challenge gender discrimination, 32, 72, 74, 155–58
   definition, 216
   liberal interpretations of, 31, 147, 155, 219

patriarchal interpretations of,
31–32, *219*
provisions on women's rights in,
180–87
recognition of polygamy in, 117–21
Shariati, Ali, 54, 73
Sherkat, Shahla, 77, 162, 200
Shi'ite clergy
views on gender equality, 2, 60, 138,
145, 155, 180–87
Shid, Nahid, 199
Shirazi, Ayatollah Makarem, 86, 88, 89,
115, *246*, *250*
Shojaei, Mansoureh, 177, 193
Shojaei, Zahra, 93, 204
Shoraye Markazi Daftar-e Tahkim-e
Vahdat [Central Council of
the Office to Foster Unity],
168, 177
Showra-ye Negahban. *See* Guardian
Council (GC)
Sobhani, Hassan, 89, 91
Society for the Protection of the Rights
of the Child (SPRC), 78–79
Society of Islamic Revolution Women,
199
Soltankhah, Nasrin, *247*
Somalia, 38
Sotoudeh, Nasrin, 175–76, 191–92
Soviet Union, 16, 53
state repression, 9, 161, 163, 169–70,
189–94, 209–10
stoning (punishment), 129, 150, *269*
Sudan, 38
Supreme Council of Cultural
Revolution (SCCR), 82–83
Supreme Leader of Iran. *See* Khamenei,
Ayatollah Ali; Khomeini,
Ayatollah Ruhollah
Syria, 14, *233*

Tabrizi, Ayatollah Mirza Jawad, 86
Tabrizi, Ayatollah Mousavi,
183, *246*, *250*

Tahmasebi, Susan, 168–70, 179–80,
187–88, 193–94
talāq. *See* divorce (talāq)
Taleghani, Ayatollah Mahmoud, 54
Taleghani, Azam, 77, 199–200, 203–4
Tavasoli, Nahid, 203
temporary marriage (siqeh),
72, 119–20, 132–36, 135, 136,
260, *264*, *276*, *278*
testimony. *See* legal system of Iran:
unequal status of women's
testimony
The United Nations' fourth World
Conference on Women.
See Beijing Conference on
Women (1995)
Tohidi, Nayereh, 17, 181, 205
Tunisia, *233*
Turkey, 14, 30
Twelver Ja'fari School of Shi'ite Islam,
58, 132–33, *218*

UN Committee on the Status of
Women (CSW), 11–15
UN Convention on the Rights of the
Child, 79, 99–100, 144
UN Human Rights Committee
(HRC), 25
United Arab Emirates (UAE), *233*
United Nations Charter, 11, 12
United Nations Decade for Women
(1975–85), 16–17, 34, 45
Universal Declaration of Human Rights
(UDHR), 12–14, 25–26, 45,
96, 164–65, 186

Vasmaghi, Sedigheh, 177
violence against women, 78, 97, 149,
207, 208
Voice of America, 170, 187

War on Terror, 5
Women's Cultural and Social Council of
Iran, 179

INDEX

Women's Cultural Centre of Iran,
  79–81, 80, 176
women's movement in Iran
  before 1979, 2–3, 15–17
  re-emergence after 1979, 76–82
Women's Organisation of Iran (WOI),
  15–16, 53
Women's Participation Centre of Iran,
  198–200
Women's Association of the Islamic
  Republic, 202

Yazdi, Ayatollah Mesbah, 90, *219*
Yemen, *222*

Zanān (magazine), 76, 77–78,
  77–78, 200
Zanān-e Esfand (women's group), 81
zenā (adultery). *See* adultery (zenā)
Zeynab Society, 172, 174, 197, 202
Zibaei Nejad, Hojat-ol-Islam
  Mohammadreza, 90, 95,
  98, 99

www.ingramcontent.com/pod-product-compliance
Lightning Source LLC
Chambersburg PA
CBHW070011010526
44117CB00011B/1517